SEEING THAT FREES

SEEING THAT FREES

Meditations on Emptiness and Dependent Arising

ROB BURBEA

Hermes Amāra Publications

Hermes Amāra Publications
Gaia House
West Ogwell
Devon
TQ12 6EW

publishing@hermesamara.com

ISBN:
SB 978 0992848 910
HB 978 0992848 903

British Library Cataloguing in Publication Data.
A catalogue record for this book is available from the British Library.

The publishers wish to thank all those anonymous donors whose kind and generous financial assistance has supported the publication of this book

Contents

Part Five: Of Highways and Byways

Foreword

The experience of emptiness is one of the most puzzling aspects of the Buddha's teaching. While we can intuitively understand and experience, at least to some extent, the truths of impermanence and unreliability, it may be difficult to relate to the term 'emptiness'. In fact, in English, the word is not all that appealing. We may think of emptiness as a grey vacuity or as some state of deprivation. Yet, in the Buddha's teaching of liberation, of freedom from all suffering and distress, the realization of emptiness plays a central role.

Rob Burbea, in this remarkable book, *Seeing That Frees*, proves to be a wonderfully skilled guide in exploring the understanding of emptiness as the key insight in transforming our lives. This is not an easy journey. Beginning by laying the foundation of the basic teachings, he explains how these teachings can be put into practice as 'ways of looking' that free and that gradually unfold deeper understandings, and so, in turn, more powerful ways of looking and even greater freedom. This unique conception of insight as being liberating ways of looking is fundamental to the whole approach, and it makes available profound skilful means to explore even further depths of Dharma wisdom.

Rob is like a scout who has gone ahead and explored the terrain, coming back to point out the implications of what we have been seeing, and then enticing us onwards. He shows how almost all of the Buddha's teachings can lead us towards understanding the fabrication, mutual interdependence, and, thus, the emptiness of all phenomena. And that it is this understanding of emptiness that frees the mind.

Following the thread of this understanding leads to great flexibility in how we view things, and it is this very flexibility that informs the entire approach to insight that is offered here. Many times throughout *Seeing That Frees* we discover how different and often opposing notions can be integrated into our practice. Instead of being caught up in a thicket of metaphysical views and opinions, the basic criterion here is, 'Does it help to free the mind?'

Such discernment and understanding make possible a greater breadth in our approach to practice, which is illustrated in many ways throughout the book. For example, different traditions often hold quite different views regarding the place of analytical investigation and thought on the path: for some, they are an indispensable part of our journey; for others, they are seen merely as an obstacle.

Rob very skilfully demonstrates the role that each of these perspectives can play as we deepen our practice.

Yet *Seeing That Frees* is much more than merely an attempt to form an approach that is broad and inclusive. Consistently, the limitations in and assumptions behind each view being considered are pointed out, and, each time, understandings that transcend that particular view are explored. Rob shows how so many of the insights that we might at first consider ultimately true are still only provisional, and yet he also shows how these very provisional perspectives can be used as vital stepping-stones towards a deeper and more complete understanding.

Another example of this progressive questioning and unfolding involves the various contrasting views of different traditions regarding the nature of awareness itself: Is awareness momentary? Is it a field? Is it the ground of Being? Rob has done a masterful job of highlighting how each particular view can help us see experience from a different perspective, and how each one furthers our ability to let go. But rather than simply resting in this appreciation of what each perspective offers, he goes on to demonstrate the conditional, fabricated nature of even the most sublime awareness, and then shows the emptiness of fabrication itself. In realizing emptiness, there is no place at all to take a stand; indeed, no place, and no one who stands.

It is rare to find a book that explores so deeply the philosophical underpinnings of awakening at the same time as offering the practical means to realize it. How does one talk about what is beyond mind, beyond concepts, beyond time? What does it mean to say that even emptiness is empty? *Seeing That Frees* does not shy away from these most difficult tasks of describing the un-describable. Although these descriptions could so easily become an exercise in abstraction, because this book is so rooted in experience, exploring with great subtlety and depth how we can put insights into emptiness into practice, it brings to life what Rob calls "the awe-inspiring depth of mystery". This great book can inspire us to the highest goals of spiritual awakening.

Joseph Goldstein
Barre, Massachusetts
January, 2014

Abbreviations

AN	*Aṅguttara Nikāya*
BCA	*Bodhicaryāvatāra* (Śāntideva)
DN	*Dīgha Nikāya*
Dhp	*Dhammapada*
Iti	*Itivuttaka*
MA	*Madhyamakālaṃkāra* (Śāntarakṣita)
MAV	*Madhyamakāvatāra* (Chandrakīrti)
MMK	*Mūlamadhyamakakārikā* (Nāgārjuna)
MN	*Majjhima Nikāya*
SN	*Saṃyutta Nikāya*
Sn	*Sutta Nipāta*
Skt.	Sanskrit language
Ud	*Udāna*

Preface

Curiosity and desire can be the most precious forces. For anyone curious about the Buddhist teachings on the nature of things and desiring to take their meditative practice and understanding deeper, my sincere hope is that this book will be a helpful resource. Its subjects – emptiness and dependent origination – are immensely rich and may be explored in a variety of ways. While purely scholastic approaches have their place and can have great value, it is primarily through practice that liberating insights are born and empowered. It is also mainly through practice that the fullness of the intimate connection between emptiness and dependent arising is understood. Guides to exploring the subtleties and nuances of practice and of insight as they deepen may therefore offer something useful.

This book is, first and foremost then, a kind of meditation manual – one that pursues into great depth a fundamental philosophical inquiry. It is a book about practice, and about the profoundly freeing insights that anyone who practises can discover and unfold for themselves firsthand. Although presupposing some experience in meditation, and particularly in mindfulness and insight meditation, there is an attempt to explain things – the teachings, most of the relevant terms, and the practices – starting from first principles.

The way of approaching emptiness presented here is based on what I have found helpful in my own years of practising with these subjects and also in teaching students both on and off retreat. Other ways of ordering the material would certainly have been possible and in some cases might have seemed simpler from a logical point of view. However, experience with the different responses of students to such teachings, the various kinds of needs that arise in the course of deepening practice, and the ways in which their insight typically tends to mature leads me to organize things in a slightly different fashion – in a structure that follows more the actual unfolding and refining of insight, and that hopefully better serves a practitioner as (s)he travels this path.

On the whole, teachings and practices are discussed progressively through the book. Often an idea, an insight, or a meditation that is introduced builds on what has come earlier. Already established understandings are either used as platforms for further discoveries or may themselves be nuanced further. It will probably be most fruitful, therefore, to read and practise with the material in the order presented. Having said that, there is no rigid formula to be adhered to, and needs vary from individual to individual. So as long as you sense your realization of emptiness is growing deeper, subtler, more thorough, and more comprehensive in terms of the phenomena it includes, and as long as you understand just how all these insights tie together, feel free to move through the material in whatever way seems most helpful.

Chapters 1 to 3 are essentially introductory. Rather than extending a rigorous and complete exposition, they try to sketch in the broadest possible brushstrokes a very brief overview of the path we will be travelling, giving some sense of both the direction and the range of insight involved. They also try to address some of the immediate concerns that can arise for many simply hearing about emptiness.

In a number of respects Chapter 4 is fundamental to the entire approach here. It presents a way of understanding what insight is and the whole movement of its development, as well as the kinds of practices we will be using as our vehicles.

The subject of Chapter 5 is the art of calming, concentrating, and unifying the mind – the vast area of *samādhi* and its relation to emptiness practices. A great deal more could have been included there but I have detailed only the minimum I thought might be relevant and helpful for most readers. Once you have digested its more essential general points, the meditation advice in this chapter may be used, depending on your experience, as an ongoing resource in parallel with an exploration of the contents of the rest of the book. You may wish to dip into it periodically, take a little that is useful, and return later to assimilate something else.

Then, beginning very simply, specific emptiness practices are introduced starting in Chapter 6. Regarding the material presented in the chapters that follow (6 to 10), again much more could have been said. Since plenty is already available elsewhere addressing that level of insight, the main concern here was to present just enough to make clear how there is in fact one principal thread of understanding we can follow into greater and greater depth. From quite easy, almost obvious, everyday realizations, following this thread can take us, surprisingly, all the way to the most profound levels of insight. Some readers, because of their previous experience, may not feel it necessary to spend much time with the meditations in these chapters. The essential insights and principles sketched out there will need to be comprehended, however, before moving on.

From Chapter 11 onward, through the step-by-step introduction of more powerful emptiness practices, a long arc of insight is gradually unfolded. In following it, the main thread of inquiry alluded to above is strengthened by weaving in other supporting and complementary strands of inquiry. And as will become apparent, there are some twists and turns on the journey as practices mature and yield various discoveries. Our understanding evolves as it penetrates and opens to deeper levels.

With respect to the different meditations described, as well as patience we will emphasize again and again the huge benefits of the attitudes of play and experimentation. Not only do these attitudes make practice more fun, we also tend to learn and discover more that way. Developing meditation is like learning a craft, and many skills are involved. In the process, inquisitiveness, playfulness, responsiveness, and improvisation are indispensable. They help build confidence and independence in practice. They help also to open the sense of the *art* of meditation. For no matter how much is explained here, there is only so much that can be communicated in words, and much that we must actually discover for ourselves.

Likewise with the various analyses (or reasonings sometimes used to penetrate emptiness) that are peppered through the book. Rather than considering every possible qualm or counter-possibility, I have tried to keep the explanation of each analysis fairly brief, allowing space for each reader's individual process of engagement with any reasoning. At least to some extent, these reasonings will need to be pondered through, wrestled with and considered for oneself to one's own satisfaction. Only then can they be used as powerful instruments in meditation.

Although many practices are offered in the course of the following pages, it is not absolutely necessary to master, or even to try, every one. What will, almost surely, be necessary is for you to develop enough of them to the various extents that enable you to follow the thread of progressively deepening inquiry and insight that is unfolded – in ways that *you* feel make a genuinely liberating difference.

The intention here is not to marshal an exhaustive collection of emptiness practices by any means. Many that could have been included have not been. And indeed, following what we said about experimentation, one can certainly discover or invent one's own practices and variations. More significantly, tied in to the thread of inquiry pursued, the book is in part an attempt to open a way of *conceiving* of practices. As we shall explain, one way of approaching an understanding of emptiness and dependent origination is in terms of 'fabrication'. And all practice can in fact be seen in those terms. Many practices that one might not usually think of in this light can actually be understood as ways of fabricating less, and through comprehending this, eventually everything in our lives bears on our understanding of emptiness. Everything becomes relevant. Eventually too this understanding unlocks the potential of a novel way of conceiving of the whole of the Dharma.

Exploring and developing so many practices will likely open up many wonderful experiences in meditation. Only a few of the countless possible variations have been described though, and those only briefly. For the most part

I have tried to portray and discuss just enough from the array of possibilities to draw attention to the essential significant features shared by any group of insights. Often it is not that we need a new, different, or 'deeper' *experience* to deepen our understanding of emptiness. It's more that we need to infer the right conclusions and insights from the range of experiences we already have. Highlighting that which needs to be understood from any experience – the underlying central principles – therefore takes priority.

A core insight repeatedly insisted on in this book is that fundamentally what gets us into trouble are the ways we typically view things, and our blind clinging to these ways of seeing. At the roots of our suffering – primary in engendering, perpetuating, and exacerbating it – are our habitual conceptions and the ways of looking they spawn. It is therefore precisely these that need to be addressed and replaced.

At one extreme, perhaps, of the spectrum of approaches to emptiness are teachings that try to reject concepts outright almost from the beginning, or somehow, as we shall explain, too soon. One of the dangers then is believing one has realized deeply the meaning of emptiness when there remains in fact much left to fathom. At the other end of the spectrum lies the danger of predominantly emphasizing a skilful mental manipulation of concepts, but ending up remaining fettered by them, subtly addicted to them. The approach we will take here tries to steer a course between these two extremes. As will become clear, we will use concepts, but only to varying extents at different times and in ways which let them lead us to the edges of their own use, and then further, into non-conceptual insight. Such an attitude can support all the subtleties and nuances of insight as it deepens, and so supports the opening of deeper liberation. It also allows great flexibility of practice.

Our practice needs to be flexible, in so many ways. This too is something we will stress again and again. It is related of course to what was mentioned above about playfulness and experimentation, and also to the whole project of freeing up views. For now let us just make one point in this connection. Often when we are suffering, some emptiness view or other is quite capable of dissolving or substantially reducing that suffering. Sometimes just dissolving it thus is fine. Sometimes though, that suffering may be felt to be an integral part of one's humanity, so that it might seem necessary to allow and to feel that particular pain and that sense of humanness more fully before viewing it as empty. Yet it is also true that on occasion an ordering opposite to this last is viable and actually more helpful. We may choose to see the emptiness of something first, so dissolving it or at least loosening it up, and then – either allowing it to reconstitute, or taking advantage of this loosening – we can draw near to it again to be with it and hold it in a different way. An open-minded experimentation and a free and pliable approach are vital.

Along with such responsive, supple, and open-minded play what is outlined in the course of these pages does involve a kind of work too. It is not necessarily always easy, or simple. But following the Buddha's teachings and putting them into practice one discovers depths and freedoms that more than repay the effort put in. Here is an invitation. The path is open. Often so much more is possible for us than we think.

PART ONE

Orientations

1

The Path of Emptiness is a Journey of Insight

Revered in the tradition as the 'crown jewels' of the Dharma, the Buddha's teachings on emptiness and dependent arising point and pave the way to the most beautiful possibilities for us as human beings. Their realization brings a truly radical revolution in our whole sense of existence in a way that opens up a profound and extraordinary freedom.

Emptiness – in Pali, *suññatā*, in Sanskrit, *śūnyatā*, which may also be translated as 'voidness' – is deep and subtle, however, not easy to see or explain, and in many respects it is even counter-intuitive. It is extremely rare for a full realization to come suddenly. Almost always a *journey* of understanding is required, one that liberates gradually. And this remarkable adventure of insight involves many facets of our being, certainly not just our intellects.

From the outset, therefore, we need to have a degree of humility and openness of mind in relation to these teachings, accepting that our understanding will keep evolving, deepening, filling out, and becoming more nuanced as we practise and inquire. Meditation is central to this adventure. Without a certain depth of meditation, voidness and all that it means, and also in fact a good portion of what the Buddha taught, cannot be fully understood, even on an intellectual level.

We therefore start our discussion not with a finished and polished definition of what emptiness is, but rather with a short introduction that will help point us in the direction we will be travelling. A much fuller and more mature comprehension will come through the practices as we develop them. As the journey proceeds, we will see too that the radical understandings progressively arrived at and opened to through deeper and deeper meditation eventually transcend concepts.

Voidness, the roots of suffering, and the way things seem to be

Let's begin by making clear at least a little of what emptiness is not. To many people, and often even to meditators, the very word 'emptiness' can evoke emotional associations with a sense of barrenness, bleakness, meaninglessness, or even depression. But that is definitely not what Buddhist teachings mean by the word emptiness. On the contrary, they point to this realization as something wonderful, supremely joyful, and profoundly liberating.

It might also be imagined that voidness is some kind of thing that can be obtained; but it is not a thing. Nor is it a state of mind or a state of consciousness. Occasionally, when using language loosely, one might talk of relative 'states of emptiness' in meditation. And it's true that emptiness is sometimes spoken of as a kind of state of mind or a kind of space of consciousness. For now though, let us set aside such conceptions. We will find in the long run that it will be much more helpful in opening out a fuller and more potent understanding if we start in a different way.

To begin to more accurately comprehend what emptiness means and why it is regarded as the most significant aspect of the Dharma, so central and vital on the path of awakening, we can follow the Buddha in tracing the question of suffering to its root.

It's clear that our lives, at least at times, involve suffering (*dukkha* in Pali) – pain, dis-ease, discontent of all sorts. This is the First Noble Truth. Beginning to inquire into how this *dukkha* comes about, we can see that there are many causes. We recognize unhelpful habit patterns – of action, speech, and thought, of reactivity, and of contraction of the heart; we notice tendencies to feed emotional states that are not nourishing, and often to somewhat neglect to nurture those that are; we see that we chase after things that will not bring lasting fulfilment. All this and more we can understand. Looking more deeply though, the Buddha pointed out that all this *dukkha* has craving and clinging as a cause.[1] This, we could say, is the short version of the Second Noble Truth. As we will see in great subtlety through practice, to crave is to be in a state of *dukkha* in the present, and although it is not always so simple, in some way or other it also brings *dukkha* in the future.

But of course this then begs the question: Why do we crave? And the answer the Buddha gave and wanted us to understand is that craving is based on a fundamental mistake in the way we see and intuitively sense our selves and the whole world of inner and outer phenomena. We feel and take for granted that

[1] E.g. DN 22, SN 56:11. For now, we will use the two terms 'craving' and 'clinging' synonymously and interchangeably, to refer to any degree of grasping, aversion, attachment, or holding-on to any phenomenon at all. Learning to work skilfully with this force and fully understanding its various effects are themes central to the whole journey of insight we will be travelling, so we will clarify and expand on the meaning just given as this journey unfolds. In so doing, we will also discuss the conventional views and definitions of these two terms sometimes upheld: that 'craving' and 'clinging' refer to two really different movements of mind; and, alternatively, that they refer to two differing intensities of the same basic movement of mind.

selves and things are as real as they seem to be, that they exist, as they appear to, in a substantial way, in and of themselves, 'from their own side', as it were. Their reality seems obvious. We assume, in a way that involves no thinking, that our bodies or this book, for instance, exist independently of other things and independently of the mind that knows them. We feel that a thing has an *inherent existence* – that its existence, its being, inheres in itself alone. Believing then that this real self can really gain or lose real things or experiences which have real qualities, grasping and aversion, and thus *dukkha*, arise inevitably.

All phenomena are empty of inherent existence

We can, at least for now, define emptiness as the absence of this inherent existence that things appear to naturally and undeniably have. In the tradition, a variety of expressions are used to say this – that all things lack intrinsic existence, true existence, self-existence, substantial existence. Many texts leave out the words 'true', 'inherent', etc., and just state that all phenomena have no existence, no nature, no reality, but the implied meaning is essentially the same. 'Emptiness', then, is more a quality that we can recognize in something, a way something is, a property it has. A thing is 'empty' of its seemingly real, independent existence. And all things are this way, are empty. This voidness is what is also sometimes termed the ultimate truth or reality of things.

To illustrate this and begin to get a hint of what it means we could consider a wooden chair thrown onto a big fire. The chair begins to burn, then gradually deform and fall apart, slowly turning to ashes. At what point *exactly* is it no longer a chair? Is it not the mind perceiving and conceiving of it one way or another that determines whether it is 'a chair' at a certain moment in time after catching fire? Its chair-ness is given by the mind, and does not reside in it independently of the mind. The lack of an inherently existing 'official' time when it stops 'being a chair' points to a certain emptiness, its lack of inherent chair-ness. In the *Upālipariprcchā Sūtra* it is declared that

> [All things] are simply posited by conception. The world is fabricated through conception… completely conceptualized.[2]

[2] Translation by Geshe Ngawang Samten and Jay L. Garfield in Tsongkhapa, *Ocean of Reasoning: A Great Commentary on Nāgārjuna's Mūlamadhyamakakārikā* [Oxford: Oxford University Press, 2006] p. 233.

We might also borrow, and extend, an often-used example to elucidate further. Imagine that you and a friend enter a large room and you see there three big wooden beams suspended in the space in the middle of the room. Two are parallel with the floor, each at a different height; the other is at a 45-degree angle to it. They are not touching, perhaps they are some distance from each other, but all three are in a line parallel to the wall. Your friend says, "It's a 'Z'!", but until she said that you had not seen it that way. Now though, you can indeed see the three beams as a 'Z'. But is it a 'Z', *really, in itself*? How near to each other do the beams have to be for it to qualify for Z-ness? How far apart to make that notion virtually implausible? It is the mind that determines whether the beams are seen as a 'Z', and just how close they have to be for that perception to arise without suggestion will vary from mind to mind. The perception of 'Z' is dependent on the mind. Needless to say, someone who does not use the Roman alphabet will not see a 'Z', but even then, it is up to their mind whether the beams are connected in one gestalt or seen as separate units. Although we can certainly perceive a 'Z', we can't say the 'Z' here inherently exists, independent of the mind. There is no inherently existing 'Z' there.

This example might be relatively easy to accept, but probably we will intuitively resist its extension to too many other things. While we might readily admit that some phenomena could, potentially at least, be perceived in different ways, we usually still feel they are, 'in reality', one way 'in themselves'. Things appear to us as being *really* this or that, *really* this or that way, as having an essential nature, or what is traditionally called 'own-nature' or 'own-being' (*svabhāva*). Emptiness teachings, however, extend the principle of this example to *all* phenomena, not only ambiguously arranged groupings of material objects. All things seem to us to be, in the most basic way, simply and exactly 'what they are', regardless of how, or whether, they are perceived. Their that-ness and their inherent existence seem evident and given immediately with our very awareness of them; they are not somehow added conceptually later. And yet this seemingly real nature that we perceive is fabricated by the mind. As Nāgārjuna stated in his *Mūlamadhyamakakārikā*:

> The world has no own-nature.[3]

And in his *Acintyastava*, a hymn of praise to the Buddha:

> You taught that the whole world is empty of reality.[4]

---

[3] MMK 22:16. (All translations from MMK are the author's own.)

[4] '*vastuśūnyam*' – void of 'reality', of 'essence', of 'substance'. (All translations from *Acintyastava* are the author's own.)

The illustration of the 'Z' thus has important limitations. While highlighting the emptiness of the Z-ness, it quietly leaves unchallenged the inherent existence of the wooden beams that are its component parts and seem to us so real and so solid. If we extend the investigative process to those beams, we might still leave undisturbed our assumptions of the inherently existent reality of the molecules of wood or the subatomic particles, the space in which those particles move, the self, or the awareness that knows all this. But voidness applies to all these too, an insight that is harder to fathom and much more radical and far-reaching in its implications than initially the 'Z' example might seem to suggest. The Buddha taught that *all* phenomena are empty of essence, of inherent existence.

Realizing voidness dissolves dukkha

Unquestioningly but mistakenly then, we intuitively sense and believe in this inherent existence of phenomena, in 'real' experiences of a 'real' self in a world of 'real' things. Now, in itself, this may strike some as a rather abstract or irrelevant piece of metaphysical philosophizing. But as alluded to earlier, the complete dissolution of this error in our sense and understanding of things is the primary thrust of the Buddha's message of liberation. This mistaken seeing is the deepest level of what the Buddha calls the ignorance or fundamental delusion (Skt: *avidya*; Pali: *avijjā*) that we share as sentient beings. We cling, and so suffer, because of the way we see. Although it may not be obvious at first, any clinging whatsoever requires this mistaken intuitive sense – of the reality of what we are clinging to, and of the self as something real and so 'invested in' through clinging.

But we do not cling to what we know is not real. Thus when, with insight and wisdom, we realize that something is illusory in some sense, we let go of any clinging to it – of chasing it, trying to hold onto it, or trying to get rid of it. Since clinging brings *dukkha,* in this release of the clinging there comes release and freedom from *dukkha*. As the Buddha said,

> One who... knows with regard to the world that 'all this is unreal' abandons the near shore and the far, like a snake its worn-out old skin.[5]

[5] Sn 1:1. (All translations from Sn are the author's own, made also with reference to the translations of Thanissaro Bhikkhu in *Handful of Leaves, Vol. 4* [Redwood City, CA: Sati Center for Buddhist Studies, and Valley Center, CA: Metta Forest Monastery, 2003].)

When this profound knowing of the voidness of all things is absorbed, beyond mere intellectual understanding, there is liberating insight into the heart of reality. There is an awakening which fundamentally alters the way in which we perceive the world. This is the realization necessary for enlightenment. Nāgārjuna, among others, pointed out that

> Without recourse to the ultimate truth, *nirvāṇa* is not attained.[6]

If you dislike such talk that concretizes 'end points' for practice, we might simply say instead: To the degree, depth, and comprehensiveness that we can realize the emptiness, the illusory nature, of phenomena, to that degree, depth, and comprehensiveness is freedom then available to us. Thus in his *Catuḥśataka*, Āryadeva wrote, concerning this fact of the voidness of all things:

> When one sees reality one achieves the supreme abode. [But] even by seeing the slightest bit of it, one is better off. Therefore the wise should always cultivate such insight in contemplating phenomena.[7]

And thus the Buddha encouraged those who seek freedom to

> View the world as void.[8]

For many, it may not yet be evident how a recognition of emptiness – that things are not real in the way they seem to be – dissolves the foundations of *dukkha*, so perhaps a different illustration might help make the connection clear. Imagine that one day when out walking you turn a street corner and suddenly hear a loud and menacing growling nearby. A ferocious and hungry-looking tiger appears in front of you seemingly about to leap. The distress of a reaction of terror there would be quite understandable. But if you notice on closer inspection that this tiger is not real, that it is actually a holographic projection with accompanying sound recording from a nearby hologram projector, the fear and the problem simply dissolve.

The release from the suffering of the situation here comes not from simply being mindful or accepting of the tiger so much as from the realization of its illusory nature. It is this that hopefully your mindfulness can reveal. And such an understanding will

---

[6] MMK 24:10.

[7] Translation from the author's notes.

[8] Sn 5:15.

not seem abstract and irrelevant; it will matter. Sometimes it is assumed that realizations of voidness will create some kind of 'disconnection from reality' or 'ungroundedness' in a person. But here we can see that to realize that this tiger is illusory is, in fact, to be more 'grounded in reality' than otherwise; and that it will make a considerable difference to how you feel. We can even say that from the point of view of what brings release from *dukkha*, the most profoundly significant and fundamental thing to understand about this tiger is its emptiness. And this we can extend to all phenomena without exception. It is the puncturing of the illusion that punctures the *dukkha* most radically and completely. As Nāgārjuna wrote:

> Whenever there is belief that things are real… desire and hatred are generated… Without that belief no defilements can occur… And when this is completely understood, all views and afflictions dissolve… [This] the supreme knower of truth [the Buddha] has taught.[9]

Voidness and impermanence

Of course, the analogy of the holographic tiger is also limited in a number of ways. Exactly what it means to say that all things are 'not real' we will uncover gradually through this book, since, as we have said, it can only properly be comprehended through the development of deeper meditative insight.

What the analogy does suggest, though, is that emptiness is more than impermanence. It is true that the Buddha also repeatedly proclaimed that *avijjā* includes a kind of blindness to the impermanence of things, and so an investment in what is not stable. But we must remember that in forty-five years of speaking to many different seekers he naturally gave teachings of different levels in different situations. To say that something is empty is to say something much deeper and more radical, harder to fathom, than that things are inconstant, in flux, in process, or even that, inspected more closely, phenomena are seen to be arising and passing with breathtaking rapidity and that we construct a solidity of continuity where in reality there is none. Even this rapid change turns out to be only a relative truth and its perception a stepping-stone. As we will explore, seeing impermanence is but the beginning of one possible avenue into understanding something more subtle and mysterious – the emptiness of things.

[9] In his *Yuktiṣaṣṭikā*. (Author's own translation.)

Emptiness is the Middle Way

We should probably say one more thing here at the outset, despite the fact that this too will be much more fully understood through the deepening of the meditative practices we will be unfolding than through mere words. On encountering such teachings, it is easy to assume that their message and their implications are of existential meaninglessness, undermining ethical concern and passionate care for the world. Or that the world of things, once their illusion is exposed, will appear to us as somehow dreary, and we will disconnect. Such assumptions and fears, however, are usually based on various common misunderstandings of what emptiness means.

This teaching is certainly not, for instance, proclaiming that only material things really exist – organisms and neurons and tiny solid atoms or subatomic particles that form the building blocks of our selves and our world. By declaring that, like all other phenomena, these too are equally empty of inherent existence, it goes well beyond that kind of reductionist materialism, which is probably the dominant cultural view in the modern West.

To say that all things are void, however, is not to say that they don't exist at all. Emptiness is not nihilism. Clearly and undeniably there are appearances of things and those appearances follow reliable laws and function in terms of predictable cause and effect. It turns out, rather, that to see that something is empty is to see that it is beyond the categories of 'existing' or 'not existing'. Asked by the monk Kaccāyana about Right View, the Buddha answered:

> That things exist, O Kaccāyana, is one extreme [of view]. That they do not exist is another. Rejecting both these extremes, the Tathāgata points out the Dhamma via the middle.[10]

The voidness of things is the 'Middle Way'[11] between the assumptions of existence and non-existence, being and non-being, and it is this that needs to be understood. In Nāgārjuna's *Ratnāvalī* it says:

---

[10] SN 12:15. 'The Tathāgata' is an epithet the Buddha often used to refer to himself. (All translations from SN are the author's own, made also with reference to the translations of both Thanissaro Bhikkhu in *Handful of Leaves Vol. 2* and *Vol. 5* [Redwood City, CA: Sati Center for Buddhist Studies, and Valley Center, CA: Metta Forest Monastery, 2003 and 2007] and Bhikkhu Bodhi in *The Connected Discourses of the Buddha: A New Translation of the Saṃyutta Nikāya, Vol. I* and *Vol. II* [Boston: Wisdom Publications, 2000].)

[11] *Madhyamaka* is the name, within the tradition, for the philosophy that treads this Middle Way of the emptiness of all things.

> It is deluded to conceive of this mirage-like world as either existent or non-existent. In delusion there is no liberation.[12]

And again in the *Yuktiṣaṣṭikā*:

> One does not gain liberation through reification. Nor does one free oneself from *saṃsāra* through nihilism... By thoroughly understanding existence and non-existence, the great beings obtain liberation.[13]

It's important also to realize that we are not asked to 'believe in' emptiness or accept in blind faith this teaching of the illusory nature of things. As with almost all of the Buddha's teachings, we can investigate the matter and find out for ourselves. When we do, we discover that as our understanding of voidness deepens through our own practice, we still very much respect the functioning of conventional reality. But we've undermined, in a way that takes the suffering out of experience, the beliefs that reify things.

Seeing emptiness opens compassion

The concern that emptiness implies a kind of moral nihilism, an attitude that 'we can do whatever we want because everything is empty', and that following this path we will not care for the plight of others and the world, we can also test through our own practice. But we will find that as insight into these teachings deepens, we become, as a matter of course, more easily moved to concern for the world, and more sensitive to ethics and the consequences of our actions. Opening to voidness should definitely not lead to a lack of care, to indifference, cold aloofness, or a closing of the heart. If I find that my practice is somehow making me less compassionate, less generous, less caring about ethics, then something is wrong in my understanding or at the very least out of balance in my approach, and I need to modify how I am practising.

Generally speaking, and although it may at first seem paradoxical, as we travel this meditative journey into emptiness we find that the more we taste the

---

[12] Translation adapted from Jeffrey Hopkins's in *Nāgārjuna's Precious Garland: Buddhist Advice for Living and Liberation* [Ithaca, NY: Snow Lion, 2007] p. 101.

[13] Translation from the author's notes.

voidness of all things, the more loving-kindness, compassion, generosity, and deep care for the world open naturally as a consequence in the heart. Seeing emptiness opens love. Just as Nāgārjuna wrote:

> Without doubt, when practitioners have developed their understanding of emptiness, their minds will be devoted to the welfare of others.[14]

We usually find too that our capacity and energy to actually serve also grow organically as our insight into emptiness matures.

Entering into the mystery…

Although, due to fundamental delusion, our habitual, ubiquitous, and almost uninterrupted tendency is to intuitively conceive of things as either existing or not existing, the Buddha's response to Kaccāyana suggests that something more profound and mysterious than our usual conceptions is being communicated in these teachings. And as we learn to deepen our understanding through meditation, we discover that not only does seeing into emptiness bring a rare and crucial freedom, sweet relief, joy, and love, there is in the seeing of it more and more a sense of beauty, of mystery. It becomes indeed a mystical understanding. We uncover a dimension of wonder in things that we hadn't known before, because the voidness of things is something truly magical when experienced deeply. We come to appreciate what is meant when in the Ch'an tradition it is said of all phenomena:

> Truly empty, [hence] unfathomable existence.[15]

We begin to open to a whole other sense of the true nature of things. As Chandrakīrti, echoing an earlier *sūtra*, wrote:

> The Teacher has proclaimed that all phenomena are primordially

---

[14] In his *Bodhicittavivaraṇa*. (Translation adapted from Chr. Lindtner's in *Nagarjuniana: Studies in the Writings and Philosophy of Nāgārjuna* [Delhi: Motilal Banarsidass, 1987] p. 207.)

[15] Translation by Gadjin M. Nagao in *Mādhyamika and Yogācāra* [Albany: State University of New York Press, 1991] p. 166.

> peace, free from arising, and that their real nature transcends every pain.[16]

We understand: this is neither nihilism nor reification. As the Zen saying puts it: "True emptiness equals wondrous being."

---

[16] MAV 6:112. In general in this book, translations from MAV are composites of translations by the following: Tyler Dewar in Wangchuk Dorje, The Ninth Karmapa, *The Karmapa's Middle Way: Feast for the Fortunate* [Ithaca, NY: Snow Lion, 2008]; Padmakara Translation Group in Chandrakirti and Mipham, *Introduction to the Middle Way: Chandrakirti's Madhayamakavatara with Commentary by Jamgön Mipham* [Boston: Shambala, 2002]; Ari Goldfield, Jules Levinson, Jim Scott and Birgitt Scott (under the guidance of Khenpo Tsültrim Gyamtso Rinpoche) in Chandrakirti and the Eighth Karmapa Mikyö Dorje, *The Moon of Wisdom: Chapter Six of Chandrakirti's Entering the Middle Way* [Ithaca, NY: Snow Lion, 2005].

2

Emptiness, Fabrication, and Dependent Arising

Dependent on the mind

The Buddha's assertion that things are beyond existing and not existing[1] is not easy to fully comprehend. One of the keys that can unlock our ability to realize, more than just intellectually, this mystical way things are is tied in with an important way in which our holographic tiger illustration is limited. For that illustration gives no suggestion of a certain aspect of the illusory nature of things – how all appearances are fabricated *by the mind*.

The examples of the chair in the fire and the 'Z' do point to how the thingness of things is dependent on the mind, but perhaps do not convey the full extent and implications of this dependence. Likewise, when we hear or read that what is meant by the voidness of a thing is simply the fact of its dependence on causes and conditions, the central import of this dependence on mind may go unrecognized. While at one level it is certainly an accurate statement to say that something is empty because it depends on various elements and conditions, it is vital to open out completely just what this means. Nāgārjuna wrote:

> Emptiness is just this dependent arising.[2]

And in the same text:

> This world arises from imagination… it is unreal.

It is this dependence of all phenomena on the mind that is most significant and that needs to be understood. Teachings on voidness are offered in the service of liberation, yet it may be that an explanation of emptiness as meaning 'dependence

---

[1] SN 12:15

[2] *Lokātītastava*. (All translations from *Lokātītastava* are the author's own.)

on causes and conditions' is grasped in only a limited way, and so yields only very limited freedom, if any at all, and misses the profundity of what is being communicated. If, for example, I own an expensive china vase, my knowledge of the many and rare conditions which had to come together for its creation – the particular mix of clays sourced perhaps from various barely accessible mountains, all the conditions involved in the formation of those clays over time, the conditions for their extraction, all the conditions involved in the development and handing down of the techniques used by the artisan who crafted it, the conditions sustaining the life of that artisan, and so on – rather than leading to my letting go of attachment to the vase, might actually increase my attachment to it.

Acknowledging dependency on causes and conditions merely at this level of materiality will only sometimes bring a release of clinging. It will often do little to undermine our sense of the reality of objects. And as we have explained, it is this belief in their reality which supports our clinging, and so our *dukkha*. A level of insight that sees the dependency of phenomena on the mind, however, will open an understanding of their being beyond existing and not existing, and so bring freedom much more powerfully. But this dependency on the mind is also a more mysterious and radical dependency to fathom.

Fabricated, therefore illusory

Certainly, then, the Buddha declared that all phenomena are *saṃskṛta* (Pali: *saṅkhata*) – 'constructed', 'fabricated', or 'concocted'. But in his more detailed descriptions of dependent arising, which we shall in due course come to work with, he explained more fully how all appearances and perceptions arise dependent on the mind, constructed by the mind. He taught how the mind, through delusion, fabricates all the aggregates of experience.

> Just as a painter... would fashion the likeness of a woman or a man, complete with all its major and minor parts, the ignorant, ordinary person, creating, creates form... creates *vedanā*... creates perception... creates mental formations... creates consciousness.[3]

[3] SN 22:100. The word *vedanā* means 'sensation', or, more specifically, the 'feeling-tone' of sensation – pleasant, unpleasant, or neither pleasant nor unpleasant.

The words 'fabricated' and 'concocted' are good words to translate *saṃskṛta*, because in English, not only do they have the meaning of being 'constructed', or 'built', but also the suggestion of being somehow 'untrue'. A 'lie' is a 'fabrication' we say. And this is also the fullness of the Buddha's meaning. When he proclaims that things are fabricated, he is declaring much more than the simple fact that they were put together from other building blocks as causes and conditions. He is pointing more radically to their illusory nature. Again this is echoed by Nāgārjuna:

> The Blessed One has said that a thing that deceives is false. Constructions are all deceiving, therefore they are false.[4]

The world of inner and outer phenomena is, in some very important sense, 'fabricated', 'fashioned', 'constructed' by the mind, so that it is somehow illusory, not real in the way that we assume, and not independent of the mind that fabricates it.

Let's elaborate our illustration of the holographic tiger slightly differently to draw out this aspect of emptiness. Imagine that you enter a room that is dark except for a lamp in one corner. There you see your friend, huddled next to the lamp in a state of great anxiety and staring transfixed at the wall opposite. "A wolf! A wolf!", he is whimpering in fear. Turning to look at the wall, you see a large silhouette of a wolf but very quickly realize that it is just the shadow of your friend's hands, cast by the lamplight on the wall. In his fear he is completely unaware of his hands or how he is holding them, or the fact that the wolf shape is merely their shadow. What will you say to him?

The ramifications for freedom here are of course similar to those in the case of the holographic tiger. This illustration has the slight advantage, however, of implicating our involvement somehow in fabricating the illusion and the appearances of things. In this scenario, although your friend may have been trying to 'be with' the wolf, 'accept' its presence, even remind himself of the impermanence of all things, at the deepest and most significant level 'insight' and 'wisdom' here must mean seeing that the wolf is a fabrication that he himself has been fabricating. Pointing this out to him would also be the most compassionate response to his plight that you could offer him, *if* he was ready to hear it and to let go of the wolf. Understanding this, there might then be the possibility that he could do something about it – stop it perhaps, or fabricate something else that doesn't bring so much *dukkha*.

Likewise, the general meanings of 'insight', 'wisdom', and 'compassion' must also include, most fundamentally, insight into how all phenomena and appearances are concocted by the mind. Rather than something to judge ourselves

[4] MMK 13:1.

for, however, this fabricating is simply what all minds, without exception, do. It's how they work, part of their nature. Liberation comes from understanding this illusory nature of all appearances. The Buddha taught that *any and all*

> … perception is like a mirage.[5]

Challenging assumptions

All the illustrations we have used, and indeed all conceptual explanations we might give at this point, are limited though. They all share a certain kind of limitation in that they each point to the emptiness of one thing, whilst leaving another part of the illustration quietly untouched. It can safely be assumed, however, that with respect to what is left unexamined and not consciously and clearly seen to be empty we will have a tacit assumption of inherent existence – it will continue to be there unless it is explicitly exposed. Our default sense of things, our habitual mode of perception, is to project inherent existence onto phenomena, *not* to see their emptiness deeply. Just because we are not publicly proclaiming that something is inherently existent, it does not mean we are recognizing its emptiness and reversing the perspective of *avijjā.*

Our various illustrations are also each limited in unique ways, and between them we are walking a tightrope that is the Middle Way. Some, like the 'Z' illustration, may not seem so radical in their implication for freedom. Others, like the hand-silhouette wolf, may seem too radical though, preposterously close, in what they are suggesting, to an assertion that only the mind is real, or that it can freely and happily 'create its own reality' as it chooses.

It may be at this point that the gist and understanding of emptiness that you are taking from our short discussion so far seems as if it wouldn't make that much difference to your sense of existence. Or it may seem to be suggesting something

---

[5] SN 22:95. As will quickly become evident the word 'perception' is being used to mean more than the mental verbal labelling of something experienced, or the recognition of a phenomenon from previous experience. Although aware that some prefer these last, more limited, definitions, we will use the word 'perceiving' in a way that implies, more fully, the forming of appearances, the differentiation into things – no matter how vague, subtle, or spacious – possessing various attributes; the word 'perception' will be used to mean the thing sensed, the experience, regardless of whether it is mentally labelled or remembered. As far as deepening practice and insight are concerned, construing it thus will be much more helpful and will in the long run allow a more complete comprehension of the Buddha's teachings. For further discussion see Chapters 19, 21, and 28.

utterly implausible for which you harbour great scepticism. Either way, please again bear in mind that it will probably only be possible for a practitioner to begin to get a truer and more balanced understanding of the subtlety of what exactly is being said in this teaching about fabrication when (s)he has developed for a little while the sorts of practices that are introduced starting in Chapters 12 to 14. Practising in certain ways, we begin to see fabrication and its radical implications firsthand.

Emptiness definitely challenges the common-sense assumptions we have of things. And typically we have all kinds of assumptions we do not even realize we have. In relation to one of them in particular, it is vital at this point to say something important about our *method*. If we are not careful, we may simply assume a common default position – happily admitting that some experiences and phenomena are somehow fabricated (illusory), while tacitly, or even more explicitly, presuming others to be true (not fabricated, not illusory). As the modus operandi of our ongoing investigations, though, we will *keep open the question* of what is and what isn't fabricated, and simply keep deepening our ability to expose the fabricated nature of more and more phenomena as far as possible. We will not arrest our inquiry prematurely by presuming from the start a limited range to what is fabricated.

The mystery of fabrication

In time, through adopting this stance of ongoing inquiry in practice, we will in fact come to see for ourselves that all phenomena, all experiences, are fabricated by the mind. It is necessary, though, to add something to this statement, because as we develop our skill and follow this investigation deeper, we witness something even more radical and astounding. As the Buddha discovered, not only appearances, but the 'whole show' is fabricated, including the mind with its various factors and its consciousness. Thus he also declared the illusory nature of *any and all* awareness, any consciousness[6] of anything. Through a potent simile he illustrated both the fabricated and the illusory nature of awareness:

[6] Depending on their background, some readers will be more familiar with approaches that make a distinction between the two words 'awareness' and 'consciousness', ascribing them different meanings and significances. In this book however, rather than defining them differently, we will for the most part use the two terms identically and interchangeably. As will become clear, such a choice keeps open a broad range of possibilities for meditative practices, which we shall explore, and from which various experiences and insights into the nature of awareness will emerge. Inquiry into this whole area – the nature of awareness/consciousness/mind – is rich and subtle and will be addressed progressively and more fully in Chapters 15, and 25 to 30.

> Suppose… a magician or a magician's apprentice should hold a magic show at the four crossroads, and a keen-sighted man should see it, reflect on it, and examine it radically. Even as he sees it, reflects on it, and examines it radically, he would find it empty; he would find it hollow; he would find it void of essence. What essence… could there be in a magic show?
>
> Even so, whatever consciousness – be it past, future, or present, in oneself or external, gross or subtle, inferior or superior, far or near – a monk sees it, reflects on it, and examines it radically. And even as he sees it, reflects on it, and examines it radically, he would find it empty, he would find it hollow, he would find it void of essence. What essence… could there be in consciousness?
>
> … Consciousness is like a magic show.[7]

It is not that while everything else is fabricated by the mind, the mind itself is somehow real, a really existing basis for the fabrication. The mind, whether conceived as mental processes or 'Awareness' – even the awareness that we can know as vast and unperturbed, that seems natural and effortless – is also fabricated in the process. We find, in the end, that there is no 'ground' to fabrication.

And as if that were not cause enough for amazement, we eventually also recognize, taking this exploration of dependent arising deeper and deeper still, that even this profound realization of the fabricated nature of all phenomena is only a relative truth. Fabrication itself is empty too. Ultimately, it turns out we cannot say that things are fabricated, nor that they are not fabricated. We cannot even say that they arise and cease, nor that they do not arise and cease. What we come to understand is that the way things truly are is beautifully beyond the capacities of our conception. Practising with dependent arising forms a thread, though, that can be followed to such great depths. For in doing so, insights of greater and greater profundity are progressively opened, until this thread ultimately dissolves even itself. It leads and opens beyond itself.

---

[7] SN 22:95.

3

"All is Void!" – Initial Reactions, and Responses

What the Dharma thus teaches, and what we will discover for ourselves as practice evolves, is that absolutely everything is empty, without exception. The self is empty. So too is the body, and the whole material world, together with its constituent elements, its subatomic particles, fields, and forces. Also all our inner experiences, emotions, and thoughts; and even whatever experiences we might have through 'bare attention' that so much seem as if they are 'direct experiences' of 'things as they are' – indeed, whatever is perceived, as the Buddha said, is empty.

Void as well are whatever might be conceived as the functional 'processes' of the body and of the mind; the 'flow' of impermanent events and experiences, inner and outer; the infinite web of conditions that support all things; and the process of fabrication too. Even such apparently obvious and undeniable givens that seem to form the very foundations of existence – space, time (and not just the past and the future, but also the present, 'the Now'), and awareness, however it is conceived or experienced – these too are empty; Buddha Nature, and whatever notions or senses we may have of 'Being' or 'Essence'; emptiness itself, and even the Unfabricated – all are thoroughly void, in some deep sense illusory.

Typically these insights unfold step by step. And as mentioned, along with the radical liberation that is opened, this realization of the emptiness of all phenomena begins to elicit from the heart and the mind a profound reverence, a deep bowing of the whole being. We are touched, amazed and awestruck at the unfathomable mystery of things. Seeing this voidness also unlocks a depth of joy. Thus, for example, Mipham wrote:

> In the infinite expanse of equality without reference point, all the phenomena of *saṃsāra* and *nirvāṇa* are perfectly complete… Thanks [to the teaching of dependent arising and emptiness] the light of wisdom's brilliant flame has shone upon me, dispelling

> the darkness of doubt and causing profound certainty to arise.
> Ema! A la la! How wonderful! How blissful![1]

And Saraha, too, sang:

> The self is void, the world is void; heaven, earth, and the space between are void; there is neither virtue nor sin in this bliss.[2]

Disbelief

On initially hearing or reading that all is empty, however, we may have a whole range of reactions. Some we have already mentioned and responded to a little, but beginning the journey it is usually helpful to explore this a bit more fully. For a minority this radical emptiness seems right from the start to have the ring of truth. Something in the intuition resonates and responds, the heart is touched or excited, even while keenly aware of not yet properly understanding quite what it all means.

Most people, though, will have a mixed and somewhat ambivalent reaction to the teachings and the prospect of their realization. Often there may be not just puzzlement, but disbelief. As explained in Chapter 1, our intuitive sense and immediate experience of most things is simply that they *are* real. The world seems so obviously real, and so the teaching of emptiness runs counter to our experience and our gut feelings about the way things are. It might strike us as being a patently incredible, even ridiculous, teaching, and so one we may be tempted to simply dismiss without further investigation. Perhaps through repeated exposure to certain more common spiritual teachings, we might find it easier to understand that the 'ego' is empty. This we might be quite happy to concede or believe. "But *all* things?", we might wonder, "How could *everything* be empty? Surely, for whatever appears, there needs to be *something* real to provide its ground and basis?"

These are very normal and understandable responses. Again, however, we need to remember that this journey asks for open-mindedness and humility. The Buddha declared often that the insights one comes to as practice deepens run counter to the common view:

---

[1] *Jewel of the Powerful Nāgārjuna's Intention that Perfectly Illuminates the True Nature.* (Translation by Ari Goldfield in Khenpo Tsültrim Gyamtso, *The Sun of Wisdom: Teachings on Noble Nagarjuna's Fundamental Wisdom of the Middle Way* [Boston: Shambala, 2003] p. 168.)

[2] From his *Dohakoṣa*. (Translation from the author's notes.)

> Whatever is considered as 'This is true' by the world, with its deities, *Māras*, and *Brahmās*, with its contemplatives and priests, its royalty and common people, is properly seen by the Noble Ones with right wisdom as it actually is, as 'This is false'…
>
> Whatever is considered as 'This is false' by the world… and common people is properly seen by the Noble Ones with right wisdom as it actually is, as 'This is true'.[3]

We need also to recognize that on this adventure we must investigate and find out for ourselves, without deciding on the truth in advance. Maintaining the openness of an ongoing spirit of inquiry is essential, and it brings the path to life.

Worries of meaninglessness

A second possible reaction that can frequently arise was also already mentioned in Chapter 1, in our brief discussion of the view of nihilism. Even after hearing that emptiness does not mean nihilism, some may still worry that, going deeply into these practices, their life will somehow become cold, loveless, or bleak, or that a sense of meaninglessness will pervade existence. "If I do eventually see there's no self, that nothing's real, won't I then feel that there's no point to anything?" Here it is vitally important not to jump to imagining what some end-point of practice will look like, but rather to proceed gradually with whatever letting go you can actually feel, in your own practice, through seeing an emptiness that's accessible to you right now.

For instance, as we will explore in Chapter 9, I might begin to notice that a certain way I have unkindly defined myself or my personality, perhaps for decades, is simply not a fixed truth of who I am. Seeing this clearly, I let go of the tight binding of this particular self-view, and begin to feel a degree of freedom, released from the familiar but painful confines of that particular prison. And although it's possible that this newfound freedom feels a little disorienting for a while, I soon get used to it and enjoy the novel sense of spaciousness. In the case of the more entrenched and invested-in self-definitions that I let go of, it may be that I feel very temporarily bereft of purpose before I discover a more authentic meaningfulness; but I certainly don't encounter in this letting go any sense of a

[3] Sn 3:12

fundamental meaninglessness to all existence. And rather than feeling barren and cold, I find that I feel more genuinely engaged and more caring and open to love.

Taking this step and finding that I feel no harm from it, only benefit, allows me to trust the process, step by step. When I see that *that* much emptiness was fine, that it actually brought joy, it's likely I can trust that a little more will also be fine. I can feel confident enough that it will bring freedom and heartfulness, not disconnection.

Fear of annihilation

Closely connected with this and with a suspicion of nihilism that may be present, there can be a strong fear of 'annihilation' that arises, a fear that the self will somehow be destroyed. The possibility of fear occurring at times during these meditations we will address later as the practices develop.[4] Sometimes though, this fear arises even when simply hearing about the voidness of the self or of things. It is important then to point out right here that we are not trying to annihilate the self through these teachings or practices. Rather, we are seeking to understand something about the self and all phenomena – their emptiness, their fabricated and illusory nature. And this emptiness is true of the self and of all things anyway, even now, whether I'm aware of it or not. Nothing changes in the actual reality -- the ontological status – of the self or of phenomena through practice. We are simply realizing a fact that has been true all along. And this realization frees.

Using dukkha and immediate experience as guides

Related to all this, another aspect of our method is worth mentioning at this point. I have found, in my own practice and through teaching, that the realization of emptiness deepens and brings more felt fruits in life if it is approached not only gradually, but also primarily in relation to whatever is immediate in our experience, including, and even especially, any *dukkha* that may be present in the moment –

[4] See, for example, Chapters 5 and 14. Although it is actually likely that fears of various kinds will occasionally come up for anyone meditating deeply on emptiness, the intensity of such fears really need not be very great. Chapter 5 explains how the depth of well-being opened to through *samādhi* practices can be helpful in minimizing the arising and the strength of such fear. And in Chapter 14 in particular we will explore ways of working skilfully with these fears in meditation, so that they need not present a problem or a block at all.

these sensations, *this* emotion, *these* thoughts, and also *this* physical pain, *this* heartache, *this* contracted self-view – learning to see *their* emptiness, and then deepening and widening the range of experienced phenomena we can recognize to be empty. As we learn to let go of grosser *dukkha* and experiences through realizing their voidness, meditation naturally refines. Then we can work skilfully with more subtle *dukkha* and phenomena, and insight too becomes correspondingly subtle.

I know one can quite successfully take a different route and begin by considering and trying to understand the emptiness of external objects such as tables and cars. Questioning such objects' ontological status so early in the journey, however, won't for the most part tend to have much impact on my felt sense of *dukkha* – unless perhaps it's actually *that* table, *that* car that I am attached to, and suffering over, that is being considered.

The approach developed here seems to me to ensure two things. First, it keeps the process feeling very alive, meaningful and relevant to my experience, to my life and the unfolding liberation I can know for myself in the present. It will not then be an abstract philosophical exercise. Instead I will feel, in this very moment, the relief, freedom, and joy that any realization of voidness brings. And second, most often it actually turns out to be easier to see and understand emptiness when it is approached via one's own *dukkha*. Though we will talk a little now and then of chairs and chariots, we will find we get a much more complete and direct understanding of how the mind fabricates both *dukkha* and experience in general when we are focusing on this particular *dukkha* and experience that is present.

Doubts about our own capacity

On hearing of the possibility of deep insight into emptiness, one other reaction that may arise is self-doubt: "How could someone like me hope to realize such profound and subtle insights?" Painful self-doubt and self-criticism are epidemic in our culture, and can wield a power that is enormously destructive and paralysing. Although perhaps the seeds of such distortions of view are only completely eradicated through seeing the voidness of self and phenomena, in most cases it is vital to find various means to at least somewhat disempower their claims right at the beginning of the path. There are so many helpful possibilities and a great deal could be said in relation to these difficult inner constellations. Here though, we will just mention a few things very briefly.

Perhaps the most important is to reiterate the wisdom of proceeding gradually, as described. By witnessing the freeing success of one's efforts step by step, confidence develops naturally. Implicit in this statement, however, is that we each need to find what actually works *for us* in meditation. Very often a large part of what underlies the proliferation of self-doubt in relation to practice is that we have not yet discovered ways of working in meditation that we can really feel for ourselves are helpful. With experimentation we can find out; and once we do, self-doubt begins to melt as confidence slowly develops.

We might emphasize too the importance of kindness in meditation in general. And in particular, the gradually transformative and inexorable healing power that comes through devotion to regular loving-kindness (*mettā*) practice should not be underestimated. Here again, it is absolutely vital to find ways of cultivating *mettā* that work for you. There is no one 'right' way of doing that. Creativity, playfulness, and experimentation are indispensable.

Often untapped, there is also an equally great power accessible in heartfully connecting with our own deepest aspirations. Self-criticism tends to squash these aspirations and obscure our connection with them. Conversely though, tuning into and sustaining a focus on the felt force of these aspirations within oneself – in ways that allow them to gather strength, and allow the being to open to that strength – can significantly undermine the dynamics of self-criticism.

Developing insight gradually

Although admittedly at the profoundest levels not always easy, the full range of insights into emptiness *is* available to us, whatever the self-critical voice maintains. The vital question is: how? As well as it being helpful for the confidence to proceed gradually, a progressive training of our capacities to see the voidness of things is usually unavoidable anyway. We need to start where it is relatively easy for us and then build on those foundations, extending the range and the depth of our penetrative insights, and developing the seeing in this way.

As we begin to experience the liberating effects of insight and the heart is touched, the whole process starts to take on a momentum of its own. While at first these may have seemed such strange ways of looking at things, and still probably involve some effort, the mind begins to gravitate towards exposing the emptiness of this and that, of situations and perspectives that we would have solidified before. To the heart is revealed a sense of beauty in the open, space-like nature of things. More able to shift ways of looking, less locked into any perspective, it wants to see the emptiness. Gradually conviction builds, based firmly on our experience.

PART TWO

Tools and Provisions

4

The Cultivation of Insight

What is 'Insight'?

Before outlining how such a gradual development of our seeing might be cultivated, a couple of pivotal concepts in relation to insight need introducing, for they will be fundamental to the whole approach we will use. Insight, it is important to point out, may viably be defined in various ways. Here, we will not attempt to set down a complete, or even a totally precise, formula for what it is. Rather, we will try to say just enough to begin to open up the possibility of a subtly but significantly different conception of practice than that with which many readers will be familiar. Then through this, the possibilities of new and different avenues of practice may also be opened.

For now, let us take as a loose definition of insight: any realization, understanding, or way of seeing things that brings, to any degree, a dissolution of, or a decrease in, *dukkha*. We should, right away, draw attention to a few of the immediate implications of such a definition, and in doing so we can also clarify more what is meant here.

First, insight defined thus is not, in itself, a certain experience that we need to attain. Extraordinary experiences may, to be sure, be important at times but they are not what actually frees. Nor is insight simply 'being mindful and watching the show', without any effect on, or input into, the fabrication or dissolution of the experience of *dukkha*. Just knowing, for example, that *dukkha*, grasping, or reactivity is present is hardly ever enough to free us from it even in that moment. And it certainly will not be enough to exhaust or eradicate the latent tendencies of craving and aversion. What is needed is an understanding that cuts or melts something or other more fundamental on which that *dukkha* relies, thus eradicating, or at least diminishing, that *dukkha*.

Second, defining insight in this way admits a wide range to its manifestation. It can be present in any situation, or in regard to any experience or phenomenon: gross or extremely subtle, easy to see or more profound, 'worldly' or more transcendent. It may manifest as the understanding of a *personal* pattern that has been problematic. Or it may involve the recognition of something more *universal* – the fact of impermanence impressing itself more compellingly on the mind and heart, for instance, or, indeed, a realization at some level of the emptiness of something. Always the essential characteristic, though, is that it contributes to lessening *dukkha*.

Third, however, it is important to stress that, as we are defining it here, only what is actually *perceivable* to a practitioner qualifies as an insight for that practitioner. I may, for example, feel anxious when I check my bank balance and see that there is no money at all in my account. But refusing to believe the bank statement and simply choosing to believe instead that I have a million dollars in the account would not in itself constitute an insight according to our definition here, even if it did have the effect of reducing my suffering. More generally, any introduction of a belief not based on perception, or similarly, any introduction of notions of unobservable entities would also, strictly speaking, be excluded from this particular definition of insight.[1]

Fourth, and related to this last point: Rather than being based upon faith in the experience of another, or upon blind beliefs – even 'Buddhist' beliefs – about how things are, insight, as we are defining it, is based primarily on personal experience of what decreases *dukkha*. When there is insight, the seeing melts *dukkha*; and that release of *dukkha* we can feel and know for ourselves.

Insight and the Four Noble Truths

Insight, then, may loosely be described as any 'seeing' that frees. For some though, despite the qualifications just listed, this might still seem a strange way to think of it. Possibly one may be wondering just what relationship insight thus conceived has with 'reality' or 'truth'. In response, we can just briefly draw attention at this point to an important aspect of the Buddha's approach and to some of its consequences.

Repeatedly the Buddha stressed that his entire Teaching addresses essentially only the question of *dukkha* and the ending of *dukkha*.[2] In effect then, the primary and unifying principle overarching the whole of the Dharma is the relieving of suffering and dis-ease. Although not immediately obvious, this conception and

---

[1] None of this is to make any judgment whatsoever on the value of such beliefs, nor on the possibility and the possible efficacy of their use. It is only that, for the most part, these kinds of approaches lie beyond the scope of this book and of the approach to insight outlined here.

[2] E.g. in SN 22:86; SN 56:31; MN 2; MN 63.

approach of the Buddha has immensely significant ramifications that we shall repeatedly return to and expand on and that will become more apparent and more fully understood with more practice. It turns out that making the relief of suffering and dis-ease the fundamental thrust and concern of practice is not only the most compassionate and skilful support for the alleviation of *dukkha*, such an approach also begins to uncover the truth of things in the process. In taking the dissolving of *dukkha* as our primary investigation, reality is gradually revealed. On the path the Buddha discovered, then, insight, discernment of truth, and freedom from *dukkha* all unfold together.

The Buddha's formulation of the Four Noble Truths[3] is basically an elaboration of this overarching Dharma principle – the cardinal orientation towards liberation from *dukkha*. And in its very direct concern with the releasing of *dukkha*, the conception of insight we are adopting may be regarded as a kind of shorthand and immediate version of the Four Noble Truths.

This is so because in approaching insight through the loose definition given here, a practitioner's focus in the moment is, in effect, channelled through the lens of the teaching of the Four Noble Truths – albeit often a slightly simplified version of that teaching. That is to say, in relation to phenomena, (s)he will, in some way or other, explicitly or implicitly, be focusing on the actual experience of *dukkha* (the First Noble Truth), on recognizing what is supporting it (the Second Noble Truth), and on finding ways of seeing, understanding, and relating that enable the experience of its relief to some extent (loosely, the Fourth and Third Truths respectively).

Now, in travelling this path of insight outlined by the Four Noble Truths, sometimes we understand something and that understanding will lessen *dukkha* in the future. Perhaps, for example, it becomes very clear to us how acting unethically in a certain way inevitably brings suffering for ourselves and others; or how crucial it is to take care of the heart and mind through cultivating beautiful qualities such as *mettā*, *samādhi,* generosity, and compassion. The clarity of realization can be enough to prevent us acting in that harmful way in the future; or enough to help us commit to a life of practice. In these instances, the insight lessens future suffering.

We can, as well, understand in ways that dissolve some degree of *dukkha* also in the moment that we are seeing. In these cases, there is a felt sense of relief, release, or freedom, through some realization and at the very time of that

---

[3] The Four are the Truths of: *dukkha*; the origination of *dukkha*; the destruction of *dukkha*; the way to the destruction of *dukkha*.

realization. The feelings of relief and release then are indicators to us that insight is happening, that we are on the right track.

As practitioners, we are of course interested in both the kinds of insight that contribute to future freedom and those that bring freedom in the moment too. For our purposes, though, we are particularly interested in the latter.

Modes of Insight and 'Ways of Looking'

Let's make a further distinction. You have probably had the experience of an insight arising spontaneously as you were being mindfully present with something. You 'have' or 'get' an insight. There is an 'aha!' moment: suddenly or gradually, you see something, you realize something, and it makes a difference to the *dukkha*. Such an insight arose as a *result* of mindfulness, or of qualities like calm or investigation.

This mode of insight practice is in contrast to another mode in which we can also work at times, where insight itself is more a *starting point*, a *cause*, more itself the *method*. In this second mode of insight practice we more deliberately attempt to sustain a '*way of looking*' at experience – a view of, or relationship with, experience – that is already informed by a certain insight or other. Here, rather than 'getting' (or hoping to 'get') an insight, we are *using* an insight. This does not mean merely to 'think something insightful', for instance that "all things are impermanent" – thinking may or may not be involved – but actually to shift into a mode where we are looking through the lens of a particular insight (looking deliberately *for* and *at* the impermanence and change in everything, for example). Then we are, intentionally, actually seeing and experiencing things in a different way than usual, one that is more in line with and emphasizing some insight or other. If insight is what frees, then sustaining any insightful way of looking will free, to some extent, in that moment. And it will keep freeing as long as we sustain it. Thus the use and meaning of 'insight' in this mode is as a '*way of looking that frees*'. And we might similarly speak of '*insight ways of looking*'.

Since insights rarely make a lasting difference if they are seen only a few times, this second mode of approach will also have the important effect of consolidating any particular insight used. Being repeated, the insight is more likely to be gradually absorbed and to become rooted in the heart's understanding in ways that can make a long-term difference.

Additionally, this second mode of approach supports an organic deepening of insight. Repeating, cultivating, and prolonging a way of looking that embodies a certain level of some initial insight should lead naturally to more profound insights emerging passively from the space and foundational ground of that sustained way of looking. Over time, any such newer, more profound insight can be consolidated. And then this deeper insight may itself be employed in turn as a more powerful way of looking. This whole movement can potentially be repeated again and again at successive levels of seeing and understanding. In the process, insight is progressively refined and deepened in a stronger and more trustworthy way.

The Inevitability of Fabrication

To some, this second mode of insight practice, where liberating ways of looking are intentionally cultivated and sustained, may initially sound unattractive. This is quite a common reaction, and there are various possible reasons for it. One may involve a belief that 'being' and 'doing' are really different. Often then, 'just being' is regarded as preferable or somehow more authentic. As we will see, however, with the maturing of insight into dependent arising and fabrication one realizes that this perceived dichotomy between 'being' and 'doing', though it might at first seem and feel self-evident, is in fact essentially mistaken and based on a false impression. It rests on three basic and connected assumptions:

1. That there actually is an objective reality that we can and should 'be with'.
2. That anything other than the awareness 'simply knowing' or innocently, naturally 'receiving' this 'reality' is somehow a laboured and artificially constructed state.
3. That since a state of 'being' is thus assumed to be a state of 'non-doing' and so to involve no effort, self will not be constructed there. This is in contrast to states more obviously involving intention, which are assumed to construct self.

It turns out, though, that whenever there is *any experience at all*, there is always some fabricating, which is a kind of 'doing'. And as an element of this fabricating, there is always a way of looking too. We construct, through our way of looking, what we experience. This is a part of what needs eventually to be recognized and fully comprehended. Sooner or later we come to realize that perhaps the most fundamental, and most fundamentally important, fact about any experience is that it depends on the way of looking. That is to say, it is empty.[4] Other than what we can perceive through different ways of looking, there is no 'objective reality' existing independently; and there is no way of looking that reveals some 'objective reality'. And as we shall also see, in states of 'just being' which we might imagine are devoid of self, a subtle self is actually being constructed anyway.[5] This fact too needs to be recognized.

Generally speaking, a full conviction that all this is the case will only be available through the deepening realizations which come mostly as emptiness practices progress. It must be pointed out, however, that all that is needed right now is an acknowledgment that different ways of looking are, at least sometimes, possible. Together with a willingness to experiment with various ways of looking, and to notice their effects on *dukkha* and on appearances, this will be enough to gradually unfold more profound insights.

It may also be that in the past a meditator has tried at times to adopt an approach somewhat similar to what is being described here, but felt discouraged for some reason and discontinued it. Perhaps there was a feeling of quickly becoming a little tired of engaging ways of looking deliberately, and then wanting to revert to a practice of 'just being with things as they appear'. Two things can be said about this here. First, as we shall explain, it is relatively easy to learn to minimize such fatigue – through learning the skills of subtle responsiveness to effort levels; and also through learning to include and enjoy the feelings such as release, freedom, and ease that insight ways of looking open.

Second, in the context of this approach to insight, a temporary reversion to basic mindfulness practice is not necessarily a problem in itself. Significantly however, without *conceiving* of practice in terms of ways of looking, it will be very likely that this reversion becomes a default and de facto reversion back to the assumption of 'being with things as they *are*', without realizing it. Without enough experience in seeing how different ways of looking fabricate different perceptions, it can be difficult to overcome the tacit assumption that things really are how they appear, or that there really is a way they are, in and of themselves. It can be difficult too even to realize that such assumptions are there. What seems like 'just being with things as they appear' will undoubtedly involve all kinds of views and assumptions, mostly unrecognized, about what is perceived. Thus it is

---

[4] As alluded to previously, this formulation of what emptiness means represents in fact only a certain level of understanding. Eventually it too is transcended through deepening practice. Nevertheless, understanding at this level constitutes a necessary and powerfully liberating stepping-stone for furthering insight into emptiness.

[5] See Chapter 11.

actually a way of looking; or, more likely, it will subsume, at different times, relatively diverse ways of looking.

This mode of approach, of actively cultivating a range of skilful ways of looking, is premised, then, on the understanding that we are *always and inevitably* engaged in some way of looking at or relating to experience anyway. But we are not usually aware of this fact. Nor are we usually aware of *how* we are looking – what exactly the view is – at any time. Even to intuitively and with immediacy feel a sensation in the body as 'mine', for instance, even without consciously thinking "mine", is a view, a way of looking at that sensation. We could say that the way of looking in any moment is constructed from the total mix of assumptions, conceptions, reactions, and inclinations, gross and subtle, conscious and unconscious, that are present at that time.

Now crucially, in any moment we are either engaging a way of looking at experience, self, and the world, that is creating, perpetuating, or compounding *dukkha* to some degree, or we are looking in a way that, to some degree, frees. Unfortunately, we mostly have a habit of looking at experience and phenomena in ways that tend to contribute to *dukkha,* not to its release and the unbinding of ourselves and the world. Certainly, with a little investigation, we can recognize this often enough at relatively gross levels; but at subtler levels we will find that it is almost always so. These habitual and normal tendencies to view things in ways that fabricate, compound, and tighten *dukkha* are deep-seated and difficult to reverse. Nevertheless, that is the great and beautiful work of the path. Insight meditation, indeed perhaps even the whole of the Dharma, could be conceived, very broadly, as the cultivation of ways of looking that lessen *dukkha*, that liberate.

Insight into Voidness

Through this exploration of various liberating ways of looking, we also begin to understand just how our perception of things is even more fundamentally flawed. As discussed earlier, we continually perceive phenomena as having a basic inherent existence. And this way of perceiving is itself, of course, also a view, a way of looking that is operating, and that supports *dukkha*. How will we see beyond it, and learn to see differently?

My experience in my own practice, in teaching, and in talking and listening to others, is that meditations using only the first mode of insight – that is, relying mostly on insight as a 'result' – will very probably not be enough on their own to overcome the force of deeply engrained habitual delusion that perceives and intuitively feels things to have inherent existence. As we have said, some element or aspect of a phenomenon will remain reified if it is not consciously and profoundly seen into. The overwhelming tendency is to unconsciously impute inherent existence to things, not to see emptiness. We need, therefore, to practise views that actually dissolve or remove this illusion of inherent existence.

Sustaining experimentation with certain ways of looking is one approach that can readily begin to reveal the voidness of appearances. And then, in time, it is also possible to practise viewing phenomena through lenses which actually include some level of understanding of emptiness. Different depths of understanding of emptiness, we will find, can be translated into different ways of looking.

Although it will be better understood as the various practices are unfolded, it is perhaps important to make something clear about such an approach right now. What is being suggested here involves much more than an intellectual assertion of the relativity of all perception, and a concomitant inability to uncover any more ultimate truth of things. For in the course of such practice we will become aware of more than just which ways of looking lead to *dukkha* and which to freedom. We also become aware of what exactly is included in any way of looking. And we can learn gradually to withdraw more and more of the elements in our looking that contribute to fabrication.

Meditation thus becomes a *journey of experimenting*: with freeing ways of looking; and in particular with ways of looking that withdraw, undermine, or dissolve various elements in the mind and heart that contribute to fabrication. On this journey something amazing is revealed. For as well as learning to drain the *dukkha* from situations and things, we are also learning to dismantle fabrication. In the process, we are moving towards opening to what is beyond conventional perception, what is unfabricated; and then there is the possibility of opening even beyond that to the fundamental truth of *all* things – their emptiness.

Seeing the Emptiness of Things: A Range of Means

As the journey progresses, we will offer for possible cultivation a whole variety of ways of looking that bring freedom and an unfolding of insight into the voidness of things. They might, broadly speaking, be initially divided into two groups, according to how insight into emptiness is arrived at. Each group will be expanded and explored in much detail throughout the book, but briefly now they are:

1. A gradually deepening inquiry into fabrication – of the self and of all experience

Here we are developing a certain kind of *understanding* of all experience, including meditation experiences. We begin by noticing the range of variability in our perceptions of self and the world. Sometimes I perceive myself or some thing one way, and at other times quite differently; and yet each time, what I perceive seems true, truly how I am, or how this thing is. What, though, is the 'real' way any thing is? I realize that how things appear always depends on how I look. And I realize too, moreover, that I cannot find or arrive at a way of looking that reveals how a thing *really is in itself.* Inquiring further into how appearances arise dependently, we begin to understand more exactly why 'this' appears and not 'that', and why things appear the way they do right now. This involves learning in meditation to be aware of how we are regarding and relating to things, what is included in our ways of looking at experience.

More than this though, as mentioned we can gradually develop ways of looking that fabricate, in this very moment, less and less *dukkha*. Clearly such skills will be helpful for us. The insights uncovered, however, are even more crucial. We realize, first, that *dukkha* depends on the way of looking. And, as briefly alluded to above, with deepening exploration we find we can discover and cultivate ways of looking that fabricate not only progressively less *dukkha*, but also less and less self, and eventually, as we shall explain, even less and less experience. Not to try and stay forever in some kind of unconstructed state, as if that were even possible, but to *understand* something wondrous about all experience in a way that fundamentally frees our whole sense of existence.

2. Realizing the impossibility of inherent existence

Here we are engaging in a thorough search for the self or for the essence of any thing. Such a search in practice considers and exhausts all the possible places or ways that it might exist, and so reveals that it simply cannot exist in the way that we perceive and feel it to. We see for ourselves and our conviction grows: not only is it unfindable, but it is *impossible* for it to exist with inherent existence as it seems to. In these kinds of practices, the way of looking hunts for, and then exposes the lack of, inherent existence in one or all phenomena. It then works to sustain the view of that lack, that emptiness, as it continues to regard that phenomenon or all phenomena.

This second group of approaches involve the use of logic and analysis *in meditation.* Depending on one's background or inclinations, there may sometimes be some resistance to these practices, or a suspicion that they will remain solely intellectual and thus not include or affect the heart. However, exploring in greater depth both our attitudes to analysis in meditation (Chapter 16) and the practices themselves (e.g. Chapters 17 and 22), we find that, like any practice, meditative analysis is an art that needs to be cultivated, and that it actually has a delightful and powerful liberating effect on the heart. And although without much questioning we might easily have assumed that it is unfeasible, we discover that, approached in certain ways, we can in fact use the logic of the conceptual mind to transcend the conceptual mind.

Intuitions and intimations of emptiness

In addition to these two more formal groups of approaches, it is important to mention a third. For it is very possible at times that something in the heart and mind – we could call it intuitive wisdom – feels the intimations of a different sense of things, intuits somehow and to some degree the truth of emptiness. Sometimes the perspective opens up dramatically and very forcefully; at other times much more faintly – perhaps we feel a subtle quality that infuses appearances with a suggestion, a whisper, of their voidness, or even of a kind of silence, a transcendent and mystical dimension, that seems to lie 'beyond' those very appearances, yet that somehow 'shines' timelessly through them, changing our relationship with them, rendering them diaphanous, less substantial. Such intuitions may arise either suddenly or gradually, and they can come in all sorts of ways – through reading or listening to teachings, even when we don't fully understand, through contact with a teacher, or at any time there is a profound openness with others, in nature, or in meditation. The possibilities are probably countless.

It is vital to trust these openings and intimations. However, they are invariably incomplete and need the support of the practices in the other two approaches to refine, deepen, widen, and consolidate the insights they bring. Indeed it seems the flame of intuitive sensibility here is often sparked and fanned by the more systematic approaches, which it can in turn then feed back into and ignite further. Through practice we then start to see that, rather than being separate, all three approaches actually overlap, inform, and mutually reinforce each other, and that used in conjunction they help to fill out the whole understanding.

5

Samādhi and its Place in Insight Practice

Vital to our path and of uncountable benefit is the quality of *samādhi*. This word *samādhi* is usually translated as 'concentration', but in many respects that does not convey the fullness, or the beauty, of what it really means. Therefore we shall keep it in the original language throughout this book. For *samādhi* involves more than just holding the attention fixed on an object with a minimum of wavering. And it certainly does not necessarily imply a spatially narrowed focus of the mind on a small area. Instead here we will emphasize that what characterizes states of *samādhi* is some degree of collectedness and unification of mind and body in a sense of well-being. Included in any such state will also be some degree of harmonization of the internal energies of the mind and body. Steadiness of mind, then, is only one part of that.

Such a unification in well-being can come about in many ways. In this book we will embrace in our meaning of *samādhi* both states that have arisen through holding the attention on one object, as well as those that have arisen through insight ways of looking. And we will also include both states where the attention is more narrowly focused on one object, and those where the awareness is more open. This chapter, however, primarily explores some more general aspects of those practices that do involve holding the attention to one thing (for example, the breath, *mettā*, or body) as a way of developing *samādhi*.

And although, as the Buddha did, we can certainly delineate a range of discrete states of *samādhi* (the *jhānas*), in this present context let us rather view it mostly as a continuum: of depth of meditation, of well-being, of non-entanglement, and of refinement of consciousness. Among other benefits suitable to our purpose, there is also less chance then that the relationship with practice becomes fraught through wondering too much if one 'has it' or 'doesn't have it', is 'succeeding' or 'failing', is 'in' or 'out'. Instead of relating to *samādhi* practice in terms of measurement or achievement of some goal, it is usually much more helpful, more kind, and less self-alienating to conceive of it as a caring, both in the present and in the long term, for the heart and mind.

The framework of the eight *jhānas* is extremely helpful in other contexts, and we will actually return later to discuss this framework in relationship to dependent arising and fabrication.[1]

I. The Blessings of Samādhi

In his teachings, the Buddha did not seem to be overly concerned with the possibility of attachment to *samādhi*. Rather, he placed great emphasis on its development and the well-being it brings as an important element of the integrated path of practice that he taught, proclaiming, for example:

> This kind of pleasure should be pursued, it should be developed, it should be cultivated; it should not be feared.[2]

In particular, he emphasized how *samādhi* supports the deepening and maturing of insight. A practitioner who is skilled in *samādhi*, he said,

> could shatter the Himalayas, the Kings of Mountains, to say nothing of pitiful delusion (*avijjā*).[3]

The development of *samādhi,* he taught, moves us in the direction of liberation:

> Just as the River Ganges flows toward the ocean, slopes toward the ocean, inclines toward the ocean, so too [a practitioner] who

---

[1] See Chapter 19.

[2] MN 139. (All translations from MN are the author's own, made also with reference to the translations of both Thanissaro Bhikkhu in *Handful of Leaves Vol. 1* and *Vol. 5* [Redwood City, CA: Sati Center for Buddhist Studies, and Valley Center, CA: Metta Forest Monastery, 2004 and 2007] and Bhikkhu Ñāṇamoli and Bhikkhu Bodhi in *The Middle Length Discourses of the Buddha: A New Translation of the Majjhima Nikāya* [Boston: Wisdom Publications, 1995].)

[3] AN 6:24. (All translations from AN are the author's own, made also with reference to the translations of both Thanissaro Bhikkhu in *Handful of Leaves Vol. 3* and *Vol. 5* [Redwood City, CA: Sati Center for Buddhist Studies, and Valley Center, CA: Metta Forest Monastery, 2003 and 2007] and Bhikkhu Bodhi in *The Numerical Discourses of the Buddha: A Translation of the Aṅguttara Nikāya* [Boston: Wisdom Publications, 2000].)

> cultivates and develops… [states of *samādhi*]… flows… slopes… and inclines toward *nibbāṇa*.[4]

The place, however, of *samādhi* on the path, and in relation to insight, is not simply a matter of it 'sharpening' the mind so that phenomena can be seen more clearly and minutely. Insight, as we have already said and shall extensively explore, is not really about seeing smaller and smaller divisions of 'reality'. Rather, it must primarily address and open our understanding of emptiness, fabrication, and dependent arising. Without these understandings, any insight actually remains rooted in fundamental delusion. As we gain more experience, we find there are in fact many ways in which *samādhi* supports the path and the flowering of insight. Some of these are not immediately obvious. They are, nonetheless, immensely significant.

A Resource for the Whole of the Path

The confidence to let go

Among its many benefits, a dedication to *samādhi* can bring a certain 'juiciness' to practice and to life, and this can provide a vital resource of wholesome and profound nourishment. In particular, the well-being that it includes can be crucial. There may be times, for example, when we know it would be best to let go of an unhelpful attachment but somehow we just can't. Perhaps at a certain level we feel somewhat desperate, and unable to imagine that we could be okay without this thing that we are clinging to. Perhaps even unconsciously we worry that letting it go would render us bereft of what we believe we need for our happiness or even our survival. If, however, we can have access to, and develop, a reservoir of profound inner well-being, it makes letting go of what is not so helpful much easier. We feel that we have enough, so letting go is not so scary.

Over the long term, repeated and regular immersion in such well-being supports the emergence of a steadiness of genuine confidence. We come to know, beyond doubt, that happiness is possible for us in this life. And because this deep happiness we are experiencing is originating from within us, we begin to feel less vulnerable to and dependent on the uncertainties of changing external conditions.

---

[4] SN 53:7.

We may also find that a relatively frequent taste of some degree of *samādhi* helps our confidence in the path to become much more firmly established. Gaining confidence in these ways will have a profound effect on the sense we have of our own lives and their potential, without making us aloof.

And while it certainly can occur, my own experience in practice and in teaching is that a stagnation in feelings of bliss and peace is really quite rare. Rather than being a source of attachment, *samādhi* is greatly supportive of letting go and non-clinging in our lives in general.

Countless gifts beyond meditation

We could in fact list a whole host of potential blessings that *samādhi* can bring which likewise overflow from practice well beyond the meditation session or retreat. Deep rest and rejuvenation of the whole being, emotional (and, at times, physical) healing, vitality, openings of the intuition, emotional strength that is yet pliable, increase in the heart's capacity and in our availabilities to others, steadiness of energy and of commitment in creative and service work – these, and more, are part of the broad range of long-term benefits that *samādhi* can make available to the whole of one's life. In general, to the degree that we can find ways to nourish this quality of *samādhi*, we will find that it nourishes us profoundly and widely in turn.

The Significance of *Samādhi* for Insight Practices

In the kinds of insight practices we will be exploring, there are, moreover, a number of qualities it brings to the *citta* (the heart/mind) that are particularly valuable, almost indispensable. One we have already acknowledged, and most obvious, is the possibility for a more stable focusing of the mind on what we choose to focus on. Periods of some *steadiness of attention* are necessary for looking deeply and seeing clearly. Something held more unwaveringly in our sight is easier to investigate. (As we shall shortly explain though, this steadiness does not *only* arise by holding the mind to one object.)

But there are other, perhaps less immediately obvious, qualities that *samādhi* engenders. First, as the Buddha pointed out, a mind that has cultivated some *samādhi* has more *malleability*. It is more able to look at things in different ways, finds it much easier to learn and develop novel approaches and practices, and can move between these with more agility.

Second, the spectrum of deepening *samādhi* is also a spectrum of deepening *refinement* of consciousness. As it develops, therefore, *samādhi* also enables us to see and work with much more subtle levels of fabrication and dependent arising. It has already been explained how this, too, is central to our approach.

Third, the sense of well-being of the body and the mind that *samādhi,* to some degree, involves has other fruits in addition to those already mentioned. As it progresses, the feelings of bliss, happiness, contentment, and peace, of stillness, spaciousness, and freedom that come and go can be exquisite and profound. They are typically also accompanied by some sense or other of emotional warmth, love, or tenderness that suffuses the being. All this, in any measure, is helpful for insight in a number of ways. Far from being merely an indulgence, the exposure to, immersion in, and accessibility of these feelings provides the *citta* with a sort of 'cushioning' that is usually crucial as the insight practice deepens.

One very significant benefit is that the 'softness' of such heart qualities helps prevent the insight practice from getting 'brittle' and *too* intense, and the energies from becoming unbalanced in ways that can be counterproductive. It can be quite common for a practitioner engaged in powerful insight practices to find, for instance, that the body starts jerking slightly in an unhelpful way at moments of deep insight. This is often easily remedied by accessing, and then inviting in, some of the softening qualities available in deeper states of *samādhi.* (With practice, such a skill is acquired relatively easily.) Then the insight practice can continue just as potently, and actually progress, in a more helpful inner space.

This well-being can also be immensely useful as a resource if fear arises in unfamiliar deep states of consciousness. It can help to dissolve the fear. It can also help to provide an important sense of a safe and trustworthy, albeit provisional, place of abiding. The well-being can be useful too if there is a propensity at times, in relation to seeing emptiness deeply, to lean towards an interpretation or a feeling of meaninglessness (as alluded to in Chapter 1). Then it will naturally incline the *citta* to a more balanced, helpful, and sustainable view, preventing the latent tendencies or misunderstandings from 'colouring' the sense of emptiness with bleakness.

Preparing the soil – supporting insights to take root

Whether through working with the breath, the *mettā*, or some similar practice, in cultivating *samādhi* alongside the insight practices, we are, in part, preparing the soil in which insight and a whole range of beautiful qualities of heart can take root and grow. Insight needs good soil. Perhaps you remember instances when you had an insight – it might have felt intense, significant, and quite freeing in the moment or for a period – only to find that its liberating power dwindled to almost nothing all too quickly, and you were left with only a shell, a memory of an experience.

There are a few things to say about this common occurrence. First: as we have already mentioned, most often, insights need *repeating* to be absorbed. Second: we need to *use* insights that we have had. We need, at least at times, to act and make decisions in life informed by their perspectives. This consolidates and empowers them greatly. Even if time has gone by and we no longer feel in touch with that insight so readily, we can in certain circumstances take a risk, act and choose *as if* we are inspired by that insight: "If that insight were true and I really knew it, how would I act or choose here?" This 'resuscitates' the insight and opens a channel for currents of freedom to flow powerfully in our life, strengthening our confidence in the Dharma. Like a muscle unused, an insight not acted on will atrophy.

Third, and in relation to *samādhi*: since the soil of the *citta* that is cultivating *samādhi* is more well-turned and full of nutrients, the insights that we have tend to be planted deeper in the being and stay alive for longer. For these reasons they are more likely to have long-term fruits and impacts. At times, the mind in *samādhi* seems to even have a way of retroactively bringing to life and organically digesting insights we may have had previously when there was not so much *samādhi* around, and which otherwise would probably have wasted away without transforming the heart at all.

II. A Wise Relationship to Samādhi Practice

All these considerations together point to how *samādhi* furnishes and opens for the *citta* an inner climate most supportive for investigation. Entering into meditation, it is important to bear this in mind as it will also inform our attitude to *samādhi* practice. And attitude is always crucial.

So much is being cultivated: seeing the bigger picture

When we invest time and effort working patiently on *samādhi,* more is happening than we might immediately recognize. Too easily we can become caught up in measuring the ups and downs of our focus of mind and miss the bigger picture of what we are cultivating. For even before the arising of any well-being or much steadiness of attention, beautiful and always helpful qualities are being strengthened and developed: patience, perseverance, and mindfulness, for example, as well as the kind of 'muscle' or power of mind that gradually accrues on returning over and over to our meditation theme. Hopefully too we are cultivating kindness in our attitude to our mind, and also gently erasing the habit of judging ourselves. These seeds too are being sown, and it may be that all these qualities are just as significant in the big picture of our practice as any others we have discussed.

Consciously acknowledging and reminding yourself of this bigger picture of what is being nourished before a formal meditation session, and as you work on *samādhi*, can be very helpful in keeping the *citta* buoyant and inspired, and in preventing the tightness or dryness that comes when the view of practice is contracted in any way.

Tending to the elements which support samādhi

Samādhi, we have said, contributes significantly to our happiness and well-being in life. But it is important to recognize too that, to a certain extent, *samādhi* is itself also *dependent* on happiness. Except in rare instances, and then usually not for very long, we cannot force the mind into stilling. The process is aided more by our taking care of a certain degree of well-being that can then serve as a foundation for *samādhi* to develop. Thus, whether on or off retreat, it can be immensely helpful to give some attention to nurturing, just as much as possible, the kinds of elements that contribute to a climate supportive for the ongoing deepening of *samādhi* practice. Qualities such as:

- inner and outer kindness
- some simplicity
- a degree of receptivity, connection, and openness to beauty and also to nature
- a love of the Dharma
- appreciation and gratitude for whatever and whoever is around you and supporting your practice

– these may not seem relevant at first glance, but they all nourish the *citta* profoundly. Caring for and supporting these qualities and attitudes should not be overlooked then, for they are indispensable to the cultivation of *samādhi*. It is definitely not simply a matter of 'trying harder'.

Playfulness and experimentation are key

This unification of mind and body is an art. As such, it is also in part a skill that we can develop, just as we learned the skills of walking, tying our shoelaces, reading and writing, or perhaps playing a musical instrument. And if we consider how we learn any skill as human beings, we see that the way we go about it makes a huge difference. Allowing and encouraging a quality of play and experimentation in practice is vital, and vitalizing. I can't emphasize this enough. Usually that's how we learn best as human beings, and it keeps things from getting rigid and feeling heavy.

A wise attitude to the hindrances

Central to the progress of practice, and particularly of *samādhi*, is our whole relationship with 'the five hindrances' – sense desire, ill-will or aversion, dullness and drowsiness, restlessness and worry, and doubt. In addition to learning to employ a range of antidotes to their specific manifestations,[5] we also need to develop a certain wisdom in our view of and attitude toward them in general.

Whether practising on or off retreat, we notice, over the days, that hindrances tend to come and go in waves. Though their force and frequency do indeed diminish over time, this attenuation still proceeds with its ups and downs. We should expect this coming and going. If we believe it should be otherwise, then a wave of hindrances is considerably more upsetting than it needs to be, for it is then interpreted as *meaning* something about the success of our practice, or, worse, about ourselves and our self-worth. It is a practice to learn not to take the hindrances personally, to let go of any self-evaluation that we might tend to attach to their arising, and to remind ourselves that all their presence means is that we are human beings still. (The Buddha stated that they do not disappear permanently until full Awakening.) This learning usually takes time, but is immensely worth it.

---

[5] Since information on working with the grosser manifestations of the five hindrances is widely and readily available, I will not include it here.

Further, if care is not taken, the habit for most is that the mind gets swept up by the *perspectives* of a hindrance when it is present. We believe what they say, their 'take' on our selves and the world. It is as if a hindrance is like a seed that has tiny hooks, and these hooks are looking for something, anything, to sink into, to suck sustenance from. When they find something, then they can grow and the whole complex of the hindrance and the thing they have hooked into grows too. It becomes an 'issue' with shoots, roots, and branches of stories, reactivities, and perspectives – all of these growing, spreading, and feeding the 'issue'. The mind gets hooked into and entangled in the stories that the hindrances tend to drag up or spin, and easily becomes ensnared in the web of unhelpful proliferation (*papañca*) thus woven. Over time though, we learn to recognize the wily ways of the hindrances and need not be taken for a ride to such an extent. We understand what is happening, and buy into their perspectives much less. Then their impact, when they do arise, is also much reduced.

It is crucial to realize that a dedication to cultivating *samādhi* necessarily involves working with the hindrances. In fact, it will actually expose and highlight them, and the ways we get seduced by and caught up in them, sometimes more than a simple mindfulness practice might do. Thus it offers us the opportunity to learn, usually gradually, the two wise attitudes discussed above: not to take the hindrances personally, and not to believe their perspectives. If *samādhi* practice had no other benefits than these, its value would still be enormous. For hindrances do not just arise in formal meditation; they are states that impact our life and our well-being every day. And if we can maintain a stance that, no matter what the conditions, asks always, "What can I learn here?", the times of hindrances in *samādhi* practice can be as genuinely valuable as the times that feel good. As we shall shortly see, even the hindrances are useful for insight into emptiness.

III. A Few More Subtle Points about Samādhi Practice

A tremendous amount could be said about the art of cultivating *samādhi*. Since that is not the subject of this book, however, our discussion here will be confined to just a few brief notes touching on some of those aspects of *samādhi* most related to the ways in which it aids emptiness insight practices. Hopefully this will be enough to provide some ideas for ways of working which can be explored further in meditation and prove fruitful. The Buddha advised seeking out and questioning those who have developed this art, to learn from them. To this we can also add, yet again, the strong encouragement to play and experiment with curiosity.

Common Difficulties

Subtle hindrances

Once a degree of collectedness is accessible to us and we have some familiarity and skill in working with the hindrances, we need also to begin to become sensitive to the presence of their more subtle manifestations. A state of *samādhi* is essentially a state of energized calm. In meditation, we are working, therefore, to support some fluid balance of both energy (or vitality) and calmness.[6] Although it might feel relatively pleasant, too much calmness without enough energy is a kind of subtly dull state, sometimes referred to as 'sinking'. The mind and the body can feel slightly heavy when this is the case and the quality of brightness is not so manifest in the mind. On the other hand, too much energy without the calm to balance it can create a subtle form of restlessness, often referred to as 'drifting'. Here, the body does not feel so settled, the attention may skit off the object more frequently, and there seem to be more thoughts or images being thrown up by the mind. Noticing these subtler manifestations of the hindrances, and playing and experimenting to discover some of the many possible ways to energize or to calm the energy body in meditation are important strands in enabling practice to deepen.

Feelings of tightness

For practitioners who already have a little experience in meditation, probably the most common difficulty and the biggest hurdle encountered in trying to develop *samādhi* is the feeling of tightness that can arise at times, both emotionally and physically. Indeed it is often a recurring experience of tightness that causes a person to despair and give up *samādhi* practice in favour of another kind of

[6] In some stages of practice when there is a lot of intense *pīti* ('rapture') arising, it can seem as if the state of being then is not very calm. In fact, there is actually a greater degree of collectedness there than in a normal state of consciousness – it is just that sometimes we may not yet recognize this, our attention captivated by the intensity, the movements and waves of energy of the *pīti*, and perhaps the accompanying emotion of excitement. At any rate, this more intensely rapturous phase is often necessary for the evolution of the *samādhi*. It is having all kinds of helpful effects on the mind, both opening and beginning to change the habits of the subtle energy body and the heart; and this too may not be obvious at the time.

approach – usually of 'just letting things be'. In order that the practice of *samādhi* can flourish then, we need to find ways to address such tightening.

To begin with it must be pointed out that an essential aspect of the larger sensitivity and awareness that is included in mature practice is an awareness of the subtle emotional relationship with the practice at any moment in time. Incorporating this delicate and ongoing wider 'monitoring' of our attitude and feeling, we are more likely to notice sooner when tightness creeps in, and there is then the possibility of responding skilfully to it. Since the feelings of tightness and our reactions to them can have such a significant effect, this is crucial. Some of what can be helpful here overlaps with a few of the approaches that can be helpful in responding to sinking and drifting.

First: Tightness is a state of contraction of the mind and body energy. So too, in fact, is any restlessness – gross or subtle (as in drifting) – and any dullness or drowsiness (including sinking). It can be very helpful, therefore, when any of these are present in *samādhi* practice, to find ways of opening up more *space* for the awareness, *without* abandoning the primary object.

Awareness of the whole body is one way this can be effected. Even if you are working with a method of breath meditation, for example, that involves a spatially narrow focus of attention as 'foreground', it is often beneficial to lightly maintain, as the 'background' to this 'foreground', a global awareness permeating fully and 'filling out' the whole body in an alive way. Among other advantages, this will automatically introduce more of a sense of space into the meditation, which can help to ease the contraction of tightness when it arises.

Second: Tightness is usually a result of, and indicates, slightly too much effort in the concentration at that time. Similarly, a slight over-efforting can underlie both sinking and drifting. There, however, the situation can be a little more complex, because both sinking and drifting may arise at any time as a result of marginally too much effort and also of too little effort. It can be difficult to tell, for instance, whether this drifting state that is present right now is caused by 'squeezing' the mind slightly too hard, so that, like a gas under pressure, it actually becomes more agitated and generates even more random thoughts and images; or whether the object in our attention needs to be held a little more firmly, and with more intimacy, to prevent its wandering. Again, we need a willingness to experiment, to play and respond.

In any case, it is necessary to gradually learn to include in our awareness a sensitivity to our moment-to-moment level and quality of effort. This is part of the art of *samādhi* practice. Such sensitivity and responsiveness to the effort level is not something we 'grow beyond' and then forget about. In fact, it only gets more subtle. Nor should we expect to find, in any one meditation session, a balanced quality and level of effort and hope to keep it statically there, on 'cruise control', with the 'effort dial' set at '5'. Part of the refinement, and beauty too, of this art of *samādhi* practice is the moment-to-moment play of sensitivity and responsiveness as conditions change. Without this, like a stationary and unresponsive surfer, it's just not much fun, and we simply get thrown off balance even by the gentlest waves.

What can help greatly in developing this subtler sensitivity to effort levels is, again, an awareness of the whole body and how it feels. Even a slight over-efforting the body will reveal, through tension or tightness somewhere in particular, or through a subtle sense of contraction of the space of the whole body. Relaxing the body in those moments can be helpful, helping organically to relax the effort in turn. More ease is opened in the practice in that moment, and this supports the *samādhi*.

Additionally though, since tightness is often an indicator of a degree of over-effort, we need not view its presence only as a difficulty. We can actually use the feeling of tightness when it appears somewhere in the body as a helpful signal to slightly back off the effort in that moment. And this subtle backing off, this delicacy of application of effort, we can learn to play with, much as one might learn to control a manual car with the clutch and accelerator pedals.

Modes of Attention

Many factors can influence the quality and subtle balance of our effort in any moment. And since this balancing is often one of the pivotal aspects of practice, these other factors will affect, in turn, the felt experience of the whole meditation. Among such elements are the ways we actually conceive of and perceive both the object that we are focusing on and the focusing itself.

Probing and receiving

For example, in breath meditation one way of working is with the attention concentrated on a small area of sensation somewhere in the body: at the upper lip, the nostrils, or somewhere in the abdomen are common points of concentration. The attention can work in a way where it 'moves toward' that point and probes it, penetrating that small area of sensation, like an arrow or a laser beam. Alternatively, at other times, it can be more useful to encourage a more 'receptive' mode of working, to let the awareness 'receive' the breath sensations. Here the breath may be conceived of, and thus perceived, as 'coming toward' the awareness, as opposed to the other way around.

Rather than being separate modes, these two constitute more the poles of a spectrum. Within this larger range, it can be very helpful to experiment with different stances of the attention. With a little practice, we can learn to feel and move our way along this continuum, sensing and responding to what seems helpful in any moment.

Playing with the intensity of attention

Related to this, we can also discover a continuum of what could be called the 'intensity' of the attention. And this too is a quality whose modulations we can grow sensitive to and control. In between the two poles just described, sometimes we find that a lightness of attention directed to the sensations serves better than a forceful penetration. Indeed, as some calmness begins to surface and spread, the breath will tend to become more subtle, as will the whole feeling in the body, or the feeling of the *mettā*. Often what is needed then is a correspondingly more delicate and subtle level of effort and intensity of attention.

Conversely, it is just this delicacy of attention, of subtle sensitivity to the breath or the *mettā*, that, at times, can allow the perception and feeling of that object to transform in some way which supports the deepening of the *samādhi*. Perhaps the sense of the breath or the *mettā* lightens, or becomes itself more delicate and refined. A deepening of refinement is in fact an essential aspect of the deepening of *samādhi*. There is a refining of both the perception of the object, and, correspondingly, of the attention itself. Often as part of this process, the object may begin to be sensed as somehow more pleasurable and lovely. As we shall shortly explore, these transformed feelings and perceptions of the object may be used to gently aid the integration of mind and body in *samādhi*. A light feather faintly brushing, touching so delicately the sensations of the breath or the body can take the meditation deeper at times than a laser beam of probing. Sometimes 'less is more'.

Sensitive to the whole body

In contrast to a concentration of the attention on a small area, another way of working is to focus primarily on the wider field of feeling of the whole body – the felt sense, the 'texture', 'tone', vibration, and energy of the whole space of the body – and to fill that space with an aliveness of awareness, of presence, that permeates the entire body.

- This feeling of the energy of the whole body space can be made the sole focus of attention.

- Alternatively, it may be mixed with the awareness of another object such as the breath or *mettā* – by paying attention to the changing effects of the breath or the *mettā* on the body's energy field.

- Either way, there will be a tendency for the attention thus deployed to keep shrinking to a smaller area. It will therefore be necessary to keep stretching the field of awareness out, expanding it so that attention pervades and encompasses the whole field of the body.

- Oftentimes just remaining lightly, delicately open and sensitive to the whole body in this way begins to reveal a subtle pleasantness to the way the space of the body feels. It can be extremely helpful to learn to 'tune into' this, and to enjoy it.

- Of course, many times we will find on inspection that there is a mixture of both pleasant and unpleasant 'frequencies', or a range of qualities, coexisting in the tone and vibration of the body space. With practice we can learn, if we wish, to tune into whichever of these frequencies we choose. Attuning to and enjoying the more pleasant frequencies in the mix is an immensely helpful skill to learn and very valuable in fostering *samādhi*.

Whether one starts from a spatially narrow focus of attention or with the whole body sense, whether the object of concentration is the breath, *mettā*, or some other object, it can be deduced from much of the above discussion just how central and vital the body sense is in the development of *samādhi*. Moreover, as 'concentration' deepens it necessarily includes and involves the perception and felt sense of the whole body as unified, harmonious and pleasant to some degree, and spacious. Clearly then, sooner or later in *samādhi* practice the whole body needs to be included in the awareness;[7] and, as the discussion here has suggested, sooner is probably more helpful than later.

---

[7] In some texts, mental 'one-pointedness' (*ekaggata*) is listed as a factor of all *jhāna*. The Pali word means, literally, 'gone to one'. From what we have seen though, it is evident that this cannot refer to a spatial one-pointedness – a contraction of attention to one small point – but designates, rather, a relative absorption, or unification, of the mind, in or with some perception, along with a degree of steadiness in time, of *temporal* one-pointedness. This is obvious too from the fact that *ekaggata* is sometimes listed as a factor of the formless *jhāna* of infinite space.

Working with Feelings of Pleasure and with the Subtle Body

Encouraging feelings of well-being

The method just described, of focusing primarily on the sense of the whole body, involves the development of a sensitivity to what could be termed 'the subtle body' or the 'energy body'.[8]

- Almost from the start in this approach we deliberately but gently work at nurturing a sense of comfort, pleasure, or well-being in the body.

- This can be done through the way we pay attention to the subtle body, as described above – opening out the awareness to encompass the whole body space, and tuning into the more pleasant frequencies of feeling that are perceivable.

- It is also possible to use the breath or the *mettā* to help elicit and support the pervasion of this sense of well-being. Simply sensitizing to, and enjoying, the way we feel the energetic resonances of the *mettā* or the breath throughout the whole space of the body – opening to and finding delight in their reverberations there – can gently move the experience in the direction of a more expansive well-being.

- And when there is a state of agitation or anxiety, we can play with ways of breathing or practising the *mettā*, and also ways of *sensing* the breath or *mettā*, that feel as if they soothe the subtle body and smooth out its energies. Delicately tuning into the felt experience of these qualities of soothing or smoothing-out will help them to gradually gain strength, and help the agitated energies to slowly subside.

- The imagination, too, can be skilfully employed in order to gently encourage this sense of pleasure or well-being in the subtle body. While simultaneously

---

[8] We can freely use a term like 'subtle body' or 'energy body', without needing either to assert or to deny the 'reality' of such a concept. It is enough for us that it is a perception, a way the body can be perceived which can be helpful. In fact, a little reflection reveals that the same could be said of concepts like 'attention'. Is there really some 'thing' called 'attention' that can 'go towards' some other thing (or mental representation of an object) or 'receive' that thing? These are all ways of conceiving and perceiving useful on the path to freedom. Perceivable, useful, and, as we will come to see, thoroughly empty.

pervading the whole body space with an awareness sensitive to the texture and tone of the energy of that whole field, it is possible, for example, to *imagine* the subtle body as a body of radiant light; then to open to and explore what that feels like. Any image formed in this way does not necessarily need to appear in precise detail, or even completely distinctly. It is, rather, the energetic sense of pleasure or well-being which it supports that is primary, since this is what primarily supports the *samādhi*.

- Likewise, one may experiment with imagining various luminous lines of energy in the body – for example, between the perineum and the crown of the head, or from the lower belly out through the legs – and sense how any such line of energy supports the whole body to feel upright, open, and energized. The imagination here may be visual or kinaesthetic, or a combination of the two. And it need not always follow exactly the anatomical contours of the physical body or its posture. For instance, if sitting or kneeling with the legs crossed or bent, the luminous lines of energy imagined radiating from the lower belly or base of the spine need not bend with the legs, but may instead continue and extend straight out at the knees, if at that time that feels more supportive of openness, energization, and well-being.

- If there is tension, or even pain, in one area of the body, rather than always conceiving of it in anatomical or physiological terms, it can sometimes be more helpful to conceive of and perceive that area in energetic terms, and to play with the perception of lines of energy in order to support a degree of comfort and ease.

There are many ways we may discover to bring about some sense of energetic openness and well-being in the subtle body. And as it is accessed more and more, this altered body feeling is one that eventually we can 'remember' and *learn to deliberately recall* – to summon by a gentle intention. We can then move, usually gradually, into the focused steadiness of *samādhi* from that basis, by incorporating this perception of pleasure or well-being more centrally into the meditation.

Towards unification

Whether it has arisen through being deliberately recalled, or through focusing on the breath or *mettā*, there are again a number of possible ways of using the sense of pleasure or comfort to help guide the *citta* into the unification of *samādhi*.

- Once it is easily sustaining for some minutes, we can gently begin to take that bodily feeling of well-being as the primary object of our focus. It is important not to 'snatch at it', but rather to ease the attention toward it gracefully, and gradually let it take up the full focus of attention. Then the attention and the *citta* can be encouraged to enjoy it as fully as possible.

- The attention can at times probe it, burrowing into one area of the pleasure, perhaps where it feels strongest.

- Or, at other times, a mode of 'receiving' it, really trying to open up to it, can be employed.

- Either way, one attempts all the while to remain intimate with its texture, and actually to relish the pleasure as much as possible. In these ways (and in others that can be discovered) we can delicately work to gently sustain the bodily feeling of well-being, and to absorb the attention more fully into it.

- Alternatively, it is possible to mix the sense of pleasure with the perception of the breath or the *mettā*, in order to support and deepen the quality of *samādhi*.

- Then it may seem, for example, as if one is breathing the pleasurable energy; or it may seem as if one is breathing into and out of that area of well-being.

- In *mettā* practice, it may seem as if the *mettā* and the pleasurable energy have become fused, so that the feeling of the *mettā* at that time *is* the feeling of the well-being. And this can become the 'flavour' of the energy of *mettā* that is radiated outwards towards beings, or that wraps around and permeates one's own body and being.

- The area of pleasurable energy may also be perceived as the source of the *mettā*.

Steadiness of feeling is more important than strength

We should point out once more that sometimes the sense of well-being is really quite subtle. Although the feelings of pleasure might also be very strong at times, this is actually not necessary in order to use them in a helpful way. Over time, their strength will in fact vary naturally (and anyway, as the practice matures, at a certain stage they begin to mellow). What is more necessary is that they sustain relatively steadily for more than a few minutes. Then we can learn to sustain them for longer.

Within this larger steadiness, any perceived waves or movements of the energy are not at all problematic. We can try to open the space of the body to these inner currents as much as possible, allowing and fully enjoying them (and if they feel very intense, even playing with surrendering and abandoning our whole body and being to them). Doing so, their intensity will in time calm.

Suffusing and saturating the whole body

Along with the steadiness of the feelings of well-being, and of the attention on those feelings, we are also gently aiming at eventually having the whole space of the body suffused by and saturated with the feeling of well-being or pleasure. Sometimes this happens by itself. But sometimes the sense of pleasure, when it arises or when it is recalled, only pervades one area of the body. There are a number of viable responses then.

- One is to simply enjoy it in the area where it is located, in the ways that we have described, without pressuring the feeling to spread. It may then expand naturally at some point to pervade the whole body.

- But even if it does not spread then, that need not be regarded as a problem. A vital aspect of the whole relationship with *samādhi* practice is to enjoy what well-being is there at any time, not to measure it and view it through a lens that somehow demands, even subtly, that it be 'better', bigger, stronger.

- Having said that, it is in fact also possible at times to gently encourage the feeling of pleasure or well-being to spread – for instance by simply *opening up the space of the awareness to embrace a larger area of the body.* Sometimes then the pleasant feeling will automatically start to expand to fill that space.

- Alternatively, the breath may be used to gently 'massage' the sense of well-being into other areas of the body. Although there is not space to enter into a full description of possibilities here, with practice the breath energy may be felt and perceived throughout the body, entering and flowing in all kinds of ways beyond the strictly anatomical movement of air into the wind-pipe and lungs. We can learn to sense the breath energy in and through the whole body. And as alluded to earlier, the breath energy can be mixed with the pleasure, so that the perceived movements of breath in the whole body space move and spread the perception of the pleasure.

- There is also, again, no reason why one cannot just *imagine* the feeling of well-being permeating the body space more fully. The perception then often begins to follow the image.

These are some of the possibilities, but with repeated practice over time it will anyway become normal for the pleasurable feeling to effortlessly pervade the whole body whenever it arises.

Unblocking and smoothing out the subtle body energies

The harmonization and unification in well-being that is characteristic of *samādhi* can also be regarded as a harmonization, alignment, smoothing out, and opening of the flows of energies in the subtle body. All day and all night long our energy body is moving in and out of states of alignment and openness, constriction and blockage, in response to a whole range of conditions, physical, mental, and emotional. This is completely normal, and with attention and sensitivity to the experience of the body we notice these fluctuations more and more. Although they may be felt in any region, perhaps most commonly a block in energy will be felt as a constriction somewhere along the central axis of the body, anywhere from the perineum to the top of the head. As we move into a state of more *samādhi* there is an unblocking, untying, aligning, and harmonizing of the subtle body energies to some degree.

When the subtle energies are blocked and agitated, *samādhi* is to some extent blocked. And when the subtle energy is unblocked and unagitated, *samādhi* is not so far away. (Perhaps all that is needed then is a steadying of the attention on enjoying the pleasant feelings of the 'unblocked' subtle body, as described.) In addition, therefore, to the ways of working to smooth out and soothe the energy body suggested earlier, it can be useful to learn means of gently unblocking the energies when there is any sense of energetic constriction, in order to open up again the potential of a degree of *samādhi* at that time. Again, with a light and playful attitude of experimentation, a variety of ways of working in meditation can be discovered.

For example, sensitive to the whole subtle body sense, the breath energy or *mettā* may be perceived and conceived in any way that feels helpful, as alluded to above:

- We may breathe into and out of an area of blockage.
- Or we may, perhaps gently, breathe the breath energy *through* that area.
- In *mettā* practice, we may experiment with situating the centre or source of the energy of *mettā* right at that point of constriction, and explore what effects that has.
- If these strategies prove difficult, it is again quite feasible to imagine the breath, the body energies, or the *mettā* flowing more freely through the area of blockage, or even flowing *out* of the body, and opening and unblocking in that way.

IV. The Relation between Samādhi and Insight

Insight brings samādhi

As well as those described above, there are many other practicable means to unblock the subtle body energies. In particular, most of the insight ways of looking that we shall introduce in the course of this book may also be used in the service of opening and deepening *samādhi*. Mindful observation will reveal that any craving or clinging is always accompanied by, and reflected in, blocks and knots in the subtle body. Now, insight, we have said, cuts that on which *dukkha* depends. And *dukkha* depends on craving. Thus, according to our definition, insight is any way of looking that releases craving. As the insight and emptiness practices are developed, therefore, they can also be used at times to deliberately undo the craving that is mirrored in the knots in the energy body. This might involve using the insight practices 'on' the experienced subtle energy blocks themselves, as ways of looking at those perceptions and feelings. Or it might involve engaging these insight ways of looking just more generally in regard to any experience in the moment. Either way, the dissolving of craving to whatever extent will, at the same time and to a similar extent, untie the knots in the subtle body to unblock those energies and so deliver the possibility of some *samādhi*. Ha!

With more practice our skill grows and we find that it is in fact possible quite often to use the 'letting go' that insight brings to deliberately unblock the energies and the felt sense of the subtle body in this way. The pleasantness, openness, well-being, delightful and alive stillness, or joy that comes with this unblocking can be felt in the space and texture of the body sense. We can then tune into that. It is this tuning in to the frequency of the pleasant, and delicately attending to it, that 'filters it out' of the field of awareness, so that it begins to become more palpable and more prominent.

Then we can rest in it, allowing it to spread throughout the body space. And if, as before, we continue to tune in to and focus on the felt sense of the energy of this well-being, gently intent on allowing and opening to an enjoyment of it, and encouraging the attention to become absorbed in it, to fill up with it, this can carry us to the threshold of some *samādhi.*

Such a skill is useful for even the most experienced meditator. There are times in meditation when we may be trying to bring the mind to some unification, working with the intention for *samādhi*, and despite all our patience and adeptness in attempting different things *samādhi* does not come. We may need some insight to help us let go of some craving or clinging, perhaps even a craving we were unaware of, and then some *samādhi* becomes possible.

In addition to the opening and transformation of the energies of the subtle body just described, there is another, related aspect to what is occurring that can be pointed out. To a degree proportional to its strength, the push and pull of craving pushes and pulls the attention. It thus agitates the mind and makes it restless; or saps its energy and makes it dull. Relaxing craving through insight will therefore allow the mind to settle more naturally and easefully into stillness and a steadiness of attention. We can see then that the quality of steadiness of attention does not *only* come through holding the mind to one object.

Aside from being a skilful 'trick', however, all this suggests a number of things. One is that although usually we might conceive that '*samādhi* leads to insight', (and clearly a certain amount of steadiness is generally needed before any insight can arise), as we explore we discover more and more that they can lead to each other.

A fluid balance between samādhi and insight

This in turn suggests the possibility of ways of working in meditation where insight and *samādhi* practices can fluidly and openly complement each other. If desired, their developments can proceed in parallel. Especially if you are practising on a longer retreat, you don't necessarily have to 'collect the mind first and then move on to insight' in any sitting.

It is the *balance* of *samādhi* and insight work that is important and so potentially powerful. Too much *samādhi* relative to insight practice, and the mind may lose its desire then to contemplate or analyse or shift ways of looking. Too much insight practice relative to *samādhi* usually tends to enervate the mind and the energetic system. It can lead to an imbalance in the energies, manifesting in over-excitement, which is unhelpful if it persists too long. Or, worse, it can lead to a subtly aversive agitation, which distorts the insights, so that they do not free or even feel freeing. The mind working on insight is profoundly supported by having a 'wholesome abiding' in which it can periodically rest and be resourced.

If you are practising with this book at home off retreat, you will probably find many times, perhaps unexpectedly, that tipping the balance of your practice towards *samādhi* in any sitting, even by as much as a ratio of five to one, greatly increases the efficacy and the felt depth of the insight practice that you are doing. As we've also said though, sometimes the mind won't settle down until the energies have been opened and unblocked through some letting go. Dare to experiment with the balance and the order of practices.

If you are practising with this book on retreat, after a few days devoted to *samādhi* at the beginning of your retreat, I would highly recommend then adopting a loose and fluid, *roughly equal*, balance between insight practices on the one hand, and *samādhi* practice (whether through the breath, *mettā*, body awareness, or whatever) on the other, in any rhythms through the day that feel beneficial and supportive. Most people need to be reminded and strongly encouraged to give as much time to *samādhi* as insight.

Meditation is not easy, and, for most of us, developing *samādhi* is certainly not easy. We need to find ways to make any practice work for us, and to make it our own; and this requires experimentation. But with persistence, patience, some creativity, and playfulness, much more is possible than most people imagine. Although in the initial stages it may be hard to believe, eventually we can even come to work with this balance of *samādhi* and insight practices in meditation the way a great eagle might ride on warm air currents, skilfully, easefully, and elegantly inclining the direction of its flight as it wills, in subtle and sensitive response to those currents.

Samādhi and fabrication

Something else also is suggested by the way insight can bring *samādhi*, which we will just mention here and return to more fully after exploring some of the deeper insight practices. It typically takes a good deal of both *samādhi* practice and insight to reverse a misconception of what is actually happening in a state of 'concentration'. For at first it understandably seems that such an altered state of unification and well-being is arrived at by ignoring phenomena other than the chosen object, so that these other phenomena, both inner and outer, are repressed from the consciousness at that time. It might seem too that, replacing them in their absence, with much 'huffing and puffing' and strenuous effort, an altered pleasant state is constructed.

Is that really what is happening though? A state of *samādhi* is indeed still a constructed, fabricated state. But keen investigation, reflection, and a pondering of the relationship it has with letting go suggest that it may be more accurate to understand *samādhi* as a spectrum of states that involve progressively less fabrication than a more 'ordinary' state of consciousness involves. It may not be obvious for quite a while but any state of *samādhi* is to some degree a state of letting go, of reduced craving. And the deeper the *samādhi,* the deeper and more comprehensive the letting go that it involves. As we shall come to see through the insight practices, less craving results in less fabricating. Therefore any state of *samādhi* is a state of less fabricating, less building of the perception and sense of the self and of the world. If we understand how to contemplate it, *samādhi* itself offers profound insights into fabrication and dependent arising.

Related to this then, yet another blessing of *samādhi* practice is that it helps us to grow accustomed to states of progressively less construction. Having experienced them gradually and imbued with a sense of well-being as part of the spectrum of *samādhi*, when we open naturally in deep insight practice to such states of less fabrication they are not so unfamiliar, disorienting, or even frightening.

Risks of Attachment

This leads us, conversely, to one final point, which we will also mention here and return to much more fully later on. Without experience of different states of *samādhi*, there is not only more chance that states arisen through insight meditation may, through unfamiliarity or fear, be fled from or not given the chance to settle; it is also in fact much more likely that attachment crystallizes around states of insight and particularly around the *views and perceptions they involve or imply*.

This is actually the most insidious of the three forms of clinging to meditation states and experiences that I see. Attachment to the *pleasure* of *samādhi* usually only occurs if experiences of *samādhi* are rare. A meditator may then hanker after it unskilfully because, even if they are told they shouldn't, and even if they know it is impermanent, they do not have the confidence that such pleasure, though not permanent, is regularly accessible. When we know we can fairly readily experience that kind of pleasure again, we naturally relax our clinging, letting it go when it dissolves.

Anyway, as the *samādhi* develops through different stages, even the bliss of *pīti* is easily let go of as the more fulfilling *sukkha* (happiness) becomes more available. And most of the clinging to this is released in turn as the even more satisfying and exquisite ensuing stage of peacefulness opens up. Likewise much of the clinging to states of peacefulness may be released as the beauty and greater subtlety of a deeper stillness and equanimity establishes itself. And so it can go, the process almost refining itself, until we are no longer attached to states of pleasure.

A second possible way of becoming attached to *samādhi* is through *pride* – believing that we are somehow special because we can experience, even at will, such states of bliss and peace. But this kind of pride usually does not last very long at all. With dedicated practice and a minimum of intelligent attention, a meditator sees fairly quickly that *samādhi* is essentially dependent on the right conditions coming together in the mind and body. It is not the 'self' that does and 'achieves' it. When the necessary conditions are present, *samādhi* arises and can sustain; when they are not there, it does not. That this is simply how it is becomes evident soon enough to a practitioner, and then (s)he just can't get too puffed-up about the arising of *samādhi*, or too self-judging when it is difficult or does not arise.[9]

The third and, as mentioned, most insidious way that meditation can provide an object of attachment pertains as much to states of insight meditation as it does to states of *samādhi*. For there can easily arise attachment to the *view* opened up or implied through any state or insight.

Here the predicament is less obvious. A person may sometimes shun the practice of *samādhi* in the belief that they are thus rendering themselves free of

[9] This kind of seeing – in terms of conditions rather than self – is explored further in Chapter 8. Opening up the view of the self specifically in relationship to its actions provides us with an insight way of looking which can allow a degree of unburdening, of liberation.

an almost certain pitfall of attachment – to its pleasure or to pride – only to become unwittingly attached to one view or other that has emerged from some insight meditation experiences. Often the view thus opened to can be extremely hard to let go of. In this case, the development of *samādhi*, as well as of more fundamental insight, may in fact be part of the solution. But without either a further deepening of *samādhi* and an intimate knowledge of its stages, or, in particular, a way of understanding fabrication and emptiness more deeply, the practitioner is without the means to effect a shift and pry the heart and mind loose from such a view. Indeed it may not even seem or feel to them like a constraint, a limited freedom.

On the meditative journey, special care in this regard needs to be taken with a number of wonderful, deeper states of consciousness that can be arrived at both through insight practices as well as through 'concentration'. These include the four *arūpa* (formless) *jhānas* – the spheres of infinite space, of infinite consciousness, of nothingness, and of neither perception nor non-perception – and *also* states that are similar to these *jhānas*, but which involve, relative to their *jhānic* counterparts, more of an openness of the sense doors, more consciousness of the diverse phenomena arising and passing in the space of awareness. Profoundly beautiful, they are also all genuinely and enormously helpful in the deepening of insight, as each opens up a view – a perception, an understanding, a way of looking at phenomena, experience, and the world – that is powerfully freeing. The perceptions of oneness, of the insubstantiality of material things, and of the vastness and imperturbability of awareness are a few such possible perceptions we could point to as common instances of this.

None of the views that are implied or impressed upon us through any of these states, however, (and certainly none of those states themselves), is complete in the depth and comprehensiveness of its insight. None is the final truth. Though necessarily *relying* on these awesome perceptions and openings and the partial understandings they bring, we will still need to understand just how exactly they are fabricated. It is this that will deliver for us the fuller understanding of the emptiness of all things. And it is to the very beginning practices of this journey of understanding that we now turn.

PART THREE

Setting Out

6

Emptiness that's Easy to See

Especially when supported by a devotion to cultivating *samādhi*, the meditation practices that reveal just how experience is fabricated are immensely powerful. So too are those practices that expose the impossibility of any thing's inherent existence. When developed, such practices are capable of cutting through the reifications of *avijjā* at the deepest levels and with respect to all things. All possible notions of self and all phenomena can thus be seen to be empty, including even those which seem to be the most fundamental givens of existence – awareness, space, time and the present moment, for instance – where subtle reification is usually unrecognized and unquestioningly entrenched.

As explained, these more radical levels of penetrating insight become progressively more available through the deepening of practice. But there are many situations in life where a significant degree of *dukkha* can be released through recognizing voidnesses that are not so hard to see at all. Through just a small shift in, or refinement of, our way of looking we realize that some element or other involved is a fabrication, and that it has no inherent existence. We start our insight investigations with these more modest shifts of the way of looking – not only because there is a great deal of suffering that can be relieved at this level, but also because, in the means by which they deconstruct the views underpinning *dukkha*, some of these ways of looking actually form the humble beginnings of a number of the deeper and more powerful ways of looking that we will learn to cultivate. The principles are in many ways the same. Let's consider a few examples to illustrate the kinds of seeing through and thinking that we might use.

Social Conventions

The whole area of social conventions is one in which we can experience all kinds of suffering. Yet often with just a little reflection we can recognize the emptiness of some convention that we have reified, and this realization can bring some freedom.

The voidness of countries

It is quite easy to see that countries, for instance, do not have the kind of inherent existence that we as a species seem so readily to believe and feel they have. A country only exists because of human agreement; it is a human convention. Even just a few hundred years ago, which from the perspective of the geological timescales of the Earth is extremely recent, there was no 'United States of America', no 'Germany'. Just like others, the concepts of these countries were at some point concocted, by humans, from various other notions. Sometimes, for example, the solidification of a notion of ethnicity is bound up in the concept of a country, often in an unhelpful way. Whether or not that is the case, though, the establishment of any country is then dependent on enough people consistently seeing it in a certain way. Without the belief in the notion of a 'USA', would an entity called 'the USA' have any reality? Other than as an idea, is there any reality to the claim that a certain patch of sand and rock is 'in the USA' rather than 'in Mexico'? And imagining even a short time into the future, we can see that if the agreements and notions on which it depends do not persist widely or strongly enough, any currently existing country may simply cease to exist. New agreements might form new countries; and what seems real now will, for most, lose its sense of reality.

Of course, a group of people in one area coming together and deciding to create a framework to support their collective well-being is not in itself a problem. It will probably be helpful in fact. But when the patently fabricated nature of countries is not recognized, the concept of 'this country', or 'my country', can gain an overwhelming force and solidity in human minds. The belief in the country as something real can give rise to a strength and rigidity of feeling beyond even the biological impulse for survival. How much violence and suffering in human history has there been with roots in this reification? How much willingness to kill and to die dependent on such a belief?

The relatively obvious insights proffered above also make clear that there is no a priori reason a country's boundaries need to be positioned where they currently are. These lines have to be agreed (or an 'agreement' on them forced) with humans in other countries. Extending this a little, however, we can see that, regardless of where exactly the borders are at present drawn, the very notion of any particular country necessarily exists *in relation to* the notion of what is 'not this country'. Usually this means other countries. 'England' only has meaning with respect to, and in differentiation from, what is 'not England' – Ireland, Scotland, Wales, or France, for instance. Any concept of 'this country' thus *arises together with*, and *dependent on*, a concept of 'those countries'. Though it might seem to, no country exists independently of other countries; none has inherent existence.

The point of this discussion is not to say that we shouldn't have countries (or that we should), but that we can be aware that they are human fabrications. It is important for us to be able to see them as such, to realize their emptiness at this simple level – partly as a very basic exercise, and partly because, if we do not, suffering is likely to somehow ensue.

Conditioned views of worth

Although not always easy to recognize, it is important to acknowledge too how often our opinions and our feelings about many things are conditioned by the views prevalent in the society we live in. Particularly significant in this regard is the conditioning of our sense of values, and thus also of our sense of what is valuable. In itself, cultural conditioning is not necessarily wrong. But it matters what we are 'taught' in this way. We are exposed to almost incessant messages from our society about what is of value, and much of this, while actually not serving our genuine happiness, is also more insidiously powerful than we might assume. The endless tidal-wave of advertising that manipulates values and desires, and thus culture, in consumerist economies is only one, glaringly obvious, example. For ourselves individually, for the continuing welfare of humanity and of other species, and for the well-being of the planet's ecosystems, the consequences of this kind of conditioning of values are enormous.

Within all this, just one of the reasons such conditioning can cause suffering for us personally is that we can often attach our sense of self-worth to that which is held as valuable by our society. In this respect, although also in others, the world-views and the value-views in smaller sub-cultures are often similar in their manipulative effects to those of the wider culture. We might consider, as an example, an educational environment that places great emphasis on one certain area of achievement – it could be academic, athletic, musical, or artistic – and frequently attempts to assess children on the basis of certain prescribed abilities in that area. For any child receiving again and again from the authorities ratings that are low relative to other children, it will be hard not to internalize a sense of self-worth dependent on this. And if the other students, children, and adults around are also collectively buying into this view of what is important, measuring each other in this way, and also attaching some sense of the worth of the person to these assessed abilities, the whole value system is being repeatedly reinforced.

Then it can be extremely difficult to see through this view and any associated sense of lack of self-worth. Even when I am rated highly, it can be painful and alienating to be entranced by such a way of seeing and measuring self and others. Myopically caught up in all this, it can be very hard to realize that the culture of this particular time and place is valuing one ability more than others. Fifteen thousand years ago, my prowess as a hunter of woolly mammoths would probably have accorded me more status in the culture than my ability to handle the kinds of abstract mathematical concepts involved, for example, in twelfth grade differential calculus. I need to see: one is not inherently more valuable than another; I am not inherently worth more or less dependent on these abilities. If I can see this, I open a door to a more natural sense of self-worth, and to a degree of freedom.

Including body and emotions in reflective practice

There are probably countless examples, large and small, where it is possible to shake off the shackles of the dominant view and expose a lack of intrinsic truth to some assumption or ideology that may be widely agreed on in our social world. Sometimes the belief in a value system is shattered in an instant of penetrating insight. Other times it is melted away more gradually. Either way, although undoubtedly we do not need meditation to reflect in the kinds of ways described, it does take a certain boldness to trust in one's own capacity to question views and to think for oneself. And while these qualities of boldness and trust are dependent on and empowered by many factors, let us mention a couple which may actually be supported by a more meditative approach.

The first is including in one's awareness the sense of strength as it manifests in the body. This sense can often be neglected, especially if we are not accustomed to having faith in ourselves in this way. But noticing, allowing, inhabiting, and even enjoying the bodily feelings that accompany the sense of confidence in our own seeing will greatly help that conviction, self-trust, and strength to take root and flourish in the being. Even if these bodily feelings are only fleeting at first, it can be a significant step in their consolidation to learn to open to them in this way. Then as our sense of strength and independence grows, it becomes easier for us to see that, just because most people around us believe it, we don't have to fall for any view that has solidified and raised what is only a convention to the status of an objective truth.

Connected to this, the second helpful element is a skilful awareness, and holding, of any difficult emotions that are evoked by what is being considered.

In order for freedom to be possible, it is vital not to ignore feelings such as anger, hurt, or powerlessness that may be associated with an issue being reflected on. Such emotions may well need caring for, in various ways, as part of the process of liberating the mind. Equally though, it is important not to sink in feelings like these, or to be consistently overwhelmed by them, or pulled down into a state where there is no space or opportunity for creative responses and movements of mind.[1]

Practice: Opening to freedom and strength through reflection

Take a little time to settle in meditation. Then see if it is possible to allow, and to tune into, a sense of energetic alignment along the central axis of the body. Feel the strength that comes from this alignment of energy, including the body as a whole in your awareness. (Alternatively, you could think of something which stimulates a sense of strength in you, then tune into the feeling of energy in the body that is present, and allow that to align the body sense.) Let yourself enjoy it for some time if you like.

Trying to stay connected to, and supported by, this sense of strength and alignment in the body as much as you are able, begin to reflect on your life and your social environment, asking yourself if there are any values or beliefs that you have absorbed from the culture and from your social environment that are contributing to suffering of some sort and that might be questionable.

Notice, allow, and feel as fully as you can any emotional and energetic responses to what you see, and notice also the mental responses. If it seems that something arises emotionally that needs holding and attention before continuing, take time to do that now.

When you feel ready, see if it is possible to reflect in a way that challenges this belief, or that recognizes it is not inherently true. Perhaps you can uncover the assumptions it rests on, or expose it as merely an agreed-upon conventionality.

Again, as you do this, notice, allow, and feel as fully as you can any emotional, energetic, and mental responses.

Especially with regard to any sense of strength that may surface, it might be important to try to let go of any preconceptions about what it should feel like. Strength can have a softness and pliancy to it; it need not feel brittle at all.

---

[1] While a great deal could be said on the subject of working skilfully with emotions, we will only offer a few suggestions occasionally, as for the most part it is an area beyond the scope of this book. I am assuming that a practitioner reading this has already developed some skill and experience here, or has access to teachings that can help acquire that skill.

Then if any feeling of strength and/or freedom arises, see if you can allow that to fill out in the body, and enjoy it. (It can be particularly helpful to feel the quality of strength filling the lower belly and the legs.) Let yourself linger in any feelings of strength or freedom that emerge.

If strong anger arises, is it possible to find the quality of strength *within* the anger, and to tune into that, thus helping it to become a more wholesome emotion?

If grief or sadness arise, what does it feel like they need right now? Sometimes in developing experience working with difficult emotions, we may have developed at the same time a habit to incline towards what is emotionally difficult at the expense of noticing and opening to the lovely. If it seems that emotions such as grief or sadness need more attention and care in the present, is it possible to do that without neglecting the sense of freedom and strength?

It is probably helpful to end the session with an awareness that this process of questioning values and beliefs is a journey. However you are feeling right now is part of that journey to a certain freedom.

Of course, as mentioned, such bold reflection needn't be a meditative process at all. What is often most significant in opening our capacity to question and to re-evaluate any assumptions of our social environment is exposure to others who are also questioning boldly or thinking differently about these things. Whether through reading or hearing their ideas, or through personal interaction or friendship, 'association with the insightful'[2] is enormously supportive.

Seeing the 'Holes' in Things

When the mind believes in and builds up certain concepts and their significance for the self, it gives them a solidity they do not possess on their own. Then we can very easily feel burdened and imprisoned in certain situations that involve those concepts.

For example, the roles we have in life are concepts, agreements (again) between human beings, and yet so often we can over-identify with them, or let them define us. We are then even more likely to fail to see their lack of solidity. One obvious area this occurs is at work. For some years now I have been the Resident Teacher at Gaia House. Being so visible to so many people so much of

[2] Cf. The Buddha's advice in Sn 2:4.

the time in a role like that, it would feel quite claustrophobic and burdensome if I were to perceive myself all the time as 'The Resident Teacher'. Until I am asked to, by someone or by a situation, however, I don't have to step into that role. And although I could, I need not conceive of myself as 'The Resident Teacher' as I am simply walking down the corridor, or reading a book, or sitting on the toilet. Even if I tried, I would probably forget at times! If I pay attention, I see there are countless such 'holes' – moments and stretches in any day when I am not, and do not have to be, 'The Resident Teacher'.

And I can also see that this role is actually only one of the various roles I have in my life at present. I am at times a friend to friends who have nothing to do with Gaia House, or even the Dharma; at other times I am a musician, a poet, a writer, a citizen, a neighbour, a brother, a son, an uncle, a room cleaner, an activist, a cook... So easily one role gets over-emphasized in an unwise way and we contract around it in identification. It becomes charged for us then, and it may begin to feel like a painful weight. Opening out the seeing to recognize the wider context can open out the contraction, so that vitality, interest, and creativity can flow more freely and widely.

The psychology involved here is not often simple, but in addition to acknowledging the life in other roles, this seeing of the 'holes' in any role can be immensely helpful in exposing its lack of solidity. By seeing these gaps, we burst a bubble we've believed in and felt constricted by, and reveal a spaciousness in which we can then move more freely. We find that it is very possible to be fully committed to the responsibilities a role entails, and to feel profoundly the sense of meaningfulness it may have for us, without solidifying or over-identifying with that role.

Deconstructing differences

This way of looking can be extended to many areas. A retreat is another example where it can be easy to solidify a perception of something and then struggle with it. Focusing too much on the perceived differences between 'being on retreat' and 'everyday life', we might feel either imprisoned in the form – the structure, schedule, and way of being – on a retreat, or become attached to that form and then have trouble letting it go and leaving at the end. Usually we do not realize, however, that the perceptions of certain differences are being fabricated, and inflated, by the mind and its tendencies of attention. We may lose sight of the fact that the elements and activities that comprise life on retreat – walking around and sitting around, eating, sleeping, washing, meditating, and talking, for instance – are actually quite similar to those of life off retreat. Admittedly retreat life involves a bit more of some things, like meditation, and a bit less of others, like talking; and it may also include a bit more of certain kinds of sensations, like knee pain, and a bit less of some other kinds of sensation. Essentially though, moments, at least, of such experiences – meditation, silence, talking, and bodily pain, even knee pain – may be encountered anywhere. The differences between situations are not as stark as we might at first suppose.

Investigating more closely, I recognize that my 'world', wherever I am, wherever I move to, is a world of inner and outer *experiences*, that is to say, *appearances* – sights, sounds, smells, tastes, bodily sensations, emotions, thoughts, memories, dreams, and intentions. Some of these fragments, these more elemental appearances, are pleasant, some not so pleasant, and some neither particularly pleasant nor particularly unpleasant. Viewing through the lens of such deconstruction frees up my sense of things. And I can begin to question whether it is really as different as it seems to be from place to place. Is any environment as solid as it seems? When I look in this way, it is hard to find 'the retreat', 'the work-place', 'the vacation', 'the travelling to', or any situation I may find myself clinging to or struggling with.

We could also apply this way of looking to 'meditation'. At some point it is almost inevitable for a practitioner to unwittingly reify the concept of meditation, and then to measure themselves, and suffer, in relation to that solidified concept. Looking more carefully, I can recognize that meditation does not have the kind of solidity that the mind might be giving it. If I am sitting in a formal meditation session and actually spacing out for a few moments, is that then 'meditating' or not 'meditating'? And conversely, if I am walking down the street in the city and spontaneously, without any effort on my part, strong mindfulness arises for just a few moments, is that 'meditating' or not? What makes it 'meditation'?

We fail to notice the 'holes' in things where they admit what seem to be their opposites. When we do, though, we see that they are not so solid, and that the contrasts between things are not so black and white. Then as our vision opens and relaxes, some ease can enter into our relationships with these things.

Different ways of looking: discerning what is helpful

Again some sensitivity and care is needed in our approach. And although we will return to it much later, one point in particular it is crucial for us to make here and continue to bear in mind throughout the journey of these practices: Any teaching on emptiness is simply a tool for freedom; that is all. When we have reified something in a way that causes *dukkha*, we can pick up these tools as ways of looking that deconstruct the reification and the solidification, and thereby bring a sense of relief, unburdening, spaciousness, and freedom. But like any tool that we have picked up and used, we can also put it down again. And we also have the choice to pick up another tool in its place, or even, in some instances, at the same time. Emptiness teachings and ways of looking are only a smaller subset of the larger set of tools for freedom that is the whole of the Dharma. The perspectives and practices of emptiness are certainly the most *powerful* tools, but that does not mean that they are in every situation of *dukkha* the most appropriate or most helpful.

So when we considered, just now, a retreat as simply another stream of sights, sounds, sensations, etc., this is definitely *not* to assert that this reductionist's world is reality; it is not. And nor would we always want to see life this way; that would be foolish. It is only that seeing in this way can at times open something up when perception is constricted. More conventional ways of looking have their validity, their place and their necessity, and their beauty too. Relating to a period of retreat as a sacred space very different from 'normal life' may be profoundly helpful and skilful – for example in supporting some sense of meaningful devotion.

Usually we will find we do still emotionally and purposefully engage with a thing or situation even as we are seeing its emptiness. There may be occasions, however, especially in the initial stages of developing voidness ways of looking, when a practitioner might tend to an unhelpful kind of dismissal or nullification of a thing as (s)he is trying to see some level of its emptiness. Perhaps then the way of looking needs to alternate for a time between a view of emptiness and a skilful reification, until the emptiness way of looking matures and there is a clear sense that it opens, rather than shuts down, the heart.

It is worth reiterating that experimentation is vital in all this, as it is in all practice. We need to notice what the effects are of different ways of looking, what is being supported. And when we feel that a way of looking brings some freedom, openness, or other wholesome and helpful quality, we know that we can trust it.

A way of looking is more than a reflection

While it is certainly possible that merely *reflecting* on a situation to acknowledge the 'holes' and deconstruct differences may be helpful, actually *seeing* and *experiencing* things in these ways will be much more powerfully liberating. And as always, our ability to engage such ways of looking grows with practice.

Practice: Beginning deconstruction – The elements of experience

When you find yourself feeling somehow imprisoned in a situation, or grasping unhelpfully at something that is not present, see if you can look within and around you in a way that 'deconstructs' your world into its aggregate appearances of sights, sounds, smells, tastes, physical sensations, and mental and emotional experiences.

Play and experiment with this way of looking until it feels that some of the oppressive solidity has lessened and you can sense some spaciousness has opened in the perception. Enjoy the lightness that this way of looking allows.

Notice too how the heart feels when you view things in this fashion. When we let go of contraction, warmth and kindness manifest effortlessly and naturally. Experiment and play until you discover a way to do it that naturally allows some warmth to permeate experience.

Practise this shift of view many times until it feels quite easily accessible, and even lovely. It's important to practise a lot also when there is no strong grasping or constriction present. Even what feels like an unproblematic perception of things can be lightened and opened up this way.

"What Was *That* All About?!"

As emphasized in Chapter 4, typically we do not deliberately choose our way of looking at any situation. It is imposed on us, rather, by the habits of the mind. And instead of helping to see the emptiness of things, these habitual ways of looking tend to solidify perceptions and compound *dukkha*. Most human beings will have experienced, many times, states in which the mind gets so caught up in a storm of reactivity that the ability to have a spacious perspective – on a thing, an event, or a person (self or other) – has been lost. Sucked into a vortex of unhelpful thinking and viewing, the mind is bound up in one lens, one way of looking at some situation (or at life in general), utterly convinced of the truth of what it thus sees. Difficult as such states are, we can in fact use them to develop some insight into voidness.

It may be, for example, that one morning, tired and not careful enough with our irritability, we have gotten into an argument over something trivial and have now lost our temper. Or perhaps we are beset by one or more of the five hindrances, either in formal meditation or out of it, and have been dragged into a state of obsessively proliferating thoughts about something. Some time goes by, however, and with a change in conditions the mind state naturally changes.

Looking back then, we recognize that the mind was fabricating something. It was 'making something' – fixating on, and drawing out, some aspect of the totality of our experience, and inflating it through *papañca*. Reactivity and obsessive thinking were pumping up the perception of this thing as a problem. Now though, from the perspective of a more balanced mind state, we wonder what the big deal was. Maybe whatever it was that we had been so humourlessly fixated on, and that had loomed so large in consciousness, doesn't seem so important now. Perhaps we feel a little foolish at how easily drawn in we were, how convinced by the mind's stories, interpretations, and ways of looking. We see that we were caught up in a way of looking that cast our view of our self and of some thing or other in rigid moulds, and in a way that brought *dukkha*. We see that the mind had concocted something illusory and fallen for it. Even if it is a little late to help the situation already past, such recognition is important. It constitutes an insight into fabrication and the emptiness of whatever view we were transfixed by.

As we practise more, however, we see more clearly that we naturally move between states of relatively greater *samādhi*, calm, spaciousness, kindness, and equanimity on the one hand, and states of relatively less *samādhi*, calm, etc., on the other, all the time. Gradually we grow wiser to the tendency of the mind to become caught in grosser fabrications when it is in a less wholesome state and more afflicted by craving, reactivity, and confusion. We can recognize what is occurring sooner, and eventually, even as it is happening we know not to trust the web that is being spun. We know that something is being blown up and distorted. It becomes more possible to see, right then, what is being concocted by the mind, how it is empty, and how we should not trust these particular perceptions.

Eventually, usually over time, the mind begins to lose its attractions to grosser levels of *papañca*. It loses also its blind addictions to certain kinds of agitation. The habitual grooves of the *citta* shift. States of calm, peace, kindness, and happiness become more the norm, and the mind, actually wiser now to where well-being lies, gravitates more naturally and effortlessly back to dwell in these more skilful states when it moves. Since the tendency to be swept up in unskilful mind states is weakened, their typical solidifications of perception are even further diminished. And the less solidifying ways of looking of the lighter, more wholesome, states become more common.

It may be that you are already very aware of how the hindrances can spin a tangle of *papañca* and solidify such compelling perspectives, and you feel that the power of your insight generally outweighs that of the hindrances. If you feel that this is not yet the case, however, repeated, careful observation of the processes involved can contribute to making it so. The following exercise may therefore be helpful.

Practice: Investigating what is being fabricated through the hindrances

Both in formal meditation sessions and as you move through your day, devote a series of practices to noticing when hindrances are present, and when they are absent. It may be useful to label which hindrance(s) is/are colouring consciousness. (Recognizing *that* a hindrance is present already informs and transforms the view.) Then, as sensitively and precisely as you are able, begin to inquire:

a) Is the mind believing a story about something or about yourself? If so, what is the story?

b) Whether or not there is a story, how is this mind state affecting perceptions right now?

In particular:

c) What do you notice about the self-view (how you feel and think about yourself, how you see yourself) in this state?

d) Is there some thing or element of experience upon which the mind is focusing and dwelling in particular?

e) What is the mind's perspective and assessment of this thing?

f) How much belief is there in the truth of such a perception?

g) You may also want to become aware of how the mind is framing and relating to notions of past, present, and future right now.

h) See if you can pay attention to the feelings of *dukkha* involved in this whole experience, and notice just how and where they manifest in body and mind.

i) Based on what you have learnt from past experiences, can you accept that something is being fabricated here by the mind state? If so, is it possible to hold this insight more steadily (but still lightly) in the mind, and to see things now through the lens of that knowing? What effect does that have?

It may be, until practice matures somewhat, that sometimes one has to wait for a particular wave of hindrances to subside to a certain extent before being able to see the voidness of whatever it is that one is reifying. So, when the above approach seems to have no effect, it may be more fruitful to work instead on cultivating a more wholesome mind state, or just sit out the storm with patience and mindfulness. When the hindrance dissolves – through insight, through somehow encouraging a more helpful mind state, or just through time – really feel how it feels when that *dukkha* has gone. Notice also then how perception has softened and is less locked-in to solidified perspectives of both the self and whatever was previously being unskilfully focused on.

As stated previously, seeing emptiness even with hindsight like this is helpful. It is a vital and genuine step in understanding the whole principle of fabrication; and it can lessen the chances of getting so taken in by such perceptions in the future.

Seeing Spaciousness

Bound up with the *dukkha* that comes from reification, and related to what we have just been discussing, is another element that we can draw attention to and begin to work with here. Whenever there is any grasping or aversion towards something, indeed whenever any hindrances are present, the mind is, to some degree or other, in a contracted state. It has, so to speak, been sucked in to some perception, some object of consciousness, has shrunk and tightened around it. Generally we experience this contraction in the mind as an unpleasant state, as *dukkha*.

We can notice this contraction, this constriction of the mental space, in relation to both internal and external phenomena. It will be evident, for instance, with regard to some unpleasant sensation in the body, like tiredness, or a difficult emotion, such as fear. And we may also detect it sometimes in social situations, if a certain relationship is charged.

The clinging mind contracts around some experience, and then, because the mind space is shrunken, the object of that grasping or aversion takes up proportionately more of the space in the mind. It thus seems somehow larger, and also more solid – its size and seeming solidity both corresponding to the degree of contraction in the mind. With the object appearing then bigger and more solid, and the experience of contraction being painful to some degree, the mind without insight in that moment will usually react unskilfully. It will unconsciously try to escape the situation by increasing the grasping or aversion, in a way that only keeps it stuck or even makes things worse. For unfortunately this further grasping keeps the mind space contracted, or contracts it even more. This makes the issue, the perception, still larger and more solid, setting up a vicious circle in which the mind is trapped.

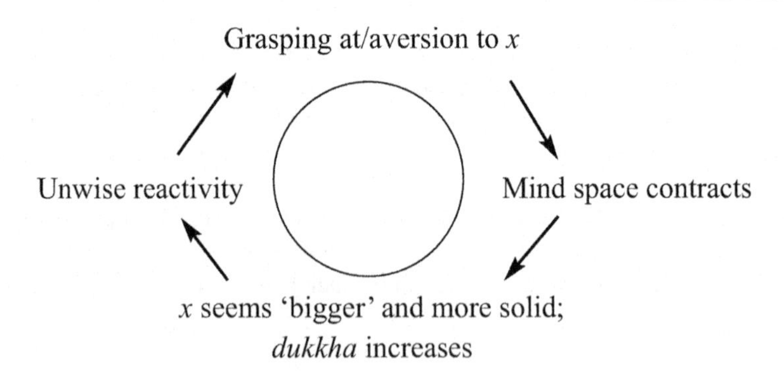

About all this, for now, we simply want to point out that it can be very helpful, when the awareness is unwisely sucked in in this way, to pay attention deliberately to a sense of space. Noticing space opens up the perception, and can begin to dissolve the vicious circle. Even attention to external physical space can help to open and ease the constriction of the mind, and can create a sense of space around an internal experience such as bodily discomfort or a difficult emotion.

Practice: Beginning to notice space

See if you can notice how attention tends to get sucked in to difficulties, or towards something else as a distraction when there is a difficulty. Can you notice that the mind space has contracted?

Be sensitive to how a contracted mind feels. Can you feel the *dukkha* of this?

Then see if you can deliberately pay attention to space, or deliberately include an awareness of space in your attention. Attending to the sense of actual physical space can be very helpful.

This may be done in a number of ways:

a) by opening the awareness to the totality of sounds that are coming and going;

b) by opening up the field of vision;

c) by intentionally noticing the space around and between objects, and the space in any room or situation.

Notice what effects this has.

As we have stated before, space is not emptiness, and emptiness is not a space of any kind. Rather, our investigation here is simply into how the mind gives solidity to experience and fabricates *dukkha* through the very ways we relate to, see, and conceive of things. We are gradually learning to untangle the tangle of suffering. And again, like all deliberate shifts in the way of looking, the more we do it, the more accessible it becomes. The more we practise inclining the mind to notice space, the easier it becomes to actually open up some space in the perception and experience some relief.

7

An Understanding of Mindfulness

Mindfulness is centrally important on the path, and is said to be always helpful. When we introduced the concept of ways of looking in Chapter 4, however, we stated that simple mindfulness practice is limited in terms of the depth of reification it can dissolve; and as we develop the different practices we will come to understand exactly why this is. Despite these limitations, though, naturally woven in to basic mindfulness practice are certain features that do make it a way of looking which, *to a degree*, both lessens fabrication and exposes some reification. It is in these ways in particular that it can help us realize a modicum of emptiness.

Some of these features were, to an extent, already involved in the approaches to the examples we looked at in the last chapter. But for the sake of fuller comprehension it may be helpful to draw them out further. Understanding how mindfulness works, from the perspective of understanding fabrication and emptiness, will be very useful for the longer trajectory of insight we are developing. Let us begin by considering two closely related aspects of mindfulness – '*staying at contact*', and '*bare attention*' – that contribute to its capacity to bring a degree of freedom through some lessening of fabrication.

'Staying at Contact'

In any moment, without a certain amount of mindfulness, there can often be a tendency for the attention to get dragged into the associations, reactivity, and stories that a simple stimulus (any sight, sound, smell, taste, body sensation, thought, or emotion, for instance) might trigger for us. This movement, the escalation of such complicating mental activity, and the entanglement of the attention therein, are all ingredients of a grosser level of manifestation of *papañca*. (For now, *papañca* may be translated as 'mental proliferation'.) In contrast, when we practise mindfulness, we are usually trying more to '*stay at contact*' – that is, to hold or return the attention to the 'initial, basic' experiences that arise at the contact of the sense doors with the sense objects.[1] Thus mindfulness practice involves a degree of putting down, or cutting off, these grosser levels of complication, self-based narratives, and proliferation.

The word *papañca* might also be translated as 'amplification'. And etymologically, it has the implication of 'spreading out', 'extending' something. As we have briefly described, it is possible to see that this is indeed what happens when the mind becomes ensnared in these associations and stories. It fabricates – constructs, amplifies, and inflates – at that time, both the sense of the self and also the sense of something else, an issue that it is somehow obsessed with and caught up in. And more often than not, both self and thing are fabricated in ways that are not so helpful, that do not feel free. Worse still, frequently the complications thus engendered seem perniciously to start to breed more of the same. The thicket of entanglement spreads to involve other issues and other perceptions.

This complicating proliferation and amplification may happen in any situation, but let us illustrate it with a particular scenario. Perhaps I am a retreatant on a silent group retreat. Early on the first day, I pass the teacher in the corridor, glance up, and see him looking at me. In that moment, however, he does not smile at me. Perhaps I don't yet know this teacher; and perhaps my experience from childhood and school has been of stern and judgmental teachers with whom I associate a (now internalized) sense of my own failures and inadequacies. I shrink a little from the contact in the corridor. Memories of these childhood teachers come up, and soon they are mixed with an imagination that this teacher now is displeased with me for some reason. I shrink more and tighten inside, though we have now passed each other in the corridor. Sitting in my room, I find I can't stop thinking about it and the encounter is replayed over and over in my mind's eye. In the process, I have somehow become certain that it was indeed a look of disapproval, and now I am fretting – wondering if his look was expressing a silent condemnation of something I had done wrong. I rack my brains trying to guess what that might have been, replaying through my mind the whole passage of events and encounters since my arrival. "Or perhaps he simply saw into my essence," I muse, "and saw my worthlessness and badness... I know it's not really possible to hide it forever... I have been found out." Soon I am asking myself if

[1] Again, for now, we will leave off questioning whether the 'initial' or 'basic' sensations involved in 'staying at contact' and, likewise, in 'bare attention' are in fact 'basic', 'initial', or 'bare', at all, and just accept them and the assumptions of 'bareness' etc. as perceptions and conceptions supportive of one skilful way of working in meditation. In later chapters, we will return to investigate these assumptions more fully.

perhaps I shouldn't have come on the retreat and start pondering possible excuses to leave early. I feel quite upset. But then I also start to feel angry at him and wonder if perhaps he is actually at fault, if he is simply not a nice or friendly person. It may even begin to seem to me now that this whole place is full of similarly unfriendly people… My mind ricochets back and forth, without rest, between all these thoughts, feelings, and conjectures, until the bell suddenly announces the next session. There the teacher gives some meditation instructions, but I cannot hear much at all of what he is saying. I am still caught in this mental whirlpool. And I have become convinced now that he does not like me. For though he moves his gaze as he talks, he does not make eye contact with me. Neglecting to notice that he has not made eye contact with quite a number of the many retreatants sitting in the hall during his very brief instructions, and despite the fact that I do not yet really know him, I believe that I do know exactly what he is like, and what he thinks of me. I may not realize I am doing so but perhaps I am also believing I know even what his opinions are on all kinds of other matters.

All this is painful, and it's tiring. Unwittingly, in the very process of constructing the self of another, my self is also constructed, and probably in a familiar and afflictive mould – in this example, as one who is indeed essentially "unworthy" or "bad" in some way. The heart is then closed in a tight grip, the seeing is locked into certain views, and all this unaware construction of selves feels like a heavy burden. The mind has been dragged away from the perceptions immediately given at contact, and become embroiled in a process where a sense and identity of one's self, of the self of another, and a solid-seeming issue are all being fabricated together. And these fabrications are *dukkha*.

If, in that situation, I were deliberately endeavouring to stay more 'at contact', the mind's interpretation of his glance, the memories of other teachers, and the momentary feelings of unpleasantness that might accompany them may all still have arisen. Noticing their arising, however, the mindfulness – supported by the intention of staying at contact – would recognize that here was a possibility of getting dragged away into *papañca*, away from the immediacy of experience in the moment. And I would then try to let go of such associations and the beginnings of proliferation.

If, at any point, I recognize that I have already been pulled in to a web, or even a tornado, of *papañca*, it is crucial to realize that all is not lost. There are still many practice options available to me then. In the context of this particular practice of staying at contact, I would simply make an effort to return the attention to the present moment and the actuality of experience at contact with the sense objects. I may need to repeat this skilful movement of the attention a number of times. But it may well be enough to calm the storm. It is also contributing to generally weakening the grip of *papañca*, and strengthening the mind's ability to stay more at contact in the future.

If we take it as a practice to move through a day, or a period of a day, trying with mindfulness to stay more at contact, we find that it is actually a delightful way of being. Lighter, more easeful, less burdened by the complexities of *papañca*, we also enjoy the vivid brightness of the present moment, the beauty of 'nowness', and the relative spaciousness of less self-building.

Practice: 'Staying at contact'

If you are not already very familiar with working in this way, experiment with periods of practice, both in formal meditation and in all kinds of situations and environments as you move through the day, where the principal intention is to try, as much as possible, to 'stay at contact'.

Experiment with two modes of doing this:

a) With the attention *directed* (at any time) *to a specific* sense object – a sight, sound, smell, taste, touch, or body sensation. Make sure that you also include objects that do seem to trigger reactions and associations.

b) With the attention more *open* to the totality of sense contact.

Expect associations, memories, and reactions to arise at contact sometimes. See if you can simply notice them, and not get drawn off by them away from the more immediate experiences of contact at the sense doors.

Expect also that the mind *will* at times get drawn off and into a story or *papañca* of some kind. There is no need to judge this. See if it is possible to simply notice as soon as you can and bring the attention back to whatever is contacting the senses.

As you try to sustain this, notice how it feels.

And when the mind is caught up in *papañca*, what do you notice? How does it feel?

Abstractions, Concepts, and 'Bare Attention'

Intimately connected with this idea of 'staying at contact' is the notion of '*bare attention*'. Not only does the mind have a habit of getting pulled off into associations and stories, but also a tendency to overlay a veil of concepts, abstractions, and images 'on top of' our 'basic' experience. Sometimes this can actually be helpful, even necessary. But we can easily become enchanted by and then caught up in those ways of looking – perceiving in terms of and through the lens of that concept, abstraction, or image, rather than attending more simply to the more 'basic' data presented by the senses.

The mental image of our body, rather than the sensations of the body, is often what the mind is engaging and preoccupied with, for example; and we feel the sensations of the body mixed with and through the filter of this image, instead of more 'barely' or 'purely'. Or, hearing a sound and recognizing a plane, the concept and image of a 'plane' can get superimposed onto the sound in a way that makes our listening at that time more vague, less intimately attentive to the actual experience of the sound itself.

Oftentimes, of course, this is harmless. But any veil on our experience will colour and obscure it, and any investigation into experience thus veiled will be similarly coloured and obscured. Along with stories, abstractions and concepts are also implicated in the meaning of *papañca*. And sometimes they are not so innocuous at all.

For example, at certain junctures of change and uncertainty, if there is agitation, a person might think, "I've no idea what I'm going to do with my life!" Believing this compelling but rather abstract thought, though, anxiety is fed and a vicious circle of reactivity and reification is set up. This is *dukkha*. What is not seen then is that the mind has painted a picture of one's whole life situation that is exaggerated, and too broad. A statement has been made that is far too general if taken literally, and falling for it, the mind now flails, painfully, in the webs of its own making. The abstraction – this over-generalized sense of 'my life' – itself a construction, also constructs a certain sense of self, and the *dukkha* that accompanies it.

Thus at times when there is *dukkha*, it can be helpful to ask oneself if the mind has fallen for some abstraction or other, to see if one can identify what it might be, and then to question whether the perspective of this abstraction is necessarily true. In addition to this possibility, though, the 'bare attention' that is often a feature of mindfulness practice seeks to get 'underneath' the veil of abstractions and concepts, and can disempower them in this way.

These features of mindfulness practice and their potential to dissolve a certain amount of abstraction can be illustrated further with another common example. Consider a practitioner who feels some sensations of pressure and constriction in his chest arising from time to time in meditation. With the best of intentions, he might interpret, perceive, and experience them through a whole heavy apparatus of constructs about his story, his past, and perhaps his difficulties with his parents. In this he may ascribe causality, and sometimes even blame. He is sure there are emotions, memories, and more sensations (all of which are assumed to be difficult or painful) somehow locked inside him. And perhaps he vaguely imagines a lengthy process of 'releasing', and thus hopefully 'healing'. Even without attaching a definite story from the past to such sensations appearing in the present, just the notion and view that they are 'past *karma*', 'stuff', or wounds 'releasing' is still a conceptual assumption that loads the perception. The attention is then not '*bare*', but heavily influenced and shaped by beliefs, theories, and assumptions. Without a doubt, an attention loaded thus will, in turn, heavily shape the experience that unfolds.

Now, it is *not* that there may not be some truth in these kinds of views. But they are only ways of looking. And as such, they may sometimes be helpful and sometimes not. We can grasp at a belief in their veracity so easily, solidifying a perspective so that we never question it, or rarely experiment with other perspectives. In doing so, we may also lose sight of the question of whether any particular assumption or view is contributing to easing *dukkha*, or actually fuelling it.

In this last example, an alternative approach to the whole experience would be to practise *bare attention*. This would mean trying to sustain a way of looking, over and over, moment to moment, that meets and notices, pays careful and close attention to, the sensations in the chest as they present themselves (pressure, heat, tightness, etc.), as much as possible putting aside, *just for now*, any story or interpretation that the mind wants to add, even if there is some truth to that story or interpretation.

It is worth re-stressing a couple of points here in relation to this example. First, that our investigations around all this need to be sensitive, and probably delicate. The whole area of emotional healing and emptiness is complex, and it asks of us not only great kindness, but also great courage, intelligence, and integrity. In later chapters we will return to discuss further some of its aspects. Second, I am not suggesting that bare attention is always a better, or even a truer, way of looking than some of those that involve more psychological complexity. Although it can often be immensely helpful, bare attention is also just another way of looking, and one that it would be limiting and unwise to attempt to restrict oneself to continuously.

It is healing and freedom that are important here. In our lives and our practices, can we be free enough to question, and to experiment with different ways of looking? What might we learn through this? What might be healed? And what might be liberated?

In this spirit of freeing inquiry then, and depending on your past meditation experience, the following practices may be useful as part of a range of available resources.

Practice: Questioning abstractions and generalizations

On an occasion when you are aware that some *dukkha* is present, see if you can identify any abstraction or generalization the mind has created and is now reacting to.

If a generalization, abstraction, or assumption is involved, can you question whether it is true? If questioning its truth does not feel conceivable, can you identify why not?

Is there another perspective on this experience that is possible? What might that be?

Practice: Bare attention

If you are not already very familiar with working in this way, practise periods of bringing and sustaining, as much as you can, a *bare attention* to experience – trying to meet experience as it presents itself, as free as possible from the veils of concepts, interpretations, and abstractions.

Make sure you experiment with all the sense doors, both when there is obviously *dukkha* present and also when there is not, and both in and out of formal meditation in different situations – for example with the *sensations* of sitting (in a chair, in a car, or on a bus), of the hands in cold or hot water, of the body in the shower; with the *sounds* around you, wherever you are; with various *smells* and *tastes* of different things. The individual possibilities are endless.

What do you notice happens when you sustain bare attention on an experience?

Is it possible to see that at least some level of fabrication cannot be supported if the attention is more 'bare'? How do you notice this?

What happens to any *dukkha* present?

What else do you notice?

As we develop skill in sustaining these kinds of attention, it is important to notice their liberating effects; but it is also important to understand how this is happening. One of the ways that mindfulness dissolves a certain amount of *dukkha* is by fabricating less, in general, than the mind usually might. The mind of *papañca* – of stories, abstractions, and images – fabricates the sense of self, and also *dukkha* and experience, in line with, and to the extent of, this *papañca*; and just to the extent that moments of mindfulness avoid, cut, or undermine *papañca*, there is then less fabrication. It is crucial to see and appreciate this for ourselves.

The Simplification of Attention

Although already implicit in, and really not separate from, the concepts of *bare attention* and *staying at contact*, we can tease out another potential aspect of mindfulness practice that likewise contributes to it fabricating less: a *simplification of attention*.

Often when there is *dukkha*, we are pulled into trying to combat it at a level of great complexity – ideas and stories and thoughts. Working with things and inquiring at this level is important and necessary too, but sometimes not helpful. Any unskilful attention to unhelpful abstractions will only feed those constructs and the associated reactivity, and thus fabricate more complexity, self, and *dukkha* in the process.

With *bare attention* in mindfulness practice we are, in effect, deliberately choosing to pay attention in a simpler way and to a simpler, less conceptual, level of experience. With *staying at contact*, we are also choosing to keep attention with a simpler object – the immediate sense experiences – so that it does not become so embroiled in complexities in ways that give them energy and cause them to grow. In both modes the mind is taken out of the pathways, or labyrinths, of unhelpful constructions, therefore not feeding those constructions so much in that moment. This can simplify the whole experience, and possibly untie a knot of *dukkha*. For less is being fabricated then – less self, less issue, and less *dukkha*. Thus we can say that one way mindfulness often helps is by deploying a simpler attention to a simpler aspect of the complexity of what is happening.

Taking this a little further, it is possible, too, to recognize that a complicated experience is actually a complex of simpler experiences. Therefore, within mindfulness practice we can also at times choose *which object*, among the many elements of an experience, we pay attention to. The attention placed on some experiences within the totality of experience will be more helpful in undoing fabrication than when placed on others. In addition to *staying at contact*, there are potentially other elements of a difficult and complex experience to which we can skilfully redirect the attention.

A Wise Attention to the Emotions in the Body

Consider again the example above where a person feels agitated and petrified with the generalized thought, "I don't know what to do with my life!" It may be possible there to untangle the knot of *dukkha* and lessen fabrication through attending skilfully to the emotions, for instance. Though they seem to be a *result* of the situation, the emotions may in fact also be partly *causal* – an element that is part of propping up the building of *dukkha* and abstraction.

Perhaps there are emotions present that are being unconsciously reacted to rather than met in a helpful way, and these reactions are feeding the whole web of thinking and perception. One way this can happen is that the attention, through aversion, recoils from or bounces off difficult emotions such as fear or sadness, away from feeling them in the body and into the mind of thought and abstraction.

Learning to deliberately bring a kind and skilful attention to the emotions that are present in the body, allowing and holding them, can allow the emotions to soften. The body then begins to soften. As the body and the emotions thus soften, the view, the way of looking, softens naturally, and right then it is possible to see 'My Life' in a different way.

We realize the perception of 'My Life' as this or that was not only a cause of, but also partially *dependent on*, the knot of emotions. We see the emptiness of the abstraction and the over-solidified perception: things are not *really* that way. Rather than rendering us irresponsible, however, this seeing frees us to respond more wisely to the situation.

Again, in addition to this softening of the emotions, a part of what may also be occurring through such a process is that bringing the mindfulness to the emotions in the first place is usually a move away from the mires of unhelpful abstraction. Because of this, and because it can be simplifying, this skilful movement of the attention can lessen fabrication.

Differentiating the emotions present

Often what we find when we look, however, is not just one but actually a whole complex of emotions present. What may be possible then is to try, slowly and delicately, to differentiate the various strands of emotions that are there (even if a word can't be found for each one). Then holding each somewhat more individually in turn, we may give each some attention, or some kindness, or whatever else it may need. The overwhelm that we can experience when emotions, thoughts, stories, and reactions all become entwined can be lightened this way. Clarity, and often some healing too, can be enabled.

This differentiation of the emotions is a further simplification of the object of attention, because instead of one big tangled and seething morass of emotion, we now experience smaller, simpler, and more 'manageable' strands of emotion. In beginning to disentangle the mass of emotions, moreover, we are untying, or at least beginning to untie, a knot that was partially supporting the whole complex structure of the abstraction and the perception.

Focusing on just the vedanā in the emotional body

Within paying attention to any emotion, we may choose at times to simplify the attention even further – by keeping it focused very specifically on the simple level of the *vedanā* (pleasant, unpleasant, or neither pleasant nor unpleasant) *of the bodily manifestation of that emotion* as it is occurring. We could find an area of the body where the moment-to-moment expression of the *vedanā* feels relatively clear. Then we might gently work to sustain the attention one-pointedly there. It will probably be helpful to play, as discussed in the *samādhi* chapter, with the balance and intensity of such an attention. It may need to be relatively bright and energized, but also soft and delicate. What will be important too is that, all the while, we are allowing the *vedanā* to appear as it does – pleasant, or unpleasant, or neither pleasant nor unpleasant – in this moment, and then the next, and the next.

Again, we certainly wouldn't want to always adopt such a way of looking. It would not be helpful, and we would miss much of the richness, depth, and wonderful complexity of our emotional life. But such an approach can be simplifying, and likewise allow the whole experience to simplify.[2]

By working with the emotions in such ways, we can gradually gain some confidence in the face of difficult emotional states and overwhelming complexity.

---

[2] Because the *vedanā* of emotions as they manifest in the body constitute an extremely simple level of experience, and because they are actually always there and available, no matter what else is happening, focusing on them like this can be a very useful way to simplify and calm the mind when one does 'wake up' to find oneself already caught in the middle of a *papañca* storm. It may often be the case that one does not catch an initial moment of reactivity and the movements of the mind from contact which spark *papañca*. As stated earlier, it is crucial to realize that one can still practise well at any moment – for example by skilfully tuning into this simple strata of the experience.

More specifically to our theme, we can also see how it is sometimes possible to undermine, disentangle, and withdraw energy from a whole tangle of abstraction and fabrication that is bringing *dukkha*. In the process of this learning, the beginnings of a liberating understanding of fabrication and emptiness are being developed too.

Practice: Choosing a simpler object of attention

When there is an experience of *dukkha* that seems to involve some complexity, see if it is possible, while remaining connected to the difficult experience and without moving the mind deliberately somewhere else (like the breath or a *mettā* practice), to tune the mindfulness to some simpler aspect of the totality of that difficult experience – for instance, the emotions, or the *vedanā* of the emotions in the body.

As you sustain the attention on this simpler element, notice what effect this has on the sense of *dukkha* and on the whole experience.

With regard to focusing on the emotions here: We are interested in finding ways of attending to, relating to, or holding the unfolding of an emotion or of the *vedanā* of an emotion, that feel like they are helping, soothing or calming the formation of the emotion or the fabrications around it. It is vital, therefore, that a portion of the mindfulness be devoted to noticing gently if this is happening, discerning if this way of attending is helpful in this moment.[3]

See if you can play and experiment and sense what may be needed. Is it possible to find a way of sustaining the attention on the emotions that feels helpful? (For instance, as touched upon, there are times when a more delicate attention will feel more helpful, just like with *samādhi* practice.)

Through practice we can see how, owing to this simplification of attention – in bare attention, in staying at contact, and in choosing a simpler object – the kind of attention we call mindfulness typically cuts fabrication and fabricates less than a more habitual kind of attention. Not only this though, we can see how mindfulness may also expose some fabrications and illusions *as* fabrications and illusions, and so undermine, to an extent, the unquestioning

[3] As we have already said, the amount that can be offered in this book about working skilfully with emotions is limited. Much can be discovered individually in practice, though, by keeping alive the crucial attitude of experimentation. And this will necessarily include using a part of the mindfulness to notice the effects that any approach is having and what is helpful in any moment.

belief we often have in their objective reality. We have discussed some of the ways in which this happens. Let us return to one in particular and take it a little further.

'Dot-to-Dot'

As practice develops, we naturally experience times when the quality of mindfulness is relatively stronger and more continuous than at other times, and we are able to pay closer attention to things, inner and outer. Then, as has been mentioned, it is possible to begin to see that what at first blush looked so solid in fact has lots of gaps in it. More than this though, we can begin to get a little sense, at a certain level, of how the perceptions of solidity are fabricated. Just as in those children's 'dot-to-dot' drawing books – where you follow and join the numbered dots with a pencil line to get a picture of something or other – close mindfulness can show that the mind joins the fragmented 'dots' of momentary experience, and thus fabricates some 'bigger' and more solid-seeming experience. And as explained, the bigger and more solid an experience seems, the greater the clinging and the *dukkha* it involves. This 'joining of the dots' happens in thinking about an impending experience in the future, and also while we are actually experiencing it.

For example, one morning, perhaps at a time when I am not feeling so fully connected with what I am doing, I think of lunch and imagine that it is going to be truly wonderful. I start eagerly anticipating it, perhaps even growing a little restless or impatient as the mind solidifies, raises up, and relishes its image of 'the bliss of lunch'. If I actually take up the meal time as a period of meditation, however, and bring all the mindfulness I can muster to the whole experience of lunch as it unfolds, what do I notice? Beginning meditators often find that mindful eating of a tasty meal increases their enjoyment of it significantly. More present and connected with the subtlety of sensations of taste, aroma, and sight, a world of sometimes exquisite pleasure can be revealed. But as the mindfulness grows more keen and continuous, I start to notice more closely what is actually happening. A mouthful of food in the mouth: the sensations of touch, warmth perhaps, and of chewing… ; chomp, chomp, chomp, an explosion of pleasant taste sensations, "Wow!" (It may even be very pleasant);… chomp, chomp, a bit more taste;… chomp, chomp, chomp, chomp, some more neutral taste sensations, amidst plenty of sensations of chewing;… chomp, chomp, chomp… maybe a taste that's not so pleasant for a moment or two; more chewing sensations, probably neutral, with actually sporadic, sometimes pleasant, taste sensations emerging among them. The whole, I find, is certainly nowhere near an uninterrupted experience of pleasant taste. Hmmnn… Even if I only pay attention to the sensations of *taste* in the mouth, I may well notice that in fact the moments of pleasant taste are significantly outnumbered by the moments of more neutral experience that are interspersed between them. Without such care of attention, however, I cannot see that the mind had 'joined the dots' in its image of lunch. Perhaps it is surprising, but the solidification and elevation of some experience seems to require a degree of inattention.

Or consider an example where aversion is an impediment. Looking out of the window at a somewhat rainy and windy outdoors, the thought might arise, "It's *terrible* weather", and there is a reluctance, an aversion, to going outside for a walk. If we have to go, it does indeed feel terrible, and our perception of it is confirmed by our lack of investigation. Paying closer attention as we are outside in the rain, however, we see here too that there are lots of gaps in this whole experience, and certainly gaps in the 'terribleness' of it. There may be some moments of coldness on the face, but one recognizes that they are in fact intermittent; then occasionally a raindrop may trickle down the neck, constellating for a few moments an experience that is a little unpleasant (even this, though, is revealed by closer mindfulness to contain gaps); maybe nothing much for a moment or two; maybe a few moments when the breeze even feels faintly pleasant; another slightly unpleasant moment when a cold raindrop splashes on the face, and so on… Without care, the mind – both in imagination beforehand and in actual perception as we are outside – may easily focus on the more unpleasant 'dots' and selectively join them to create the "terrible" experience, fabricating a sense of solidity and more *dukkha* in the process.

Mindfulness supports the possibility of investigation, and of our asking, in a way, "What is actually so terrible here?" It sees through the construction of a big terrible thing from tiny discrete moments of experience. We realize that the 'whole', unwittingly built from such separate and smaller moments, is actually empty, a fabrication.

Beliefs in grosser generalizations and abstractions can also sometimes be undermined in this way. Returning again to the earlier example of the generalization of 'not knowing what I'm going to do with my life', either a reflective self-questioning or a more steady mindfulness would reveal that there are many moments in the day when there is in fact a 'knowing what's next': "I'm going to have a shower", or "I'm going to meet my friend for a coffee." Abstractions and generalizations, like 'My Life' and 'unknown', are exposed as fabrications partly through such simple realizations – for instance here that there is, in the totality of diverse experiences, both knowing and not knowing; it's certainly not all unknown. Mindfulness and inquiry support a kind of puncturing of some abstractions in a way that can be calming, opening, and freeing.

This 'joining of the dots' is also evident, more subtly, with emotions. If a curious and unpressured, moment-to-moment care of attention is brought to the experience of sadness, for example, we will not find an uninterrupted continuity of that emotion. Instead we typically find what is more like a string of beads of sadness, with gaps in between the beads. We may find, for instance, there is a moment of sadness, perhaps followed by another moment of sadness, but one that is not so intense; this followed by perhaps a moment of another emotion, peace, say; then a moment of sadness again; a moment of what feels like an absence of emotion; another moment of stronger sadness; a moment in which a feeling of love, compassion, or tenderness comes more to the fore; and so on…

Sensing previously that this sadness was around, there may have been fear of this emotion – fear of letting ourselves feel it at all, or perhaps of getting overwhelmed by it. We find, though, that it is not as solid and heavy as we assumed. In the experience there is more spaciousness, more lightness, than we imagined. Only a relatively close and delicate mindful attention will reveal this however. It is quite possible to experience sadness as a continuous emotion, but only if the mind has a chance, through lack of intimate attention, to join the dots, to stitch the moments together without us realizing.

So we could say here, for now, that mindfulness actually reveals a way we are constructing something by solidifying its perception, giving it a continuity it does not inherently possess. And close mindfulness actually undermines that process to some extent.

Practice: 'Dot-to-dot'

Experiment with giving a whole range of different kinds of experiences a steadiness of intimate, careful, and precise, moment-to-moment attention. Can you notice the 'gaps' in the experience of a 'thing'?

See if you can sustain for some time that level of mindfulness that sees the gaps. What difference does it make then in your sense of that thing?

How does it feel to see this way?

In your investigations, be sure to include various emotions and mind states, as well as pleasant, unpleasant, and also 'neutral' physical experiences involving different sense doors. (Taste, touch, and bodily sensation are particularly conducive to this kind of investigation.)

§

An important thread running through the discussion of this chapter is worth summarizing: Although it can be useful to think of mindfulness as 'being with things as they really are', it is in fact more accurate, and more helpful for our purposes, to understand basic mindfulness practice as *a way of looking that merely fabricates a little less* than our habitual ways of looking. This is because, in leaving aside stories and *papañca*, and in paying attention in a closer, simpler, and more continuous way to simpler aspects of experience, it both sees through a certain level of abstraction and fabrication, and does not engage in perceptions and processes of the *citta* that fabricate quite so much. There are, too, other features of mindfulness practice responsible for it fabricating less, but we will return to these later.

8

Eyes Wide Open: Seeing Causes and Conditions

Beginning to Understand Self-Construction

As we've said, the Buddha taught that not just the self but *all* phenomena, without exception, are empty. Some streams of the tradition divide this comprehensive emptiness up into 'the two selflessnesses': 'personal selflessness' – the emptiness of persons – on the one hand; and the 'selflessness of phenomena' – the emptiness of all other phenomena – on the other. Such a scheme may be useful at times in the unfolding of practice and insight. In these next few chapters, we will focus predominantly on the emptiness of the personal self, although it will soon become evident, in contemplating fabrication and dependent arising, that seeing how the personal self is fabricated cannot really be separated from seeing how phenomena are fabricated.

And as we navigate this journey it is crucial to remember that emptiness practices seek not to obliterate the world of phenomena, nor to erase the self, but rather to understand the deepest nature of all phenomena and all selves – their voidness – in a way that frees us and also frees up compassion. As we have explained, one way in which this happens is through seeing how our perceptions of things, which seem so convincingly to be true representations of what is inherently real, are actually fabricated by the mind.

This concocted and illusory nature of things we can learn to expose first in its more obvious manifestations. And then we can keep inquiring, developing our ability to see through these constructions of perception in different ways and at different levels, gradually uncovering a greater range of more subtle fabrication. As we do so, a broader and deeper range of freedom is opened. For where there is belief in inherent existence, there is *dukkha*, there is an imprisonment in the cages of reification. And to the extent that there is insight, there is liberation from that prison.

In regard to the sense of self and the various self-views in which we become ensnared, a significant strand of practice therefore involves beginning a) to *recognize when* the self-sense is being more grossly and rigidly constructed; b) to *understand how* it is being constructed; and c) to *learn how to undermine this construction*, so that there is less self fabricated at that time, and a degree of binding in *dukkha* is thus loosened. This strand of practice, involved implicitly to a degree in some of the approaches already discussed, we can pick up and further a little now from a couple of other perspectives.

Blame as a Constriction of View – Opening the Vision

One of the ways self becomes exaggeratedly and inflexibly built up is through blame. There a view is solidified, not just of a situation in the past, but of the role of our self, or the self of another, in that situation. And though arising with respect to one specific event, self-blame that we have not seen through can petrify over time into a conclusion about how we, or others, truly are. The blame and the conclusion can become encrusted together, and encrusted into whatever chronically afflictive and rigid mass of more general negative self-views a person might hold. Then, of course, these more pervasively critical self-views make it increasingly likely that the way of seeing self or other in response to some new problematic situation will also be blame. Another vicious cycle of *dukkha*. Like all such cycles, though, it is open to defusing and dissolution from a number of angles.

One of these, and one that can bring much-needed relief and healing, is learning to 're-view' an event in a way that melts blame, because it looks in an altogether different way. Blame is an extreme example of our instinctual way of seeing, which tends to focus on, and solidify, the perception of self. Too easily and too quickly – when we make a mistake, when something goes wrong, when we or others act, or fail to act, in a certain way, when what manifests through body, speech, or mind is not what we wished for or might approve of – we point at and blame our self or the self of another. Usually in adopting such a stance the mind is adopting a shrunken view. Seeing only in terms of self, and habitually placing self at centre stage of whatever situation or event transpired, it is not recognizing and including in its understanding the wider confluence of conditions that give rise to anything at all in the world. But seeing in terms of the wider web of conditions that come together to give rise to any action or result is a different, more open and more compassionate, way of looking at what has happened or is happening. It is a seeing *not* in terms of self, not through the lens of self.

Perhaps, for example, you are with a friend and she is telling you of some difficulty she is going through. You are listening as attentively and sympathetically as you can but at the same time you are also aware of some disquiet within yourself. In response to what your friend is sharing with you, surely, you vaguely worry to yourself, you should be feeling more empathy and compassion; yet somehow you are left mostly unmoved. Later, this bothers you and you wonder if there is something wrong with you, perhaps suspecting that your capacity for empathy is small, that you are, after all this practice, rather a cold-hearted person.

That way of looking – focusing only on your self and holding the self responsible for how things went – fails to see, and to take into account, a whole range of other factors that contributed significantly to limiting the extent of the compassion that you felt at that time. The rather unfulfilling connection may have been simply a result of something as basic as being tired, from overwork or for any other reason. (If that is so, then in a similar situation in the future it might be more helpful and kinder to both of you to tell her that you really want to hear about what she is going through, but that you want to respect her by being fully present, and make another appointment.) Believing that you should be feeling more, however, and then pressuring yourself subtly in the moment or judging yourself, the cues of tiredness are likely to be discounted. What's more, the pressure you put on yourself to feel something is also itself more likely to strangle any emotional resonance that might have arisen. Of course, there could also be other more complex reasons why you did not feel so much in response to her story at that time. It may be that there was already between you some slight tension left unresolved from a week ago, something small and that might be judged as insignificant, but enough to affect the openness and empathy between you this evening. Or, although even after the fact you find that you cannot put your finger on it easily, there was something in the way she was herself relating to her story, and in how she was telling you, that somehow inhibited your heart's resonance. Perhaps she was holding back. Or perhaps she was, at some level, offhand with it all, disconnected herself, or maybe hamming it up in an artificial way; perhaps, even, her sharing came across as subtly aggressive toward you for some reason. If any of this was partly the case, it is definitely not that we then blame her, for there will similarly be conditions that contributed to her speaking that way. The point is that it will all have an effect on what arises in your heart as you sit listening, and it is crucial to realize this.

Conditions are inner, outer, past, and present

What we can practise then, at first *after* an event that we are seeing with blame, is a 're-viewing', a looking again in a different manner, in a way that takes at least some of the suffering out of it. There is a deconstruction, a softening of a view that has calcified. And this requires the head and the heart working together. Clarity and thoroughness are here in the service of compassion.

Since, in blame, our vision tends to be too narrow, it is vital to take into account a broad enough spread of contributing conditions to open out the view. Thus it can sometimes be helpful to make sure to consider four kinds of possibly relevant conditions. We can search for and acknowledge the force of what we might call the 'present, inner' conditions – the states of mind, beliefs, perceptions, etc. that were active within us at the time. In the situation above, your tiredness would be an example of a 'present, inner' condition. We should also scrutinize the 'present, outer' though – those conditions present in the outer environment at the time that were impacting – for instance, the manner in which your friend was sharing her story. Likewise, it will be helpful to ponder the 'past, inner' conditions – for example, states or habits of the *citta* set up within us before the event. Perhaps in the above situation, the feelings left unresolved from your last meeting might be regarded as 'past, inner' conditions. And fourth, the effects of 'past, outer' conditions – external impressions and influences from our history – can also be brought to mind.

As we reflect this way in practice we may well find that these four categories sometimes overlap. Or we may be uncertain to which exact group a particular factor belongs. It is important to realize that these are only loose categories. The purpose here is merely to stretch open the view into corners that may have been overlooked.

Even then, thinking in this way might at first seem slightly contrived. In time and with practice, though, our reflections and awareness are able to encompass the range of conditions in a very fluid and natural way. Indeed, this more open, less solidifying way of seeing can more and more come to be the natural way we see. And it can also become accessible even in the midst of a situation as it is happening. We do not have to be locked in to a way of looking that binds the self.

Let's illustrate this liberating deconstruction through another scenario. At lunchtime I need to catch a train, and I have tried to fit too much work into the morning. I rush to pack so that I can leave in time but I find, halfway to the station, that I have forgotten the train tickets: they're still in my desk. I rush back home, grab the tickets, drive (too fast now) toward town, park, run (with my not-so-light bags across the muddy field) to the station (where the train, I discover, is late anyway), then, standing, lightly perspiring still a minute later on the platform, a thought dawns in the mind: "Did I close the car windows?"... Too late to go and check now, the train is coming... If I had been more present, more mindful, when leaving the car, I would be able to remember now whether I had closed the windows. Easily I could blame myself for this lack of mindfulness. Even though

I might realize that mindfulness is impermanent and comes and goes like everything else, still I could believe it was 'I' who failed to intend or to remember to be mindful.

Investigating further, however, one could ask what it is that supports a moment of intention, or of remembering, to be mindful. Briefly, we may consider our four kinds of conditions. The 'present, inner' conditions certainly contribute. For example, a moment or mind state of mindfulness is more likely than a moment of distractedness to spawn a next moment of mindfulness. And if in the 'present, outer' environment there are many reminders to be mindful, these aid its arising. Conversely, time pressure is a significant 'present, outer' condition, one which often affects the 'present, inner'. When there is outer hurry, the mind state easily becomes correspondingly hurried and off balance, and such an inner mind state is less likely to generate a next moment of mindfulness from itself. Then also, although they may be distant in time, the 'past, inner' conditions exert their influence in shaping what happens in the present. The more often there have been moments of intending and remembering to be mindful in the past, the more likely it is for a moment of intention and remembering to arise in the present. And likewise, the 'past, outer' conditions are also influential. A history of being repeatedly reminded to be mindful, for example by teachers, friends, and books, makes it more likely that there is a more 'spontaneous' remembering to be mindful at some future time.

Looked at in this way then it is clearer that, when I do remember, the self cannot claim that its remembering really comes purely 'from itself', from its own power. Nor can it accurately take all the blame for the moments when mindfulness did not arise. In opening the seeing out to a broader array of conditions – inner and outer, past and present – this way of looking does not point at a self with blame. In fact, engaged more thoroughly, this process does not even find a self. For it becomes evident that actually none of the conditions that might be considered can be regarded as really being the self; nor can it be said that the self truly owns any of them. Through broadening the way of looking to respect the contributions of a variety of conditions, a certain level of self-view, including the painful self-view of blame, can be dissolved.

Guilt, remorse, and responsibility

We will look much more at this unfindability of self later, but one point should be stressed right now. We are not adopting and clinging to a view here that would have us never take responsibility, or never be able to accept someone's appreciation for what we have done. For sometimes it is of course important to feel ourselves take responsibility for our actions and choices, and similarly to appreciate the good that we and others have made manifest.

As always, the crucial and overarching question is: What way of looking contributes to suffering, and what way of looking to ending suffering? And the answer will vary from situation to situation. To emphasize again something we have already voiced: in this area, and in so much of the work with emptiness practices, we seek a *flexibility of view* – to be able to pick up a view of self and situation when it is helpful, and, when it is not, to put it down and look in a different way that is more helpful.

When what has happened feels very significant or has had significant consequences, views of blame, inflamed by the emotional charge, easily become repetitive. Then the self can become bound in a tight and painful orbit of obsession – both with the past and with whatever self-view has been crystallized and clung to. That is to be trapped in feelings of *guilt*. If the view can be opened up in the way suggested, it may still be that we feel *remorse* for something in the past we have done or neglected to do. This emotion of remorse may in fact be an important part of healing. And it differs from guilt. Less rigid and constricted, softer and more compassionate, remorse actually has its own kind of beauty. Significantly, it recognizes and is more concerned with the skill and beneficence of *actions*, rather than making conclusions about *selves*. And rather than being caught in obsession about the past, it looks to the future with a sense of possibility and of heartfelt aspiration to choose differently next time.

In the not-so-emotionally-charged example of rushing for the train, I certainly could take some lessons from the escapade, but not blame or guilt, nor conclusions about my self. It would be more helpful for me to reconsider such factors as how much work I try to do on the morning of travelling, or the possibility of packing at least a little in advance. Then I would be considering in terms of conditions rather than self. And I would be looking creatively and helpfully toward the future rather than being stuck in the past. Of course, a similar re-orientation is possible in instances when the blame is more painful. Opening the view to the wider convergence of conditions, a measure of space, ease, and lightness are liberated, and both caring and taking responsibility are naturally included.

A web of inter-dependence

The fact that any thing that exists or that comes into being does so dependent on countless other things as supporting conditions is one of the basic meanings of *dependent arising*. With reflection the assumption or view that some effect or outcome is due to just one cause can seem quite naïve. And as we look more openly, more thoroughly, and with more intelligence, we can see how complex and far-reaching, infinite really, is the confluence of conditions that gives rise to anything. For each condition is fed by others, without a beginning or an end to this web of dependency.

Moreover, conditions affect and feed each other too. In the example of listening to your friend, it may be that she picked up somehow on your lack of empathy or on the awkwardness you vaguely felt. Perhaps at the time she was not quite aware of what it was she was sensing and did not stop to check it out with you. But it had a significant effect on the openness and flow of her communication, because usually the way we feel we are being listened to affects what and how we speak in that moment. Thus the web of conditions in the present becomes further multiplied and entangled.

Much of this is actually noticeable in many relational situations – whether speaking or performing or whatever – but it can often be overlooked. In a public talk, for instance, it can be common for both speaker and audience to assume and feel that the qualities of, say, aliveness, warmth, or intimacy that the talk seems to have, or not to have, are due to the speaker. A performer or speaker who pays attention to this will notice, however, that the way the talk is (the particular words that come out of the mouth, the turn of phrase, the tone of voice, the energy level, etc.) arises symbiotically with the quality of the listening, with the energies and attitudes in the room as the talk unfolds. They influence each other hugely. How one is listened to depends on how one is speaking of course; but it also depends on all kinds of other factors, including, for example, the histories of those listening, their interests, their capacities to understand, and their energy levels. And just these last, for example, might in turn be dependent on such things as the prevalent mood of each listener, how rested they are, what they have been doing recently, and what and how much they have eaten in the last few hours. 'How it is' depends on the total mixing and interaction of an extensive range of conditions. In a very real and palpable sense, everyone gives the talk, not just the speaker.

As we have explained, so easily when we have a difficulty in any kind of relationship, the mind falls into a view that it is 'your fault' or 'my fault' – in the language of blame. But such a limited perspective is rarely completely true, or helpful. In relating, our reactions, interpretations, communications, and subtle signals, intended and unintended, feed off and impact each other all the time, whether we are aware of it or not. Thankfully though, if we can acknowledge this and become interested in it, the possibilities of reconciliation open up. If it becomes our shared basis for understanding, then two people having a difficulty can become two *looking together at the dynamics* of their relating, on the same team untangling the dependent arising of a problem, rather than two accusing, two at war.

From this less restricted and restricting perspective we can recognize too that the kind of self or persona that arises is similarly contingent. Again this is noticeable in any relational context. How I am, or appear, when I am teaching in this or that situation is not necessarily how I am or appear in another teaching situation or another non-teaching situation. The way of using language, the tone of voice, the humour or gravity, gentleness or fieriness, the quality of kindness, and the feelings that arise in me – all this comes from the fullness and openness of the situation. It is clear to me that what arises is dependent on the totality, inner and outer, of that situation.

This does not mean though that how I am then is somehow inauthentic. I feel it is just as authentically and fully 'me' as any other expression or persona in my life. Understanding that what arises does not arise from any essence, but rather dependent on the meeting of wider (or even infinite) conditions, brings an openness and lightness to the perception of any situation, and a freedom to let this or that persona manifest, if it is helpful.

The way of looking is always a significant condition

As alluded to earlier, in the complex interplay of causes and effects, the way of looking operating at any time – the amalgam of perspectives, assumptions, conclusions, and reactions – also constitutes an immensely significant factor. A crucial element of the 'present, inner' conditions, it will always have an effect on the *perception* of what is happening. For example, when there is blame or judgment in regard to something, the self that has grown – that has become inflamed around and in relation to that issue – then tends actually to perceive that issue with *more* bias and intensity. In so doing, it thus reinforces not only its own solidity but the perception and view of that thing, and also the emotions and reactions experienced as a result. Another example of a vicious cycle of *dukkha.*

In addition to such effects on perceptions (and we will come to talk much more about the fundamental and far-reaching effects any view, or way of looking, has on perception) it may also be that the view affects, to some extent, how the whole situation unfolds externally. For it is immediately clear that if the view softens, emotions and reactivities soften too, and this softening is naturally communicated into the whole mix of conditions. The 'present, inner' conditions being then different, the web of conditions is in fact different. And this difference may be enough sometimes to affect the situation so that a different outcome ensues. You can imagine, in any of the examples we have used, what effects on action or speech a different view in the moment might have had. Sometimes all we are able to change in a situation is the view; the other conditions may now be past, or may not be in our control.

§

While this explanation of the dependence of any outcome on a wider set of conditions may seem clear enough intellectually, it is vital to practise re-viewing events and situations *often* in this way. As we have said, the habit of seeing in ways that solidify self is immensely strong and deep rooted, and will not be transformed without, usually repeated, practice of alternative ways of seeing.

It may be too at times that we are not able to open out the comprehension of a situation sufficiently without help from others. Asking a friend, or someone whose wisdom and care you trust, to help you to see the wider conditions that you may be missing can be enormously supportive.

Practice: Ending blame through recognizing the confluence of conditions

If there is something from the past for which you are blaming yourself, take some time – either in formal meditation, or quietly reflecting, or with a spiritual friend – to consider the broader range of conditions on which whatever happened was dependent.

Make sure you include the loose categories of 'present, inner', 'present, outer', 'past, inner', and 'past, outer' conditions in your considerations.

Notice if there is a condition that you come to which you feel is 'you', or for which you believe you are to blame. Can you see that this too is dependent on other conditions that are not 'you', and identify what they are?

Notice what effect this re-viewing has on your perception of and feelings about what happened, and on notions of self-blame or guilt.

Re-view this event many times in this way. Even if it feels immediately helpful, the shift in view probably needs consolidating. Alternatively, if it feels like it does not help much, it may yet be that it gains power through repetition, or with the help of a friend kindly pointing out your 'blind spots'.

It is also important to practise this shift in view on many events and situations, ones that feel quite difficult and charged, and also those that feel less so.

See if you can practise viewing a situation or a phenomenon that has arisen in the present in the same way. What effect does this have?

If there is some apprehension regarding an impending situation, could you also consider that situation in this way?

Whenever there is a lingering blaming of another person, a similar contemplative process may potentially be directed toward them. Although we usually have less knowledge of the specific variety of conditions that were operating for another, the same principles hold, and reflecting on this can often dissolve blame.

Of course, sometimes self-views have hardened into a more pervasive shame that tends habitually to regard situations, events, and much of what arises and transpires, in ways that blame self. While the practice above will still be helpful, it can be greatly supported by other practices (such as *mettā*, or other emptiness practices). Whether alone or together, but usually over time, such practices have the power to melt even the most rigid and painful self-views, allowing a greater unbinding of the sense of self, and enabling profound healing.

9

Stories, Personalities, Liberations

Respecting the self

Before continuing our exploration of the ways self-views are fabricated, it may be important to reiterate and explore a little further another point crucial to the navigation of our path. Though all self-views and all things are fabricated, this emptiness of self and phenomena does not mean that we cannot engage with, and view in terms of, the self or any phenomenon on a conventional level. A part of the freedom that comes with any degree of realizing emptiness is a freedom to view in different ways. And in fact there will be countless times when it is not only necessary, but most helpful, *not* to emphasize the view of emptiness. Sometimes seeing in terms of self is the most appropriate way of seeing, and the one that relieves the *dukkha* of a particular situation most satisfactorily.

We have already mentioned, for example, the importance of adopting at times the viewpoint of ourselves taking responsibility. A view of a somewhat autonomous self, with a measure of free will and choice, is usually basic to and necessary in establishing the kind of relationship with ethics that can sustain our Dharma path in a healthy way. Very often too there are instances where communication, and in particular the resolution of conflict and hurt, between two people needs to be in terms of selves, and not simply because the language of self is a convenient 'conventional shorthand'. If my friend is aggrieved at me for something I have said or done, and I respond only by reminding her that, like everyone else, she "has no self" and that she should therefore just "let it go" and "get over it", I am hardly being sensitive, respectful, or caring. Such a perspective and its expression may just be unskilful and inappropriate to the situation. It may well be that what is needed instead for the easing of the *dukkha* here is a view wherein two 'selves' talk caringly and honestly to each other, in terms of their 'selves'.

A great deal of Dharma practice is at the level of the self, and this is necessary. For many, learning how to care for the self, *in the terms of the self*, is a crucial strand in practice. To recognize and honour needs, to communicate and voice what is true and important for us, to connect with and learn to relate well to the emotions – these are vital skills. And so too are the learning to hold one's self in tenderness and kindness, and to cherish and even celebrate oneself.

Something about stories

Central, usually, to the sense of self are the stories we tell, both internally and externally, about ourselves and our lives. Self-blame, which we discussed in the last chapter, would be one example of a kind of story we tell, but there are countless others. Certainly, like all things, these stories are empty; they are not ultimately true. And we can begin to at least glimpse this at a relatively obvious level. In addition to what we have already explored, if we are honest we can notice, for example, how we might tell, and even perceive, the story of our past differently at different times – depending on present circumstances, our mood, the perspectives we are currently favouring, and what we are now emphasizing. We start to realize, or at least to entertain the possibility, that our story is not inherently one way, independent of such factors in the present.

With regard to the emptiness of our stories too, however, we must tread with care and sensitivity, for we may again miss the point of emptiness teachings. It is frequently the case that in circles prioritizing meditation we can come to regard any and all stories as something to be dropped and avoided. The question, as always though, is whether this narrative that I am entertaining is helpful or not.

Commonly we do not realize quite how malleable is the story of our life, how much flexibility is possible in the way of seeing it, interpreting it, and expressing it. The narrative of my journey – not only my present and my future story, but also the story of my past – is not completely fixed, simply and objectively 'given', engraved in stone. Significantly, we can see our story, and thus also ourselves (who must be central to the story), in ways that imprison and disempower us, or render us, for instance, as a victim in some way. Alternatively, we can loosen a little the chains of the stories that bind us, and see our journey in ways that heal, that empower and inspire us, give us energy, possibility, direction, and meaning.

Certainly the Buddha did not refrain from telling his story, even after his Awakening, but he framed it in certain ways. And this storying was not just to others. On his path before his Awakening, he was seeing his own life and journey in particular and skilful ways – as a 'noble quest', as a 'battle' even at times, and seeing himself in those narratives as a dedicated 'seeker', and a heroic 'warrior'. Given his family background, his mother who died in giving him birth, his controlling father who enforced on him an extreme seclusion from the outside world, and also other events, such as the break with the group of five ascetics and the consequent solitude of his journeying – he could have storied himself and his life in quite a different way.

The story we end up telling and the identity we adopt necessarily go together as a package. Just as do a theatre play and a character within that play, narrative and identity must imply and weave into each other. And as with the story of our life, to a certain extent at least, we may well have more choice of identity than we believe. Sometimes we are locked into both an identity and the story that goes with it, not because of something real in the story but because of assumptions and ways of looking that we absorb unquestioningly from the cultures around us – including, occasionally, those ways of looking that are intended to be healing and helpful. And any identity we adopt, although not ultimately true, will have considerable effects on how we see and relate to our journey and the events of our life. Just the notion of where 'success' and 'failure' lie, for instance, will be significantly altered if we let ourselves 'choose' – that is, be drawn to and fill out – an identity that feels more meaningful for us. For that new way of seeing ourselves will naturally reorder our priorities, and also recast the meanings assigned to certain things and events. Identifying oneself as a 'seeker' rather than a 'college dropout', for example, will bring a considerably different interpretation to and evaluation of many facts of one's past, present, and future, changing the whole relationship with these aspects of life. What such things as 'work', 'money', 'status', and 'security' mean to us depends on the identity we imagine for ourselves.

It is therefore not simply that stories are a problem and to be transcended once and for all. We are not endeavouring through practice to exist in some constant state of 'being in the now without story'. Stories are, in fact, a finally inevitable dimension of our existence. And at an important level they matter greatly in giving our life its meanings and directions.

Being *locked into a story*, however, believing that this narrative and the fantasy of self-identity that it involves are ultimately true, with no room or freedom to story ourselves and our life differently, nor any ability to experience times of letting go of narrative ways of looking and seeing through other lenses – that is the problem. What we seek, then, are both the means of recognizing the emptiness and the malleability of stories and self-views where they have been petrified, as well as ways to move, at times, out of the narrative mode so that other and more radical insights are possible. Part of this, again, will be understanding *how* a particular self-view has been constructed. In so doing we realize *that* it is a construction, and so see through it. A significant measure of liberation and an ease of spaciousness are thus made available to us.

Questioning self-construction

Whether as part of a longer story or not, construction of any more obviously problematic self-view or sense of self is always dependent on *other* views, gross or subtle. In our exploration of blame we began to expose one way of looking typical of the root delusion of self: a tendency to 'self-reference' things and events. Too quickly, for example, we infer that the arising or the presence of this or that *means* something *about ourselves*. This pain or tightness in the body, this hindrance arising, this strange or violent thought or image that pops into the mind, is taken to strongly imply something about ourselves, often then impacting our self-worth. We can do this too with the more 'positive' occurrences – feelings of bliss, or a sense of freedom that arises, for instance – but is it helpful, or even true, if I take a conclusion about 'me' from it?

It is such a liberating shift of understanding and perspective to see in terms of conditions, and so not make conclusions about 'how the self is'. At times, therefore, when we feel the contraction of *dukkha* around some thing, it can be powerfully helpful to ask:

What am I making this mean?

We need to see precisely what the mind is doing, and particularly what it is concluding. For the meaning of something is given by the mind's perspective.

Closely connected, and also in line with themes we have already touched on, it is interesting as well to see what it is we tend to blame ourselves for, *which* things seem to matter. And to see too *how* it is that those things come to have more significance than others. For 'this thing mattering' is also something that arises dependent on all kinds of conditions. In particular it is very much influenced by the messages of our immediate environment. In a situation like a retreat where we are placing so much repeated focus and emphasis on mindfulness, mindfulness of course can then be what easily comes to matter. It then also comes to be a concept we tend to measure our selves in relation to, and an issue that self is constructed around and on.

So when there is suffering around a certain thing that has occurred or a certain element of experience, a related second question we can ask is:

From the huge variety and totality of moments of sense impressions today or in a certain situation, why is this phenomenon fixated upon and not something else?

Correspondingly, of course, we may ask a third question:

What am I not giving significance to then? What am I perhaps not even noticing?

This kind of investigating may be vital to freedom at this level. Through questions such as these we can begin to expose the building blocks of painful self-construction and undermine the assumptions and ways of looking on which grosser self-views are built. Then the possibilities of new and different pathways are opened for the mind and the heart.

Imprisoned in self-definitions

Because of the depth and force of fundamental delusion it is unfortunately normal for us, without profound practice, to be trapped in views of ourselves, locked into identities, at least at some level or other. And for complex reasons, in our modern Western culture a great deal of the pain that most people experience is at and in relation to what might be called the 'personality level' of the self – how we think about, feel, and see our personalities.

At any level there is much to fathom about how the self is fabricated, but let us consider one significant element here, that of *self-definition*. We can, and do, of course define ourselves in all sorts of ways (socio-political, human, existential, etc.) and at all sorts of levels. It is the personality-definitions adopted, however, when believed in too completely and taken too rigidly that can often be a source of the most palpable sense of suffering and constriction, both acute and chronic.

Many possible ways exist through which we come to grasp at and imprison ourselves in more fixed self-definitions. The blame that we were discussing is an example of self-view being built around, and constricting around, specific events in time. As mentioned, blame may lead to a *conclusion*, not only about what we, or someone else, 'did wrong', but also about '*how we are*'. The shrunken self-view of blame festers, swells, and transforms into a more pervasive and abiding self-definition.

Some of these ways we define ourselves are obvious but some may be more hidden from us; we may not even be conscious that we have them. Often in our culture many seem to be quite harsh and negative: "I'm a failure", "I'm a hopeless case", "I'm bad", "I am weak". And although all self–definitions typically wear the guise of objectivity, some may indeed hold a degree of truth at the relative level: "I am wounded", "I am sick", "I am an angry person", "I am passionate about everything". It can be very instructive to notice what we repeat, to ourselves and to others, about ourselves, but it may take a subtlety of attention to notice the more subtle manifestations of self-definition. Sometimes we only voice these definitions of our personalities inwardly; sometimes they are forcefully operating within us, but in a primarily non-verbal way; and sometimes the presence of a self-definition is announced loudest through our repeated communication of its message to others – either directly, in words, or more indirectly, by habitually adopting certain roles or personae in groups or communities.

A negative self-definition is, of course, a painful view, and like any view, it has significant effects on perception. Looking at ourselves through the filters of such self-definitions, our attention is continually pulled toward and impelled to focus on our negative qualities. Moreover, what we see then, through these tinted lenses, is inevitably coloured, distorted, and made to appear more negative. Through the co-operation of factors such as these – the fixating of the attention on the negative, and the colouring of perception – the self-definition automatically and repeatedly culls 'evidence' for itself. Thus that self-view is indeed reinforced.

Again though, a continuity of mindfulness as we go through a day punctures the pervasiveness of the view, exposes the holes in what we assume to be the seamless fabric of how we are. If, for instance, I am clinging tightly and rigidly to a self-definition that I am an angry person, then sustaining attention carefully I cannot help but notice that there are times when I am not angry. Thus we witness clearly and undeniably the *absences* of the qualities we believe define us. And more than likely, we witness too the *presences* at times in ourselves of qualities opposite to those 'self-defining' ones. If I were *really* 'an angry person', how could this be? Such a fixed and real essence of my being would not admit of absences in anger, nor of other qualities in its place. Plainly seeing this again and again, it becomes simply impossible to rigidly maintain the old self-definitions. Something is loosened in our view of our selves, and some freedom, openness, and relief can thankfully come into our experience.

When the insight is based thus on a simple attention that simply notices more broadly and evenly through the day, there is much less chance that a negative self-view is then replaced by its opposite and that we cling to some positive self-definition. In some instances, such positive replacement really is a necessary intermediate step. But it too will become a prison soon enough. Under the burden of this positive self-definition, I will somehow probably feel obliged to keep proving its veracity to myself and to others, which will quickly come to feel like a tiresome pressure. (Not to mention the irritating fact that I will inevitably encounter people who don't seem to agree with my elevated self-definition!) At some point we realize that any self-view that we believe is really true is a way we bind ourselves. As such, it will be felt as a constriction at some level in the being.

As briefly discussed in Chapter 3, sometimes a practitioner is unsure about taking steps into emptiness practice, and this questioning of the self-definitions can be an excellent and gentle place to start. Taking the times of suffering as our lead, we can notice if this *dukkha* present, here, now, has an element of self-definition wrapped up in it. And if so, we can look to uncover the lack of ubiquitous and immutable truth therein. We find that when we let go of the tight binding of that self-view the heart softens and there is more capacity and more availability to care for ourselves and others. We realize we can trust this process and look forward to exposing other self-definitions as falsities. If there is one that we are afraid to let go of or whose lack of complete truth we are ambivalent about recognizing, then it can sometimes be useful even just to imagine what it would feel like not to believe that self-definition.

Practice: Examining, and loosening, self-definitions

Take some time to notice and make a written list of self-definitions that you hold on to – both the more obvious and the more hidden ones. What reveals that a self-definition is operating?

Once you have the written list, look at it. Writing a list like this on a piece of paper is a way of externalizing it, and so engendering a little space around these views. Notice how it feels to read the list slowly. Notice also how true these definitions seem as you read them.

Pick one of these self-definitions and see if it is possible to lightly sustain an attention over some days that notices both the presences and the absences of the qualities it implies. During this time, notice also the opposite qualities when they arise (for instance kindness, if you have a self-definition of being unkind; or unkindness, if you have a self-definition of being kind).

How does it feel to see these various contradictions to the self-view? What effects does it have?

Freeing the expressions of self

This kind of loosening of some of the tightness in which we bind ourselves can be furthered a little, without yet jumping to a level of view that emphasizes the voidness of all notions of self. For it is also possible to expand and open up the personality-view by acknowledging, honouring, and loving the diverse aspects, manifestations, and expressions of the self.

Often we simply do not see all that is within us. There may be certain thoughts, emotions, intentions and drives, and even sub-personalities that we are habitually inclined not to notice and acknowledge. It can be instructive to ask oneself therefore:

What do I tend to miss or ignore when I look at myself?

This non-acknowledgment is sometimes simply a matter of a lack of mindfulness; and a question such as this may serve to open up, energize, and direct the looking.

But there can also be other more complex reasons why we fail to recognize certain aspects of our being. Oftentimes we may assume too hastily that something we glimpse within is an expression of an element of ourselves not to be trusted. Perhaps then we may go so far as to block our own self-seeing, without realizing that we are doing so. Or we may just not give an open-minded, close, and caring attention to some movement in us, some feeling or behaviour manifesting, because of this presumption that we already know what it is and 'where' it comes from within ourselves – when it may in fact be the expression of something else entirely or in part. A young man told me, for example, of his habit of procrastinating by watching TV; and he saw in this pattern only a sign of weakness or an expression of fear of failure. As we talked, though, it became clear that such procrastination was also hiding a deep love of doing things well, of abandoning himself to a work project. There were other, not immediately evident, reasons why he was holding back from giving himself and from letting his love initiate action. And somehow in the partiality of awareness that love was going unacknowledged. In such ways and in others, parts of ourselves can remain obscured and their expression blocked. They are not being watered – through attention, and appreciation, and through allowing ourselves to feel into and openly explore them.

Or, to take another example, a woman related her assumption, having noticed herself often avoiding groups and company, that she was somehow either simply fearful of or just not interested in connecting. On more open and careful inspection, however, she saw that actually she had an intense desire for truly intimate and deep connection; and that it was in fact this that was causing her to shun those situations where it seemed connection was inevitably limited to a more superficial kind. Not what it seemed at first – when such a behaviour and the feelings behind it are approached with greater care and without so much presumption, something surprising may be revealed.

It might also be important therefore to ask ourselves at times:

What quality within me, or what aspect of myself, am I assuming is the reason for this behaviour (or this thought, or this mood)?

Again it is so crucial to become aware of our presumptions. Questioning like this can create more space wherein we can look more freshly. Then we may be able to see if what we are assuming is actually the case, or if in fact some other aspect of our being is coming through.

This freeing of the self-view can be given still greater power, though, even at this level. In the last example, to illustrate, once she uncovers this deep desire for intimacy that had been hidden by assumptions, there remains a further possibility. It may be very helpful for her to let herself really feel that desire – conscious of its wholesomeness and its beauty, to feel its energy in the body and to allow it to fill out the being. In some instances this may take some practice of course. But in doing so, the self-view can expand, and not just intellectually. Dwelling meditatively in the different and expanded sense of self that the process of inquiry opens will make it less likely that habitual self-views are so easily re-established once this particular experience ends. Allowing and feeling, as fully as possible, both the newly acknowledged quality (desire for connection, in this case) and also the relatively unbound sense of self, will greatly consolidate such openings.

So much more could be said at the level of freeing the personality-view, but one last thing for now. (The practices at other levels we shall explore should also have a liberating effect on this level of personality anyway.) Often due, again, to the usually unrecognized force of influence of those around us, we can easily believe that we should be – i.e., act, dress, talk, feel, etc. – a certain way. Too readily we may have absorbed and taken on certain collectively held assumptions of the particular sub-cultures we move in. It is therefore powerful also to ask ourselves, as freshly as possible, and with an intent to expose old assumptions:

What do I stifle within myself?

There should not be any implication, lurking behind such a question, that we always have to act on and express everything that arises within us. Nevertheless, sometimes when we recognize that we are holding back a certain expression, unless it would harm ourselves or others it can be freeing, empowering, and hugely enlivening to experiment with expressing it. Here again, it may be very helpful to feel into the (perhaps less habitual) sense of self when we do so.

Any such experiment, it is crucial to realize, would not be for the purpose of then concretizing and identifying with whatever new sense of self it supports. Rather, playing in this way may serve to open up a wider and freer space for the movements and expressions of self. And in breaking out of rigid moulds and exploring more unfamiliar senses of self, the more habitual self-views are unbound, and also questioned, more powerfully. We may better understand the malleability of the self-sense through witnessing and feeling it thus more directly; and this understanding eventually aids our understanding of all self-construction. Although still limited to the personality level, such playful experimentations can therefore constitute a significant beginning to loosening the bindings of all self-views.

To emphasize once more what was stated at the beginning of the last chapter: Dharma practices are not to lead to an erosion of our personalities. It is not a sign of spiritual growth to have the personality dampened down, or blanched to some kind of uniform ideal. Yet in sometimes subtle ways, variations of such a pernicious idea can commonly be grasped at and take root in the mind. And even if it is only half-conscious the effects of that kind of assumption will usually be enormous. Similarly, these practices are not to lead only to a *tolerance* of the expressions of the personalities of ourselves and others. It may be that, given certain messages from a spiritual sub-culture, a view is adopted of personality as merely an unavoidable manifestation of past conditioning, not really interesting or spiritually important in itself. Probably then one's aim will become the development of an attitude which does no more than try to patiently put up with and spaciously allow these manifestations. If you do notice in yourself a tendency to regard personality in these ways, check carefully to see what assumptions and inclinations are operating in your mind.

Yes, the self and the personality are empty. But the emptiness of some thing does not make it essentially worthless. Being empty, indeed partly because it is empty, *how* a thing manifests – its particular appearance – can, more than merely being tolerated, also in fact be celebrated. For when any phenomenon, including personality, is deeply understood to be void, other dimensions of its beauty become apparent.

One of the fruits of such understanding here may be that we are liberated from restricted views – again perhaps absorbed from various sub-cultures – which approve of or regard highly only certain personality types or manifestations. Instead, the distinctive value and the specific loveliness of what is being expressed through diverse personalities across a much wider range can begin to become more visible to us.

Additionally, when we realize more fully the emptiness of some thing – such as personality – not only do we perceive it as lighter, but we are also able to perceive it more creatively and in manifold ways. In this way too a sense of the beauty of a thing becomes more readily accessible to us. And knowing the emptiness of self-view and personality, we are free to lightly pick up different ways of seeing, and conceiving of, the self – *if and when* they prove helpful. As discussed earlier, it is not that story, self, and personality-view should never be engaged or adopted. Rather, given an understanding of their lack of inherent existence, it is *how* self is viewed that matters. A profound realization of voidness, perhaps more than any other means, allows us to recognize, to freely play in, and to delight in the wondrous and unique, magical and empty nature of all appearances.

These are themes we shall return to much later. For now let us simply stress that if the kinds of questioning, investigating, and experimenting outlined here are engaged again and again, then, through that repetition, insights can gain the strength to melt or shatter self-conclusions of a certain level. We see through the tight bonds of self-definitions. There is a freedom to know and express our individuality, our non-normalcy. Then we honour the full, vibrant colours and vital ranges both of our own personalities and those of others.

10

Dependent Origination (1)

A good deal of what we have explored thus far could be expressed in the terms of the Buddha's teaching on *dependent origination* (Pali: *paṭiccasamuppāda*). Although it can be interpreted as describing the processes of rebirth of sentient beings from one life to the next, this teaching can also serve as an explication, or a schematic map, of how both *dukkha* and the self-sense are constructed – in the moment and over time – within one life. It is from this perspective that we will explore it here, though not in great detail.[1] Later we will return to this schema of dependent origination at greater depth, where it yields its most powerful and mysterious fruit.

Introducing this map at this preliminary level of understanding then, it should be noted that, for now, we will emphasize only certain aspects of what is implied by each of its terms. In due course though, we will fill out, expand, and refine the meanings of many of the links introduced here. That said, a common formulation of *paṭiccasamuppāda* reads:

> With delusion (*avijjā*) as condition, there are concoctions (*saṅkhārā*);
> With concoctions as condition, consciousness;
> With consciousness as condition, mentality-materiality (*nāmarūpa*);
> With mentality-materiality as condition, the six sense spheres;
> With the six sense spheres as condition, contact;
> With contact as condition, *vedanā*;
> With *vedanā* as condition, craving;
> With craving as condition, clinging;
> With clinging as condition, becoming (*bhava*);

[1] In part because relatively detailed expositions of *paṭiccasamuppāda* at the level of understanding addressed in this chapter are now more easily available, it does not seem necessary to expound it at greater length here. Instead, I will try to provide enough at this level to: (a) be useful (for a certain depth of letting go of *dukkha*, and of understanding fabrication); (b) fit into the longer arc of insight that we are developing; and (c) furnish a foundation for the deeper explorations to come.

> With becoming as condition, birth;
> With birth as condition, aging and death, sorrow, lamentation, pain, distress, and tribulation.
> Such is the origin of this whole mass of suffering (*dukkha*).[2]

Let's consider an imaginary scenario to see how this works. Your boss has asked you to give a presentation at work tomorrow for a group of your more senior colleagues. Exposed to what felt like harsh criticism for some of the presentations you have delivered in the past, both in this job and also previously, the idea of tomorrow's encounter fills you with dread. That dread, even before the actual experience, is already *dukkha* of course, and from the map of dependent origination we can see how this *dukkha* is engendered, and reinforced, in multiple and complex ways.

As we've already said, the most fundamental meaning of *avijjā* is ignorance of emptiness. Since this necessarily includes ignorance of dependent arising, *avijjā* also implies a way of looking at your situation that is ignorant of – and ignores – this process of the arising, and possible ceasing, of *dukkha*. Rather than a way of looking at the circumstances and your experience in these terms – which would be to look at them through the lens of dependent origination and the Four Noble Truths – you automatically view them from the perspective of your own story, which has hardened over time into an unquestioned truth (also *avijjā*).

Belief in this story generates expectations of how you will be seen and treated tomorrow. Such expectations would be an example of *saṅkhārā*. Unchecked, they fuel fear, and you begin to imagine tomorrow's humiliation over and over in your mind – *consciousness* contracting around the obsessive thinking and the fantasies. This, together with the fear, causes contraction, tension, and other unpleasant changes in the state of the body and the mind (*materiality-mentality*). There is *contact*: in the *sense sphere of the mind*,[3] with the thoughts and imaginings; and in the *sense sphere of the body*, with the experience of tension and fear as it plays out in the body. Both of these instances of *contact* involve unpleasant *vedanā*.

---

[2] See, e.g., MN 38, Ud 1 – 3.

[3] Buddhist psychology counts six sense 'spheres': the five familiar to traditional Western psychology (sight, sound, smell, taste, touch) with cognition of mental objects (thoughts, images, and mental perceptions) as the sixth. The Pali word *āyatana*, rendered here as 'sense sphere', can mean: 'stretch', 'extent', 'reach', 'compass'; 'region', 'locus', 'occasion'; 'doing', 'working', 'performance'; 'sphere of perception or sense', 'object of thought', 'sense-organ *and* object'; 'relation', 'order'. In some instances all of these meanings are implied. Especially where it relates to the six senses, no one English word can adequately encompass its meaning. On occasions when it seemed more helpful to render it with another term, such as 'sense base', I have done so.

Now, the instinctual reaction to unpleasant *vedanā* is aversion – wanting to get rid of these feelings, or distract oneself from them. This aversion is a form of *craving*. (Sometimes such *craving* can also be for a kind of annihilation – wanting to somehow just blank out all experience, for example by going to sleep.[4]) With the mind already caught in the tendency to obsess about tomorrow, the unpleasant *vedanā* of these thoughts do not disappear however. The very movement of repulsion from these thoughts seems actually to empower them, and also your anxiety. All this impulsive reactivity and rejection serves only to entangle the mind further. You begin to get even more obsessed and filled with dread in relation to these images. *Craving* thus intensifies into *clinging*.

At this point the *clinging* is already complex, for several strands may be wrapped up in this knot of anxious obsession about tomorrow. Included there may be, for example: a more desperate desire to get rid of these images that won't stop; views that this suffering is actually the fault of your boss, or else your own fault for being inadequate; fantasies of various strategies to avoid the situation, perhaps by calling in sick; but worries then that if you do simply evade the presentation you will be seen as a coward or as not 'up to the job'.[5]

All this supports *becoming*: shaped by the *clinging*, there is the desire to not be one who is shamed, and the mind starts groping toward some decision about what to do. Without insight, however, your only option is to try to control the situation, and there don't seem many possibilities for doing that. Depending on which of the strands involved in the *clinging* are strongest, a particular direction of *becoming* emerges and gathers momentum.

It may be that, partly due to past habits, the fantasies of avoidance win out. You pick up the phone and leave a message saying you're sick and won't be in tomorrow. This now is *birth* – an action taken, its consequences committed to. You breathe a sigh of relief, and after a few moments even begin to look forward to what feels like a much deserved lie-in tomorrow morning. But although you feel briefly better, this relieved self that has just been born and constructed contains within it the seeds of its own instability. For now you can't seem to evade thoughts of self-judgment that start to creep in for the course you have taken. These thoughts, and the low-grade feeling of lack of self-worth they engender,

---

[4] The Buddha in fact enumerates three kinds of craving: craving in relation to sense objects of the six senses; craving to be or to become; and craving not to be, i.e. for some kind of annihilation. (See, e.g., DN 22.)

[5] In MN 18, the Buddha lists four types of clinging: clinging to sense objects; clinging to views and beliefs (Pali: *diṭṭhi*); clinging to what is customary, including habits and practices (Pali: *sīlavatta*); and clinging to the doctrine of self (Pali: *attavāda*).

begin to spread cracks in the structure of the relieved self that was constructed, so that soon there is the *death* of this self, together with *pain and distress*.

Unfortunately, in the *pain* that now ensues, *tendencies* to view yourself as inadequate have been reinforced. And these *tendencies* form part of the *saṅkhārā* that may influence future reactions in unhelpful ways. This would be one example of how experiences of *dukkha* can end up fuelling more *dukkha*. They may feed something back into, and so reinforce, the very processes that generate and support further suffering. For often there is confusion in the mind when it is in a state of distress, and what flows out from that confusion (as grasping reactivity, lack of clarity, or mistaken notions) will most likely compound suffering, and exacerbate confusion.[6]

Of sub-loops and manifold connections

Thus far, however, this descriptive sketch has oversimplified the process and suggests a kind of linearity that is not really there. It would be more accurate if we added the realization that any link can feed into and reinforce any other link, so that all kinds of sub-loops and vicious cycles can occur.

For instance, without wisdom, the painful memories from the past that are triggered will in all likelihood reinforce, right then, any associated personality-level self-view you might hold woven into your story – perhaps of being a lousy public speaker or lacking in charisma or intelligence. This, already, is *birth*, a self re-constructed. And this particular self-sense now re-constellated significantly empowers the *saṅkhārā* arising in that moment – for example the expectations for tomorrow's encounter – as well as various manifestations of *avijjā* – such as the degree of unquestioning belief with which those expectations are held. Since these expectations involve emotionally charged self-images and self-fantasies, they reciprocally reinforce the construction of self and the concomitant self-views, right then in that moment. Unexamined, self-views and expectations serve to strengthen each other here.

---

[6] The Buddha pointed out (e.g. in MN 2, AN 6:63, Iti 3:7) three kinds of 'effluent' or 'outflow' (Pali: *āsava* – a word which might also be translated as 'fermentation' or 'festering') from *dukkha*: sense desire; desire for being or for being in any state; and fundamental delusion (*avijjā*). Some passages in other texts (e.g. *Vibhaṅga* 373) add a fourth: attachment to views and beliefs. Perhaps these latter – and certainly including attachment to any self-views – may be seen to be implied anyway in the meaning of *avijjā*. Regardless of whether they are delineated as three or four, notice, for now, how the descriptions of the *āsavas* overlap with, and replicate, the lists of types of craving and of clinging.

It is clear, too, in this example that *pain and distress* do not arrive only at the end of the process. They are already involved, in fact, in the thoughts, memories, and imaginings that the mind is bringing to the situation; and the grasping reactivity of the mind in relation to all these thoughts, memories, and imaginings is itself also painful, as we shall shortly discuss.

Additionally we could point out, as described in Chapter 6, that *craving* brings a contraction of the body and mind (*materiality-mentality*). In the usual formulation of dependent arising, though, the ordering of these two links might seem to suggest that the direction of causality runs from *materiality-mentality* to *craving*, not the other way round. Actually, the two links feed each other. And because they do, a sub-loop is created between them that can easily set up a vicious cycle.

It is important to understand and explore the possibilities of non-linearity in the conditioning processes of *paṭiccasamuppāda*. Rather than elaborating more of these potential sub-loops, however, it would probably be more useful to ponder many situations for yourself in these terms, in order to gain some familiarity with comprehending the workings of dependent origination at this level. Since *avijjā* is a lack of awareness of *paṭiccasamuppāda*, such familiarity will contribute generally to lessening the ways the mind becomes entangled in suffering. And in any particular situation, looking at it in terms of *paṭiccasamuppāda* will mean that *avijjā* is lessened, to a degree at least, right there, and therefore does not feed then so forcefully the *saṅkhārā* and the other links that support suffering.

A Map for Relieving Dukkha

It is vital too to see that the map of *paṭiccasamuppāda*, even at this level of understanding, offers not only a description of the tangles we get into, but also multiple possibilities for untangling and lessening *dukkha*. In fact, this very non-linearity just discussed, as well as adding significantly to the complexity and reinforcement of knots of *dukkha*, is also an aid to our freedom, since it makes available diverse entry points for undermining the fabrications of self and suffering. Let us briefly consider a few of the many options.

Recognizing saṅkhārā

Even an *awareness* of what particular *saṅkhārā* (patterns and tendencies of reaction, view, expectation) are operating for you can be helpful. These *saṅkhārā* may be long-term habitual tendencies. Or they may simply arise due to the state of *citta* at the time, since any state of the heart will tend to spawn reactions and views that are shaped by it. (Consider how a state of irritability conditions the perceptions and reactions in certain ways, compared with a state of fear, or a state of *mettā*, for instance.) Alternatively the *saṅkhārā* may themselves flow out of something else that has just occurred – an incident, a thought, or a memory, for example, to which you are now reacting.

Being alert to the presence of such *saṅkhārā*, or at least to the possibility of their arising, already effects a slight reduction of *avijjā* in the mix of conditions. We are less ignorant, in that moment, of the mechanisms of dependent origination that are active. Those particular *saṅkhārā* may be deprived thus, to some degree, of the empowerment that comes from an ignorance of their presence. Seeing them *as* tendencies can allow a modicum of helpful suspicion into the mind. Realizing that in fact a tendency to perceive, think, believe, or react in a certain way is functioning, it is possible that its force in fabricating more *dukkha* at that time is diminished.

Attending to craving and to vedanā: Two strategies

The link between *vedanā* and craving is one of the more common points at which to try to pacify the fabrication of *dukkha*. Craving, it is relatively easy to see, is actually a normal and automatic response to *vedanā*. We can witness, for example with unpleasant physical sensations such as pain, discomfort, or even itchiness, the presence of aversion to the unpleasant *vedanā*, a craving for them to cease, to be rid of them. The typical craving reaction to pleasant *vedanā*, conversely, is to grasp at them – to try to hold on to that pleasantness when we experience it, or to somehow chase after an image of the pleasant.

Interestingly, though one may not be aware of it in the moment, the craving for pleasure is sometimes conjoined with a craving to be rid of some unpleasant sensations. And likewise, the impulse to reject the unpleasant is sometimes mixed with a movement toward an image of the pleasant. Is the craving for a cigarette, for instance, in one who is addicted to smoking, a craving for pleasant sensation, or a craving to escape the unpleasant sensations that come when it has been a while since the last cigarette? Or both?

Exploring this whole nexus of craving and reactivity a little further, we find, on more mindful inspection, that the *experience of craving itself is an experience of dukkha*. It is unpleasant. It may be, as described above, that the mind feels uncomfortable in the prison of its obsession, or unpleasantly contracted around that to which it is clinging. And although often there might not be clear awareness of it, craving is felt in the body too – perhaps, when it is relatively intense, as a kind of pressure that is usually hard to tolerate. In seeking the object that we are craving, we are partly seeking the end of the difficult-to-tolerate experience of the pressure of craving.

These gut reactions to *vedanā*, and to craving itself, will frequently be fuelled by thought and proliferation about the object craved. The thinking mind unhelpfully obsessing and circling around the object of grasping or aversion only stokes the fires of craving and the energetic impulses of reactivity. Conversely, without care, the unpleasant pressure of the craving can fuel the proliferation of usually unhelpful thought. It is important to see these feedback loops and how they ensnare the mind in *dukkha*. To effect a degree of liberation from their grip, though, it is often the case that a more focused mindfulness needs to be employed – one in which the mind is taken out of the circuits of unhelpful thought.

One possibility would be to pay attention to the experience of craving itself, and the feelings of pressure or tension that go with it, particularly in the body. Without wise awareness, there is typically an impulsive grasping for any possible escape from the feeling of growing pressure or tension that accompanies craving. This blind reaction, itself a movement of craving, simply propels the whole process of fabricating *dukkha* forward. But actually sustaining a focus of mindfulness on these feelings, and particularly giving them some space in awareness to be there, the sense of craving will, left to itself, typically intensify, reach a climax, and then begin to reduce. With it, of course, the feeling of pressure will rise and then fall.

Usually, the mind would have been hooked and dragged into compulsive reaction before the pressure of craving even reached its apex. Intentions of body, speech, and mind can arise that are merely unwise attempts to flee, or to quell, the felt discomfort of craving's pressure. We may act then in some way that perhaps we later regret. One can learn, however, to *tolerate* the pressure and tension of craving, by mindfully allowing it the space to wax and then wane. Repeating this begins to bring a crucial confidence, so that it feels easier and easier to do. Over time then, the very force and pressure of the craving can be diminished. The compulsivity of the cycle is thus weakened, and eventually broken.

A second possibility involves stationing the attention on the actual experience of *vedanā*, moment to moment. Fixing the mindfulness at this point means that the mind is less swept along by the impulses of craving, so that clinging and the constructions of *papañca* are not fuelled. Thus they can die down to some degree. Less self is built then, and less suffering too. It may even be that by concentrating intently on the *vedanā* in this way, the movements of craving also begin to be attenuated.

This possibility of a skilful focusing on *vedanā* we already presented in Chapter 7, in relation to emotions and a helpful simplifying of attention. Partly for its practical usefulness, a crucial point mentioned there is worth reiterating now in this expanded context. It can often be assumed that our mindfulness needs to 'catch the moment of contact' between consciousness and a sense object or a thought as it arises, and that if it does not, we have missed our chance to pacify the process of fabrication. It will have inevitably rolled on to clinging, *papañca,* and *dukkha*, and all that is available to us then is a kind of post-mortem explanation of how we ended up in that particular mess. In practice, with strong mindfulness we may indeed be able to catch that moment of contact on occasion. But it is not actually always necessary that we do. For at any time after an initial moment of contact, even if we already feel that the mind is lost in a thicket of *papañca*, it is possible to tune into a much simpler level of the experience – the *vedanā*, or the experience of the pressure of craving, as described in Chapter 7 and here. Skilful attention at that point, no matter what degree of complexity and reactivity has built up, will almost always be helpful and can calm the fabrication of *dukkha* through calming the ongoing processes of *paṭiccasamuppāda*.[7]

Practice: A skilful tolerating of craving

When there is craving – a grasping after, a holding on to, or an energetic movement to be rid of, something – practise bringing a spacious mindfulness to the experience of the craving, and particularly to the sense of pressure or tension that it involves in the body.

Notice how the felt pressure of the craving unfolds in time, intensifying, peaking, and then gradually subsiding. Can you get a sense how mindfully allowing it to do so develops a capacity to tolerate the experience of craving, and gradually disempowers it?

Notice too the corresponding rise and fall in the experience of *dukkha* accompanying the craving.

What else do you notice when you do this?

---

[7] The assumption that one needs to catch the moment of contact comes out of a certain incompleteness in the understanding of dependent origination. Such limitations of understanding are actually to be expected, perhaps partly because the teaching of *paṭiccasamuppāda* has been handed down most often in the same linear ordering of elements in which it was presented at the start of this chapter. The very consistency of this ordering seems to imply certain facts about the process, and only with more careful investigation are these realized to be inaccurate. As we move on, and attempt to open our understanding of dependent origination to deeper levels, we shall repeatedly return to such considerations and gradually explore their more profound ramifications.

Practice: Focusing on *vedanā* to temper the force of craving

When you notice that there is craving or clinging present in relation to some object of any of the six senses, practise sustaining a focused attention on the experience of the *vedanā* (the shifting quality of pleasantness, unpleasantness, or 'neutrality') of that object, moment to moment.

As you do so, see if you can get a sense of the moment-to-moment arising of the craving from the *vedanā*.

If the *vedanā* seems to be feeding reactive thoughts and *papañca*, notice what effects staying concentrated on the *vedanā* has on the strength and amount of these thoughts and *papañca*, and on the degree of entanglement in them.

Pay attention also to what effect such a stationing of the focus has on the craving and clinging.

Observe the effects too on the whole sense of *dukkha* involved.

Again, what else do you notice when you do this?

Later, in Chapter 13, we will explore how the craving with which we tend to react to *vedanā* can be worked with, and diminished, in yet more powerful ways, allowing an even greater calming of the processes of *paṭiccasamuppāda*, and the unfolding of deeper insight too.

Some other possibilities – Softening the view

But still reading the map at this level, there are also other practice options for withdrawing some of the fuel from the process of dependent origination. For example, we saw in Chapter 6 how opening the attention to a sense of space can be helpful in countering the contractedness of *nāmarūpa* (*body and mind*). And the force of *avijjā* manifesting as beliefs in various self-views may be undermined through the kinds of questioning discussed, for instance, in Chapter 9. Indeed many of the strategies we have explored in other chapters could be mapped onto the links of *paṭiccasamuppāda* at this level. Reflecting yourself on how these approaches can be understood in terms of dependent arising would be useful.

Let's consider again the scenario described earlier to draw out still other possibilities. The thoughts and *clinging* that arose might have shaped a different direction of *becoming* so that, despite your ongoing agitation, you do actually go into work the next day. Then dependent origination still continues to operate – shaping your perceptions and reactions to the presentation as it unfolds.

For example, as discussed in Chapter 8, you may view yourself, through *avijjā*, as being solely responsible for how it goes, ignorant of the influence of a whole host of wider conditions. And this shrunken view will probably support a sense of stress and pressure.

Still holding, too, the assumption (through *avijjā*) that your boss and your audience are the true causes of your suffering will influence the *saṅkhārā* to colour your perception of the entire situation, including how you perceive your listeners. Perhaps you will be much more likely to interpret their facial expressions as being critical of you. Such a challenging perception will then probably be reacted to, and reinforce the self-views and the *saṅkhārā* operating.

There may also be a priming of the *sense spheres*, a heightened alertness to any sense information that might be signalling this threat of criticism. The whole field of perception might then even contract oppressively around these perceptions of seeming disapproval, the attention pulled there repeatedly as you deliver your presentation. All this *colouring and shaping of perception* is in fact included in what is meant by *nāmarūpa*. And of course it conditions the *vedanā* that are involved, and so the other links.

In addition to some approaches we have already explored – for instance opening the attention to a sense of space in the room as you are talking – such unhelpful perceptions could be addressed in all sorts of other ways.

Deliberately encouraging an attitude of *mettā*, for example, toward your audience members may soften your view of them, so that they actually appear to you as less critical and less threatening. Or there is the possibility of deliberately bringing in a way of looking wherein you see their mortality – holding a strong awareness that in not very many years everyone in the room, including yourself, will be dead. You might even see them as skeletons sitting there listening to you. This awareness of mortality may relativize the perceived import of the whole situation in a helpful way. And in acknowledging your shared fragility and fate as human beings, this awareness may also soften the heart – and so then the view – with compassion. Less perception of difference between self and other is being supported when we contemplate what we share, and so less separation between self and other is sensed. Because there is less sense of separation, there is less fear, and less self is constructed.

Self and Phenomena: A Mutual Construction

In this last example, and in others we have discussed, we can see how different practice approaches can begin to unravel a tangle of *dukkha* from different points and perspectives. Sometimes it is the *self-views* operating that are directly addressed – perhaps through questioning, as suggested in Chapter 9. Often though, the lessening of the construction of the self is enabled by directly addressing views and reactions to *phenomena.* These latter would include phenomena that we conceive of as being experienced internally, such as emotions and thoughts; and also those we conceive of as being experienced externally, such as the perceptions of others or a situation.

From this observation, one immensely important insight can be drawn out. Notice that self-fabrication is always tied up with the fabrication of one or more phenomena. We can see that self-construction *depends on some thing being reacted to*, made an issue of, or viewed in certain ways. That thing may be conceived as an inner phenomenon or an outer one, but the sense of self cannot be supported without depending on some thing or other as a kind of base. Self-construction always relies on clinging, on reactivity and view, with regard to some thing. The phenomenon thus regarded, though – just like the self-sense and self-view – is *also* pumped up, constructed, in the process of constructing the self. Fabrication of a thing and fabrication of the self are mutually dependent. In fabricating one, the other is also fabricated. This insight into mutual dependency turns out to be of radical significance for liberation, and will be revisited at greater and greater depth as we go on.

The Need to Probe Deeper

Looking at and working with situations, self-construction, and *dukkha* from the perspectives of *paṭiccasamuppāda* outlined in this chapter is enormously helpful, and time should be taken to digest the teaching at this level. Nevertheless, as we ponder and practise more, we can notice important limitations to any understanding of dependent origination that is restricted to this level.

For example, in considering the map to the extent that we have, and related to the just-discussed reliance of the self-sense on clinging to phenomena, we can recognize the important implicit insight that the self does not exist, and is not findable, separate from this web of links. We can see, further, that self cannot be equated with just one of the links in isolation, not even *birth*. It might be tempting then to assert, as a definition or a description of its true nature, that 'the self is a process'. This is not, however, an assertion the Buddha ever made or endorsed. While it might be helpful for a time as a provisional way of looking, such a conception is limited in its understanding and thus in the freedom it can deliver.

As we go on we shall see more fully just why this is so. But we can point out for now that such limited understandings stem in part from inadequacies in the way we have explained *paṭiccasamuppāda* in this chapter. Principally, the level of understanding of dependent origination discussed so far only addresses a certain degree of fabrication. It therefore leaves the inherent existence of many elements of the process unquestioned. For example, in explaining the mechanisms through which the more extremely contracted and solidified constructions of self-sense are fabricated, instances of such grosser degrees of self-construction are clearly revealed *as* fabrications. But the fabrication of any much more subtle sense of self is not yet exposed, or explained, by this level of understanding.

Also, the elements that make up the self, or the process of the self, are assumed at present to be real. For instance, this level of explanation describes some of the ways in which craving in relation to the experience of *vedanā* can intensify the fabrication of the self-sense and of *dukkha*. But the *vedanā* themselves are taken as givens, and really existing, at contact. Although they are perhaps conceived of as momentary elements in a complex process, they are nevertheless assumed to be basically just 'what they are', in themselves. Implicitly or explicitly, they are still conceived of as inherently existing.

This is likewise true in regard to *perception*, and the external reality of a situation. To be sure, this level of explanation points to the emptiness of any more exaggerated '*distortions* of perception' – for example, that those in the audience at your presentation are glaring at you critically. But it is still assumed that certain perceptions will arise as givens of the 'fact of the situation'. That 'basic' situation is presumed to be self-evidently real; and the corresponding, 'basic' perceptions of that situation are presumed to be automatically and necessarily occurring objective reflections, or representations, of that reality.

At this initial level of investigation, the elements that seem to make up the process do indeed seem fundamentally real enough for the most part, so conceiving of a process seems justified and valid. A conception of a process seems reasonable enough also because we tend not to question the seemingly independent reality of *time*. It is one of our most ingrained presumptions and perceptions, just 'common sense'. Yet the whole notion of a process and the whole understanding at this level rest too on this assumption that time – *as some kind of necessary base, or vessel, for any process to unfold in* – has inherent existence.

In many instances, of course, we can actually witness a process in time. We see one element have an effect on another, and then this second element feeding back *later* on the first element. We should be cautious, though, to conclude that this is the whole of what the teaching of dependent origination is pointing to, merely with a complexity and at a rate that is impossible for us personally to see. It is important to admit, and be aware, that more often we may be merely *assuming* the operation of such feedback loops that are too fast to witness. The very normal tendency of fundamental delusion is to conceive of causality as a process in time.

Basically characteristic, too, of *avijjā* is the conception of causality as a process wherein real causes and conditions deliver real effects. Thus also, in considering the mutual dependence and the multiple sub-loops that have been mentioned, there is a particular assumption about the reality of the elements of *paṭiccasamuppāda* that would be normal, but that we should draw attention to. We might easily assume that what dependent origination involves is the extremely rapid back-and-forth, or circling, of impacts between links in this web that, though connected, are *different from each other* and clearly *separate*. However, just as we can see that the self does not exist and is not findable as something separate from this web of links, and that it cannot be isolated as only one of these links, we can, with more penetrating insight, realize that the same is true of all the other terms. The more one probes, the more one realizes that the links are not really referring to separate entities or phenomena. Instead, they are overlapping and interpenetrating; they are not self-existent. And this very fact will be part of realizing deeper levels of emptiness.[8]

At present, this brief discussion serves just to alert the reader to the fact that the explanations of dependent origination given earlier in this chapter must be regarded as merely provisional. For at this level of understanding, emptiness and fabrication are only exposed to a degree. In due course we can realize for ourselves that although it is immensely useful to approach *paṭiccasamuppāda* with the conception of it as *a process in time*, and as a description of the complex interactions and connections between *discrete and real constituent elements*, this is actually not the ultimate truth of it. We will, therefore, gradually develop the facility to transcend these assumptions. Then our understanding of dependent

---

[8] This overlapping and interpenetration of supposedly discrete elements will become more evident through practice as we proceed. It may have been glimpsed, however, even in the rudimentary practice exercises discussed in this chapter. Nevertheless, it is usually necessary to develop a meditative working understanding of the links of *paṭiccasamuppāda* at the level that conceives of them as separate before attempting to refine the insight to levels beyond that.

arising and its freeing power can go far beyond what has been described in this chapter.

It is crucial to realize, in this connection, that although it would certainly be possible to try to delineate the links and describe the process of dependent origination at the level adopted in this chapter in much more detail, that is *not* the same as understanding it more deeply. While sharply demarcating this link from that might perhaps give us a comforting or satisfying feeling of clarification and of comprehending something, clinging too rigidly to these definitions will in fact block deeper understanding. Likewise, holding on to the conception of a process occurring in time – and tacitly assuming therein that time itself has an independent reality – will also limit the liberating potential of the teaching of dependent arising for us.

Paṭiccasamuppāda, it must be understood, is a teaching that can be meditated on, and offers fruits, at different levels of comprehension. Only up to a certain level can it be regarded as an *explanation* of the arising of *dukkha*. Rather than primarily for the sake of constructing a view – an explanation – the Buddha offered the teaching of dependent arising in the ultimate service of the thorough deconstruction of all views. For it is this that finally opens the deepest freedom. And as we have said, it is freedom, above all, that is the primary concern of the Dharma.

Recognizing that it is a teaching and conceptual framework that can be engaged at different levels, we begin to seek out and explore the different ways of looking that it suggests at these different levels. As indicated, even at the levels contemplated in this chapter the explanations given in the map of dependent origination present various indispensable possibilities for a degree of untangling of *dukkha*. Learning, eventually, to see the teaching of *paṭiccasamuppāda* as containing a way of looking that can lead ultimately even *beyond itself*, will in the end, however, be even more profoundly liberating. And this we will unfold as the practices develop.

PART FOUR

On Deepening Roads

11

The Experience of Self Beyond Personality

The Sense of Self

So far we have mostly discussed ways in which self is fabricated through self-definitions and self-views operating at the level of *thoughts about the self*. We have therefore emphasized how necessary it is to notice these thoughts in the investigation of self-construction. In order for greater insight to be possible, though, it is vital also to develop a sensitivity to other aspects of the experience of self.

Besides whatever thoughts about the self are present or absent, with every state of the *citta* there will be a way the self – along with the body, and the *citta* – is *felt* and *sensed*. We can call this aspect of the perception of self the *sense of self* or the *self-sense*. When we feel embarrassed or afraid, for example, the sense of self tends to feel more contracted, more solid, and also more separate from others and from the world. In contrast, when we feel relaxed, or generous, say, the sense of self is more open and spacious; it usually feels lighter then too, and there is less of a sense of separation from others and the world. Generally, the self-sense will be mirrored in the feeling and sense of the body, which will correspondingly feel and be perceived as more or less contracted, solid, and separate.

A spectrum…

Careful attention to the sense of self, in and out of meditation, over as broad a range of *citta* states and experiences as possible yields a number of crucial insights. First, that there is a *spectrum* or *continuum* to our self-sense. In a temper tantrum, for example, when we are extremely upset about something, the sense of self feels highly contracted, solid, and separate; and likewise when there is intense self-judgment or when we are locked into a painful identity or story. This is one end of this spectrum of self-sense. In a more normal state of the *citta*, the self feels less contracted, solid, and separate. The sense of self in this more usual state, we can notice though, is in fact more contracted, solid, and separate than, for example, in some state of meditation where we feel more relaxed and less entangled than usual. Then at times – practising staying at contact perhaps, or in moments when there is more *samādhi* or when *mettā* is strong – the sense of self is even less solid, separate, and contracted. And we can notice too that there the manifestations of the personality are quieted, also to varying degrees – a little, a lot, or completely. At the other end of the spectrum, there may be occasions in very deep meditation when there seems to be only a sense of awareness aware of phenomena, and barely even any identification with that awareness. Completely beyond personality, such experiences may not seem to involve any suffering and may feel very light and very spacious. Yet still there is an extremely subtle sense of self alive then *as* the mere sense of awareness – a very refined subject – knowing phenomena – objects of experience.[1]

In addition to the sense of solidity, contraction, and separateness, we could say too that the self-sense is experienced along this continuum as more or less gross or refined. A state of anger, for instance, towards one end of the spectrum, involves a quite gross sense of self, whereas a state of deep *samādhi*, for example, towards the other end, involves a very light, refined sense of self.

The movement of the self-sense along this spectrum presents us with one aspect of a basic and pervasive opportunity for comprehending voidness. It may take some practice, but *recognizing that there is a spectrum* to the sense of self, *becoming familiar with the range* of that spectrum and the manifestations of the self-sense within it, as well as gradually *developing a sensitivity to the subtle differences along the continuum* – these are all indispensable to our approach to insight into emptiness.

Certainly, when we are puffed up with pride, or overly concerned with looking good, when there is a storm of hindrances and *papañca,* or an attack of self-judgement, or if, to borrow a common illustration, we imagine being suddenly pointed to in a crowd and accused of stealing, it can easily be recognized that a sense of self is being constructed in our experience at those times.

[1] How can one know, or at least accept, the assertion that there is still a self constructed there? It may in part be a matter of defining self thus – as one half of even the most subtle subject-object duality. More significantly though, it may be something we realize only once we have gone beyond such a state. Much as a meditator who has had some experience of profound inner stillness realizes then that her relatively unhassled, normal state of being, though it may not include any palpable *dukkha* or much gross sense of self, does in fact involve self-construction, so too, going beyond even this extremely refined state of awareness, one can recognize in retrospect that it comprises a very subtle self-fabrication.

As we have just said however, such instances exemplify only one end of the continuum of self-fabrication. With the development of meditation practice, we typically move more up and down this spectrum. And we experience a greater range of it than most non-meditators would – meditation making accessible to us at times the more refined end of the spectrum.

Such extension into the quieter areas of the range is lovely in itself, but in seeking insight into dependent arising and emptiness we must be interested in the whole continuum. It is not only the grosser, more obvious manifestations of self that need to be attended to and addressed. Nor is it that we are simply trying to hang out as long as we can at the more refined end of the spectrum. It is, rather, an intimate awareness, an investigation, and then an understanding, of the shifting of the self-sense along this entire continuum that will provide a principal key for the unfolding of our realization.

There is always some kind of self-sense

Although almost implicit in a recognition of the full spectrum of self-sense, we should draw out a second insight that can be gained through becoming familiar with this continuum: There is always a sense of self, to some degree, whenever there is any experience of any thing.[2] It may be extremely subtle, as we have already pointed out, but the self-sense will *always* be situated in any moment somewhere along this spectrum.

We might highlight here two reasons why recognizing this fact is important. One concerns the assumptions and conclusions that can quickly form regarding certain kinds of habitual afflictive states of *citta* and what these states might need in response. Practitioners with strong patterns of harsh self-criticism, for instance, can frequently hold to a belief in the notion: "I have no self. What I need to do is somehow develop a sense of self, before trying to get rid of it."

That emptiness practices do not seek to destroy the self but rather to understand its empty nature we have already made clear though. We could also add that such states of self-criticism are in fact hugely and grossly constructed states of self – only involving strongly *negative* self-views. Without a doubt they rest on, and create, not an absence of self-sense but a surfeit. Intense and painful is the sense of contraction, solidity, self-consciousness, and separation in such a

[2] In later chapters we will see that only in moments of *cessation* could it more accurately be said that there is no sense of self fabricated at that time. However, we will leave the exploration of the relationship of cessation to the spectrum of self-sense until then.

sense of self, not to mention the amount, and strength, of proliferation of self-view in thoughts. And all these may well have become the norm, the habitual mode of self. Rather than 'developing a self', what might be more needed then is actually seeing a level of the emptiness of certain self-definitions and self-views, as we have discussed; as well as rebalancing the self-views in a more realistic, kind, and positive direction.

A second reason it is crucial to realize that a self-sense is always present we already touched on in Chapter 10. In attempting to thoroughly undermine *aviijā* and gain a more complete and profound understanding of voidness, it is necessary to recognize the full extent of fabrication. It will not be enough merely to expose the grosser manifestations and constructions of self. When self is not so built up – for instance when we are witnessing, relatively simply, something that feels fairly neutral, or in those times of more profound quietude and spaciousness – it is in fact still being constructed to some degree. It may not involve the personality, and may not seem to involve much *dukkha*, but without extending our meditative investigations to include those very subtle manifestations of self, the deeper seeds of *avjjā* will be left unchallenged. Something needs to be *understood* in relation to this spectrum of self-sense, and it can only be fully understood if the full spectrum is acknowledged and explored. To reiterate something we stated earlier: *any* sense of a subject (or an object) will be felt and assumed, usually without realizing that we are doing so, to possess inherent existence, unless it is specifically, consciously, and deliberately seen to be empty. And if we do not see its total emptiness, it serves then as a seed for more ongoing *avijjā*.

We need to comprehend states of less self-construction

In relation to this, one more remark should be made. Discussing how insight into voidness develops, Tsongkhapa famously wrote that

> One should draw the distinction between the non-engagement of the mind with the two selves, and the engagement of the mind with the two selflessnesses.[3]

[3] From his *Great Treatise on the Stages of the Path*. (Translation from the author's notes.) As briefly delineated in Chapter 8, 'the two selves' are the 'self' of a person, and the 'self' of any phenomenon – the 'self' in both cases meaning here the mistaken perception of their inherent existence. Correspondingly, the 'two selflessnesses' are the emptiness of the personal self, and the emptiness of phenomena; and these are to be realized.

He explained that there are times of seeming absence of self and also of the world of phenomena, but where there is no contemplation or understanding of the emptiness of self or phenomena. Such times would include being unconscious or fast asleep without dreaming, for instance, but also states of deep *samādhi*. All such states, he declared, are equally ineffectual in weakening the view of inherent existence that is at the core of *avijjā*.

This is an important point. However, it may be grasped in a way that overlooks a couple of things. For it will only be true under certain conditions: when there is no contemplation of the fabrication involved in states of *samādhi*, and no recognition of what is involved in fabricating the appearances of self and phenomena to different degrees at different points on the continuum of self-sense. When the movement in and out of different states of consciousness is accompanied by an insightful investigation into fabrication, though, and the implications for inherent existence are understood more and more, then any and all states yield insight into emptiness. Moreover, those on the more refined end of the spectrum of self-sense can reveal subtleties and depths of understanding that are not available in grosser states.

What accrues thus through adopting such investigation as an essential facet of method is in addition to what we already explained in the chapter on *samādhi* – that it is generally helpful for the digestion and stabilization of insight to dwell for periods in states of less self and fabrication.

Practice: Noticing the sense of self

Begin to include in your practice, both in and out of formal meditation, an awareness of the sense of self, and how that sense fluctuates and moves along a continuum.

Notice how the self-sense feels at times of different degrees of *dukkha*, and when there is upset about something or other. Pay particular attention to the sense of contraction and the perceptions and feelings of solidity and separation that comprise the self-sense at one end of its spectrum.

Notice too how the sense of self feels at times of more ease, and particularly at different times in meditation. Especially important is to notice the quality of the self-sense in periods of greater quietude, when *mettā,* mindfulness, or *samādhi* are stronger.

Notice how the sense of the body mirrors the sense of the self.

What else do you notice about the experience of the sense of self at different times?

How it is that the self-sense moves along this continuum, and what this movement *means* for emptiness, we will unfold more fully as we go on. But without a recognition of, a sensitivity to, and a familiarity with this spectrum, a central thoroughfare for insight into fabrication and dependent arising will be unavailable to our practice.

The Conception of Self

As well as this spectrum of sense of self, there is too another aspect of the experience of self that it is very helpful to notice. That is: the range of possible ways we habitually *conceive of* the self, and particularly how we conceive its more general relationship with the body and the mind. In Chapter 9 we explored the formation and power of self-views and definitions at the level of the personality. More fundamental than that though, we can also investigate the kinds of self-views and definitions that operate at a more *existential* level, in terms of more basic elements of existence – body and materiality, mind and awareness.

Sometimes this conceiving is conscious and involves thought: a person will adopt, intellectually, a certain philosophical position about the self and how it relates to the body, to the mind, and to consciousness; or (s)he may choose, as a matter of faith, to uphold a certain belief about the nature of the self. In either case, (s)he may then be able to articulate these views about the self to others. More often though, this conceiving is not so conscious and does not involve thought. It exists and operates as an intuitive feeling or conception, perhaps vaguely, and of which we may not be aware. Like the sense of self we have discussed, this conceiving is present in any moment when there is any experience. And it too, we should note, is not fixed – the actual conception can be different at different times. Now all of this we can begin to notice, and to question. For this level of self-view also needs to be addressed.

The teaching of the aggregates

In exposing more precisely and fully the ways we tend to conceive of the self's relation with body and mind, it can be helpful to conceptually divide up 'body and mind' into smaller constituents. One way of doing this is to use the Buddha's formulation of 'the five aggregates' (Skt: *skandha*; Pali: *khandha*).[4] We can list and define them, for now, as follows:

[4] In SN 22:48, AN 9:36, DN 22, etc.

rūpa – 'body', 'matter' or 'materiality', and also any 'form' perceived possessing shape etc.;

vedanā – 'sensation', but specifically the 'feeling-tone' of sensations, i.e. the quality in any experience of pleasantness, unpleasantness, or neither-pleasantness-nor-unpleasantness;

saṃjñā (Skt.), *saññā* (Pali) – 'perception';

saṃskārā (Skt.), *saṅkhārā* (Pali) – 'mental formations' or 'concoctions', including thoughts, intentions and volitions, and mental factors like attention etc. which play a part in fabricating experience;[5]

vijñāna (Skt.), *viññāṇa* (Pali) – 'consciousness', i.e. any of the six sense-consciousnesses (consciousness of any phenomena of the five senses and of mental phenomena).

Rather than being his *definition* of the self, the aggregates are better regarded as one helpful way the Buddha offered through which we can break down for investigation the complexity of our existence. Two related benefits of such an approach may be pointed out here. First, in this list the totality of experience is partitioned into piles more manageable to work with in meditation. This can help prevent overwhelm and confusion, and also lessen the degree to which the aggregates feed each other in vicious cycles. We have already seen, for example in our discussion in Chapter 7 of some of the various helpful facets of mindfulness, how within the complexity of difficult emotional and mental reactions, choosing to sustain the attention on just one aggregate of the total experience – in that case, the *vedanā* of an emotion – can simplify and calm the fabrication of *dukkha* at that time.

---

[5] Sometimes this aggregate also becomes a kind of catch-all in which are placed any phenomena that do not neatly or obviously fit into the other four aggregates. This need not always be seen as a deficiency; and neither is it necessarily a deficiency on the part of a practitioner if at times (s)he is uncertain in exactly which category a phenomenon should be placed. Rather than being a scheme of ultimate reality, the *khandhas* are merely a helpful way of looking, which, as we have already suggested, is all any Dharma concept or category of phenomena can ever be. The purpose of the aggregates teaching is not to accurately categorize phenomena, but to provide a lens we can use for freedom. What matters more here than 'correct' categorization is that *any phenomenon with which we might identify can be regarded instead as not-self* (see next section, and Chapter 14).

Possible conceptions of self

It is the second benefit of this approach, however, that is of greater interest to us right now. The frame of reference of the *skandhas* provides us with a loose, but comprehensive, kind of checklist for exposing all possible self-conceptions, and then learning to let these go. For included in this list of five aggregates are all the phenomena of existence with which we might conceivably identify or which we might assume a possession of. Everything in phenomenal existence may in fact be placed somewhere in these piles. The teaching of the aggregates thus presents us with a framework for meditatively investigating and flushing out even the more subtle and perhaps hidden conceptions and views of self. We can be sure that no stone goes unturned, and that, with practice, absolutely nothing will remain clung to as 'me' or 'mine'.

Actually, a little more thoroughly, the Buddha pointed out four basic ways that the self tends to get conceived in relation to the aggregates, all of which support *dukkha*:

> Just as a dog, tied by a leash to a post or stake, keeps running around and circling around that very post or stake, an ordinary person… not well-versed or trained in the Dharma, regards form (the body) as self, or self as possessing form, or form as in self, or self as in form.
> He regards *vedanā* as self, or self as possessing *vedanā*, or *vedanā* as in self, or self as in *vedanā*.
> He regards perception…
> He regards mental formations…
> He regards consciousness as self, or self as possessing consciousness, or consciousness as in self, or self as in consciousness.
> Thus he keeps running around and circling around that very form… that very *vedanā*… that very perception… those very mental formations… that very consciousness. Running around and circling around form… *vedanā*… perception… mental formations… consciousness… he is not freed from form, not freed from *vedanā*… from perception… from mental formations… from consciousness. He is not freed from birth, aging, and death; from sorrow, lamentation, pain, distress, and tribulation; not freed from *dukkha*, I tell you.[6]

[6] SN 22:99.

In other words, typically and almost incessantly we cling to varying permutations of four kinds of conception of the self – either explicitly, or more immediately and intuitively through our normal ways of looking. Sometimes we may feel or conceive of the self *as* one or more of the aggregates. We identify with the body at times as ourselves, or we identify with the mind, or with one aspect of the mind such as emotion or intelligence – we feel and think that is who we are. Or, it is possible at times that we conceive of the self as somehow other than the aggregates, but *possessing the aggregates* – owning the body, or owning the mind, the emotions, perceptions, or other mental factors. Alternatively, we might at times believe or feel that the self is somehow *in* the body or *in* the mind. And it is possible also to conceive, feel, or believe that the aggregates are somehow *in* the self – the self being thought of then as something more vast, *containing* the aggregates.

Conceiving of the self in any of these ways is not only not conducive to liberation, but actually prevents it. The Buddha taught, therefore, that we should abandon such conceptions of the self in order to know freedom.

Two important points need to be made here to more fully support the thrust of this teaching. First, if it does not immediately seem to be included on the Buddha's list of permutations (a list that was intended to be exhaustive), it may be that we assume that some other conception of the self is unproblematic, or correct, or corresponds to reality. However, the Buddha actually taught that clinging to *any* theory of self will be limiting and will give rise to *dukkha*.[7] It is therefore necessary at some point to become clearly aware of the conceptions of self we are entertaining and investigate if they are ultimately true, and if they are helpful.

Second, while we may be willing to drop an intellectual, philosophical formulation of the self, perhaps out of faith in the Buddha, the more important and more difficult work is to expose and let go of the clinging to these conceptions as they operate in us at a more intuitive level.

Let us briefly take a closer look therefore at some of the ways the self tends to be conceived in our own experience. We can notice on inspection that very often we tend to intuitively conceive of the self as somehow *the controller of the aggregates* of body and mind. Here the conception of the self is that it exists within the body and mind and as part of them, but also as somehow separate, as that part of them that calls the shots, gives the orders – similar perhaps to how a sergeant in charge of a small group of soldiers on a mission, or a conductor of an orchestra, is the same as his fellows yet controls them to a degree and makes the

[7] See, e.g., MN22.

decisions that move them (the other aggregates). Sometimes referred to as *the innate conception of self*, this is the most common way of conceiving of the self. Indeed, even when there is some belief or philosophical position held that is contrary to this conception, the intuitive conception will usually keep sliding back here as a kind of default.

Closely related to this, it can seem often as if the aggregates are dependent on the self, in a certain sense. First there is 'me', and then the body or the mind that 'I' own and control. Many of us might easily feel at times that we would gladly exchange this body for a younger, healthier, more attractive, or more energetic one, if we could, or exchange our minds or the mental factors for fresher or somehow better ones – and feel that, all the while, the self would remain unchanged in some fundamental way by that process. In some way a self that is *somehow vaguely independent of the aggregates* is assumed here.

We might also conceive at times of the self as *the totality of the aggregates*, as if the self is the sum of its parts, or a collection of elements. Or we might posit the self as *the continuum in time of the aggregates – a process*. This latter is slightly more sophisticated and less likely to be an intuitively held default conception.

In fact, in addition to more common-sense notions of self, regularly used in communication and acceptable to most people, there are a range of possible conceptions of self that will tend to arise and be held onto on the basis of either a philosophy or some meditative experience, rather than innately or without such instigation.

For instance, the self can be posited – more often on the basis of a philosophy, but certainly sometimes through an intuitive or meditative sense – as *the present result of an infinite web of past conditions*, material and mental. Among other things, these would include: the cells from our parents; all the food, air, water, and other material elements that over time we have ingested and that have become us; and the ideas, conditionings, and sense impressions from countless different sources in our environments that we have absorbed over years and that have their influences. The self is then asserted and conceived of as something that exists only contingent on, and as, the amassing and interaction of other conditions.

Then there can also be a conception, and a strong sense in meditation or at other times, that actually '*all is one*' – *there is only one, cosmic, self.* This can take different forms that we do not need to elaborate here. Possible too in many variations, and arising through certain practices, philosophies, or intuitions, is the conceiving of the self as being *independent of the aggregates*, something that somehow encompasses them, carries or holds them. One of the more common variations is a conception that *the true self is awareness*, or is a kind of *vast, imperturbable, permanent or universal awareness.*

None of these conceptions at all, however, was endorsed by the Buddha as the ultimately true nature of the self. They will all involve, either explicitly or implicitly, assumptions of the inherent existence of such a self, no matter how rarefied or cosmic. And likewise, they will also involve assumptions or assertions that this or that formulation or perception really is the true nature of the self.

We should refine this essential point, however, from the perspective of our central method and theme of ways of looking. For it may well be that many of these views and conceptions are extremely helpful and beautiful ways of looking at the self, which bring, in some cases, a profound degree of freedom. They might then serve as necessary stepping-stones of insight – as ways of looking that liberate to a certain extent, and that may then also be helpful en route to yet more radically freeing ways of looking. Without such stepping-stones it will usually not be possible to realize the deeper insights in ways that involve more than the intellect, and so actually make a difference.

Even as we feel the blessings it bestows, however, the freedom opened at the level of one of these stepping-stones will still have limits to it. When there is any self-conception, and when there is any assumption of inherent existence, some *avijjā* remains and, despite its subtlety, will seed the continuity of fundamental delusion and of *dukkha*.

We will, in due course, develop practices that make it possible to go beyond all such views, and to see, in each case, why they cannot be ultimately true. For now, what will be helpful is to begin to just notice the ways self is conceived, both intellectually and intuitively.

12

Three More Liberating Ways of Looking:

(1) – Anicca

Our explorations up to now have begun to reveal a little how different ways of looking at experience tend to fabricate self, *dukkha*, and sometimes also the perceived solidity of some experience, to different degrees. The presence, for example, of a great deal of reactivity, identification, and *papañca* will constitute a way of looking which supports a greater degree of construction than when there is less reactivity. In contrast, practices such as basic mindfulness or staying at contact are ways of looking that involve a certain amount of calming of reactivity, entanglement, and fabrication; thus they deliver, in that moment, a greater measure of freedom than our more normal ways of looking.

But we can also cultivate ways of looking that are even more freeing than basic mindfulness and staying at contact, because they involve an even greater degree of letting go and so fabricate even less. Such ways of looking are important not only for the lovely sense of freedom they bring right then in that moment. They also make possible a progressively deepening understanding of dependent arising and emptiness that is unlikely to be available through basic mindfulness alone.

Within the variety of such powerfully liberating ways of looking which the Buddha recommended practitioners develop, he often emphasized training in three perceptions in particular. All conditioned phenomena, he noted, can be seen to be impermanent (*anicca*), unsatisfactory (*dukkha*), and not-self (*anattā*). Used skilfully as a meditative lens – a way of looking – each of these three perceptions provides a vitalizing and significant avenue that opens joy, peace, and freedom, as well as various possibilities for the unfolding of yet deeper insights.[1] We will

[1] In the tradition, *anicca*, *dukkha*, and *anattā* have commonly come to be referred to as 'the three characteristics' or 'the three marks' (Pali: *lakkhaṇa*; Skt: *lakṣaṇa*) of existence. While we will also use this designation at times, it should become clear that we are treating them more as skilful ways of looking than as descriptions of reality that are ultimately true. Likewise, the Buddha, although

take some time over the following three chapters, therefore, to describe the cultivation in practice of each of them.

Anicca means inconstancy, instability, impermanence. That phenomena are impermanent and that they change is fairly obvious. More helpful and more potent than simply acknowledging this when the fact strikes us, however, is the development of a practice of deliberately and repeatedly attending to the appearances and disappearances, the changing nature of things. This entails much more than merely *thinking about* impermanence; it involves seeing and sensing it.

Noticing *Anicca* at a Relatively Gross Level

Such attention to inconstancy is possible in different ways and at different levels of subtlety. *Anicca* is perceivable over a range of timescales, for example, and it is important that our meditative explorations encompass this range. Clearly impermanence is evident in all kinds of things at what we could call the everyday level; and recognizing it there more often and more deliberately may be more profitable than one might suppose.

At the end of any day, we can, for instance, take time to reflect and remember the many different states that the *citta* has moved through over the course of that day. *Citta* states change; they are never permanent. Simple as this is, carefully noticing it over and over at this everyday level, the insight and its implications start to impress more genuinely into our minds. We start to digest the insight of this level of *anicca* more profoundly.

And then we can begin to bring that insight to bear on what is *currently* arising, and in this way open some freedom. For beyond mere awareness of a particular *citta* state that is present, we now have the possibility of deliberately empowering the awareness in the moment with our understanding of that *citta* state's impermanence. Bringing to mind, right then, our firsthand knowledge that it will change, we are effectively looking at that state through a different lens. We are employing our insight into inconstancy as a skilful view. This way of looking lessens clinging in the moment – it lessens, for example, our sometimes semi-conscious fear that we may be trapped in any state; and it lessens too a tendency to try to hang on to a state when it is not appropriate.

---

certainly on occasion referring to them in objective terms, spoke also of *anicca-*, *dukkha-*, and *anattā-saññā* ('perception') and *-anupassanā* ('looking at', 'contemplating', 'considering', 'viewing', 'observing') – stressing how cultivating each as a perception, a way of looking, brings liberation. See, e.g., AN 10:60; and also SN 22:40 – 42.

All this is usually also true of the sensory impressions of our surroundings. Unless we barely move in a day, we can recognize that there are relatively gross shifts and changes over time in whatever stimuli impinge on us from the outside. Over a day or part of a day, the patternings of sense impressions (visual, aural, tactile, etc.) almost always undergo considerable transformations. And again, taking care to notice this simple fact can at times be surprisingly helpful, offering a door to the possibility of some relief and spaciousness when the mind is contracted in craving and reactivity.

Practice: Awareness of change at an everyday level

Regularly take some time at the end of the day to view the day's experiences from the perspective of *anicca*. With regard to different aspects of experience – mood, energy levels, and the various sense impressions of your surroundings, for example – carefully recollect and acknowledge the changes and shifting phases that occurred.

What other transformations are you aware of?

The period framed for reflection in this way may actually be of any length. It could be longer – perhaps a portion, or the whole, of a retreat; or shorter – just one session of formal meditation, or the duration of a meeting at work, for instance.

Notice each time how it feels to see events and experiences from the perspective of *anicca* like this.

After you have gained some familiarity with this reflection, practise bringing this *knowledge of the fact of change* to your current experiences – of mood, energy levels, sense impressions, etc. – at any time. Regard whatever the experience is with the clear and conscious knowing that it will transform.

Notice, with as much sensitivity as you can, what effects this way of looking has in the moment.

Perceiving Moment-to-Moment Impermanence

Meditation on inconstancy can be refined further by attending deliberately and closely to the sense of moment-to-moment change. Here, we endeavour to sustain a way of looking which, with some intensity, prioritizes the noticing of impermanence and fluctuation in phenomena from one moment to the next, and the next. Over and over, we try to *tune in* to this one aspect of experience – this perception of fluidity and evanescence, and the momentary births and deaths of things. And this very sense of flux, this shifting of the textures of appearances, is what we attempt to *remain focused* on.

An example: The patterning of sound

Consider a gong that is struck: the sound rings, and then eventually fades. In this way of looking, the sound's attenuation and disappearance should be viewed through the lens of *anicca* – recognized and felt as an instance of impermanence. But close attention can also be brought to the sound itself, and in particular to the *fluctuations* in the texture of the sound. Including thus both the dying of the sound and the micro-fluctuations within it, what is of almost exclusive interest in this way of looking is the experience of flux and alteration. The fact of change is what is repeatedly attended to. In many ways, this practice is an extension of the practices we looked at in earlier chapters, where we began to notice the gaps in things. It is simply that here we are not just passively noticing gaps, but are making more deliberate the attending to any momentary manifestations of change.

Including the distracted mind

Let's follow the thread of this example to explain the practice more fully. If, as the gong is ringing, the mind is distracted away from tuning into the moment-to-moment change in the quality of the sound, then, just as with any other object of focus, the attention can simply be brought back to the shifting of the patterning of sound.

In addition though, the very distraction of the mind can itself be viewed with an eye to the fluctuations involved – of mental object, and of mental qualities (mindfulness and one-pointedness, for instance). In this way, distraction may actually be included in the contemplation of impermanence and not regarded so much as a problem.

Attention can be both narrow and broad

With this example we can see how the attention can be deliberately *directed at,* and remain focused on, the impermanence in, and of, any one sound. But in general, as well as such directing of our attention in a more narrow way, we are also able to *open out a wider space of attention*, and let the awareness *receive* whatever is present in that wider field. With regard to listening, we can listen in a more global way to the totality of sounds from all around. And again, we can practise tuning into, and remaining focused on, the fact of change – the arising and passing, the shifting of textures of sounds.

Other objects: The sensations of the body and the other physical senses

Similarly with the sense sphere of bodily sensation: it is possible to direct the attention to one particular area in the body, and deliberately sustain a focus on the perception of flux in the sensations there. Or we can open attention out to envelop the whole body at once, and attempt to remain tuned in, as much as possible, to the changing, the ebb and flow or flickering, of sensation in that whole broader space.

Likewise, of course, with taste and smell. With regard to the visual sense, we can attend to the variation in the visual patterning from one moment to the next. When either our eyes or objects in our field of vision move, this shifting in the visual pattern is obvious. Nevertheless, a more subtle sense of inconstancy is noticeable too even when the eyes and the objects seen are still, and attending also to this can be helpful.

Vedanā

It is useful as well to deliberately focus on the impermanence in *vedanā*. This may be in one specific object – a particular pain, or emotion, or sound, for instance – paying careful attention to the perhaps subtle changes in the quality of *vedanā* within that one perceived object. Alternatively, we can choose any sense sphere, such as bodily sensation, taste, or hearing, and try to remain brightly attentive to the moment-to-moment fluctuation of the *vedanā* in that sense sphere.

Thoughts

The fleeting, quicksilver nature of thought is usually easier to contemplate when the *citta* is a bit more settled. Thoughts can be quick, slippery, and seductive, so the attention is easily dragged off into entanglement if mindfulness is not strong enough. Attention to the impermanence of thought is therefore better left to times when there is a degree of *samādhi* that can sustain it.

Generally, this ephemeral nature of thought is also more productively contemplated when the attention is more spacious. To enable this in a meditation session, it can be helpful to first spend some time focusing on the whole body at once, tuned in to the *anicca* of the body sensations.

When this feels stable as a contemplation, and you can feel the ease and freedom this supports, the attention can be opened out further to also include sounds and their impermanence, *together with* the body sensations and their impermanence. Spend a while here, again allowing the state and its way of looking to become stable, and feeling the freedom, peace, and release that it delivers.

This space of awareness, once it is settled, will effortlessly begin to reveal the *anicca* of thought in a similar way. One can then remain there, attuned to the impermanence – the birth and death – of thoughts in a way that will automatically include, too, an awareness of the impermanence of body sensations and sounds. This stage also should be developed to a point of some stability, and the freedom and sense of beauty it opens should be tasted.

Intentions

Another mental object whose impermanence it may be fruitful to notice deliberately is intention. For instance, at the end of a walking meditation path, or standing by a door ready to turn the handle, one can remain attentive to the arising of the intention to take the first step, or to raise the hand. This intention may come as a thought, but more often it will be felt as an impulse within the body, a brief and slight sort of energetic surge that accompanies the movement in the *citta*. It may or may not result then in physical movement, but its arising and its passing, its impermanence, can be clearly known.

The totality of objects

Once you have practised and gained some confidence with focusing on *anicca* both through directing the attention to specific sense objects as well as through sustaining the attention on one sense sphere, you can also practise opening up the attention to the impermanence in the totality of experience. Simply, and more freely, tune into the changing nature of whatever is noticed in the whole field of awareness. Engaged in this way of looking, it is *anicca*, again, that one is almost solely interested in.

As suggested above, this inclusion of all the senses together may emerge naturally from working with a more spacious awareness contemplating impermanence. And in fact it will usually be more helpful for the simultaneous investigation of the *anicca* of all phenomena if the attention is more open and spacious, rather than more narrowly focused. When attention is employed in a narrower way, and is moving very quickly from one object in one location to another in another location – a sound over there, then a sight somewhere else, to a body sensation in another place, then another sound elsewhere – the rapid flittering of focus that this involves may actually be agitating and disturbing to the mind, and unhelpful for insight. In this case a wider awareness often allows insight to strengthen and deepen with more stability and ease.

Consciousness

There is too the possibility of recognizing and tuning into the *anicca* of consciousness. Doing this requires more subtlety of attention. However, it can usually be developed fairly easily with practice, once some facility with attending to the inconstancy of different sense objects has been gained. Although we will not enter into a fuller discussion of consciousness until later[2] let us just say enough about it here to enable this strand of practice.

The Pali word for consciousness or awareness is *viññāṇa* (Skt: *vijñāna*). Literally, this means 'knowing': to be conscious or aware is to know some object in at least one of the senses. Any moment of experience is actually a moment of knowing, no matter how subtle, refined, or diffuse the object known, or whether we have a word for it. Being a moment of knowing some object or other, a moment of experience is thus a moment of both consciousness and perception, regardless of whether there is a mental act of verbally labelling the object of experience. Any moment of knowing, then, must be a moment of perception, and any moment of perception must be a moment of knowing. These two are really the same phenomenon conceived from different perspectives. We might say that consciousness is perception regarded from the perspective of the knowing. The same coin from its other side.

Now, usually when we see or hear or cognize anything in the senses, most of our attention is on the object perceived *as an object*. Yet at any moment of

---

[2] See Chapters 15 and 25 *ff.*

awareness, there is also present, as a natural and effortless aspect of that awareness, a simple knowing that we are aware.[3] This awareness of awareness can be made more prominent just by noticing it more and tuning into it. Rather than viewing the experience, the perception, in a moment primarily as an *object* then, at times we can try to view it and to get a sense of it primarily as a *moment of knowing*.

At first, recognizing this awareness of awareness might seem quite subtle. For some, an initial recognition will come through remaining focused lightly on one sense sphere, or an object in one sense sphere. For others it emerges more easily with a more open and inclusive attention. Either way, over time we can develop the ability to sustain this sense of the knowing. This can be extremely valuable, because it opens up many possibilities. One of these is that it is then only a small step to see the moment-to-moment impermanence of consciousness – of these moments of knowing.

More to Mention About Seeing Moment-to-moment Anicca

An invigorating practice

Attending to inconstancy moment to moment is enormously beneficial. And along with the insight it is cultivating, we can usually notice other effects. Repeatedly engaging and sustaining an attention that intently seeks out the perception of flux in all things tends, for instance, to raise energy in the mind and the body. Sometimes markedly so. In part this is a result of the letting go that this way of looking supports, and in part it is due to the keenness of attention that is involved in tuning into moment-to-moment *anicca*. Such

---

[3] There has been a longstanding and sometimes fierce controversy in the Buddhist tradition about whether consciousness can know itself or not. Those who have claimed that it is impossible have argued that it would be "like a knife cutting itself", or "like a fingertip touching itself". Such an argument, though, is aimed at the possibility of awareness somehow taking itself as its own object. What it overlooks then, as *Śāntarakṣita* pointed out in his *Madhyamakālaṃkāra*, is that it is simply a defining and commonly acknowledged property of consciousness that it knows that it is conscious. It does not take some other consciousness to know this moment's consciousness, nor does this aspect of awareness suggest an infinite regress. When we are ordinarily aware, we know that we are aware, automatically. Such reflexive knowing of itself is included in what is meant by 'being conscious'. It is in fact, as *Śāntarakṣita* observed, what makes it consciousness and not something else. Nothing more than that is being implied or suggested here; nor is it needed for the meditative practice we are presently developing.

energization can of course be useful, as well as delightful. For similar reasons a strengthening and steadying of attention may also be supported through this way of looking.

The possibility of noting

Some practitioners find, at times, that repeating inwardly – very quietly and sparsely – a word such as "*anicca*", "impermanence", or "inconstancy" during this practice helps to keep the attention attuned to change moment to moment. Rather than labelling each micro-instant of perception as "impermanent", noting like this can function more as a gentle reminder to guide and tune the intention and attention. It will anyway be the case, more often than not, that as the practice settles, the rapidity of change noticed will preclude a discrete and overt labelling of each arising and passing.

Any mental noting, however, should only be used to the extent that it supports the view of impermanence being practised. It should not be obtrusive or itself take up much attention. For the primary focus is always on the sense of change. Experiment to find what is helpful for you. There may be times when a light labelling is conducive to the way of looking, and other times when it seems more helpful to drop it.

No need to press for a perception of more rapidity

Despite the benefits of attending to and witnessing the momentary fluctuations in appearances, it should be made clear that we do not need to force an awareness of a more and more rapid rate of change, or a quicker and quicker tempo of the appearing and disappearing of phenomena. Simply tuning in to the impermanence as fast as it is revealing itself, moment to moment, without pressure, will allow the attention and the perception to refine at times and enable us to see more subtle levels of *anicca*.

Anicca and the ultimate truth

Connected to this last point, it is important to understand that the purpose of the contemplation of impermanence is not to uncover some ultimately true level of reality comprised of the smallest possible indivisible atoms of sensation or experience. Nor, likewise, is it to come to a conclusion that the true nature of existence is some kind of 'flow', and thus that the experience of existence as 'flow' is an experience of what is ultimately real.

It has, rather, two main purposes. First, attention to *anicca* should, for the most part, organically and effortlessly engender a letting go, a release of clinging, in the moment that we are engaged in it. And this letting go brings a sense of freedom.

Second, this practice should also furnish a degree of insight into emptiness and fabrication. In addition to making evident the gaps in things, and how the mind fabricates by 'joining the dots', it also offers a simple entry point to begin to see the emptiness of self at a certain level. If sustained attention to the totality of phenomena reveals nothing that is fixed, that does not change, where then is this self whose essence we intuitively feel as somehow unchanging? What could it possibly be, other than these momentary phenomena that are all we encounter? It simply cannot be found.[4] We begin to glimpse then, at an existential level, beyond the personality level of self-definitions, how the sense of self too is stitched together.

Furthermore, while attending carefully to moment-to-moment change there is typically less 'joining of the dots' in habitual ways. So we may experience, through this way of looking, times when the self loses some or even much of its solidity. And we can begin then to understand more directly how the self-sense is dependent on a projection of temporal continuity. With, thus, less cementing of and investment in the usual sense of the self as continuous, there are actually a variety of ways in which the experience can open, and each imparts its own flavour of wonder and freedom. There can be a fragmentation, or dissolution, of the self-sense to some extent: perhaps an atomization, as if into a fine and exquisite mist of particles; perhaps simply a sense of the process or flow of the aggregates unfolding automatically in time. Or perhaps the self we perceive then appears as only instantaneous, as if we are paper thin, barely existing, while a

---

[4] Actually, such an insight from the *anicca* practice does not yet refute a view that the self is the *process in time of the arising and passing away of the aggregates*. Whether held as a result of logical assertion or as a possible conclusion from this kind of meditative experience of *anicca*, such a notion is still a reification of the self. Other practices and insights will be needed to go beyond this view of the self as a process. (See, in particular, Chapters 17 and 26.) Nevertheless, it may still be an important insight at one level, and certainly the *anicca* practice, and even a way of looking that incorporates deliberately viewing the self as a process, may be immensely helpful. Such views can bring a degree of freedom in the moment, as we have discussed, and also provide a potential platform for deeper insights.

breathtaking sense of nothingness might pervade or surround experience. This last, in particular, with its intimations of more radical insights, can produce a striking and heart-melting unburdening. Unfindable apart from the insubstantiality of this brief moment's perception, who then are we? What then is the self?

As well as such experiences of liberating disintegration, we shall soon see there are other ways too in which the contemplation of impermanence can work to somewhat calm the fabrication of self. With practice then, this way of looking at *anicca* can provide an avenue in to some insight into the emptiness of self.

Practice: Attending to *anicca* moment to moment

For a part or for the whole of a meditation session, or continuing as you move about your day, practise sustaining attention on the moment-to-moment changing that you notice in objects.

Take time to familiarize yourself with contemplating the impermanence of phenomena in this way in each of the six sense spheres.

Make sure that you choose objects that are experienced as *dukkha*, and also those that are not. (Particularly if you are feeling unwell or tired, and believe that this is preventing you practising or practising well, try to keep attending, as closely as possible, to the momentary fluctuations in these very experiences.)

Practise working with both an awareness directed towards a specific phenomenon, and also with a more spacious, open awareness simply attuned to a certain sense sphere and the *anicca* that is observable there.

In similar ways, practise contemplating the moment-to-moment fluctuation in *vedanā*; and also in the experience of different emotions or mind states, gross and subtle.

At times when the *citta* is a little more settled and spacious, practise remaining focused on the ephemeral nature of thoughts in the ways outlined earlier.

Experiment for yourself with contemplating the *anicca* of any other appearances. (As suggested, it can be helpful to use the five aggregates as a kind of comprehensive checklist of phenomena for moment-to-moment impermanence contemplation.) Some will naturally feel easier to practise with than others.

Experiment with seeing the impermanence of consciousness in the way explained earlier.

Once you have established some familiarity and ability in regard to phenomena and sense spheres taken singly, practise opening up the attention to the moment-to-moment impermanence in the totality of all experience.

> Notice always, and as carefully as you are able, how it feels to look at things attuned to their changing nature.
>
> Notice too how the sense of self is affected by this way of looking.
>
> What else do you notice when you look this way? (This investigation will eventually be vital for the development of further insight.)

The Heart's Responses to Impermanence

It is often important, with the deepening of exploration in meditation, to address the various responses of the heart to what is experienced. In relation to these practices of attending to inconstancy we can say a little about this now and add more to the discussion later.[5]

As we have asserted, generally this way of looking should bring some sense of release and unburdening, of freedom, peace, and even joy, right then as we are practising. It is crucial to notice this. However, we can also have different emotional responses to seeing *anicca* at different times, and these need to be acknowledged and addressed as part of our humanity. With regards to any individual phenomenon, of course we may feel glad, sad, or indifferent to see its impermanence, depending, for instance, on whether that phenomenon is experienced as painful, pleasant, or more neutral. With regards to the more universal fact of *anicca*, that all things without exception decay and die sooner or later, we may also have a range of different feelings.

Listen to the powerful lines from the *Vajrachedikā Sūtra* ('The Diamond Sutra'):

> Thus should you think of all this fleeting world:
> Like a drop of dew, or like a star at dawn;
> A bubble in a stream, a flash of lightning
> In a summer cloud,
> A flickering lamp, a phantom, and a dream…[6]

---

[5] See, in particular, Chapter 14.

[6] The translation here is actually a composite of two translations: one by Kenneth Saunders, reprinted in A. F. Price and Wong Mou-lam (translators), *The Diamond Sutra and The Sutra of Hui-neng* [Boston: Shambala, 1990] p. 53; the other by Edward Conze, in *Perfect Wisdom: The Short Prajñāpāramitā Texts* [Totnes: Buddhist Publishing Group, 1973] p. 138.

At times we may feel the poignancy of these words – they may evoke in us a sense of melancholy, or sometimes fear or existential anxiety, or a disappointed, deflated kind of feeling. Alternatively they may give rise to a sense of mystery, of beauty, of thrill, and of joy. In contemplating impermanence, very often we might experience a bitter-sweet fusion of contradictory emotions. As always, what we actually feel depends on a whole host of conditions, inner and outer, that come together in the moment of response.

It seems to me important, though, to be able, and willing, to open the heart to the pathos of *anicca*, to accommodate, and to care for, these feelings. There is loss in life of all kinds. No matter how we might try, nothing at all can be preserved forever just as it is. Material things change or fall apart, or we move away from them. The shared intimacies with those we love become memories, fade and disappear. Our own physical and mental capacities erode with the years. And there appears no end to this unstoppable torrent of phenomena passing from existence. The entire journeys of our lives can seem so brief at times, and our death is not distant at all. Like loss, decay, and separation, it is inevitable; only the exact timing is uncertain. *Anicca* is everywhere, all around us, and all through us too. It is behind us in our wake, and waiting for us in the future. Allowing ourselves to open to and be touched by this dimension of our existential situation is essential to our humanity, and also to our practice. As the capacity of the heart grows and we are more able to embrace the heartbreaking side of *anicca*, we may find, at least at times, the possibility of a tender kind of beauty in the reality of impermanence and in our relationship with it.

Whether difficult or beautiful, however, as practitioners we can get blinkered by and stuck in these more tragic emotions, just as with any others. And while they are undoubtedly valuable, we should be clear that experiencing them – opening to or bearing with them – is certainly not the goal of the path. Of course it may also be that through repeated awareness of *anicca* and repeated exposure to teachings about it we develop a much greater sense of equanimity in relation to impermanence in general. But even this should not be regarded as a final aim. In and of themselves, none of these emotional responses should be regarded thus. Clinging to a view that does so limits the potential of practice. Instead, recognizing that they are all simply part of our being human, and realizing how each, perhaps at different times, may be helpful or unhelpful, we can learn to cultivate the space and skill to know, hold, and respond to them all.

In contrast it should be pointed out that feelings such as release and freedom that come while engaging *anicca* as a meditative way of looking are actually vital as elements of the pathways to more profound insight. And this deepening of insight is indispensable to a deeper freedom.

For what we do in fact eventually seek through this practice is an understanding of things that goes beyond the notion of their being permanent or impermanent. Such insight is sought not in order to take away our humanity but to open another dimension of perspective on existence, one that liberates more radically. No matter how much we have accustomed ourselves to the changing nature of things and grown to feel more okay about it, where there is still some unchallenged belief in impermanence (or in permanence) as being ultimately true, there will remain in us something unfulfilled through that. A dimension of freedom that it is possible to know will be inaccessible.

Of Death and Vast Time

An awareness of impermanence *on timescales much longer than the everyday* can be helpful too and can also inform the seeing and the relationship with experience in this moment. The contemplation of our death, for instance, of the fact that we are bound to die one day, is an immensely valuable practice for all kinds of reasons, and certainly counts as a valuable contemplation of *anicca*. Such practice may be approached in many ways. Here though, we will just mention one possibility: that of deliberately viewing this present moment's experience with a simultaneous awareness of the certainty of our death. Even this can actually be done in many ways. Again it is worth experimenting with to find out what works best for you.

As you do, it is important to remember all that we have discussed regarding the range of the heart's responses, and to practise with care and sensitivity. For our purposes, as already explained, feelings such as release, freedom, and joy are, generally speaking, the indicators that insight is working, that the way of looking we are then engaged in is useful. If a way of looking or a mode of working elicits more difficult feelings, it may be that those emotions need some compassionate holding and exploring; or it may be that the way of working and contemplating can be altered to allow a freer flow of liberating insight. As always, a wise responsiveness and a willingness to experiment is crucial.

Let us at least outline one viable way of approaching this practice. Consider that this moment of experience right now can be viewed as a moment in time, a moment of knowing, in the context of almost unimaginably vast spans of time and space. My life, too, has this immensity of space and time around it. 'I' only exist for a few decades at most – a tiny, almost non-existent stretch relative to the timescale of this universe. Before 'I' was born, there extended an unthinkably great expanse of time without 'me'; and after 'I' die and disappear, there unfolds an equally great sweep. The absence of 'me', the non-appearance of 'me'. My life is surrounded by this enormity of absence. Within it, this experience – this instant of sense impression, of sight, for example, or body sensation – is like the briefest flash that appears in that vastness.

Actually looked at this way, an experience may be powerfully unmoored from its usual encumbrances, and deprived momentarily of the ways it gets solidified. With this can come a corresponding unburdening and sense of liberation. It is only a way of looking, of course, and we can see this moment from other, equally valid, perspectives. Nevertheless, intently focusing on a sense impression in the present, while simultaneously supporting such a way of considering, and allowing it to silently inform the awareness, can be thrillingly freeing.

Practice: Viewing experience from the perspective of death and vast time

Reflect on the fact of your birth and death – your appearance and disappearance in the universe. Consider, or even imagine in some way, the vastness of time and space that surrounds your life, and that also surrounds this moment's experience.

Play, many times, with bringing attention intensely to any sense impression in the present moment, while at the same time allowing this awareness of the greater context of this flash of experience to inform the way of looking. (You may have to experiment to find your own way to make this work for you.)

How does this way of looking feel?

What effects do you notice of viewing the moment's experience this way?

13

Three More Liberating Ways of Looking: (2) – Dukkha

It is necessary to take some time developing each of the three characteristics as a particular way of looking in practice, and to familiarize yourself with working with each of them, in different postures, and with as broad as possible a range of phenomena. Since they are each ways of letting go, notice, as you experiment, which of them opens up the greatest degree of freedom and peace for you. This will differ from person to person, but without doubt you should develop the one which seems to work best for you. I would strongly suggest though that you keep cultivating at least two of them.

The three characteristics as three ways of looking are certainly related to each other. In some respects they are simply slightly different perspectives on phenomena. In some respects too, they imply each other. Indeed, eventually there develops the option to sustain at times a way of looking which views phenomena through a lens that includes all three characteristics together instantaneously. Yet they are also distinct, and in some ways, as they are developed and are followed into more depth, they will unfold somewhat different avenues of insight. Retaining and cultivating at least two of these characteristics as ways of looking is therefore helpful in supporting the fullness of insight.

***Dukkha* (Method 1)**

The second characteristic, *dukkha*, we will divide into two possible ways of working that are related. The first approach is in fact implied by, and only a very slight extension of, the *anicca* practice. Phenomena are *dukkha*, that is, *unsatisfactory*, in part because they are impermanent, finite and unreliable. They cannot provide lasting satisfaction or fulfilment, even when they are lovely.

Sustaining a way of looking, moment to moment, that regards phenomena as 'unsatisfactory', organically engenders some degree of letting go – of release of craving – in that very moment. This deliberately practised view of phenomena as 'unsatisfactory' has, then, as its implicitly understood but silent subtext: 'because they are fleeting'.

Just as with the other characteristics, in order for it to work effectively as a way of letting go it must be a meditative seeing. It is not a philosophical position to uphold. And in practice, this regarding of any thing that arises as unsatisfactory should not be a laboured pondering with thought, but rather an instantaneous, and very light, way of looking, repeated over and over. Again it is worth experimenting to see if a quiet and delicate labelling of "unsatisfactory" feels helpful in supporting this way of looking. Here, such inner voicing may at times be directed towards a single phenomenon in attention, or, especially at times when it is tied into a perception of rapid impermanence, it may also work to guide and sustain the perception of 'unsatisfactory' more generally.

'Holy discontent' and 'holy disinterest'

As always, such a way of seeing things forms a lens, one among many, that we can pick up, use, and put down, rather than a final statement about reality. Although, for many people, to regard all things as unsatisfactory might at first appear to express a somewhat life-denying attitude, in practice as a way of looking this should not be the case at all. It has, rather, the potential to unfold a wonderful freedom and the mystical beauty of a radically different sense of existence.

Just as any of the three characteristics will, it forms an avenue of exploration. Our intuitive notion of life is usually bound up with and confined to experiences, but there is the possibility of a seeing that is not limited in these ways. What happens, we are inquiring, if consciousness is not so caught up in or limited by phenomena? For when we meditatively regard things as unsatisfactory, at that time we are sustaining a view that could be called one of *holy discontent* with almost everything, curious in what opens up as a result of that view. This is categorically *not* an attitude of aversion towards things, of trying to push them away, of disgust, or repulsion. It is much more a natural letting go in the moment that comes from viewing things as unsatisfactory, a lessening of the compulsive and deep-rooted tendencies to constantly pick phenomena up, grasp after them, fuss over them, or try to get rid of them.

Related to this, when we are practising with any of the three characteristics as ways of looking, there is too a dropping of many of the usual kinds of interest we might have in phenomena. Except for an interest in seeing repeatedly the particular characteristic we are working with, and an interest in the effects of this way of looking, we are sustaining what could be called a *holy disinterest* in phenomena. Clearly this is not the same as just ignoring things, or being in denial about the presence of some thing or other, or any of the usual kinds of lack of interest that can occur for us at different times. It is a conscious choice to skilfully engage in a particular way of looking. At other times of course we can pick phenomena up, draw intimately close to them, and investigate them in different ways.

'Letting go' means 'letting be'

As mentioned, generally this way of looking liberates joy in the very moments we apply it. And this it is vital to notice, to feel, and at times at least, to enjoy. If, however, as you are doing this practice, feelings of disconnection or boredom or the more normal kinds of lack of interest arise, this is actually a sign that some aversion has crept in, perhaps even subtly disguised as 'letting go', and needs to be addressed, and softened.

Rather than 'getting rid of', here letting go means 'letting be'. And letting be means the pacification of the push and pull of craving – of mentally and energetically grasping after, rejecting, and preferring. This is crucial to understand. Instead of a typical relationship with momentary phenomena that is to some extent contracted in aversion or grasping, there is more of a dropping of the struggle and the entanglement with them. It is the seeing of all phenomena uniformly as 'unsatisfactory', the holy discontent and the holy disinterest, that allows us much more to let all things be. For if all things are *dukkha*, there is a kind of equality to all things, and the tussle and agitation of preferring one over another, of pushing and pulling, calms. A different and lovely sense of things begins to emerge. It may be surprising perhaps, but as we practise letting go and releasing craving in this way, we discover clearly for ourselves that it does not lead to a coldness or a closing of the heart, either in the moment or more generally in our life.

Practice: Viewing phenomena as '*dukkha*' moment to moment

Once you have developed a little familiarity with the *anicca* practice – particularly at the everyday and moment-to-moment levels – you can begin to play at times with a slight transformation of that way of looking, sustaining a meditative view of phenomena, moment to moment, as 'unsatisfactory'.

Make sure this way of seeing phenomena is uniformly applied to what is experienced as lovely, what is experienced as difficult, and what is experienced as neither. Here the unsatisfactory nature of things is not tied to their being unpleasant.

Take time to explore this way of looking with the same range of phenomena as in the *anicca* practice, and in all the same ways – with attention narrowed down to a particular object, and also opened out in a more spacious way to the totality of experience in one or more sense spheres.

Try to be as comprehensive as possible in the practice of this view. Make sure you include the more subtle states of *citta* that arise – such as any state of relative clarity or relative concentration – as well as states that are relatively less clear and concentrated.

Notice also how it *feels* to regard phenomena as unsatisfactory. It is important to feel the letting go, the letting be, and the release, that this way of looking involves.

If joy or some other lovely state of being arises as a result of this practice, you can simply acknowledge, allow, and enjoy these feelings while you continue to view phenomena as 'unsatisfactory'.
Importantly, at other times, these feelings themselves can also be regarded in the moment as 'unsatisfactory'. If you do this, notice what effect it has.

Sustaining a 'holy discontent' and a 'holy disinterest' should open up a sense of freedom and bright peace in the moment. Notice, though, if aversion creeps in and colours the experience with feelings such as boredom or dullness. If it does, experiment to see if it is possible to shift the way of looking – back to one that supports a letting be of all phenomena. (At times, one way of doing so might be viewing the very boredom, dullness, disconnection, or aversion, as 'unsatisfactory'.)

Notice again, with care, how the sense of self is affected by this way of looking.

As before, what else do you notice when you look this way? (Such further noticing will come to be crucial for deeper levels of insight.)

Dukkha (Method 2)

Viewing phenomena as unsatisfactory is one skilful way of letting go, of letting them be. In fact, all of the ways of looking that we are interested in developing over the course of this book are actually ways of letting go, ways of pacifying the compulsive push and pull of craving and clinging to phenomena in the moment. This release and relaxation in the relationship with things can also be practised slightly more directly in a second approach to the characteristic of *dukkha*.

Recognizing Craving

In order to enable this second method, we may first have to become sensitive to the relationship in that moment with the particular phenomenon in attention. How do we actually know when craving is present? Certainly, grasping and aversion are indicated by any preoccupation with an object, and are also revealed by our thoughts when they voice a wish to have, or to be rid of, some thing.

But as meditation deepens and thought grows quiet there will still almost always be more subtle clinging present, and we need ways of recognizing it. As mentioned in Chapter 5, the body can reveal the presence of clinging, because any grasping or aversion will be mirrored in a palpable feeling, usually of contraction or tensing, either in a particular area of the body or in the whole body sense.

This felt sense of contraction may be quite subtle if the clinging is subtle, perhaps felt less then in the gross physical musculature of the body, and more in a slight contraction in the subtle energy field of the body. However it manifests, our capability to pick up on more subtle levels of clinging grows as practice progresses. (Interestingly, at first it is usually easier to notice subtle aversion than it is to notice subtle grasping. As sensitivity develops with practice though, even a very subtle movement of the mind toward something can be known clearly too.)

Another way that craving is signalled is through a sense of contraction, or shrinking, of the space of awareness. In deeper states of meditation, when the body sense may have become extremely refined or may even have disappeared, this becomes a very useful and sensitive barometer of craving.

Ways of Relaxing the Craving

When clinging is noticed in any of these ways, this practice involves easing that clinging as an organic next step. We could say that we are then relaxing the relationship with a phenomenon, for when there is either grasping or aversion toward a sense object the relationship with that sense object is one of tension. Relaxing, or softening, the relationship relaxes this tension.

Thus in this way of looking we are developing a moment-to-moment sensitivity to the presence of craving – to how the pushing and pulling of the mind actually feels when it is present – and relaxing that craving, again and again. It is vital to feel well both how craving feels, and also how it feels to relax and let go of some degree of craving in all its expressions.

This relaxation of craving can be effected in a number of ways. Sometimes merely the awareness of grasping, aversion, or resistance, is all that is needed to release it. Experience shows, however, that many times awareness alone will not be enough. Then we need other means.

Relaxing the body

One interesting way of releasing clinging is made possible through taking advantage of the mutual dependence of bodily contraction and clinging. Clinging, as we have pointed out, gives rise to a sense of contraction in the body, it makes the body tense somehow; correspondingly though, *relaxing the physical contraction can often relax the clinging* with respect to some phenomenon.

Using other ways of looking

Another option, when we are aware of grasping or aversion, is to tune into the sense of impermanence in some way, to bring attention to the rapid moment-to-moment disappearance and dissolution of phenomena. Like watching a shower of fine raindrops hitting the surface of a lake and dissolving, dissolving, we can focus on the *anicca*, and *particularly the passing away*, of momentary phenomena. This might be looking more finely and minutely at some thing that we are craving, or it might be in regard to phenomena in general. As already explored, such a way of looking should function to release the clinging, if we can allow that seeing to support an attitude right then of *letting* things disappear moment to moment, not holding on.

Similarly, when we are aware there is some craving, the mode of viewing things as 'unsatisfactory' relaxes the push and pull with regard to phenomena. (This will likewise be the case, of course, regarding things as *anattā*, the third characteristic, which we shall discuss in the next chapter.)

An alternative approach: Fully allowing, welcoming

Let's explore another important possibility for relaxing the relationship with phenomena. We can adopt a way of looking wherein we draw attention close to sense objects, become intimate with them, and then shift to a mode of relating that *allows* them, *welcomes* their presence, in this moment, *as totally as possible.*

We could also see this as *opening* consciousness to the impression of that sense object – sometimes even as if there is a 'door' of awareness which we are opening wider to that particular impression. To the extent that there is any such opening, welcoming, or allowing, there is, effectively, a corresponding relaxing of both aversion and of grasping.

What is given overwhelming priority of emphasis in the moment is the relationship of allowing or welcoming, again and again, moment to moment. Rather than with a clarity of perception of the phenomenon, or a precise attention to the sharply defined details of the sense object, the aspect of mindfulness with which we are more concerned in this way of looking is the *relationship with* the object in awareness.[1]

Here again it may be that as attention focuses on a phenomenon, a quiet and sparse mental repetition – "allowing", "welcoming", or "opening", for instance – can at times help to support and sustain this attitude.

Unlike before, in this mode of allowing there is actually no need necessarily to be aware of the relationship with a phenomenon first, before allowing. However much clinging there is in regard to any object at any time (and we can safely assume there will always be at least some), by simply allowing, welcoming, or opening, in the moment, the relationship is softened to one of less clinging.

At times when one *is* aware of the presence of clinging, though, there is the additional possibility to shift to a mode of relating that allows, as fully as possible, not just the object resisted or craved but the very sense of resistance, or the pressure or contraction of craving, itself. At the very least this should have an effect on the *dukkha* experienced, since clinging is then not being compounded so much through 'secondary reactivity'.[2]

---

[1] For some, it might be tempting to assume that, since a simple mindfulness practice will already involve an allowing and acceptance of whatever is present, there is no need to experiment with this way of looking. And to be sure, a certain amount of allowing and welcoming will also have been involved in the practices, introduced in Chapter 10, of simply focusing on *vedanā* and on the felt sense of craving. The degree of allowing or welcoming in these other practices, however, can be significantly increased, and doing so will yield the possibility of insights otherwise unavailable. I would therefore strongly advise spending some time experimenting with the way of looking outlined here, and differentiating it from both a basic mindfulness practice, and a simple stationing of the attention on either *vedanā* or the experience of craving.

[2] The effects of allowing, as fully as possible, the very felt sense of clinging or resistance could certainly be explained in terms of feedback loops between the links of the dependent origination map. As mentioned in Chapter 10 though, while useful, such an explanation is not complete, and practising repeatedly with many of these approaches will actually begin to reveal more the interpenetrating nature of the links of dependent origination. This radical inseparability and its implications is a theme to which we shall return later.

It is vital to understand that 'allowing' a thought, or 'welcoming' sleepiness, does not mean that the mind is dragged off by a thought into a chain of association and daydreaming, or lulled to sleep by the sensations of tiredness. Both of these movements in fact would actually involve, and be a result of, craving – the mind being hooked by a thought, clinging to thought, or to sleepiness and the craving to sleep. Allowing the experience of a thought, or the experience of the sensations of tiredness, to arise, means instead that craving's push and pull with these phenomena is reduced. Without the necessary clinging, the mind is not dragged off.

More About the Second *Dukkha* Method

All these various means of relaxing the clinging can of course be combined, and there are other possibilities too. Experimentation is always key. As do many of those that we are exploring, this way of looking requires practice to develop a feel and a skill for it.

Settling the citta

In this connection, two more general points that have already been made are worth reiterating. They will apply here as they do to the cultivation of almost all the practices in this book. First, our skill and confidence with any way of looking usually builds gradually. And it is usually most helpful if the potential of a way of looking with respect to body sensations and grosser objects that are easier to work with is developed first, and then built on as a base. Second, these ways of looking go better for the most part when there is a certain degree of *samādhi*.

On occasion, however, when the mind is in a state of preoccupation or distraction that involves lots of thoughts, it may sometimes be possible to work with this state more directly, rather than having to shift to a practice such as the breath or *mettā* with the intention of quieting and steadying the *citta*. One possibility is to pay attention to the whole body and the physical sensations that accompany and reflect this busy or turbulent state of mind. Often there can be then, for example, something like a slightly unpleasant buzzing sensation in the body. (This includes the actual head, but it may be anywhere.) Sustaining attention on these physical sensations and simply *allowing* them to be however they are, and to change, can be very helpful. As explained in Chapter 7, this would constitute a simplification of the attention, and so would simplify the whole experience. It would also pacify the reactivity of aversion to these sensations that is actually part of sustaining the thought-thick *citta* state, thus potentially allowing the whole experience of agitation to deconstruct, and the *citta* to settle into more stillness and unification.

Releasing craving is actually 'doing' less

Partly because it involves a more direct softening of the relationships with phenomena, this second *dukkha* method will generally feel softer than the *anicca* practice. It should also become apparent, with respect to the concerns (mentioned in Chapter 4) that some have regarding 'doing' in meditation, that rather than a practice of doing more it is in fact a practice of doing less. Clinging is actually something we do. In this way of looking, releasing clinging, we are letting go of doing. It is only that we have deep habits of clinging that we are unaware of, and letting them go feels unfamiliar at first and takes a little work. Doing so involves, however, less doing than our normal state of *citta* involves, left to itself to follow its habitual impulses. This may not initially be obvious, but for the sake of understanding fabrication more fully it is important that it becomes clear.

Both wider and more specifically directed attention are necessary

At times, sensitivity to the relationship with phenomena may be supported by working with a slightly more spacious awareness. When attention is less completely funnelled into an object, we can usually notice more easily other aspects of what is occurring in the moment, including the quality of the relationship with that object. Thus even just a fractionally wider awareness may at times make it easier to be sensitive to the relationship with any particular phenomenon.

Just as with the *anicca* practice and the first *dukkha* method, though, this relaxing of the relationship with phenomena can be practised in a fashion *directed at a single phenomenon*, or with a more *spacious awareness open to the totality* and letting everything go. And in this practice, for the sake of the fullness of insight *it is crucial that both ways be developed*. Restricting practice to only one of these possibilities will limit the insights later with respect to dependent arising and emptiness.

Insights Emerging

Dukkha depends on craving

With repeated practice in this way of looking, we are more and more able to release craving, and to sustain a relationship with phenomena that attempts to let go moment to moment. As we do so, we witness and feel clearly how the sense of *dukkha* is eliminated from experience exactly to the degree that craving is calmed. Less craving, less *dukkha*. Alongside the relief and peace experienced, a fundamental insight begins to make itself clear to us, evident in all these ways of looking but perhaps more directly here. *Dukkha* depends on craving: it comes primarily from our *relationship* with experience, not from the experience itself. This is an insight that typically needs to be repeated many times for it to be assimilated enough to make a significant difference.

We begin then to see that things in themselves are not inherently problematic. They are empty of problem. The sense of problem, of *dukkha*, with respect to anything, requires a relationship of clinging with that thing. Without this it cannot arise.

What is vital in properly digesting this realization is to notice and sense, in the body and in the mind, just how craving and the *dukkha* associated with it feel; and to notice also just how it feels when craving is attenuated, and there is an experience of relative release, freedom, or relief, of even slightly more spaciousness, peace, or joy.

Deepening into subtlety

As it develops, this practice of repeatedly softening the relationship with phenomena can deepen in very lovely ways. Letting go moment to moment through this way of looking the *citta* will normally grow more calm. This is because it is actually the incessant push and pull with respect to phenomena that agitates the *citta*, and this push and pull is being somewhat pacified.

Then sometimes, just as a day with much less wind makes it easier for us to discern fainter movements of air, this relative calmness of the *citta* may allow a greater degree of sensitivity to more subtle levels of clinging, of which we had previously been unaware. It might then be possible to relax these subtler manifestations of clinging. And that may allow a further deepening of the calm of the *citta*. This subsequent level of calm may reveal levels of grasping and aversion even subtler still, which then can also potentially be softened. And so the process might go, into more and more stillness and subtlety of awareness.

To some, this might sound like a daunting process of excavating buried contraction and dissatisfaction, and suggest a journey into more and more suffering. This is not, however, what is really happening here. Nor is it how the experience usually unfolds through this way of looking. Rather, because of the depth of letting go, the repeated sense of relief that this brings, and the sensitivity of awareness that can evolve, such an exploration into *dukkha* and its release tends to open up great beauty and ease in the moment. To be sure, every meditation session won't necessarily deepen in the way described above. But whether within a single session, or more generally over time, that will be the direction of this practice, offering with it crucial possibilities of deepening insight.

Craving and the emptiness of self

In addition to making clear that *dukkha* depends on clinging, this way of looking also furnishes insights into the fabrication of self. As grasping and aversion clearly wax and wane in this practice, it becomes quite evident that the self-sense, too, is dependent on clinging. We can witness the sense of self moving up and down the continuum discussed in Chapter 11 – more or less gross, separate, solid seeming, as craving intensifies or attenuates. When there is more push and pull with regard to phenomena, this tends to fabricate more sense of self. With less clinging, less self is built.

Seeing this, we might very well ask: What is the perception of self that accords with the truth? How am I 'really'? With only a limited exposure to the way clinging and its relaxation move the self-sense up and down the spectrum, one may tend to assume, especially returned to a more normal state outside of meditation, that the more usual sense of self is the more real. With enough repeated experience this simply becomes a no longer tenable view. We begin to understand something of far-reaching significance: There is no real or objective way we are. How 'I' arise, the perceptions of my self, are dependent, empty of existing inherently.

And as this way of looking is refined yet further, and more and more subtle levels of grasping and aversion are softened, we may realize that without craving the sense of self cannot actually be constructed at all.

Taking all this in repeatedly through our meditative experiences, the normal, intuitive, and deep-seated notion of this self – as something that exists independently – is gradually undermined. We can begin to understand, palpably and first-hand, how the sense of self is a fabrication, is empty. In doing so, of course, we are also experiencing and growing accustomed to times of less construction of self.

This lessening of self-fabrication is also partly what is happening in the *anicca* practice, in regarding phenomena as 'unsatisfactory', or indeed in any of the ways of looking we will develop. Since they are ways of looking that release clinging, they also fabricate less self, because the self-sense is fabricated through clinging. Understanding what is occurring here is crucial.

To this, though, we could add a curious twist. Self-sense, we have been saying, is dependent on clinging. But clinging is dependent on self-sense. Dependent on the sense of self, there is the wanting of this or that, or the craving for something to go away. Grasping and aversion are the normal, automatic expression of the self and its self-interest. And in fact, the more constructed the sense of self, the more the grasping and aversion that result. Without a sense of self there would be no impetus to cling. Yet we have seen just now that without clinging there can be no sense of self. Which then comes first, the clinging or the self? Are they really separate things existing inherently, on their own and independently? Can we rightly even talk of a self that does not cling, or clinging that is not born of a self? This co-arising of two things in reciprocal, mutual dependency we shall return to in later chapters, since its implications for emptiness and liberation are considerable indeed.

Practice: Relaxing the relationship with phenomena

In a meditation session, as different phenomena arise, practise developing sensitivity to the presence of clinging, particularly through its expression in some sense of contraction in the body space or of the space of awareness.

See if it is possible to gently and deliberately relax that clinging, relaxing the relationship with the phenomenon clung to.

You can experiment with different means of doing this:

a) by *simply intending* to let go in relationship to that phenomenon;
b) by *relaxing the bodily contraction* that accompanies the clinging;
c) by *allowing*, *welcoming*, or *opening to* the phenomenon *as fully as possible*;
d) by *tuning in to the moment-to-moment disappearance and dissolution* of the phenomenon clung to;
e) by regarding the phenomenon as '*unsatisfactory*';
f) by *any other means* you may discover for yourself, or find in this book or elsewhere.

In order to sustain this way of looking, repeat this sensitizing to and relaxing of the relationship, over and over, as often as you become aware of any clinging.

Feel how it feels in the body and in the mind to cling, and feel the *dukkha* that clinging brings.

Feel, too, how it feels in the body and in the mind to release a degree of clinging; and feel the relative release from *dukkha* that accompanies a release of clinging.

Experiment also with sustaining a way of looking which utterly *allows* or *welcomes*, without first pausing to become aware of the relationship with objects. As phenomena arise, gently draw the attention close to them, and then, as fully as possible, try to emphasize a total allowing, or a complete welcoming of, or a wide opening to, the sense impression of that object, over and over. Let almost all the emphasis of the practice be on repeating and sustaining this quality of allowing, welcoming, or opening to whatever is present – its arising, its abiding, and its passing.

Also include an awareness of how it feels to do this.

It is very important to work at times in a way that focuses on relaxing the relationship with one phenomenon at a time; at other times working in a more open way, focused on the totality of phenomena, is helpful.

Remember to include the possibility that releasing clinging allows the *citta* to calm, so that *subtler levels of clinging can be similarly worked with.*

Alternatively, experiment at times with focusing more on any bodily experience of well-being, pleasure, or pleasant stillness that arises through this way of looking, in order to incline the *citta* towards resting in *samādhi* for a time, as explained in Chapter 5. This may be for a short while before returning to the insight way of looking, or for the rest of the session if you like.

As you practise this way of looking notice carefully variations in the perception of the self, and how the sense of self depends on the degree of clinging at any time.

§

A last point, already alluded to on occasion, needs to be mentioned again. In order to deepen insight further, it is necessary to pay careful attention in practice to the effects of this and other ways of looking not only on the sense of self and *dukkha*, as we have begun to discuss, but also on the perception of objects and on their *vedanā*, indeed on the whole realm of perception. This essential investigation we will pick up in later chapters.

14

Three More Liberating Ways of Looking: (3) – Anattā

As explained in Chapter 11, our habitual way of looking at existence, influenced by *avijjā*, involves identification with the aggregates as 'me' or 'mine'. We usually feel either that we *are* the body or the mind (or both), or we feel that they are somehow *ours, belonging to the self.* Sometimes this normal appropriation by the self is conscious, but most often it is not – it is simply and intuitively felt as part of our experience of things and of ourselves.

The Buddha taught that, for the sake of freedom, this mistaken intuition should be let go of:

> "Monks, what do you think? If a person were to carry off or burn or do as he likes with the grass, twigs, branches, and leaves here in Jeta's Grove, would the thought occur to you, 'It is us that this person is carrying off, burning, or doing with as he likes'?"
> "No, venerable sir. Why is that? Because those things are not our self, nor do they belong to our self."
> "Just so, monks, whatever is not yours: let go of it. Your letting go of it will lead to your welfare and happiness for a long time. And what is not yours? Form is not yours… *Vedanā* is not yours… Perception… Mental formations… Consciousness is not yours: let go of it. Your letting go of it will lead to your welfare and happiness for a long time."[1]

Again though, a general teaching like this needs to be translated into actual practices, ways of looking that are ways of letting go, and that can eventually

[1] MN 22.

also penetrate more deeply to uproot the *avijjā* underpinning such identification. More than just thinking, or believing, differently, we need to actually perceive differently. We need to cultivate a different perception.

Such a way of looking may in fact emerge naturally out of those we have already presented. The last two chapters discussed ways that both the *anicca* and the *dukkha* practices contribute to revealing the emptiness of the self. As well as what was explained there, however, one should also notice, in the engagement of any of these practices, another, related, aspect of the letting go that is occurring. Practising the *anicca* and *dukkha* ways of looking, there is a natural decrease, in the moment, in the degree of identification with the aggregates as 'me' or 'mine'. At least some phenomena will be perceived as unhooked, to some extent, from habitual self-appropriation. This kind of release of identification can also come about when qualities such as *mettā*, *samādhi*, or mindfulness are strong, indeed in any practice that involves some attenuation of clinging.

Then rather than appearing in the usual way as 'me' or 'belonging to me', phenomena (body sensations, or thoughts, for instance) may seem instead to be just happening, coming and going by themselves, floating in space perhaps, less tied to or referenced to the self. A wonderful sense of freedom generally accompanies this unhooking, and one realizes that, even if it is only subtle at times, it is *dukkha* to identify with anything. One can see too that any such identification is actually a kind of clinging.

Gaining at least a little familiarity with this altered perception of the aggregates is important, as it may form a helpful springboard to enter the way of looking of the third characteristic, *anattā*, more directly. At some point then, instead of waiting for this lessening of identification to come about as a result of *another* practice, it will become possible to more immediately practise sustaining a view of phenomena as 'not-self', 'not me, not mine'.

The Buddha recommended that each and all of the aggregates be regarded with the understanding: "This is not me, this is not myself, this is not what I am;" or "I am not this, this is not mine."[2] In practice, actually repeating such lengthy phrases in the mind as one views phenomena is likely to prove cumbersome and prevent the refinement of this way of looking. For we will need to be able to regard as 'not-self' phenomena that are sometimes very subtle, and often in rapid succession. We need a way of working that is more usable, more agile and artful. As with the other characteristics, you may need to experiment to find out if a very light and succinct labelling helps this way of looking. Possibilities for such quiet verbal support of this view might include moment to moment delicately labelling

[2] E.g. in MN 22, SN 22:79, SN 22:93, and SN 4:16.

phenomena as "*anattā*", "not-self", or "not me, not mine". You can also modify the way of looking by quietly voicing within, for example: "*there is* sensation", or "*there is* awareness" – that is to say, 'sensations or awareness are *just happening*' – in contradistinction to the typical, intuitive sense of phenomena as belonging to or being the self.

Developing the *Anattā* Practice

External possessions

It can be interesting to extend this way of looking to external things too, such as material possessions. You can sustain attention, in actuality or in imagination, on the house or apartment where you live, on your car perhaps, your watch, your clothes, your phone, or anything else, and recognize, whatever the conventional legal relationship with these items, that they are also, at another level, not you and not yours.

Since appropriation by the self is a kind of *papañca*, and mindfulness cuts *papañca* to some extent, such a recognition may emerge naturally from a simple sustained mindfulness on any phenomenon. Alternatively, a little reflection can be helpful. For apart from any other considerations, sooner or later you will be parted from these things – they are not ultimately attached to you; nor are they completely under your command. The relationship with them is merely a temporary social convention. Reflecting thus, sometimes the perception can shift then into another mode where it actually *perceives* these things as not ultimately belonging to you.

If you have never experienced this before, it may feel slightly disconcerting at first, but soon you can sense the delightful unburdening and spaciousness that accompanies this shift in perception. As always, the rooting of the insight is aided by opening to this sense of relief. You need not fear that irresponsibility will follow such a shift in the way of seeing, as typically we can, and naturally do, accommodate the two views – 'mine' and 'not mine' – at once. It is only that now a degree of freedom and flexibility has entered our relationship with these possessions.

We can likewise practise regarding even our loved ones – partners, friends, and family – at times in this way. Of course at one level they are ours, but not at another level, and we can play with this altered perspective. Rather than creating a sense of alienation, we actually find that such a contemplation seems to increase the feelings of love, and also the sense, for example, of spaciousness, in those relationships.

The material body

The aggregate of *rūpa*, the body as material form, should also be worked with in this manner. The body as a whole, or parts of the body (the fingernails, the hair, the teeth, the bones, the individual organs, etc.) may be focused on and deliberately viewed as *anattā*.

Again, the perspective can sometimes shift as a result of *sustaining mindfulness* – in this case *on the body as material body*. Looking intently for a while at the hand or another part of the body, for example, aware of the organic complexity of this material form, may occasionally allow a spontaneous alteration of view, so that that part of the body is seen and felt then as not-self.

As an alternative way of stimulating this non-identification one can reflect that the body arises from, and is in fact continuously formed by, the material elements it ingests from the environment. It belongs in some sense not to me but to nature, and will inevitably fall apart and dissolve back into the environment in due course.

Rather than resulting in a state of disconnection from the body, such a way of looking tends for the most part to open up a sense of beauty and mystery alongside the ease and sense of relative liberation that it delivers. Nevertheless, for some, a little *mettā* practice may be helpful – before, after, or even at the same time as regarding the body in this way. And here, again, we can realize the essential wisdom of a flexibility of view – respecting self-view at times, viewing not in terms of self at others.

Gradually expanding the range of the practice

Just like with the other characteristics, we need to gradually develop both our skill and our range in this way of looking. In beginning to learn this practice it is imperative to ascertain and *work first with the group of phenomena from which it feels easiest to disidentify*. This will vary depending on a practitioner's meditative background and also on personal differences, so that, once more, experimentation is vital.

For many, especially those whose main training is in the kinds of insight meditation that place a strong emphasis on mindfulness of the body, it is often easiest at first, naturally enough, to sustain a disidentification with the *body sensations*.

Whatever the least difficult aggregate turns out to be, once a facility with that one is established it can serve as a foundation from which to expand the range of the *anattā* practice. Step by step, other phenomena can be included – separately, or at the same time – in the way of looking. Playing thus, discovering and consolidating, progressing by building gradually on the foundations of what feels easier, this meditation deepens and gains power, and much unnecessary frustration in practice can be avoided.

And although there is no universally shared order of readiness in which a widening of the range of this way of looking proceeds, some aggregates are usually more difficult to regard as not-self than others. As mentioned above, *the materiality of the body* may feel straightforward, or it may require a little more sensitivity in the approach. *Vedanā* can typically be included quite soon after one is able to dwell for a while experiencing the freedom that comes from disidentifying with body sensations. Similar to what was explained in Chapter 12, a spacious awareness that embraces body sensations and sounds – and in this case views body sensations as not-self – often forms a helpful platform to begin to view *thoughts* also as not-self. *Emotions* may be regarded this way too of course, although depending on the emotion this can be experienced as more or less straightforward, and will at times demand a sensitivity and wisdom in the approach. *Perceptions* and *intentions* may be more subtle, and so may require more *samādhi* or more practice.

Consciousness

Letting go of the identification with *consciousness* is generally much more subtle, and will not be possible until a facility has been more firmly established in letting go of identification with a wider range of the grosser aggregates. Such a breadth of foundation usually takes some time to develop, but once it is there, it is a much smaller step to practise non-identification with awareness.

Sometimes a practitioner may hold a consciously articulated view that identifies self with 'the witness', or with awareness in any of its manifestations; oftentimes, though, such identification happens intuitively, automatically, and without recognition. Either way, we need eventually to be able to let go of all and any identification with consciousness, and know the freedom and insight that this opens.

Learning to view any perception also as 'a moment of *knowing*', rather than only as an *object*, as explained in Chapter 12, it may then be possible to view consciousness as *anattā*. Whether holding the sense of awareness with some intensity or in a more relaxed way, more narrowly in relation to one object or with a sense of more spaciousness to it, this knowing can be viewed as 'not me, not mine', this moment of knowing as 'just happening'. Instead of as self, or as belonging to self, we can regard any awareness through a lens that sees simply: '*There is* knowing (of this or that)'.

Even having established a foundation in practising non-identification with the other aggregates, this usually takes some practice and patience. It may be that it is easier to disidentify with certain sense consciousnesses than with others, and this will differ between practitioners. Experiment with them all. Often for quite a while at first there may be just brief moments when the identification with consciousness is dropped. Still, these moments, when identification with the aggregates is extremely minimal, if it is there at all, can be immensely significant and powerfully fruitful.

Even more subtle phenomena

Perhaps even more subtle than this is the possibility of becoming aware of the moment-to-moment *intention to pay attention* to any object. Such subtle intention will become apparent most easily when the *citta* is relatively still, and the attention is relatively steady on some thing. (Here, once again, states of *samādhi* can be highly useful.) Then this specific intention too can be deliberately seen as *anattā*.

As with the practice of seeing consciousness as not-self, disidentifying with the intention to pay attention acts as a particularly potent letting go at a very deep level in the *citta*. Despite its subtlety, therefore, and the delicacy and patience it may require to develop it, such a refinement of practice has the potential to open astonishing insights and thus to bear tremendous fruit.

The same might be said of the very *activity of regarding things as not-self*, and also the moment-to-moment *intention* to do so. These can in fact be viewed as *anattā* too, without any danger of an infinite regression.

Some Tips and Reflections about *Anattā* Meditation

As before with the *anicca* and *dukkha* practices, we can work sustaining attention and the *anattā* view on one phenomenon, on one sense sphere, or on the totality of experience. Making sure too to include what is experienced as pleasant, unpleasant, or more neutral is important. And again it can be interesting to begin to notice also how this way of looking affects the quality of experiences.

Two possible perceptions

Regarding things as not-self, there are – at least *initially* in practice – two different ways that the perception of phenomena can open up, and these should be distinguished at this point. Abiding in meditation, sustaining a simple and direct view of 'not me, not mine' with regard to all phenomena will, sooner or later, likely result in a perception of them as arising *out of nothingness*, floating in space somehow, and disappearing back into this nothingness. This important perception and its variations we will return to discuss in the next chapter. It is one way that things can appear with less self-referencing, more disengaged from the self.

Alternatively, one could see that phenomena arise, in the moment, not from or as the self, but from a coming together of many, even infinite conditions, none of which are self either. This is another way that things can be experienced with less self-referencing and appropriation by the self.

It might be pointed out that, on a conventional level, it would be more accurate to say and perceive that phenomena arise not out of nothingness but out of an infinite web of conditions. However, for now let us just say that these are both immensely helpful ways of seeing phenomena, and that both should be cultivated. The direct practice of *anattā*, as described in this chapter, will lead most commonly at first to a perception of phenomena arising out of some kind of space or nothingness, and dissolving back into that space. For our purposes now, as a significant step on the journey of insight, this sort of perception can certainly be trusted and developed.

Skilful responses to aversion and grasping

As with almost any practice, it is of course possible that grasping or aversion sometimes creep in unnoticed. The ways aversion in particular may distort the process can be quite subtle. If you sense at any time that there is even a slight pushing away, or wish to be rid of, any phenomenon, it can be useful to remember that, as an attitude of holy disinterest, regarding things as *anattā* means that they actually *can* be there. Seen from the perspective of *anattā*, since they are not-self their arising and existence, whether they disappear or remain, is not a problem to me. And likewise, with respect to any lovely experiences that might open up as a result of the way of looking, this attitude of holy disinterest supported by the *anattā* view is also one of the skilful options available to us. In regarding things more wholeheartedly as 'not-self' then, the craving that ordinarily accompanies whatever is pleasant or unpleasant can be released or reduced.

As the *anattā* practice develops, a further possibility becomes available as a skilful response to the presence of clinging. We can actually view the clinging itself – the very grasping, aversion, and even identification – as 'not me, not mine' in that moment. For reasons that will be explained more fully in later chapters, this seeing of the movement and force of clinging as 'not-self' may relax or dissolve it, at least to some extent.

As always with these insight ways of looking, we can ascertain whether we are engaging the view in the moment by the sense of release that it opens. If this is not present, at least in some measure, it may simply be that the view has not truly shifted from our habitual one into the *anattā* way of looking. Or, more particularly, it may be that some degree of grasping, aversion, or identification remains in operation then, with more force than the letting go that is supported by the not-self view. In that case we can gently employ one of the suggestions outlined above for skilfully working with it, and so enable the practice to open and deepen at that time.

The curious problem of the 'kink in the carpet'

One particularly insidious manifestation of clinging that can enter the *anattā* practice in sometimes subtle ways is worth mentioning. Many times when sustaining this way of looking on one of the aggregates, you may notice that the self-identification has simply moved elsewhere temporarily. While viewing body sensations, for example, as not-self, there may well be identification with awareness, or even with the very doing of the practice itself – the intention to regard things as *anattā* – or indeed with anything else.

This is actually not a problem at all. However, on noticing it, practitioners can very commonly then create and become ensnared in what we might call the 'kink-in-the-carpet predicament'. Just as a person trying to flatten out a kink in a wall-to-wall carpet that is slightly too big for the room it is in might step on the observed kink here at first, then spot it form over there, so step on it there, and then there, and there, and so on without end wherever a kink reappears, so we might find ourselves erasing self from this place of identification, only to notice it arising elsewhere. Moving to that place to disidentify, the identification pops up in yet another location. Much like a dog chasing its own tail, without wisdom this probably futile endeavour can quickly become frustrating.

It is crucial to address this movement, for here the thrust of the practice has been subverted. We may have slipped into a mode of trying to obliterate the sense of self, which is subtly, yet significantly, different than a mode that attempts to sustain a view of this or that phenomenon as 'not me, not mine'. The former will surely end up in frustration; the latter opens over time into a sense of more and more freedom and subtlety. And although it may well be that, as the range of the *anattā* practice is extended into a disidentification with more subtle phenomena, a dropping of all self-view and a dissolving of all self-sense may be experienced, that is not the primary intention of the *anattā* practice.

Re-aligning the understanding behind the intention of the way of looking is vital if it slips like this. Knowing that it is not necessary, at that moment, to try to eliminate whatever other identification or sense of self is residually present, it can also be important to enjoy whatever sense of release arises from viewing even a limited range of phenomena as not-self. In this way we are gradually consolidating an ability to view this or that aggregate as not-self. Certainly this flexibility of view can eventually be extended, but what is in fact more important in the process, alongside the sense of relative freedom in the moment, are the insights that such letting go brings.

Engendering the perception of not-self

For some, the *anattā* practice may prove the most difficult of the three characteristics to master and may take a little while to develop. Even if so, it is easily worth the investment. I sometimes think, in fact, that one of the most precious skills a human being can learn is this way of looking at things as 'not me, not mine'. The joy, freedom, and understanding it can open are profound indeed.

On the occasions when this *anattā* way of looking does feel less workable, there is certainly the option to shift to another practice – for example, *mettā, samādhi,* basic mindfulness, or the *anicca* or *dukkha* ways of looking – which, as it deepens, might make it easier to perceive the aggregates then as not-self. Continuing in that other practice for a while, this more naturally arising perception of things as 'not me, not mine' can begin to gain some strength and stability, and eventually be gently encouraged and more deliberately sustained, so easing into a more direct *anattā* practice. In this way, these other approaches might be used as entry points or springboards from which to gain familiarity with the perception of not-self, until it is more immediately accessible as a shift of view.

Strengthening the not-self view

Especially when it is first glimpsed thus through another practice, developing this 'not-self' way of looking usually feels relatively straightforward. Regarding some phenomena as 'not me, not mine', however, can occasionally give pause for reflection. A memory, for instance, that arises is unlikely to be considered as 'me', but, even more perhaps than with other kinds of thought, it would seem more obvious to regard it as 'mine' than as 'not mine'. At the times when the *anattā* way of looking has a strong momentum this issue is probably not pressed, since then it might seem quite easy to subsume phenomena into the view and simply to regard any memories that arise as 'not mine'. At other times we might think, "These memories don't arise in someone else, they are particular to this person – me – so they must be 'mine'."

As the Buddha pointed out,[3] part of the reason the aggregates should not be viewed as truly belonging to the self is because they are not completely under the self's control. And such an understanding – evident in many processes of body and mind – certainly comes into this meditative lens of *anattā*.

In addition though, (and more helpful in regard to such questions as that above of memories) it is possible to include implicitly in the view of 'not mine' the comprehension that there is no inherently existing self as an entity that could own the aggregates or anything at all. The *anattā* view would then also be informed by the silent subtext: "This phenomenon is 'not mine', because there is not *really* anyone, any real self, to whom this phenomenon could belong."

Such an understanding of the emptiness of the self has been strongly suggested by insights emerging in particular from the *dukkha* ways of looking, but also, though less thoroughly, from the *anicca* practice.[4] It may well be that from these insights, originating in either practice, enough conviction in the absence of a real self has grown to enable this more complete view of 'not mine'.

But it may also be that this realization of the emptiness of a self that could own anything has not yet reached a point of thorough conviction for a practitioner. Then one possibly very helpful way of filling out and deepening the *anattā* way of looking is the practice of the sevenfold reasoning (see Chapter 17). Once some confidence and meditative facility has been developed with that analysis, it can be easily incorporated into the *anattā* practice if needed or desired. Comprehensively establishing, to our own satisfaction, that there cannot be any such entity as an

---

[3] SN 22:59.

[4] See the discussions in Chapters 13 and 12, respectively.

independently existing self that might own any phenomenon, this understanding can then be used to inject a certainty and greater power into the view of 'not mine'.[5] To be sure, the potency of the *anattā* way of looking will evolve on its own with practice, and is also aided by the cultivation of *samādhi* and *mettā*, but this is an important example of the way the various emptiness practices can support each other and work together to provide more rigorous and penetrating insight.

Working with the Sense of Release in Insight Practice

As mentioned, when employed as ways of looking, the three characteristics have great power in practice. Since they are ways of letting go, of releasing clinging, they will naturally lead to a sense of freedom, relief, and release, of joy, peace, stillness, or spaciousness, as they are engaged. When such qualities are opened in meditation, we are presented in that moment with three basic options:

1. We may simply acknowledge that these feelings and perceptions have arisen in the *citta*, while continuing to regard as *anicca, dukkha,* or *anattā*, some other phenomenon that is present.

2. As described in Chapter 5, we can begin to pay more attention to the quality of well-being in the body and mind that accompanies this release – with the intention of inclining the *citta* more into a state of *samādhi*. It is possible to place more emphasis then on enjoying, focusing on, pervading, and resting in this sense of well-being, than on the moment-to-moment repetition of the insight view with which we had, up to then, been working.

   Sometimes this sense of well-being, which can manifest and be experienced in many different ways, will not seem particularly prominent. It may be then that as we tune attention into it, it begins to *filter out* from the mix of perceptions, so that it does grow and become more prominent. Allowing or gently encouraging it to spread so that it fills the body and the *citta*, and absorbing the attention into it, there is then the possibility of resting in and enjoying it more fully.

---

[5] When developed, the sevenfold reasoning practice actually has the power to dissolve all reifying views of self, so that, if skilfully drawn into the *anattā* practice, it can in fact potentially also eliminate any hidden or residual self-view in the moment.

If desired, we can return after a while to the insight way of looking. Or we can choose to continue prioritizing the quality of *samādhi* until the end of the meditation session.

This graceful movement of the *citta* between emphasizing insight ways of looking and emphasizing *samādhi* is very helpful in the maturing of many important elements of practice.[6] However, the shift in emphasis it involves is actually only a matter of degree, for we can continue with the insight way of looking to some extent as we enjoy and open to the *samādhi*. With practice we realize we can modulate, in the moment, the balance of the relative intensities between the focus on the sustained way of looking and the focus on the sense of well-being.

3. We may sustain the insight way of looking, moment to moment, on the very perception of well-being, in any of its manifestations – regarding it too as *anicca*, *dukkha*, or *anattā*.

   Through playful experimentation, we will eventually find that this third approach too allows a gradation of emphasis – between enjoying the sense of release, on the one hand, and subjecting it to any particular view of insight, on the other.

§

Practice: Seeing what is external as 'not mine'

Choose a number of your material possessions for contemplation as 'not mine'. Take some time to hold each within some intensity of attention. Notice if and how the sense of ownership is affected when the mindfulness is relatively strong and the mind is less taken by thoughts about the object.

See if it is possible to *deliberately* view these things, one by one, as 'not mine'. If, through holding any object in mindfulness or through some other practice, you have

---

[6] Whether it is nourished, as described here, through skilful manipulation in insight ways of looking, or through focusing steadily on some object such as the breath, the body, or *mettā*, remember also how especially supportive it is to the deepening of insight to devote a very generous proportion of practice time (fifty percent is certainly not too much) to the cultivation of *samādhi* alongside the various insight practices.

glimpsed this dropping of the sense of ownership at times, you may find you can gently nudge the mind back into that way of looking.

Notice any emotional responses to this way of seeing.

Bring a loved one into your mind's eye, and hold the image or sense of them in attention with mindfulness. Notice whatever feelings arise. When you feel ready, practise shifting the view to seeing them free of the construct of truly being 'my friend (partner, child, parent, etc.)'. Carefully notice again any effects this has on your feelings and your perceptions of them.

If you would like to, you and a loved one could also practise this together, sitting facing each other and attempting, moment to moment, to sustain a way of looking at each other as 'not mine, not my… ' Afterwards, take some time to share with each other your experience of this exercise.

Practice: Regarding the aggregates as *anattā*, moment to moment

Perhaps, based on experience with the other practices, you have a sense of which aggregate is the easiest for you to regard as *anattā* moment to moment. If you are not sure, take some time in meditation to experiment and find out. (If you are still unsure, starting with the body sensations is usually a good bet.)

For all, or a substantial part, of a meditation session, practise sustaining a view of this aggregate as 'not me, not mine'. (If it seems difficult, remember that you can always shift to another way of looking, such as the *anicca* or *dukkha* practices or even simple mindfulness practice, *mettā*, or *samādhi*, and let the perception of 'not-self' arise out of that, until you can sustain the *anattā* view more immediately.)

Notice how this letting go feels.

When some feeling such as peace or release comes from this way of looking, at times simply let yourself acknowledge it while continuing to regard your chosen phenomena as *anattā*.
At other times, see if you can regard this experience too as *anattā*.
And at other times, practise allowing yourself to rest in the experience, fully enjoying it, and learning to consolidate it, thus leaning the *citta* into more of a state of *samādhi*, as discussed.

Once you are generally able to sustain a view of that chosen aggregate as not-self, and experience a sense of some freedom doing so, add another aggregate, or element of an aggregate, to the contemplation, and practise until that too can be sustained in the view.

As explained, gradually you can add more and more. It is possible to work individually with any phenomenon, or to include together in this way of looking a pre-determined range of phenomena, and to work with a more spacious awareness.

(For some practitioners, it will not suit the temperament to work so systematically through the aggregates in any order. If this is the case, you still need to make sure that all phenomena are eventually included, and the list of the aggregates is useful then simply as a checklist.[7])

If it feels helpful, once you have some meditative facility with the sevenfold reasoning (as explained in Chapter 17), practise incorporating it into the *anattā* way of looking to give it fuller power.

Notice how any release of identification affects the sense of self.

After gaining some familiarity with this practice, begin to pay attention also to the ways in which viewing phenomena as *anattā* affects other aspects of the perception of experience.

---

[7] In addition to the aggregates, the Buddha sometimes taught another system of division as a tool for meditative letting go. Based on the six senses, it usually comprised eighteen constituents: the six internal sense bases, their six respective phenomenal objects (the six external sense objects), and the six consciousnesses based on each. Some formulations omit the consciousnesses; others may add the respective contact, *vedanā*, and even craving and clinging, in each sense sphere. AN 10:60 explicitly describes using this as a framework for the *anattā* practice:

> And what is the perception of not-self? Here a monk – having gone to the forest, to the foot of a tree, or to an empty building – discriminates thus: 'The eye is not-self, forms are not-self; the ear... sounds... ; the nose... aromas... ; the tongue... flavours... ; the body... tactile sensations... ; the mind... things cognizable with the mind are not-self.' Thus he remains focused on not-selfness with regard to the six inner and outer sense bases. This is called the perception of not-self.

(That the respective consciousnesses are also to be included in developing this *anattā* way of looking is clearly implied in SN 35:85.)

Whether one uses the structure of the aggregates or that of the constituents, a thoroughness of disidentification is what is eventually aimed at in practice. Approached in either way, the fundamental intention in engaging the way of looking is finally the same: *nothing at all should be clung to as 'me' or 'mine'*. And by means of such practices, ultimately all conceivable self-views are to be seen through.

Of Fear and Loathing in Emptiness Practices

As well as the joy, peace, and sense of liberation that it opens, it is quite common for any way of looking that effects profound letting go to stimulate also a degree of fear at first, or at times when its practice moves to different levels. This is certainly not always the case, but when it is, often it is simply that we are unfamiliar with the new territory of perception opened up through the letting go, and unsure if we can trust it.

We have discussed how practices such as these using the three characteristics fabricate less self and less *dukkha*. There are also other significant changes in perception that deep letting go produces. The world of things can seem to lose its solidity, for instance, and a sense of empty, sometimes vast, expansiveness can often open up.[8] Mostly, however, we are accustomed to a sense of self that feels relatively solid and separate – our experience traversing only a small range at the grosser end of the spectrum of self-sense. The world of things too ordinarily appears quite solid. And we are likewise usually unaccustomed to states of great expansiveness. Thus, in these more open states of less fabrication it may be, perhaps even without realizing it, that there is some feeling of being deprived of the familiar landmarks of experience and self, and an inability at first to get our bearings. It may also be for some that a state of less self-fabrication, as a felt loss or disappearing of the sense of self, is interpreted as an annihilation, and brings up associations with death and dying that trigger fear. There are a few things that can be helpful here.

First, it is important to remember that we can retain a sense of being in control of the process in meditation. We can decide to put the brakes on and explore these states of less fabrication more slowly, if that feels more comfortable. Though it is anyway extremely rare for consciousness to get stuck in a state of altered perception, if we do not feel ready we can always, for example, shift to another practice that is more familiar, such as *mettā*, or simply end the meditation, open our eyes and do something else.

We can also choose, more than might initially be obvious, how much we let go into any state, and how long we linger there. Perhaps at first we let go only a little into the space or perception that has opened up, and only for a short period – just dipping into and out of it. Over time, we naturally become more accustomed to a certain level of expansiveness, for instance, and learn gradually that we can trust it. We can play with letting go into it slowly more and more, until it holds absolutely no fear for us,

---

[8] These, and other, changes in perception that typically occur with deep insight and letting go are in fact highly significant and indispensable for a more profound understanding of fabrication and emptiness. In Chapters 15 and 19 we will begin to discuss them in depth.

and we are able to let go there with confidence and complete abandon. What was a source of trepidation will then have become a delicious and profound resource.

Second, as mentioned in Chapter 5, *samādhi* and *mettā* have a very important function with respect to fear: in colouring consciousness with positive qualities that soften the fear-oriented perception; and also in providing, in ways that generally feel safe, a parallel gradual familiarization with states of less fabrication. Once again then, it is helpful to remember that increasing the proportion of *mettā* or *samādhi* in the mix is always a possibility.

Third, we can help the familiarization process through the way we direct the attention. For it is typically the case that when fear arises in meditation, the attention is pulled into that fear in a way that is not helpful. And the sense of loveliness that usually comes with letting go is then not noticed. When there is fear, therefore, it is in fact often possible to look with a slightly more spacious perspective, and recognize that *two* things – fear *and* some kind of sense of loveliness – are present. Rather than being sucked into the fear, we can gently incline the attention toward experiencing, and enjoying, the feelings of well-being, particularly as they are manifesting in the sense of the subtle body space. Such a move pulls the attention out of a probably unhelpful spinning in the fear. But it also helps in a deeper way, because then the very feeling of well-being begins to work, on the bodily level, to reassure us that we can trust the letting go. The more often we do this, the more trust develops.

And just as with anything else, the way we look at the fear, our view of it, makes a difference. It may on occasion be very helpful to regard an experience of fear that arises in meditation through the very insight lens of whatever way of looking we are practising at the time. It is then simply another phenomenon to view in this way, and to let go of. Regarding it thus will often have a liberating and transforming effect.

As we will see in some depth in later chapters, the views and way of looking in any moment can actually determine what experiences arise. Sometimes, for various reasons, a practitioner *expects* dread, terror, disgust, or depression to come with deep meditation, even interpreting emotions like these as signs of progress, as necessary stages to pass through in the progress of insight. This very view and expectation, though, may in fact be stimulating the arising of such feelings. It needs, therefore, to be experimented with, and investigated.[9]

---

[9] A related possibility can frequently be the case too, and likewise requires open-minded investigation. The arising of such states of disgust (or even horror) at phenomenal existence may in fact simply be reflecting the presence in the moment of strong aversion, rather than deep insight. And this aversion – perhaps even disguised now as insight (if there is a clinging to the kinds of assumptions mentioned above about how practice should unfold) – may actually be the primary support for these difficult states and their continuation.

Three Characteristics: Three Avenues of Insight Unfolding

In addition to this effect of assumptions and expectations, we should point out too that the different practices often tend to develop in different ways. The *anattā* way of looking will likely unfold a different progression of experiences and insights than the *anicca* practice, for example. In fact, the *anicca* practice, although enormously helpful, actually has limits built into it, since through its very view it tends to reinforce a subtle degree of reification – at least at the levels of elemental, momentary phenomena and of time.[10] Such reification has significant consequences. It will operate in this way of looking as one of the factors that will keep fabricating, solidifying, and holding in place, these particular levels of perception. And it will probably contribute to delivering feelings like dread and disgust with regard to things. Then for as long as they are being unwittingly fabricated thus, these feelings, which are clearly *dukkha*, will without doubt continue to arise.

It turns out, though, that the emptiness practices which are not so based on *anicca* – for instance, the *anattā* way of looking and the second *dukkha* method, as well as many others – for the most part do not issue in such emotions and experiences. One of the main reasons for this is that since, as we shall see, they more easily reveal the emptiness, the unreality, of all phenomena, the fear and horror of endlessly losing seemingly real things is significantly undermined. Whether it is the self, a particular thing, or fleeting momentary phenomena in general, when we know that, *really*, nothing truly existent is being lost, neither their apparent impermanence nor their dissolving in meditation is felt as a problem. And when through practice we understand more just how perceptions are fabricated, this too punctures the delusion that keeps us in the grip of its spells and that keeps the recycling of this or that experience in motion.

For insight, as we have defined it, includes an understanding of how experience in general is fabricated. Deep insight eventually reveals that *all* ways of looking are involved in the fabrication of perception, and it comprehends well how different ways of looking fabricate different perceptions and fabricate to differing degrees. This, therefore, is what must be investigated. If the way of looking or practising itself is actually fabricating certain perceptions and feelings, such as repeating cycles of difficult experiences, a practitioner needs to find ways of realizing *that* this fabricating is happening, and of understanding *how* it happens. Any map of the progress of insight that does not address and include an understanding of the dependent arising and fabrication of all experience – and in

---

[10] We will explore and explicate this more fully in Chapters 23, 26, and 27.

particular an understanding of its own ways of looking as fabrications that fabricate – is grossly incomplete.

Although without the particular limitations that the *anicca* practices can carry, some meditators find that they eventually arrive at a stage where the second *dukkha* method feels limited too in its own way. Not for everyone but for some, as clinging is released at deeper and deeper levels, the practice may reach a point where any residual grasping seems too subtle to notice or to release. If that sense occurs, supplementation with another insight way of looking can then offer a profitable way forward.

Of the three characteristics, perhaps the *anattā* practice is the most powerful, and the one that can be taken most deeply. It is applicable more easily to the most subtle phenomena without the tendency the *anicca* practice has of reifying and solidifying time and momentary phenomena. But alongside these comments we must repeat what was stated in Chapter 13: all three characteristics are enormously helpful as ways of looking, and a practitioner should develop the one that brings the most freedom in his or her practice, as well as at least one of the others.

In time it is possible, when desired, to sustain a view of phenomena through a lens that combines all three ways of looking implicitly at once – repeatedly letting them go moment to moment because they are *anicca, dukkha, and anattā*. Naturally this can form a very skilful way of looking in itself. Care should be taken, however, to develop the three practices separately, retaining some clear distinction between approaches so that they are available as unique ways of looking if desired. If they become enmeshed all into one for the practitioner before each has been developed and become familiar, and before their different avenues of insight have been journeyed down somewhat, much of the potential for refinement and deepening of insight will be lost, and the practice may stagnate to a certain extent.

§

Through the cultivation of such practices, we can soon appreciate how the Buddha's teaching on the three characteristics offers more than simply a statement about existence for us to believe; and that it also involves more than just advice about how to live, or how, generally or philosophically, to consider the world. When used as instructions for meditation we find these characteristics develop into three powerfully liberating ways of looking. Most significantly though, as we will see, they gradually lay bare deeper insights about the nature of reality, the fabrication and the emptiness of things. And it is this understanding that eventually opens up the deepest freedom.

15

Emptiness and Awareness (1)

We have already drawn attention to the fact that when there is a sustained looking at phenomena through the lenses of the three characteristics, both less *dukkha* and less self are then fabricated in the moment. We have pointed out as well that it is crucial to pay attention to, grow accustomed to, and at times enjoy, these changes and how they feel, and essential also to comprehend how they come about, and what they imply.

As practice with the three characteristics develops though, it is not only that the self-sense and the sense of *dukkha* die down. The experience of phenomena, too, can open up in a variety of significant ways. These various alterations in the perception of phenomena are in fact related, and they can provide vital platforms for further empowering the practice and deepening insight. Some of these transformations are indispensable to explore and understand if dependent arising is to be properly understood. Others, though not necessary for every practitioner, can be extremely beautiful openings of experience and offer profound resources for the being. A familiarity with them can also be important for mapping out and understanding the meditative territory at deeper levels.

A Vastness of Awareness

Practising the kinds of release of clinging that any of the three characteristics views involve, one very common possibility is that the sense of consciousness begins to become more noticeable. Through an attitude of holy disinterest, less entranced by and entangled in the particulars of phenomena, a perception of awareness as a vast and clear space in which all appearances are contained may naturally begin to emerge. In contrast to the habitual sense of consciousness as somehow 'over here' (perhaps in the head) directed toward some object 'over there', consciousness can now seem less localized, more pervading, like the open space of the sky. It can seem to hold within it the arising, the abiding, and the dissolving of phenomena, effortlessly accommodating whatever is present. In this vastness there is plenty of space for every thing, making it even easier to let go of any need to control or interfere in the play of appearances. Sensations, sounds, thoughts and images, indeed all phenomena, can seem to float free in this open consciousness, like fireflies flickering in the blackness of night, like clouds in the wide sky, moments of experience appearing and disappearing in the vastness of awareness. And just as physical space seems undisturbed by what appears within it, so the space of awareness rejects nothing, holds and embraces everything, no matter what it is. A meditator can tune into this sense of the space and use it to deepen the letting go.

As it opens and becomes more steady, it can seem more and more that all phenomena appear to *emerge out of this space* of awareness, abide for a time, and then *disappear back into it*, while the space itself can have a sense of profound stillness, of imperturbability, to it. Like shooting stars, or like fireworks, bursting into view against an immeasurable backdrop of night sky, phenomena live for a while and then they fade back into the space. Seeing experiences this way allows one even more fully to let them all arise and fade; and to *let them all belong to the space of awareness*.

As the letting go deepens further, and this more open perception consolidates, phenomena may seem to recede somewhat, while the space of awareness as a kind of ground of being can begin to become even more prominent. Gradually attuning more to the felt sense of it, various subtly delightful qualities that seem inherent in the space can be appreciated.[1] It may seem to sparkle with a joyous aliveness, for instance, or express an unshakeable and unfathomable peace; there may be a quality of eternity, of timelessness, that it seems to possess; it may appear luminous, or be radiant somehow, or it can be dark, imbued with mystery and a sense of the infinite. All this and more, if it is present, it is important to explore and appreciate, and be touched by too.

---

[1] Very occasionally, on first opening to such a space it may strike a practitioner instead as somewhat cold and barren, and so be a little off-putting. In relation to this we have already stressed the benefits of including a healthy dose of *samādhi* or *mettā* in the mix of practices, and of playing responsively with that mix. Here it is also a matter of time: just as on entering a darkened room the eyes take a little time to adjust to the relative darkness. Although the first impression may be that there is nothing in the room at all, gradually one begins to be able to discern a variety of objects in the darkness. So too here the receptivity begins to adjust and a discernment of a range of more subtle qualities manifest in the space is possible. It is also an issue of familiarity. An initial reaction of fear, for instance, may colour and dampen the qualities of the space; with more familiarity and less fear the space begins to reveal more. Either way, one soon realizes that such spaces are not in fact bereft of warmth or a whole host of lovely qualities. In due course we shall return to this theme of the perception of qualities such as love to explore it further and at increasing depth.

In time, phenomena may also start to *lose their sense of substantiality*, appearing less solid in the moment. They can seem to be merely *impressions in awareness*, something like reflections on the surface of a lake. Then even any image, or sense, of self, or of anything else that appears, can be regarded as just an impression in awareness too. The stillness and space of awareness can also begin to pervade and permeate everything that arises, so that *all things seem to be made of the same 'stuff', the same ethereal 'substance', as awareness*. Then it matters even less what appearances arise. Just like the ocean, whether it is the waves on the surface or the still depths, all is water, and all waves dissolve back into the sea.

With less distinction thus being perceived between inner and outer, and between phenomena and awareness, there may naturally be *a sense of oneness*, of unity of all things, that emerges, perhaps gradually, at this point. Every thing appears then, mystically, as having the nature of awareness. And this awareness seems to have very little to do with the personality; it seems more as if one has opened into something universal, shared and available to all. Allowed and supported by this sense of oneness and universality, a perception of love may also arise organically and permeate experience.

Supporting this kind of openness

This sense of a vastness of awareness I have been describing is one possible direction of transformation of perception that may occur through practising with the three characteristics. It may also emerge naturally, and become more accessible, from deeper states of *samādhi*. Perhaps you have already experienced such openings in your meditation. If so, as they emerge in the course of practice they can be allowed and encouraged, to aid a more potent letting go, until they become more available through familiarity. You may also gently seek to repeat them, to incline the perception back to them, and consolidate them as a new base for insight. With repeated practice, such perceptions can become relatively easy to access and can eventually be re-established fairly quickly simply by remembering them.

It is possible, too, to encourage this kind of opening even before it has emerged in meditation.

- One way this can be done is by working with a more spacious attention from the beginning. We have stressed the importance of practising the various ways of looking both with an attention focused more narrowly on one object at a time, and also with a wider attention, inclusive more of the totality of phenomena that arise and pass. Practising the three characteristics in this latter mode, however, will much more likely support the opening of a sense of space as we are now describing it.

- Open listening meditation can be helpful too therefore. Since sounds may come from all different directions and distances, paying attention for a while to the totality of sounds, and allowing them to come and go, may naturally aid in the awareness opening up more spaciously.

- You should experiment practising with the eyes open as well as closed. Paying attention to the sense of visual space – particularly, at first, to a more vast space such as the sky, or the space of a large room – can also greatly assist an expansion of the sense of the awareness. This attention to visual space or to the totality of sound may well be profitable by itself, but in conjunction with the three characteristics views, it may be more helpful.

- Sometimes a perception of open space may be kick-started by *imagining* it. You can, for example, imagine the mind like a vast, clear sky containing and allowing all phenomena within it. With repetition this will gradually become less strained and feel more authentic.

As has been stressed, eventually we want to understand just what is happening, and why, when perception opens and changes in such ways. We will return to this question shortly, but let us say a little right now that may be helpful.

The sense of space that opens up through practice may be vast, or even infinite, at times. The immensity of it cannot be forced, however, and should not be regarded as the goal here. For at any time it is actually a sustained diminishment of craving that is most fundamental in allowing and supporting this perception of a vastness of awareness. And anyway, as we will later see, this opening to a vastness of awareness is not in fact necessary for insight to deepen.

When it is experienced repeatedly though, it can be discerned through observation and inquiry that the three characteristics views, a sense of spacious awareness, and the factor of equanimity all mutually reinforce each other. Since the three characteristics views are ways of letting go, they lead to equanimity, which is, by definition, a calming of the push and pull of the mind with regard to phenomena. The calmness of equanimity can, in turn, allow the three characteristics to be seen more easily. This calming of craving can also tend naturally to open spaciousness at times, because it effectively includes some releasing of the contraction of mind that is typically involved in craving. And as described above and in Chapter 6, spaciousness too can support equanimity and letting go.

It is possible to take advantage of this mutual reinforcement in practice, and use any of these elements to feed the others. We can use the three characteristics as ways to open up a sense of space; and conversely, we can encourage a sense of space to assist both the letting go and the view of the three characteristics. We can eventually use it also as a platform for further insight.

Practice: A vastness of awareness

(Experiment with different approaches to the following practice. You may want to employ the three characteristics ways of looking for a while in a session before encouraging the perception to open in the ways suggested below. Or you may let go entirely of any deliberate use of the three characteristics. Alternatively, you may incorporate them into the meditation as much or as little as feels helpful in supporting the opening to the space of awareness.[2])

In a meditation session, once a little calm is established, settle for a while with an open attention that allows the coming and going of the totality of body sensations in the whole body. As you do so, be aware too of the sense of space, and perhaps stillness, around and within the body.

After some time, open the attention further to also include a bare attention to the totality of sounds. Let them all arise and pass, allowing the awareness to be receptive as much as possible, rather than moving toward and focusing on each sound.

Listen to the silence between the sounds as well. Notice how sounds seem to arise out of, and fade back into, the silence.

Allow, or imagine, the awareness to be like an open sky, clear and vast. Sensations, sounds, thoughts and images appear and disappear, like fireflies or like shooting stars in this space. Feel that in this vastness of awareness there is space for everything, no matter what it is.

Notice that the awareness itself does not struggle or become entangled with what appears within it. As you sense the arising of any impulses to control or interfere with phenomena, let the undisturbed nature of the space support a relinquishing of that craving.

[2] If you are using the *anicca* practice, it is probably best to avoid contemplating the *anicca* of awareness at this stage, since the meditation outlined here encourages the sense of awareness as a more *steady* backdrop for experience.

See moments of sensation and experience appear, float freely, and disappear within the vastness of the awareness.

Aware of the clarity and the immensity of this empty space, notice how every thing that arises is held within it effortlessly.

Over and over, watching *phenomena emerge from and then melt back into the space*, see if you can practise *letting all phenomena belong to this space of awareness*.

Notice too how experiences seem gradually to begin to lose their substantiality. Is it possible to see whatever arises as *just an impression in awareness*, like a reflection on the surface of a body of water? Include whatever image of your self, or self-sense arises – see these too as just impressions in awareness.

Just as silence permeates all sounds, gently allow the stillness and space of awareness to pervade and to permeate every thing that arises. Is it possible to *see all phenomena as having the same 'substance' as awareness*?

Watching phenomena dissolve back into the space again and again, is it possible also to get a sense of the vastness – its imperturbability or any other qualities it seems to embody?

(Make sure you practise this meditation in the walking and standing postures, as well as sitting. Experiment too practising both with the eyes open, and with eyes closed.)

Beginning to Inquire into Experiences

When the perception opens in the kinds of ways described earlier, the tremendous sense of peace, freedom, and beauty that it may involve can often affect a meditator profoundly. It can be very tempting then to suppose that what is experienced is somehow ultimate. A practitioner might assume (s)he has arrived at the deepest level of understanding. Things might then be understood to be 'empty' because they are seen in meditation to be insubstantial, like space; or because they are seen to really be consciousness in their essence, not the separate, solid objects that they appear to be.

It may be too that the space of awareness itself is reified in various ways. Even before a perception such as oneness emerges fully, the sense of the unshakeable vastness of awareness, its mystery and its endless capacity to accommodate all things, can be awe-inspiring. Perhaps it is surmised to be truly transcendent, truly free of all conditions that arise in it. The notions of emptiness and the space of awareness may get equated, so that the space of awareness itself is regarded as 'Emptiness'. Similarly, because the experience of the space seems to accord with various descriptions one might have heard or read, it is also relatively common for this awareness to come to be referred to, for example, as the 'Ground of Being', as the 'Cosmic Consciousness', 'Big Mind', 'The One Mind', 'The Absolute', 'The Unconditioned', or 'The Unfabricated'. And since a sense of divinity often permeates experience, a practitioner may begin to speak in theistic terms.

Whatever appellation is used, what unites them is the belief in the inherent existence of this space; and often too a belief in its status as an ultimate object of realization. Then a practitioner may believe that, having reached the ultimate, they only need to familiarize themselves with this state, so that its perspective becomes more continuously accessible.

As we will shortly discuss, this is a delicate and pivotal stage in practice, for in fact this is not yet the deepest understanding. Although a meditator may actually be served by becoming attached to such views for a while, clinging to the belief that it is ultimate may well prevent further insight.

Even in the very loveliness of the space, though, is a hint that it is not ultimate. With more practice, a meditator may experience the space that opens up as possessing at different times different qualities that all seem inherent to it. We have been exploring, and guiding perception towards, the quality of awareness. But it is possible that the character of the space expresses more a mystical silence, or an infinite love permeating the universe, or similarly compassion, or joy; or it may manifest simply as an unshakeable peace, without seeming to be awareness at all. It may appear with, or without, any emotional colouring of warmth or tenderness. It can also seem to be just a nothingness beyond all this. All these, and more besides, may arise in the course of deep practice. And everything that we have described above, regarding the way the perception of the space of awareness unfolds and affects the perception of other phenomena, could be repeated for any of these other perceptions of space – for example as mystical silence, love, or peace. A meditator may also develop the skill to navigate between these perceptions. All these observations hint at the conditioned nature of such perceptions.

One might simply want to assert that the ultimate has many qualities inherent in it. But it is quite possible for a meditator eventually to discover also *how* to colour the space in any of these ways, as (s)he chooses, and this discovery begins to cast some serious doubt on the notion that any of them are ultimate. Seeing this fabricating of perception for oneself, the assumption that any of these spaces is unconditioned begins to be undermined, and their status, rather, as perceptions that are still fabricated begins to become more obvious.

'This vastness of awareness is still an object in awareness'

As well as beginning such a subtle inquiry into fabrication, there is another, perhaps cruder, way of moving beyond this objectification of the space of awareness. We can consider that this kind of sense of a vast space of awareness cannot be awareness itself. In the sorts of experiences described, it is still in fact a perception, an object of awareness.

Employing this insight meditatively would begin in a fairly similar fashion to what we have already outlined. One can practise sustaining a view, within a more global attentiveness, that everything that arises, arises 'in' awareness. This will gradually open up the sense of the space of awareness.

Once this space is established for a while, the understanding that this global sense of awareness cannot itself be awareness – specifically, that it has become an object of awareness, and that therefore it too must be 'in' awareness – can be quietly and subtly, but firmly, introduced into the way of looking. This may release any clinging in that moment to a view that reifies the sense of awareness. And in so doing it may take the experience beyond what we have described in this chapter.

Openings of perception as skilful ways of looking

As we have pointed out, the perception of the vastness of awareness will often arise organically through practising a release of clinging. In turn it can provide an immensely helpful support for even deeper letting go with respect to phenomena. As such, although it is still a fabricated perception, it is a way of looking that it can serve us to cultivate.

In fact, within this view, a number of potent perceptions emerge, and each of these perceptions individually can also become itself a helpful way of looking. Each, or all together, may be deliberately cultivated and employed. Viewing phenomena as held in the space of awareness, as arising out of it and dissolving back into it, letting phenomena belong to the vastness, seeing them as just impressions in awareness, and seeing all things to be of one nature with awareness – all these are refinements of the way of looking. Of course, in many respects they are simply extensions of the three characteristics views. For example, the view that *lets every thing belong to the space* is just a small extension of the *anattā* way of looking, allowing the sense of space to support the unhooking of identification with phenomena. Ultimately, regarding these transformed perceptions fundamentally as ways of looking, rather than as arrival points, will keep open the possibility for deeper insight.

An Alternative Approach: 'No Difference in Substance'

There are actually a number of related approaches that engage the sense of awareness as a way of letting go. Some have the advantage that they may be practised with an attention focused more narrowly on one object, as well as with a spacious and more inclusive attention. Let us briefly explore one of these. Like the vastness of awareness, this view may emerge naturally as a meditative perception, and then be encouraged and sustained as a way of looking; or it may be supported by an initial reflection, and then employed meditatively in practice.

In some ways it takes as its starting point an element that it shares with the practice just outlined. We have mentioned that at times in many practices, including *samādhi* practices and even simple mindfulness practice (when the mindfulness is strong), the outer world can seem much less solid. Inner and outer phenomena may seem to lose their substantiality, while the sense of consciousness comes more to the fore. All things can seem at that point to share the same 'substance' as awareness, and all experience may be seen as essentially a 'manifestation of awareness'. Then, not just the knowing, but the content of experiences too is sensed as having the nature of consciousness, being made of the same 'stuff' as awareness. Through familiarization with this seeing, it is possible to encourage and sustain a meditative view that is a slight variation on the practice described earlier in this chapter. Rather than focusing on the sense of awareness itself though, one can focus, moment to moment, on this sense of an *absence of a difference in substance* between awareness and experiences. In practising this way of looking, whatever is perceived is regarded in the same way, through the lens of this view of 'no difference in substance'.

And instead of a vast and unchanging consciousness as before, the view here is of a continuum of moments of consciousness having both a knowing and a known aspect. Being regarded as essentially two aspects of the same moment of consciousness, the knowing (consciousness) and the known (the perceptual object) can be seen to lack any essential difference, and this lack of essential difference may be sensed or remembered, and then tuned into. What is 'empty' in this view is the duality between awareness and matter, or, more fully, between awareness and both inner and outer phenomena.

This *emptiness of difference* that is repeatedly focused on and sustained as a meditative view actually constitutes a slightly more subtle object of focus than the sense of awareness. Partly for this reason, and partly because in its way of looking it is not so much supporting that sense of awareness as a kind of 'ground', this approach will typically have an even lighter feel than the vastness of consciousness. It may be, therefore, that it is the sense of moment-to-moment release of clinging, together with a certain groundlessness, that feel most prominent in this practice.

By thus withdrawing some of the perceptions and assumptions of solidity, reality, and separate existence from things, release of clinging is greatly empowered in the moment. At the same time, as with any way of looking, the view that it encapsulates is being reinforced, while addiction to habitual ways of seeing is being disempowered.

A few points about practising this second method

In practice, it is likely that such a shift of view will be more accessible initially with some sense spheres and their objects than with others. This will vary between practitioners and is not a problem. Take time to develop some facility and confidence where it feels easiest, before extending the practice to the other senses. If, for instance, meditating with the eyes open is less familiar, this way of looking may at first feel more difficult with the visual sense. Then as you gain some facility practising with another sense sphere, you may find that the shift in view naturally spreads at times to the visual sense, and so becomes available that way.

Similarly, it is possible to take advantage of the 'after-effect' shifts in perception which sometimes follow meditation sessions. On opening the eyes and leaving a formal session – whether you have been practising this last way of looking in a sense sphere that feels easier for you, or engaging any other practice – you may notice, as you look around, that perception is altered somewhat, in accord with whatever view was being practised. (These alterations are anyway important to notice and give attention to, since generally what we are seeking is an understanding of the fabricated nature of perception.[3]) Here, included as part of such after-effects may be this very shift in view of the visual field that we have been describing. Familiarizing yourself with it then, eventually it can be brought more deliberately into a formal session with the eyes open. The range of the view can thus begin to expand more stably into the visual sense sphere.

Relaxing the gaze in this way of looking is usually helpful as well, as this can relax the tendency to objectify and solidify perceptual objects, and can open up the sense of what is seen as simply a field of visual image.

---

[3] For further discussion and brief descriptions of some of these 'after-effects' on perception, see the *Insights from the Formless Realms* section in Chapter 19.

Likewise, although it certainly can be employed within a narrow focus of attention, this practice may, for some, initially feel easier with a wider and more inclusive attention. When we focus on one object, there is usually a tendency to solidify that object.

Whether the attention is wider or more narrow, the key to this way of looking is to recognize that what is seen or experienced is just that – an experience – and then to see it that way – as an experience, a perception – rather than in the usual way of looking, which carries with it the imputation of a solid object 'out there'.

As you develop some facility with this practice, you may also want to experiment with modulating the *intensity* of the way of looking in any moment. For the view may be held within the looking in a more relaxed or a more forceful manner, and it is useful and interesting to notice what effects this has on how the meditation unfolds.

As will be the case with many of the ways of looking offered in this book, you may find you have to play with it a little until it clicks and there is, sometimes suddenly, a shift in the way of looking. Even if it is only for a moment or two, such a shift is very valuable and forms a basis that can then be built on.

Questioning conclusions

One may also arrive at such a view through considering the nature of awareness. We mentioned in Chapter 12 that consciousness and perception are like two sides of a coin, not really separable. In any moment of experience, whatever object is perceived, the knowing consciousness of that object cannot arise without the perception of that object. Nor can the perception of the object arise before the knowing consciousness of it. There cannot be such a thing as a perceiving consciousness with no object of perception, just as there cannot be such a thing as a perceived object without a perceiving consciousness. They both have to be there simultaneously; neither one can arise before the other. Therefore they have no independent existence. We can use this understanding of perception and consciousness to help support the view of the second approach described above, by deliberately bringing it in to inform the way of looking, moment to moment.

Sometimes the analogy of dreaming is used to help support such a shift in view. Just as with perceiving consciousness and perception of objects, a dream appearance cannot exist independent of the dreaming mind. This dream object arises together with the dreaming mind; it cannot appear before, or after, that dream consciousness, and, conversely, that dream consciousness cannot appear before, or after, that dream object. But the analogy is also stretched by some to suggest that the everyday world of outer objects has no more reality than a dream. Although dreaming and waking states are not declared to be without difference, their difference is not regarded as one of essential nature, since, as manifestations of consciousness, they share the same essence. Thus, based partly on the understanding of the inseparability of consciousness and perception, and partly on the dream analogy, some assert that there is no proof that any outer objects actually exist at all, other than as projections of the mind. The notion of separate, truly existing objects, both outer and inner, is argued to be an unnecessary and erroneous mental construct.

However, this conclusion – that perception and consciousness are inseparable in the way just outlined – in itself constitutes nothing more thus far than the most basic *phenomenological* observation. That is to say: in considering phenomena, we recognize, as stated before, that what we actually consciously perceive are 'perceptions'; 'perceptions' and 'perceived objects' refer here only to the objects of *experience*. As such then, alone or even together with the dreaming analogy nothing is yet proven as a consequence about the actual ontological status of external objects. The facts that a belief in external objects may be seen as unnecessary, and that, as millennia of philosophers have discovered, it is really very difficult to conclusively prove their existence, do not amount to proving conclusively that nothing at all exists 'out there' externally from the mind, or that only mind has real existence.

Rather than making any such overly simplistic conclusions about external reality, and grasping at what is basically an unsophisticated species of philosophical idealism, I would suggest merely using this view as a way of looking in meditation. We can learn to move in and out of such a view, without needing to believe it rigidly. Employed as a way of looking it can be powerfully freeing, and can serve as an important platform for further insight, if not clung to as a truth. Such flexibility of view is very skilful. For what is actually of primary interest to us is to see the effects of different ways of looking on perception, in order to realize the fabricated, empty nature of all things, even including, eventually, all ways of looking.

Practice: 'No difference in substance'

Both within formal meditation sessions and outside of them, practise holding an object in attention while recognizing that what is actually perceived is a perception, an experience.

Notice how this affects the experience.
Is it possible to sense how a degree of the solidity that is habitually imputed to objects of perception is dropped?
You may notice too how the usual distinction between inner and outer also becomes somewhat pacified.

Whether based on shifts in view from previous meditation or on some reflection, practise sustaining a way of seeing, moment to moment, that focuses on the emptiness of any difference in substance between objects of perception and awareness. Some may find a very light labelling to this effect supportive.

Practise this way of looking in the sense spheres in which it feels easiest at first, gradually adding the others until they are all included.

Experiment both with an attention focused more narrowly on one object, and also with a wider, more global attention, inclusive of whatever arises.

Experiment also with modulating the intensity of the view, relaxing into and resting in the view, or directing it in a more forceful manner.

Notice how it feels to view phenomena this way.

If feelings of release, of joy, or of physical bliss arise, you have a choice how to respond, as discussed in Chapter 14. At least some of the time though, make sure that these feelings too are regarded through the lens of this particular view.

Whatever arises, and however perception changes, notice what effects repeating this way of looking over and over has on perception.

A Skilful Use of Views

That inner and outer phenomena are ultimately of the nature of awareness could be construed perhaps as a very crude and elementary version of *Cittamātra* ('Mind Only') Buddhist philosophy. Such a view seems to be expressed in various texts. The *Laṅkāvatāra Sūtra*, for example, says:

> Apparent things, external to the mind, do not exist;
> They are the mind, in various forms, appearing to itself.
> Bodies, goods, locations – all such things
> Are but the mind alone I do affirm.[4]

[4] Translation by Padmakara Translation Group in Chandrakirti and Mipham, *Introduction to the Middle Way*, p. 258.

Nāgārjuna, however, in his *Bodhicittavivaraṇa*, stressed that

> The teaching of the Sage that all these [all internal and external phenomena] are mind-only is in order to relieve the fears of the childish. It is not [a teaching of] reality.[5]

And this caveat was echoed and expanded by Chandrakīrti:

> The *Sūtra* says that outer things are not at all real – it is the mind that manifests in various ways. This teaching that dismisses outer forms was only a device to counteract the strong attachment that we have to things. The Buddha gave such teachings as expedients; their nature is provisional.[6]

Indeed, as Mipham pointed out, the *Laṅkāvatāra Sūtra* itself actually goes on to say:

> According to the ailments of an ailing man,
> The doctor will apply his doctoring,
> And likewise the Buddha, for the sake of living beings,
> Has said that mind alone is true.[7]

This view – that all things, inner and outer, are really in essence only awareness – may be very helpful then, but it is important to realize that it is merely provisional and has a number of shortcomings.

Mipham additionally pointed out that, although in the *Daśabhūmika Sūtra* too the Buddha seems to deny the existence of materiality and an external world, and to imply that all is of the same substance as an inherently existing awareness, in the same *Sūtra* the Buddha states that awareness too is a product, fabricated by fundamental delusion and *saṅkhārā*.

This last statement we will investigate later, when we explore dependent origination more deeply. We will actually come to see then that there are much more sophisticated and profound understandings from which it could likewise be said that phenomena are 'nothing but mind' – that they are fabricated by the mind.

---

[5] Author's own translation.

[6] MAV 6:94 – 95.

[7] Cited by Mipham in his commentary to Chandrakīrti's *Madhyamakāvatāra*. (Translation by Padmakara Translation Group in Chandrakirti and Mipham, *Introduction to the Middle Way*, p. 259.)

But these understandings need not over-extend to an assertion that there is nothing 'out there' at all. Nor will they reify consciousness in any fashion.

It is the reification of awareness in various ways that eventually constitutes the greater obstacle to deeper insight and liberation, and that must therefore be seen through sooner or later. In this connection there are a couple of observations we might call attention to. The second approach introduced in this chapter, since it includes the notion of a stream of momentary consciousnesses, does not immediately lend itself to the view of awareness as some kind of eternal 'ground of being', as the first approach might. One may imagine then that it does not reify awareness. But it is quite possible that this stream of moments of consciousness is assumed to be truly existent, the moments of consciousness themselves taken in some way to be fundamentally real. And at some point it must be realized that moments of consciousness and the streams they form in time are empty, utterly lacking inherent existence. This we will explain in later chapters.[8] Alternatively, despite not seeming to at first, it may well be that in due course the practice of the second approach opens experience up to another level where some sense of an eternal awareness reasserts itself and is concluded to be ultimately real. The realizations involved in that case are more subtle, so we will for now postpone exploration of that particular development. But the conclusions there will also eventually need to be questioned further.

Two opposite views – but both powerful, both helpful

In regard to these and in fact to many discussions of using insight into the nature of awareness in meditation, something interesting can be noticed. Some approaches adopt a view of awareness wherein awareness and objects of awareness are of the same essence. In contrast, other approaches, or stages within an approach, adopt the opposite view: that awareness is radically other than the phenomena and events that are its objects; and in being other, it is undisturbed. Things arise and pass and awareness remains pure, unmoved and unsullied by any object. Many analogies may be given for this latter view. What they point out in common is the fact that we are habitually entangled in, and myopically reacting to, the objects of awareness, and miss the free and unperturbed nature of awareness itself. Just as, watching a movie, we can be engrossed in the action and story, and fail to recognize the screen on which the movie is projected, or (in a modification of the analogy) fail to turn around and become aware of the light of the projector behind us.

---

[8] See especially Chapters 25 – 27.

Both of these views are available to us. In practice, we may sometimes have, and encourage, a sense of awareness as separate from its objects, and this view can be very helpful; and at other times we may have, and encourage, a sense of the sameness of objects and awareness, and this view too may be helpful. In both cases, however, as part of the view, a nature of awareness has been asserted which will not ultimately stand up to scrutiny. We will see, eventually, that the nature of awareness is neither the same as nor different from its objects of perception. These views and insights then are still provisional. It is interesting, though, to see how opposing ways of looking can both be powerfully freeing.

Whether phenomena are regarded as being of the same substance as consciousness, or whether awareness is regarded as other than, and free of, its objects, both views tend to reify awareness. Even though it may be regarded nominally as 'not a thing', because it is not materially substantial, an intuitive belief in the inherent existence of awareness has not been destroyed yet. Nevertheless, this fundamental omission does not alter the fact that both views may be ways of looking that support a great deal of letting go, of freedom, peace, and heart opening. And they may, if employed skilfully, act as stepping-stones to deeper insight and a fuller realization of emptiness.

Maturing through practice

Notwithstanding all that we have said – that awareness is not 'the Deathless', not unfabricated, that the space of awareness is not 'Emptiness', and that the nature of awareness is neither separate from nor the same as its objects – it may be a mistake merely to protest against the views described in this chapter on purely intellectual or partisan grounds, without actually experiencing their power in practice firsthand. If this is the case, or if one only has a handful of such experiences, the overwhelming tendency will be for the default views of reality to reassert themselves. Nothing more potent than a surface level intellectuality, or received opinion, will have challenged the deeply ingrained assumption of the inherent existence of phenomena.

Practising the views described in this chapter, however, can wield enough power to begin to shift the deeply held, normal views of reality, and so move toward more ultimate insight. Even though they are not the final truth, many meditators, perhaps the majority, may need to linger in these practices and views long enough for them to do their work, and to taste the relative liberation they bring. At the very least, learning to see things as less substantial will reduce some of the clinging to those things.

In the Dzogchen tradition there is a priceless saying:

Trust your experience, but keep refining your view.

Remembering it and heeding its wisdom will serve a practitioner very well over the long term. It allows us to deepen our insights by building on those we have already realized, developing confidence and freedom, but without getting stuck.

It may be necessary then, as a stage in practice, for some meditators to reify awareness in any of the senses we have described. We reify continually anyway of course. A stepping-stone view of reifying one phenomenon in a way that allows a prying away of attachment and reification to a whole range of other phenomena is almost certainly preferable to simply remaining stuck in a habitual, albeit more conventional, reification of most things.

And it may be for many practitioners that a kind of falling in love with awareness, in any of the manifestations we have described, is part of this process, and part of what allows the view to transform the heart and the understanding – the very love and the loveliness of the experiences opened by the view thus doing their work on the being.

Some, it is true, will need a little cajoling to move beyond this view they have arrived at through practice. It can occasionally be difficult for a teacher or a practitioner to discern when it is time to move on. But at some point, as skill in practice develops, if there is open-mindedness and an ongoing questioning, there is the possibility that the reification of awareness can be seen through. What was a reification comes to be seen as a skilfully fabricated perception, and a view, a way of looking. In this way it can support deeper insight. And this we will elucidate in due course.

PART FIVE

Of Highways and Byways

16

The Relationship with Concepts in Meditation

As outlined in Chapter 4, insight into emptiness can be supported by a number of broad approaches. In addition to an investigation into the nature of fabrication, which we have begun, analytical practices that use thought and logic may too have an important role. And the combination of these two approaches can prove enormously powerful. Before introducing an analytical meditation in the next chapter, however, it may be useful, for some, to explore a little the relationship to, and assumptions concerning, concepts and thought in meditation in general.

In any case it will be essential to recognize that we can't help but bring to our practice a whole host of attitudes and preconceptions about all sorts of things; and that these affect how our practice unfolds. Since liberation must include a certain freedom from the narrow prison of assumptions and biases, and since we do not want what is unexamined to impede our path, boldly exposing and exploring such presuppositions is vital.

This is certainly true with regard to the role of conceptuality in practice. We human beings are so often painfully entangled in, agitated, and led astray, by thoughts. Depending perhaps on one's exposure to different teachings, it can be relatively common, therefore, for meditators to regard the thinking mind generally with some suspicion, and thought in meditation simply as something of a problem to be removed. Without doubt it is both lovely and immensely helpful to develop the ability to bring the *citta* into a state of some *samādhi*, where it is more quiet and unified, and less disturbed by thoughts. But it is also true that what we finally seek is a *freedom in relation to* thoughts and the thinking mind. And this includes an ability to *use thought skilfully in the service of insight*. Both this freedom and this skilful use of thought can be practised as elements of the path, as well as the stilling of thought in *samādhi*.

Bare attention, suchness, and 'things as they are'

Sometimes this undifferentiated notion that thought is an enemy of meditation is also mixed up with ideas about the goal of insight. A practitioner might conceive that 'being with things as they are' is the aim of meditation. Often the attempt then is to 'not think, just experience', to dwell in a state of 'bare attention', where perception is 'pure', free of any distortions that thought might add.

All this already involves quite a degree of assumption and conceiving, it must be pointed out, however. And while this way of conceiving may be very helpful as one mode of practice, it is only that – one mode of practising. It is worth taking the time to develop this kind of simple mindfulness practice though, as it can serve as a foundation for deeper practices. As discussed in Chapter 7, such a way of looking does indeed penetrate beneath concepts; but it does so only to a certain extent, as we will find out.

Generally such practice can also bring a degree of vividness to experience, which may be beautiful, but may be misleading too. Free of the grosser levels of *papañca*, and the dulling of the senses and clouding of the mind that it can bring, the objects of the world can appear almost dazzling in their brightness and clarity at times, and seem so obviously to be just what they are, in and of themselves. Their 'suchness', we might think then, is realized. It may strike us as foolish to question or deny what seems like the very simple reality evident in the way they appear; and in comparison, the conclusions of reasoning and thinking can seem much less believable.

As we have stated before though, insight involves much more than this. It is just this kind of intuitive realism – the normal confidence in the assumption that a world of objective things exists independently of our minds and their ways of looking, and that we can know these objective things as they are in themselves – that needs to be overcome.

When the Buddha taught that liberation is dependent on "knowledge and vision of things as they are",[1] he was not referring to simply being with things directly as they appear in the moment, but to the penetration of their true nature, which includes their emptiness. And realizing the suchness of things means, in fact, realizing their emptiness, since 'suchness' and 'emptiness' are actually synonymous in the tradition,[2] for the most part. It is the ultimately illusory nature

---

[1] '*yathābhūtañāṇadassana*' (e.g. in SN 12:23).

[2] Many examples may be offered where this is explicitly stated. See, for instance, Vasubhandhu's *Pañcaskandhaprakaraṇa*, where it says:

of all phenomena that needs to be known thoroughly for Awakening. Nāgārjuna's *Śūnyatāsaptati* says:

> To imagine that things born from causes and conditions are real
> is called ignorance by the Teacher...
> But when one, by seeing correctly, has understood well that things
> are empty... that is the cessation of ignorance.[3]

And many others in the tradition have made clear that realizing the ultimate truth of things will involve more than just the arresting of thoughts, or the quieting of the mind's linguistic apparatus. Gorampa, for example, citing *sūtra* passages and comments in Jñānagarbha's *Satyadvayvibhaṅgavṛtti*, emphasized that what needs ultimately to be seen through, or beyond, is not so much "linguistic convention", but the very "*way things appear* to the minds of worldly beings".[4]

As was explained previously, the delusion of inherent existence is woven right into perception and the way we experience things. It is not at all only a problem of language and thought. Fundamental ignorance cannot be removed merely by removing thinking. No matter how simple, direct-seeming, clear, and thought-free our experience of things might be, if the subtle sense of inherent existence in that thing is not consciously overturned, *avijjā* is still present.

Attachment to 'not knowing'

Similarly, we have already alluded on several occasions too to the fact that simply realizing and taking impermanence to heart, no matter how thoroughly, does not

---

> What is suchness? It is the true nature of phenomena, their lack of a phenomenal self (*dharmānaṃ dharmatā dharmanairātmyaṃ*).

And in Śāntideva's *Śikṣasaṃuccaya*:

> 'Suchness' – that is a designation for emptiness (*tathateti śūnyatā etad adhivacanam*).

It is only more recently in some Western translations and interpretations that, for a variety of reasons, this essential meaning has been lost and replaced by a meaning that is almost, in fact, its opposite.

[3] Translation from Chr. Lindtner in *Nagarjuniana*, pp. 64 – 65.

[4] In his *Distinguishing the Views*. (Translation adapted from Jose Ignacio Cabezón and Geshe Lobsang Dargyay's in *Freedom from Extremes: Gorampa's "Distinguishing the Views" and the Polemics of Emptiness* [Boston: Wisdom Publications, 2007] p. 135. My italics added.)

constitute full enlightenment. *Śūnyatā* is a more radical and profound insight than *anicca*; they cannot just be equated. And ignoring the deeper teachings on emptiness will have all kinds of consequences.

Anicca implies the impossibility of being completely in control in life, and also includes in its meaning the element of uncertainty in existence. Emphasizing only impermanence may thus sometimes lead to notions of practice and Awakening that put the accent on ideals such as 'going with the flow', and 'not knowing'. These ideas, which without doubt have a beauty to them, can feel intuitively attractive for various reasons. In contrast, the assertion that something, the absence of inherent existence, needs to be understood, and known, may feel less attractive for some practitioners. Coupled with this, the idea (perhaps foreign to many) that realization might be aided by analytical practices may stir up a whole range of *attachments and views in regard to knowing and unknowing* in general.

Probably there is much in this existence that we cannot know. We can be profoundly touched and humbled by the impenetrable and inexhaustible mysteries of the universe, its vastness, its origins, and our uncertain place in it all. But such existential wonder, whether felt as beautiful or terrifying, or the sublime mixture of the two, will not alone free us from suffering. As it is with anything, it is possible to become attached to the notion of 'not knowing', perhaps over-elevating its significance in practice, and to grow resistant even to the possibility of knowing. Then the crucial distinction between what we *can* and *need* to know, on the one hand, and what is unknowable for us, on the other, can be lost. When that is the case, our bearings on the path are lost. For in the Dharma tradition, liberation is predicated not on unknowing, but on fully *knowing* the lack of inherent existence of all phenomena. It is this, ultimately, that releases the craving which causes *dukkha*. As Dharmakīrti wrote in his *Pramāṇavārttika*:

> Without refuting the object, it is impossible to let go of it.[5]

Attachment to simplicity

Other uninvestigated inclinations may be at play, too, in our attitudes to conceptuality and to realizing emptiness. There may be an assumption, for instance, that the path, and the Teaching, need to be *simple*, and a suspicion of any teaching that is not simple, a supposition that it cannot be true. Certainly there is a danger in attachment to complexity, intellectualization, and precision where

[5] Translations from *Pramāṇavārttika* are the author's own.

it is not necessary, and such attachment will hinder the unfolding of deeper insight. But the same could also be said of an attachment to simplicity and to imprecision where precision is needed. Even when it is based on meditative experiences, to cling to a simple notion – for example that emptiness and oneness are equivalent – without further discriminative investigation, will stagnate the practice at a level where the insight could go deeper.

To try to be more precise in one's awareness and understanding, and to wrestle with complexity and subtlety, can feel like hard work at times. Simplicity will usually feel easier and more comfortable. But when our movement toward simplicity is, even unconsciously, an attempt to avoid the hassle and difficulty of what may require precision and may not be simple to understand, a measure of integrity may be lost from our practice. Sakya Paṇḍita wrote:

> Wise people suffer when they learn. If you want to be comfortable, forget about becoming wise. People who seek small pleasures don't get big ones.[6]

Another reason that we might cling to simplicity and shun the use of conceptuality in practice may stem from occasions in the past when perhaps the openness of the heart, and its capacities to feel, seemed to be inhibited as we engaged the thinking mind. It is certainly vital to protect the heart's capability for sensitivity and aliveness, but it is definitely not the case that analytical practices necessarily close the heart. And in fact, analytical meditation need not feel complex at all. Once a reasoning is understood and digested, with practice we can develop the ability to handle it in meditation with ease and lightness so that it does not feel cumbersome to the *citta*. As we do so, the release that the analysis brings when used meditatively becomes palpable much sooner in a session, until eventually it is almost immediate. And with it can come easily all the opening of the heart that typically accompanies ways of looking that bring release.

Likewise, eschewing precision and complexity in teaching and speaking about emptiness, and speaking instead in more open, vague, and mystical ways often moves the heart more. But it can, on occasion, have the drawback of lacking a level of clarity of discriminating wisdom when that might be helpful. Words that are more poetic, simpler, and less precise, on the other hand, have the advantage that they can sometimes penetrate deeply into the *citta* in ways that ignite the sparks of intuitive realization.

---

[6] Translation from the author's notes.

Questioning predilections

Indeed, with respect to using the intuition and the thinking mind in practice, we may similarly have emotional biases, favouring one or the other. Each has its own strength and its particular incompleteness though, and rather than being mutually exclusive the two can actually aid one another. Given the profound and counter-intuitive nature of voidness, a multiplicity of approaches may be needed or at the very least prove more potent than limiting ourselves to only one tack.

Besides, it is often the case that we grow and discover more through approaches to practice that do not initially feel attractive, or natural, for us. It would be a mistake therefore to be ruled completely by our preferences in these matters, and the Buddha clearly cautioned against being led merely by what we like with respect to teachings and practices:

> How could one commanded by his impulses, settled in his likes, overcome his own views…? Views settled in are not easily overcome… For a person takes up or rejects a teaching in light of these settlements.[7]

The demands of decisiveness

In practice, there is also another aspect of using logic that can be challenging. As we will see, the logical reasoning on which analytical practices are based requires a certain *decisiveness* of mind in the practitioner. For example, a rule of logic that often underpins the meditative reasonings is that a thing, *if it is really existent*, must be either A or not-A (permanent or impermanent, say) and cannot be both. If some thing is seen to be neither A nor not-A, then this principle implies, decisively, that that thing cannot be inherently existent. A firm conviction in this principle is necessary for the practices to work well and to open some freedom.

Sometimes this is troubling to us though, and we hold back from such decisiveness. Often, for various reasons, we may habitually lack confidence in our own capacities for clear reasoning. But we may also find that, put under this kind of pressure that demands decisiveness, our trust of reasoning in general wavers. While we may dispute the logic involved in any particular analysis, we might also be tempted to suggest, usually vaguely, the limits of logic in general.

---

[7] Sn 4:3

For instance, this might occur in regard to the logical principle mentioned just above. But if so, it may well be that something fundamental has not yet been clearly realized. Wrapped up in our basic perception of phenomena is an intuitive sense that they inherently exist; and this instinctive notion includes the tacit belief that a phenomenon is either A or not-A *in itself*. This is, by and large, how we automatically *feel* and *perceive* things to be. And it is this habitual, intuitive conception and perception that is proved false through the various analyses. Recognizing, then, that a phenomenon is neither A nor not-A is not something that can simply be shrugged off with a "So what?" It cannot just be dismissed as 'an issue of logic'; and it is not merely our typical *thinking* about objects that is being challenged and undermined. It is primarily, rather, our very *sense* of the thingness of things at the most basic level that such seeing calls into question and melts.

Used well, meditative analyses are not a matter of fiddling intellectually with abstract and irrelevant logical postulates. Again though, the appearances of things are so compelling and seem so unquestionable that being asked to be decisive can feel like we are being asked to choose between reality and reason.

The Transcending of Concepts

Some of this elevation of unknowing and this reluctance to engage the conceptual mind is understandable too for other reasons. We may have encountered a variety of teachings asserting that the actual ultimate truth of things is, in fact, beyond any conceiving, and that the transcending or dropping of concepts is the goal of the path. The Buddha definitely alluded to such a seeing beyond concepts:

> The Tathāgata, when seeing what may be seen, does not conceive[8] an [object as] seen. He does not conceive an unseen. He does not

[8] '*na maññati*': admittedly this could be translated as 'does not *think* about the seen, etc.'. Clearly, though, the Buddha used the thinking mind regularly in teaching and formulating the Dharma, and in fact stated many times that he did so. Considered in the wider context of his Teaching, some of the other possible translations of *maññati* – 'conceive of' or 'construe', 'suppose', 'believe in', 'declare' – make more sense here. A seeing with insight, that the nature of all phenomena is beyond conceiving, is being voiced.

(Interestingly, *na maññati* may also partly imply in its meaning 'does not care about'. This would then relate back to the Buddha's use, earlier in the same discourse, of the phrase *na upaṭṭhāsi*, meaning 'does not honour', 'does not care for' phenomena that are sensed and cognized, so that the whole then also describes something like an attitude of holy disinterest. However, since the phrase in which *na upaṭṭhāsi* occurs exists in variant forms in the original Pali sources, such a rendering is not certain. And anyway, seen, again, in the context of the Buddha's teaching and engagement, this could probably only convey one aspect of the intended meaning; it could not be the exclusive meaning referring to a pervasive attitude. For clearly the Buddha cared for beings and was carefully involved in teaching.)

> conceive an [object] to be seen. He does not conceive a seer… When hearing… When sensing…
>
> When cognizing what may be cognized, he does not conceive an [object as] cognized, does not conceive an uncognized, does not conceive an [object] to be cognized, does not conceive a cognizer. Thus… the Tathāgata, being as such with respect to phenomena that can be seen, heard, sensed, and cognized, is 'Such'. And I proclaim there is no other such higher or more sublime than this.
>
> Among those that are self-fettered, one who is 'Such' would not posit as ultimately true or even false anything seen, heard, or sensed, hung onto and supposed true by others.
> Having already seen that arrow onto which mankind hangs and clings – 'I know, I see, that's just how it is' – the Tathāgatas hang onto nothing.[9]

And he also taught that,

> In conceiving form… *vedāna*… perception… fabrications… consciousness, one is bound by *Māra* (Death). By not conceiving form… *vedanā*… perception… fabrications… consciousness one is freed… [10]

There are many passages, both in the Pali Canon and in later texts, that encourage a meditative realization beyond concepts – *and beyond even the conception of emptiness*. In the *Ratnakūṭa Sūtra*, for example:

> Kāśyapa, this which is called 'self' is one extreme. This which is called 'non-self' is a second extreme. The middle of the two extremes is what cannot be examined, cannot be taught, is not a basis, is without appearance, without cognition, and without abiding. Kāśyapa, this is what is called the 'Middle Way', the understanding of phenomena correctly.[11]

And in the *Prajñāpāramitā Saṃcayagāthā* it says:

---

[9] AN 4:24. Here, 'Such' or 'one who is Such' (*tādī*) is an epithet for a fully Awakened being.
[10] SN 22:64.
[11] Translation from the author's notes.

> If a bodhisattva determines, 'this aggregate is empty', he is occupied with attributes, and then the unproduced is not experienced.[12]

Nāgārjuna pointed this out too:

> 'Empty', 'non-empty', 'both', or 'neither' – these should not be asserted. It is expressed thus only for the purpose of communication.[13]

We may wonder, however, quite what it means to let go of concepts. Clearly, it is not simply to drop thinking, as we have already explained. This is made very obvious too by studying the contexts of the passages quoted above. Conceiving is actually much more subtle and pervasive than thinking, so transcending concepts will involve much more than merely stopping thoughts.

How then might such freedom from concepts be arrived at? It can be quite normal to doubt that concepts themselves might have a part in this movement beyond conceiving. Within Buddhism, though, a long and diverse tradition exists strongly encouraging the use of logical analysis in meditation. Kamalaśīla, for instance, in his *Bhāvanākrama*, wrote:

> The conceptuality of one who does not cultivate in meditation individual analysis on the nature of things with wisdom, but cultivates only an abandonment of mentation will never be overcome… Due to not having the illumination of wisdom, they will never realize the lack of self-existence of things.[14]

And in the *Samādhirāja Sūtra* it says:

> If the selflessness of phenomena is analysed, and if this analysis is cultivated in meditation, it causes the effect of attaining *nirvāṇa*. Through no other cause does one come to peace.[15]

---

[12] Here 'attribute' translates the Sanskrit word *nimitta*, which may also be rendered as 'sign' or 'object of perception', or even 'ground' or 'basis'. See Chapters 27 and 28 for further discussion of this term in these contexts.

[13] MMK 22:11.

[14] Translation adapted from Jeffrey Hopkins's, reprinted in Elizabeth Napper, *Dependent-Arising and Emptiness: A Tibetan-Buddhist Interpretation of Mādhyamika Philosophy* [Boston: Wisdom Publications, 2003] p. 125.

[15] Translation by Jeffrey Hopkins in *Emptiness Yoga* [Ithaca, NY: Snow Lion, 1987] p. 140.

Even in the Dzogchen tradition, Mipham Rinpoche frequently stressed the power and importance of rational analysis – for instance in his *Precious Beacon of Certainty*. While admitting the possibility of realization without analysis, he pointed out that it is extremely rare, and declared that

> Without endeavouring to investigate with a hundred methods of reasoning, it is difficult to achieve liberation [and] gain a glimpse of reality…
>
> [But] if, by… rational analysis, one sees the nature of things precisely, one will profoundly realize [the essence of] the illusion mind, which is like an illusion.[16]

For it is a conviction, a certainty in the emptiness of things, that analysis can bring. And this conviction is necessary for any meditative realization of emptiness to begin to deepen and mature to the next stage. Explaining this process, Mipham taught:

> As long as certainty in truthlessness[17] has not been born, one should induce it with skilful means and analysis. If certainty is born, one should meditate in that state without separating from that certainty. The lamp-like continuity of certainty causes false conceiving to subside. One should always cultivate it. If it is lost, then induce it again through analysis.

But logical analysis is not itself an end-point in practice. Rather, it is an important first step on a meditative journey:

> Having realized emptiness through analysis, you should not rest content with analysis… you should meditate again and again on… [that] apprehension [of selflessness]. By meditating on selflessness the view of self is uprooted, so it has been called necessary by many seers of truth who practised intensely… This is the fail-safe entry way for beginners.

Understandably of course, there might be the concern that the use of concepts

---

[16] Translations from Mipham's *Beacon of Certainty* in this chapter are by John Whitney Pettit in *Mipham's Beacon of Certainty: Illuminating the View of Dzogchen, The Great Perfection* [Boston: Wisdom Publications, 1999] pp. 205 – 211.

[17] 'Truthlessness' is a synonym for voidness.

in meditation would only lead to a proliferation of more concepts, and could never possibly lead to a transcendence of conceptuality. In practice, however, we find this is not the case. When reason and concept are used skilfully in meditation to undermine the conception of inherent existence, those initial concepts and the conceiving mind will then be dissolved in the process too, for there will be nothing left to support them. In the *Ratnakūṭa Sūtra*, it says:

> Kāśyapa, it's like this: Fire arises, for example, when the wind rubs two branches together. Once the fire has arisen, the two branches are burned. Just so, Kāśyapa, if you have the correct analytical intellect, a Noble One's faculty of wisdom is generated. Through its generation, the correct analytical intellect is consumed.[18]

Mipham echoed this. The repeated use of analysis having developed a steadier and more and more accessible conviction in the view of emptiness, one need not then cling to analysis at that point in meditation:

> Finally, if even without analysis certainty arises naturally, rest in that very state; since it has already been established through analysis, there is no need to accomplish it again.

For eventually analysis too dissolves in the resultant gnosis:

> When realization of the sublime paths occurs… in the context of extraordinary certainty free of [all] elaborations, there is no occasion for analysing or focusing on 'this' and 'that'.

In Chapter 30, we will see just how, eventually, a full realization of the actual ultimate truth of things goes beyond even the conception of emptiness. Such a realization, though, requires the view of the absence of inherent existence as an indispensable stepping-stone. As Mipham asserted,

> In recognizing the ultimate, one must definitely realize the absence of true existence.

We may fancy that we should, and can, just drop concepts and attachment to

[18] Translation adapted from Alex Wayman's, reprinted in Elizabeth Napper, *Dependent-Arising and Emptiness*, p. 105.

them, and that then the ultimate will reveal itself. It is easy to be fooled here however. Simply attempting to abandon concepts may well feel freeing and peaceful in the moments when there is some pacification of gross conceptuality. But without more careful investigation, this will often merely amount to a refusal to pick up more unfamiliar concepts, and a temporary quieting of thought. Without something more powerful to undermine them, attachment to habitual views and concepts – such as of a subtle sense of self, of objects, of the present moment, and of awareness – will typically return unabated. And although it is true that ultimate belief in any concept will, finally, have to be relinquished, trying to do so too early will almost certainly only leave a practitioner with a whole host of such concept-beliefs and default views remaining firmly in place.

Some of these concepts and views are so deeply ingrained in the mind, so habitual, that they require the power of profound insights to reverse them, before they can be abandoned. And this reversal almost always needs to be repeatedly practised.

Some conceptual constructs are so subtle too, and so unconsciously woven into the fabric of perception, that without a corresponding subtlety of discriminating awareness they will escape unnoticed and will continue to operate unchallenged. Conceptuality of all kinds wields its power even when the thinking mind is quiet. To drop thought, then, is definitely not, necessarily, to drop conceiving; thought and conception cannot simply be equated. Indeed, unlike thought, conception is actually a part of our normal and basic experiencing of anything, as we shall later discuss.[19] And since all of our normal conceiving actually involves, implies, and is supported by, the intuitive conceiving of inherent existence, deep and full relinquishment of concepts is not possible without insight into emptiness.

This insight into emptiness, in turn, requires *at least some* meditative handling of concepts. Endeavouring to comprehend fabrication and dependent arising through practising with the three characteristics, for example, certainly involves the use of concepts, albeit not in such an obvious and intense way as in analytical meditation. Essential to the approach that looks at fabrication is an *understanding of the implications* of what one sees happening in meditation – an active inquiry into the dependently arisen nature of transformations of perception. Thus the skilful use of concepts – in ways that eventually free us from all concepts and transcend the conceiving mind – is, in fact, a feature common to both the investigation of fabrication *and* analytical meditations.

---

[19] See Chapter 27 especially, where, in more deeply exploring the dependent origination of things, we will see how conventional perception of any phenomenon – even without a thought that labels it as 'this' or 'that' – is dependent on conceiving.

We need not therefore make too sharp a dichotomy between the two approaches used in this book and insist absolutely on the necessity of logical analysis practices. I offer a selection of such practices, though, because they may, for some, be helpful and even necessary. Many practitioners will find that complementing the approaches that eventually emerge from the three characteristics with the approaches of logical analysis significantly fills out, and makes more firm, the understanding and realization of emptiness.

§

Practice/Inquiry: Attitudes to using thought and concepts in meditation

Devote some time, either alone or together with a friend, to carefully exploring and inquiring into your relationship with the use of concepts on the path. Is it possible to uncover any assumptions you may be holding in this area, and then to question these assumptions?

Investigate, in particular, to see if any of the kinds of suppositions and biases discussed in this chapter are operating within you. For instance:

Are there are any attachments to simplicity?

Or to presuppositions of 'being directly with things as they are'?

Are there ways in which notions such as 'not knowing' have been elevated in your view of the path?

Is there a doubting of your capacity to learn to work skilfully with concepts in meditation? If so, how does the presence of that doubt feel? And what might it need?

Or is there a worry that the use of thought and logic will somehow close the heart? If there is, can you identify on what experience or teaching this concern is based? Does it necessarily have to be the case?

Of course, there may be many other inclinations and suppositions at work too. What else can you discover?

How does it feel to unveil these assumptions and biases? And what effects does it have to see them as such, and to question them?

17

The Impossible Self

The Argument of the Sevenfold Reasoning

A number of the practices we have explored so far work to reveal, to some degree, just how the self-sense is fabricated. In this way they begin to expose the self as an illusion, as empty. The analytical practices we will describe also expose the illusory nature of things, but by a different route. They prove that the way in which things seem, so compellingly and unquestionably, to possess inherent existence – the way they appear as if they are clearly differentiated units of 'this' or 'that' existing in and of themselves – cannot in fact be how they really are. Thus these meditative analyses expose the appearances of things as deceptive.

And among the practices that work more directly with the self, we can draw out another distinction. The *anattā* practice introduced in Chapter 14 is a way of looking *at* phenomena as not-self. In contrast, *the sevenfold reasoning* is a practice that looks *for* the self that seems so obviously to have inherent existence. Recognizing that such a self cannot be found in any possible manifestation at all, it proves, and convinces us of, the impossibility of a truly existing self.

Originally using an investigation of the relationship of a chariot with its parts to illustrate the deconstruction of the self's relationship with the aggregates,[1] the sevenfold reasoning can actually be employed to refute the inherent existence of any phenomenon. Once it is practised with the self we will extend its range.

---

[1] Among classical Buddhist texts, the sevenfold reasoning receives perhaps its most exhaustive treatment from Chandrakīrti in his *Madhyamakāvatāra* (see especially 6:120 – 167). Neither the thrust of the reasoning nor the chariot analogy originated there however; they have been alluded to and explicated to varying degrees since the time of the Buddha. See, for example, Sister Vajirā's teaching in SN 5:10.

Absorbed and then used in meditation, this analysis can bring profound and powerful realizations of emptiness.

In Chapter 11 we explored some of the ways the self might be conceived in relationship to the aggregates. The sevenfold reasoning expands on the permutations we mentioned there to create a more finely meshed net with which to try to seek out the self. It is the thoroughness of the search that makes it convincing. And this conviction is, in turn, critical for the meditative process.

The sevenfold reasoning will conclude that, just as a chariot or car cannot inherently be:

1) exactly *the same as* its parts (the wheels, the axle, the frame, the seat, etc.);
2) *other than* its parts;
3) *in* the parts;

and just as, really:

4) the chariot's parts are not *in it*;
5) the chariot does not *possess* its parts;
6) it is not the *collection* of its parts;
7) nor is it their *shape*;

just so, the self too cannot inherently be:

1) *the same* entity as the aggregates;
2) *other than* the aggregates;
3) *in* the aggregates;

and so too, really:

4) the aggregates are not *in* the self somehow;
5) the self does not *possess* the aggregates;
6) it is not the *collection* of the aggregates;
7) it is not the *shape* of the aggregates, nor is it their *continuum* in time.

Let's consider each of these in turn.

1) *The self cannot be equated with one, some, or all, of the aggregates.*

If we sustain attention on the aggregates, or on any aggregate in particular, it becomes clear that the self cannot simply be regarded as the same as the aggregates, or equated with one or more of them, for a number of reasons.

Each aggregate, on closer inspection, reveals itself as a plurality. In fact, one of the meanings of the word *khandha* is 'a multitude', 'a quantity', or 'a heap'; so each aggregate can itself be regarded as a heap, a collection – of material elements, or of momentary experiences of *vedanā*, or of momentary perceptions, etc.

Now, if the self were equated with the aggregate of perception, for instance, it obviously could not be equated with any single perception. Which perception would it be after all? And since all perceptions appear and disappear, such a self would only exist for an instant.

If, instead, the self were equated with perception in general, that would mean that since many perceptions arise and pass away, there would be many selves. The usual feeling and intuitive sense of self, though, seems to be singular. Alternatively – were the self to be equated with perception in general – we would have to say that since the self is one, all these many perceptions are one also. This too is evidently untenable. (Some may want to simply assert then that the 'true' nature of the self is multiple, perhaps that it is really just the stream of momentary arisings of the aggregates. But as we shall shortly see, such conceptions ultimately run into problems too.)

It can also be helpful to sustain attention on anything that may be conceived of as part of the self – a part of the body, for example, or an instance of some mental aggregate – and ask: "Is that 'me'?"

Sometimes it quickly becomes obvious that it cannot be me. At other times a little reflection or imagination helps. When we have a haircut or clip our toenails we usually don't then feel that we have lost our self, or that we somehow then have 'less self'. So one may also consider a body part, or an instance of a mental aggregate, imagine being without it, and notice that the sense of self is not diminished. It cannot therefore be 'me'. Likewise, with the arising of a thought, we do not typically feel as if our self is all of a sudden different, although there now exists a part that did not exist before. It seems to us that parts can come and go without affecting some essential sense of self.

Scrutinizing the parts of the self, we find that whatever we encounter we cannot regard as actually being the self. And if we say, "It's all the self," then, as explained, that self would have to be many. Alternatively, all these parts and instances would have to somehow be one, since the self is singular. But clearly they are not one.

When practising this stage of the analysis it is important to develop a strong sense of only being able to find what cannot be 'me'. This will make it easier to discount the sixth possibility – that the self is the collection of the parts – when you get to it.[2]

2) *The self is not other than the aggregates.*

In practice it is possible to imagine 'clearing away' the aggregates, or putting them to one side and seeing if there is anything else left over. When we do so, however, we see that there would be nothing remaining then that we could call, or identify as, self. If the self were separate from the aggregates, it should be apprehendable separately from them. But without the aggregates of body and mind, there is no self found.

Moreover, if the self were other than the aggregates it would be an entity without form, consciousness, or perception. It could not do anything or have any experiences. That is not the self that we feel attached to. Put another way, if the self were separate from the aggregates, then the experiences of body and mind would have no relation with or relevance for the self, for 'me'.

Each of the remaining five refutations in the sevenfold reasoning is actually a variation on one or other of the first two. Logically, these first two refutations – that the self is not the same as the aggregates, and that it is not different – exhaust all the possibilities. For any two phenomena must be either the same or different from each other. One might say that these next five are therefore unnecessary, but, for most practitioners, going through the other possibilities and seeing that they too cannot be the case makes the impossibility of an inherently existent self much more convincing.

[2] Apart from being impermanent and multiple, there are other reasons why the aggregates cannot be taken as the self. As we shall see, they are actually empty of inherent existence themselves. They can, for instance, be seen to be: fabricated and dependently arisen (Chapter 19); neither one nor many (Chapters 22 and 26); and not separable from, nor independent of, the rest of the universe (Chapter 24). Empty in themselves, the aggregates cannot possibly constitute a real basis for a real self, a self that is inherently existent, non-empty. Any of these particular insights just mentioned – each providing a slightly different angle on the voidness of the aggregates – can be incorporated into the sevenfold reasoning quite easily as these other practices are learnt and developed, if you feel they give more conviction to the refutation. This is one example of the many possibilities for flexibility and improvisation with all these practices, and of how, once some facility is established, practices may be combined to great effect.

3) *The self is not in the aggregates.*[3]

What is refuted here is the notion that the self is somehow among the aggregates, the way a person could be said to be in a house. It can easily be seen, though, that such a possibility is just a version of the second option – that the self and the aggregates are different, separable. Since, here, the person is one thing and the house another, we could imagine removing the person from the house, or demolishing the house and being left with the person. However, as in the refutation of the second possibility above, when we remove the aggregates it is evident that no self can be found to remain.

4) *The aggregates are not in the self.*[4]

Here the conception being refuted is that the self somehow contains the aggregates, the way, for example, a bowl might contain muesli or any other food. In this case again though, the bowl (the self) would be different and separable from the muesli (the aggregates), so that this fourth option is also essentially a variation on the second option. This possibility that the self and the aggregates are different and can be separated may be refuted just as before.

5) *The self does not possess the aggregates.*

The notion of possession may be entertained in two different ways. The first is the manner in which a person might possess, for example, a watch. Then the possessor (the person) and the possessed (the watch) are two different entities. The second is the manner in which a person possesses their own head, or a tree possesses a trunk. In that case, possessor and possessed are actually the same entity.

---

[3] Sometimes this branch of the reasoning is worded in different ways and in more technical language, such as: *The self is not inherently dependent on its bases of imputation.* (The 'bases of imputation', or the 'bases of designation', refer, here in the case of the personal self, to the body and mind or their parts – the aggregates.) However this branch of the reasoning is worded, its meaning remains essentially the same.

Note too, of course, as we shall later come to see in numerous ways, that no basis of imputation, whether for the personal self or for any phenomenal object, has inherent existence. That 'basis' is itself also empty. No ultimately true basis exists for anything anywhere.

[4] This branch too may be encountered with differing wording and more technical language, such as: *The self is not the inherent base of support of the aggregates.* Again though, the essential meaning is the same.

If the self is conceived of as possessing the aggregates in the way a person might possess a watch, then clearly the possessor (the person) is different from and separable from that which is possessed (the watch). This option thus becomes again another instance of the second possibility – that self and the aggregates are different and separable. So it can be refuted as before.

But if instead the self is conceived as possessing the aggregates in the way a person might possess their own head, or a tree its trunk, then we may ask: What, and where, actually, is the self that does the possessing of the aggregates? Other than the aggregates themselves, the possessing self cannot be found, since there is nothing else but the aggregates. Whether or not we choose to say that things or the aggregates "possess themselves", the notion of possession here is in fact just equivalent to the notion of 'being the same as'. As such, it is a variation of the first possibility – that the self is identical with the aggregates – and can be similarly refuted.

6) *The self is not just the collection of the aggregates.*

If we took all the different parts of a car or chariot and just dumped them on the ground in a pile, that collection of parts would not equate to the car or chariot. Similarly, a random heaping together of body parts and diverse and unordered moments of *vedanā*, thought, intention, etc. cannot be regarded as the self. This sixth possibility is actually an instance of the first possibility, and can also be refuted in similar ways.

7) *The self is not the shape of the aggregates, nor their continuum in time.*

Since the mental aggregates have no physical shape, it would be meaningless to take the physical shape of the aggregates as the self.[5] One might want instead to conceive of the self as the 'temporal shape' of the aggregates – that is, as their arrangement in time as a continuum. Such a conception would still be prey to many of the objections raised in relation to the first possibility.

A self that is a continuum would be changing as experiences and events are added and disappear in time. Intuitively though, we often feel that the self is essentially the same despite the coming and going of many of its elements; and

[5] In Chapter 22, we will consider and refute the possibility that the *phenomenal self* of any object – such as a chariot, a car, or a human body – can be equated with its shape, or the arrangement in space of its parts. Here let us just focus on the personal self and the 'shape' of its parts (the aggregates) in space or time.

the same also whether or not some of these are left out of the continuum entirely. Furthermore, if the self were essentially a continuum, its essence would effectively be altered by the slightest reordering in time of even the most trivial experiences and events. A reversal of the temporal sequence of even two very simple and uncharged perceptions occurring close together in time would constitute a different self. Yet this is not our sense of the self. Whether, for instance, I perceive the carpet one second before I hear a car go by outside, or vice versa, my essence feels unaltered.

Another problem with the notion of the self as the continuum of the aggregates is that, since the past is gone and the future has not yet come to be, most of the temporal continuum is not actually in existence at any time. Most of the self, therefore, would not exist at any time. Sensing ourselves or another though, we intuitively feel that we or they are all here – a self complete – right now. This reasoning may be pushed a little further. Since the present moment could be said to be infinitesimally small, it follows that at any time this self would in fact barely be in existence at all. Carefully contemplated in meditation, the possibility that the self could be equated with the continuum of the aggregates is seen to collapse.[6]

---

[6] Later, in Chapter 26, we will apply another reasoning – the neither-one-nor-many reasoning – to all temporal phenomena. In practice, this provides perhaps the most powerful refutation of the notion that the self could be the continuum of the aggregates. Many of the objections put forth above rely on a mismatch between our usual, intuitive sense of self, on the one hand, and the conception of the self as the continuum of the aggregates, on the other. Someone may want to assert then that it is *only* such an intuitive notion that is to be refuted, that the true nature of the self *is* the continuum and as such just does not correspond with our intuitive sense of self. The neither-one-nor-many reasoning applied to the temporal continuum refutes not just the intuitive sense of self we usually have, but also any assertion or conception of the true nature of the self as a continuum.

Briefly, its argument runs as follows: Since it is made up of a series of many moments, a continuum is not really 'one'. But it cannot really be 'many' either. To be truly many it would have to be made up of moments that are truly one. No such moment can exist though, because a moment that is truly one would have no differentiable times of beginning and ending. (For a moment to function and give time a direction, its beginning needs to *precede* its ending: its beginning and ending need, effectively, to be *different moments* in time.) Being neither truly one nor truly many, continua – and also, as we shall later emphasize, moments of time – have no inherent existence. And a self that is supposed to have inherent existence cannot be equated with an empty continuum.

As mentioned before, when some facility has developed with the neither-one-nor-many reasoning, it can be incorporated very easily into this stage of the sevenfold reasoning to great effect.

Developing a Personal Understanding and Conviction

In order that this analysis can be converted into a meditative practice with the power to liberate, we should make clear a few more things. Although the brief explanation of each branch of the sevenfold reasoning just given may feel sufficient for you, it is more likely that it represents only a skeleton of reasoning around which to base your own reflections. It is vital to think through each branch for yourself, and to find reasons that convince you. Perhaps some reasons will be filled out, added to, or replaced with other reasons. Much of this pondering may be done outside of formal meditation. We need to be quite convinced of all the reasonings, and also develop some familiarity with them, in order for this analysis to work well in meditation.

It is also important to realize what is the fundamental principle involved in the analysis. Naturally and typically – that is, unless we sign up to some philosophical doctrine formulating the nature of the self in a particular way – we do not consciously conceive of the self as existing in any of the seven ways listed in the analysis. The sevenfold reasoning is not principally, therefore, aimed at refuting a specific theory of self that we may be espousing or clinging to. What it is saying, rather, is that *if* the self had inherent existence, it would *have* to exist in one of these seven ways. There is no other possibility. That the self is not findable in any of these ways implies that it cannot really exist in the way that it seems to.

Again it may take a little time initially to recognize that there are no other possibilities for an inherently existing self, and for this recognition to reach a point of conviction. However, without this conviction, and also the understanding of its implication that the self is empty, the analysis will have very little power. Once the conviction is reached though, it can be re-established in practice very quickly – as a step in the meditative analysis, and thereafter whenever needed.

Working in Meditation

Let's briefly outline the meditative process here. In some traditions, a first step, referred to as 'ascertaining the object of negation', is prescribed. This means identifying what exactly the reasoning is refuting, what the analytical practice is taking aim at.[7] For now,

[7] In due course we will have more to say concerning this concept since there has been, between different streams of Buddhist tradition, considerable controversy surrounding it. And the debate here is in fact neither abstract nor irrelevant: as we will eventually see, the depth of liberating potency that any realization of emptiness opens hinges on what we consider the object of negation to be. See Chapter 31, in particular, for further discussion of this issue.

let us just say that in this case the object to be negated is the appearance of the self as something real. Simply paying attention to the sense of self, as explained in Chapter 11, will suffice. As an aspect of the experience within this sense, we can recognize too how the self feels so obviously real, so independently existent. Once we are familiar with noticing the spectrum of self-sense from previous practice, only a moment or two is in fact needed for this step.

Actually then considering each of the seven possibilities in turn, and seeing that none of them is a feasible way for the self to be, comprises the second step. This exhaustion of the possibilities is referred to as 'ascertaining the pervasion'.

Going through this search for the self in meditation and not finding it, we certainly recognize intellectually then that the self must therefore be illusory, empty, that it cannot exist in the way that it appears to. But something more than this begins to happen: a sense of emptiness begins to open up. The self-sense begins to dissolve right then as we realize that the self is not findable.

This vacuity that gradually appears to the perception in place of self is not simply a blanking out though; it is pregnant with meaning. It embodies the implication of the emptiness of self. Usually this significance permeating the vacuity – its indication of the voidness of the self – is obvious at this point for the meditator, both intuitively and also probably through some very light and sparse thought. We need to *focus the attention wholeheartedly on the sense and perception of the vacuity, and also on its implicit meaning.* This is the third step.

If at any time the vacuity's significance is no longer appreciated, then it is important for that sense to be resurrected, to keep deliberately remembering that this vacuity has the meaning of the emptiness of self. Whether it is obvious or whether we have to remind ourselves, whether it is through thought or more silently recognized, as we concentrate the awareness on the vacuity we need to let its meaning impress upon the *citta*. And just as we can get a feel for the seeming inherent existence of the self, we need to get a feeling for its emptiness. As the vacuity begins to appear, our focusing intensely on it and on the sense of emptiness is vital for deepening the insight into voidness.

With practice, as we concentrate on it, the sense of separation between the mind or awareness, on the one hand, and the vacuity, on the other, naturally begins to gradually fade, and they move toward fusion. As they do so, the sense and appreciation of emptiness become more direct and involve less and less conceptualization.

It is important, however, not to grasp at the perception of a vacuity as the goal of the practice. Rather than trying to find emptiness or a vacuity, the practice is best conceived of as a search for the inherently existing self – and then the realization that it cannot be found, because it does not exist. This realization is what is fundamental.

When the intensity of focus on the vacuity is relaxed, the self-sense reappears, and attention should be paid to how it feels. The self appears again but there is a knowing of its emptiness to some degree, and *this sense of it as an empty appearance should be explored, and enjoyed.* This is the fourth step.

On occasions when the meditative analysis of the self has gone deep enough, it is possible that, as the focus is relaxed, the sense of emptiness will spread naturally to other phenomena, so that they too can be seen and felt as empty appearances. Spending some time looking at other objects through this lens constitutes an optional fifth step. It is sometimes said that seeing the emptiness of any one thing profoundly, we understand the emptiness of all things equally.

As mentioned too, this particular meditative analysis can take *any* phenomenon as its object. It is not restricted to the personal self. Any physical object or any of the aggregates may be subjected to the sevenfold reasoning.

Creativity and fluidity in the practice

Although there is clearly a kind of formula for this analytical meditation being spelled out here, in practice it actually need not be ordered with complete rigidity. What matters is that it works for you. Certainly a thoroughness of reasoning, and a conviction in it, are indispensable. But as with any practice, eventually we want to make it our own, and this comes only through familiarity and the willingness to experiment. Responsiveness, as always, is crucial too. The whole meditation can then be a very fluid process.

So for example, as long as they are all covered, the order of the branches of reasoning is not necessarily fixed but may be varied at will. The pace at which they are moved through will vary greatly too. At first it might be relatively slow, and this is fine; it should not be rushed. The impact of the reasoning is what is important, and that should be the guide for pacing. With familiarity, the reasoning stage may be moved through very rapidly and still be very powerful.

A certain amount of fluid movement between the stages of the practice is also possible. Once you have gone through the reasonings and a sense of the emptiness of the object has been established, it may still be helpful sometimes to return to the reasoning and engage it again when that sense of emptiness, or conviction in the object's lack of inherent existence, weakens. Even once a vacuity has appeared in place of the object analysed, revisiting the steps of the reasoning – perhaps only very briefly or lightly, as appropriate – may help to maintain the perception of the vacuity, or to maintain a sense of its meaning for the object.

Like all insight practices, the sevenfold analysis meditation requires a certain amount of *samādhi* in order to be engaged in a fruitful way. But also like other insight practices, as it develops it will itself lead to a deepening of concentration.

This fortunate fact, together with the possibility of relaxing the focus on the vacuity – so that, as described, the object analysed reappears now qualified by and imbued with a sense of its emptiness, or so that other objects may similarly be viewed – opens up much potential for fluidity in practice. Notwithstanding what we have said about the importance of focusing on the vacuity and the sense of emptiness it implies for the object then, the practice may eventually move freely and as feels helpful between its various elements. These include: resting in a *samādhi* concentrated on the subtle body sense or some other object; engaging the reasoning; focusing more intensely on the vacuity; and viewing the object analysed, or other objects, with an understanding and felt sense of their lack of inherent existence.

Practice: The sevenfold reasoning in meditation

Spend some time reflecting on the principle underpinning the sevenfold reasoning until some conviction is reached – that the self, or anything else, if it is inherently existent, must be found in one of these seven ways; and that if it is not, it must mean that it lacks inherent existence.

Spend some time too pondering each of the seven branches of the reasoning so that they become familiar, and you find reasons refuting each possibility that convince you.

When you feel ready, you may engage the analysis more meditatively.

Take a little time to settle the *citta* in meditation. (As discussed, you can move back and forth between a concentration practice and the sevenfold reasoning practice as feels helpful.) Once a degree of *samādhi* is established, become aware of the sense of self, wherever it is on its spectrum. Become aware too of the way it feels as if it has inherent existence. If you have chosen another object to analyse, focus on that object and notice too the sense that it exists inherently.

Remaining focused on the object of analysis, remind yourself, based on the conviction you have established, that it has to exist in one of the seven ways if it has inherent existence.

Begin to go through the seven possibilities refuting each one. This can be done in any order that feels fruitful, and at whatever pace feels helpful at that time.

When you have gone through all seven, you may want to consciously remind yourself of the conclusion again – that since it cannot be found in any of these ways, and since there are no other possibilities, it is empty, it cannot exist in the way that it appears to.

Linger in and pay attention to the feeling that accompanies this conclusion.

Pay attention, too, at that point, to the perception of the self or the object analysed. If a perception of a vacuity has replaced the object then that vacuity may now be focused on. (It may take a little practice to be able to do this.) Make sure, though, that it is pregnant with the meaning of the emptiness of the object.

When you need to, you may revisit the analysis to any degree in order to reconsolidate the sense of the emptiness of the object.

You may also relax the focus on the vacuity and allow the perception of the object to reappear. Again though, notice the sense of the object, and how it now appears with a greater sense of its emptiness. Notice too how this feels.

At this point, you may also let the attention wander to other objects. Notice how they appear now, and how it feels to view things this way.

18

The Dependent Arising of Dualities

Any of the insights and practices that see all phenomena as having the nature of awareness will inevitably then see a certain kind of equality, or sameness, of all things. Sometimes it is proclaimed that all phenomena are of 'one taste'. We could also say that in those ways of looking there is a measure of insight into non-duality, since the duality between objects and consciousness is seen to be false.

Moreover, since in that view all objects, whatever their appearance, share the same essential nature, implicit too in this non-duality is the non-duality between things which seem to be opposites. Pain and pleasure, both being awareness in essence, are only apparently, but not essentially, two dissimilar things. And if the space and the unity that had opened up for a practitioner were characterized more by some other quality, such as mystical silence or love, any two apparent opposites could be seen to share *that* quality as their essential nature, so this insight into non-duality would be effectively unchanged.

Non-duality may be approached from various other angles too though. Before considering some of these possibilities, however, it is necessary to make clear one aspect of what is also contained for us in a sense of duality. Certainly a pair of obvious opposites constitute a duality. But even when we do not clearly define an opposite to some thing, a fundamental duality is made in our minds, consciously or sub-consciously, between that thing and what is not that thing. This would include then, as the Buddha declared to Kaccāyana,[1] the duality we typically assume between any thing's existence and its non-existence, and also between its presence and its absence.

[1] SN 12:15. We quoted and very briefly discussed this passage in Chapter 1.

'No Preferences'

A first option for working with dualities is to simply be aware of them, and to drop investment in them, without actually considering their emptiness. *Faith in Mind,* a much loved text by the Third Zen Patriarch, Seng T'san, begins:

> The Supreme Way is not difficult if you do not pick and choose.
> When love and hate are both absent, everything becomes clear and undisguised.
> Make the smallest distinction [between things], however, and heaven and earth are set infinitely apart.

It is possible to use this teaching as a meditative way of looking. In a meditation session, we can attempt to sustain an attitude of not picking and choosing, moment to moment, in regard to whatever is present or not yet present. We can practise, over and over, a dropping of any preference for any pole of any duality that presents itself.

Often though, we are not even aware that dualistic conceiving is operating in us. The felt sense of any *dukkha* and any clinging can provide a way in, for a duality is implicated through their presence. The arising of even the most subtle *dukkha*, grasping, or aversion must rest on some perception of duality. *Dukkha* requires clinging. And when there is clinging, it is always to one pole of a duality: grasping at some thing's presence and aversive to, or fearful of, its absence; or aversive to a thing's presence and desiring its absence. Noticing *dukkha* and clinging, we can identify what duality we are invested in, and practise a view of 'no preferences', 'not picking and choosing'.

Of course, this is a way of calming the typical push and pull of the mind's reactivity with regard to phenomena. Thus it will be effectively equivalent to the letting go that comes from the three characteristics views or from any practice of holy disinterest. Indeed it could be seen as a version of the *dukkha* characteristic practices. And like any of those ways of looking, it has the potential to deepen in subtlety – in this case, to the degree to which more subtle preferences are let go of.

Along with the beauty opened through this practice and the release it brings, at this point on our journey what we are particularly interested in are the effects of such a way of looking on the actual perception of dualities.

Practice: 'No preferences'

In a meditation session, take some time to gather the *citta* in a state of *samādhi* to a degree, and then attempt to sustain an attitude of 'no preferences', of not picking and choosing between experiences at all.

Whenever you become aware of the presence of *dukkha* or clinging, see if you can identify what duality has been seized upon.

Then see if it is possible to drop any preference for one pole of that duality over the other.

Notice what effects this has – both on the sense of *dukkha* and also on the sense of self.

Use any calming of fabrication that this practice allows to support a sensitivity to more subtle picking and choosing, which may then also be dropped.

What effects does this way of looking have on the perception of these dualities?

What else do you notice?

Seeing the Emptiness of Duality

Echoing a *Prajñāpāramitā Sūtra*, Shavari gave the instruction:

> Do not see fault anywhere.[2]

In practice, one way of not seeing fault anywhere is to view things through a lens informed by a conviction in the emptiness of duality. For 'fault' is a dualistic concept. Any 'fault' is in dualistic relation to its own absence, or to an instance of something conceived as 'without fault'. Recognizing the voidness of dualities can melt the notion and perception of 'faults'. And more generally, insights into the emptiness of dualities make possible a number of options for working with them, beyond merely trying to 'not pick and choose'.

Through sustaining a view which knows that dualities are void the investment in any duality is automatically dropped. Thus a release of clinging is supported through the insight in the way of looking. In addition, as is always the case with views, the particular insight embodied in that view is consolidated through practising it. And the practice of such a view also opens the possibility for certain new insights to be gained. Let us investigate two ways of realizing that dualities are empty, each suggesting a profoundly helpful way of looking.

---

[2] Translation by Ken and Katia Holmes in Jé Gampopa, *Gems of Dharma, Jewels of Freedom* [Forres: Altea, 1995] p. 248.

1. Recognizing How Dualities are Fabricated

Exaggerating through clinging

The emptiness of dualities may be exposed through exploring how their perception is often exaggerated. Various factors may have a role here. For example, when, believing in its real existence, we favour or desire one member of a dualistic pair over its opposite, this craving actually accentuates the very sense of duality for us. "Make the smallest distinction... and heaven and earth are set infinitely apart." Grasping after one pole and pushing away the other the apparent contrast between the two poles is highlighted. Without insight, this drawing-out of the appearance of duality only elicits a further response of clinging, and so simply perpetuates a vicious cycle. 'Silence' and 'noise', as an illustration, may seem to be real opposites, and meditators can often crave silence as an absence of noise. With this craving will inevitably come, as well as the *dukkha* of irritability, a degree of contraction of the mind around 'noises', and also an exaggeration of the sense of the difference between 'noises' and 'silence'.

Thus the more a *citta* state involves clinging, the more it will exaggerate the perception of certain dualities. In a state of restlessness, for instance, the perceived disparity between 'here' and 'there', and between 'now' and 'later' grows, and is also given greater significance. 'There and later' seem so different from, and so preferable to, 'here and now'. And this belief that 'there and later' are really very different from 'here and now' will, conversely, feed restlessness. *Citta* state, perception, belief, and clinging are locked into mutually supporting each other. To the extent that restlessness dies down, the apparent differences between 'here and now' and 'there and later' also die down. Correspondingly, to the degree that a belief in the reality of these differences is punctured, restlessness loses its support. A similar web of mutual fabrication is sometimes evident, for example, in the duality between 'security' and 'insecurity'. A grasping at the dualistic notion of 'security' (whether financial, emotional, or existential), a perception of 'insecurity', and the emotion of fear, can all feed each other.

In any of these examples, the more we cling to one pole, the more the other looms for us. The more we grasp at something, the more its absence or opposite stands out for us. Through clinging, the perceived intensities of opposites are mutually dependent. Seeing a little of how such dualities are fabricated in this way at least suggests to us the fundamental emptiness of their elements. With enough release of clinging though, it may be quite possible for the seeing in this way to completely undermine a belief in the elements of the duality in question.

Artificially separating continua

In our lives we regularly encounter all kinds of dualities – complex or simple, gross or subtle, more or less obvious as a duality. Some can seem innocuous enough, but not comprehending the emptiness of dualities, we may instinctively seize on what seem like opposites, and create *dukkha* there, often without even realizing what is happening. Consider the following opposites: tiredness and brightness of mind; happiness and sadness; calm and agitation; mindfulness and distractedness; illness and health; pain and absence of pain; stillness and movement of mind; aversion and acceptance; grasping and non-grasping; conceiving and non-conceiving; realization and delusion; wisdom and ignorance; freedom and bondage. The distinction can seem so real within each pair – one pole desirable and the other to be rejected or somehow overcome. Inflating the difference through clinging and ignorance, the mind can feel further ensnared in and oppressed by the duality it perceives.

But a closely related insight can be teased out too here. Carefully inspecting these pairs above will reveal that each pair of opposites more accurately forms a *continuum*, without an inherently existing demarcation between them. For each pair, the areas of delimitation of both elements are in fact conceptually constructed, together. Already in Chapter 5 we regarded *samādhi* in this way. Clarity and lack of clarity, comfort and discomfort, contentment and discontentment – these dualities too are in a relation only of continuous degree. Yet the mind can so easily seize on and reify these poles, imputing them with inherent and separate existences.

Solidifying what is not solid

Moreover, in so doing the mind may also fail to see that many of these reified poles have minute holes in them, where they may actually contain their opposites or their absences, as explained in Chapters 6 and 7. (We can notice this, for example, even in states of *samādhi* that at first sight might seem utterly homogenous and solid.) Through clinging, not only is the difference between poles exaggerated but the poles themselves become further solidified, painted black and white. Now though, as suggested above, we may well ask: Where, really, does one end and the other begin? And are they really as black and white as they seem?

Developing a Liberating Way of Looking

Although not all dualities are solidified from a continuum, for the ones that are we can use these insights to empower another way of looking. More than simply dropping preferences then, it is possible to regard any such duality through a lens informed by the understanding that the difference is not as stark and real as it seems.

This insight will need to be consolidated somewhat before it can be employed as a way of looking in meditation though. Some reflection, and some closer scrutiny of apparent dualities – *samādhi* and lack of *samādhi*, clinging and non-clinging, for instance – may be required to reveal that the distinctions between certain things are not as clear cut as they seem. And it will also be necessary, in order to secure the insight that such opposing pairs are empty of having the kind of solidity and separateness they appear to have, to notice repeatedly how the perception of any duality – for instance between pain and its absence – is affected by clinging and its release.

Transported into practice then, the recognition of the emptiness of such opposing pairs may still initially require a little reflection in some cases. But with familiarity, it can become very quick and feel very light. This realization can then be held in the view without strain as attention focuses on one or both of the poles of a duality.

In this way of looking, as well as in the one offered next, we can again use a sensitivity to the presence of any *dukkha* and clinging to alert us to the operation of dualistic conceiving. We can then identify the object of clinging as a pole in some duality. Having identified the duality, we can remember that it is empty, begin to view it as such, and feel the relief and freedom that this view brings.

Occasionally though – and despite the recommendation in Chapter 3 that we mainly contemplate the voidness of those things whose reification seems to cause palpable *dukkha* – we may choose to meditate on the emptiness of certain phenomena even when their reification does not seem to be problematic in that moment. The *dukkha* supported by assuming that *avijjā* or grasping, for instance, are inherently existent will not be immediately apparent unless they become charged themes for us in practice, and the mind has contracted around trying to eliminate them, for example. Still, it can be very instructive, and surprisingly liberating, to contemplate that they too are conceived dualistically, and to contemplate their emptiness in these ways.

In due course it will be crucial to see that such phenomena are void. For now, however, we can trust that starting to work for the most part with more obviously relevant dualities, such as pain and its absence, the less obviously problematic ones will in time become more relevant and central elements of practice. They will also become easier to work with as our skill in handling more subtle phenomena in meditation develops.

Practice: Seeing dualities as empty because fabricated

Once a degree of calm is established in a formal meditation session, whenever you notice *dukkha* or clinging is present, see if you can identify the dualistic conceiving that underpins it.

Having done so, practise viewing both the duality and the pole or object clung to knowing that, although they are perceived, they are empty.

Experiment with using a very light label such as 'empty' to help hold this insight within the attention to the object.

(The understanding underlying the view of emptiness here is that the apparent difference is not as substantial as it seems – that the dualistic perception is exaggerated by clinging to reified and solidified poles of what is essentially a non-solid continuum.)

Notice how this way of looking feels, and the effects it has on the sense of *dukkha*.

Notice also the effects it has on the sense of self, and *particularly* on the perception of any phenomenon clung to.

The need for sensitivity in practice: a reminder

In viewing duality as empty, it is important to understand what we are trying to do, and not to throw the baby out with the bathwater. While *dukkha* can easily be bound up in such dualities, clearly many of the pairs mentioned above actually constitute helpful distinctions, necessary for a genuine deepening of insight. We need, therefore, to use them, but to take care in our relating to them. Eventually, seeing their emptiness will allow a freedom to pick them up or put them aside, to use them without any danger of *dukkha* or of becoming trapped in them. More central to our purposes at this point, though, is the illustration of their voidness; and also the development of other meditative ways of looking.

As always with emptiness practices, sensitivity and care are required along with a spirit of experimentation. We may recognize within ourselves marked individual tendencies to perceive in terms of certain dualities in ways that cause suffering. Realizing their voidness can be immensely freeing. But some of the dualities we repeatedly suffer with are also quite complex psychologically. Loneliness and togetherness, feeling rejected and feeling loved, feeling understood and feeling misunderstood – dualities such as these may be part of more consistent and multifaceted knots of pain in a person's life, and may need to be approached with more delicacy. There may be times when it is appropriate and helpful to regard them as empty, and other times when other ways of relating to them might be more helpful.

2. Understanding the Mutual Dependence of Dualities

In many respects this understanding of how things are solidified and how the sense of duality is exacerbated through clinging, ignorance, and a lack of careful inspection is quite similar to some of what has already been discussed in previous chapters. We may go a little further now though, and call dualities into question at an even more fundamental level – through seeing the *dependent arising* of things which seem to be opposites. Nāgārjuna, in his *Ratnāvalī*, pointed out that

> When there is this, that arises,
> Just as when there is short there is long…
> [And] when there is long, there has to be short –
> They do not exist through their own nature.[3]

The very notion 'long' depends on the notion 'short'; and, equally, 'short' depends on 'long'. They arise dependent on each other. Of course, as Tsongkhapa and others stressed, this is not to say that 'short' is the producer of 'long', or vice versa, in the way that a sprout produces a seed, for example, but rather that they are meaningless concepts without each other. This will be the case for any thing that exists as a duality with, or in relativity to, something else. Thus 'left', 'right'; 'here', 'there'; 'beautiful', 'ugly'; 'calm', 'agitation' – none of these have independent existence either.

We saw earlier that the perceived *intensities* of a pair of opposites are dependent on clinging. Here this mutual dependency is shown to extend to the most basic *conception* of any of these phenomena. Each is actually constellated in mutual dependence on its opposite, and is unable to stand alone. From this

[3] Translation adapted from Jeffrey Hopkins's in *Nāgārjuna's Precious Garland*, p.100.

perspective too, then, we can say that, because they lack any reality independent of each other, they are empty, they have no inherent existence. In addition to the formulation of the twelve links that we began to explore in Chapter 10, and the dependency on clinging we began to explore above, this mutual dependency of pairs of opposites constitutes another important aspect of the meaning of dependent arising.

A lack of deeply understanding that each member of a duality fundamentally depends on the other is one of the manifestations of *avijjā*. On an intellectual level it may be relatively easy to acknowledge that concepts arising in mutual dependence are empty concepts. On a more intuitive level, however, our belief in the inherent existence of dualistic concepts forms a support for *dukkha* more basic even than clinging. For this belief radically shapes not just our thinking, but our very perception. We do not only conceive dualities on an intellectual level; through conceiving them intuitively, we perceive them. And this is so even when we perceive without verbally labelling the percept in our mind. The conception of duality between pain and non-pain, for example, is actually wrapped up in our very perception of pain, whether or not we actually think "pain". Out of this dualistic perception arises clinging, which, as we explained before, then exacerbates the dualistic perception.

It is possible, though, to practise a way of looking that deliberately includes the realization that the elements of any duality are mutually dependent and therefore empty. Again, it may be necessary to spend some time first digesting this understanding. Then, as always, it will probably be useful to experiment with ways of incorporating this knowing into the view in the moment. For some, a very light and brief thinking may be involved, and this is not at all problematic. More likely though, once the understanding has been digested, with practice we can simply summon the knowledge of the emptiness of duality in a very delicate yet powerfully effective way as we hold it in attention.

Practice: Seeing dualities as empty because mutually dependent

As in the previous practices, once you are settled in a meditation session, whenever you notice *dukkha* or clinging is present, see if you can identify the dualistic conceiving that supports it.

Having done so, practise attending to both the duality and the clung-to object within the knowledge that, although they are perceived, they are void.

Experiment with using a very light label such as 'empty' to help hold the understanding within the attention to the object.

(Here, the label 'empty' would have at times the tacitly understood subscript: 'because it arises in mutual dependence within a duality'.)

Again, notice how this way of looking feels, and the effects it has on the sense of *dukkha*.

Notice also the effects it has on the sense of self, and *particularly* on the perception of any phenomenon clung to.

§

It will almost certainly not be enough merely to reflect intellectually that dualities are empty because they are mutually dependent or because they are conceptually carved out of a continuum. These views must be meditatively employed in order to be more deeply digested into the *citta*. As has been stressed, as we practise any view and feel the freedom and release it brings, the understanding expressed in that view is consolidated. And it may also deliver further insights. In this case, it is vital, therefore, to notice also the effects on the perception of phenomena.

PART SIX

Radical Discoveries

19

The Fading of Perception

Through the different practices offered so far, we have seen clearly how *dukkha*, the sense of self, and the apparent substantiality of inner and outer phenomena are all dependent on clinging. We also explored a little how the sense of duality between things is exacerbated by clinging. As they are developed, many of the practices already described will follow this thread of insight even further and reveal more.

A meditator practising diligently will notice that, often, through many of the insight ways of looking the perception of phenomena will *fade* to some degree. It may be a little, a lot, or completely, but even as attention is focused on an object, for example a pain somewhere in the body or the body sensations as a whole, when the view releases clinging enough in one way or another, the experience of that object under view begins to soften, blur, and fade. In the case of painful sensation, the unpleasant *vedanā* will also become less and less unpleasant, before the apprehension of any sensation at all gradually dissolves. Again depending in part on the background of the practitioner, this fading will initially be evident more easily in some senses than in others, but to some extent there begins to be, in meditation, a melting of all appearances, of 'things', of objects of perception.[1]

This fading of perception – or, as Nāgārjuna and others sometimes called it,

[1] This should be the case for all the practices from Chapter 13 on. The *anicca* practice, however, because it reinforces through its very way of looking beginnings and endings of experiences, will often sustain, rather than a fading, merely a sharper delineation of phenomena at a finer level, which will thus likely be reified. Since the essential insight into dependent origination that is suggested by the dependent fading of phenomena is therefore not so apparent through the *anicca* practice, I would stress again the importance, if you are developing the *anicca* meditation, of developing at least one of the other ways of looking too.

'pacification of perception'[2] – it is crucial to experience many, many times, and to reflect on. It is easy to miss the insight here. Without giving it a second thought, a practitioner may just assume that things disappear 'because they are impermanent', or 'because the attention is concentrating on something else'. More careful investigation, though, reveals that something more surprising, radical, and mysterious is going on here than either of these conclusions suggests: *The experience, the perception of a phenomenon, depends on clinging*. For a thing to appear as that thing for consciousness, to be consolidated into an experience, it needs a certain amount of clinging.

As alluded to above, this insight is in fact merely an extension of our previous insights into how clinging fabricates self-sense and apparent substantiality of phenomena. A fading of perception is, in a way, just a further loss of substantiality. And it is actually possible to see this dependency of phenomena on clinging at any level, from the grossest to the most subtle. At a more gross level, we can see that when we are swept up in a tantrum about something, for instance, the self-sense certainly becomes more pronounced, but so does the solidity, and also the very prominence, of the thing we are upset about. All of these perceptions are fabricated less – they are 'pacified' – as we calm down.

That the perceptions of certain grosser *citta* states are dependent on clinging becomes obvious too if you deliberately try, in a state of boredom or fear, to become *more* bored or *more* fearful. It is actually very difficult, and may even decrease the intensity of the boredom or fear. Both these states, like any afflictive emotion, require aversion to the states themselves. Trying to make them stronger is a movement opposite to aversion, so reducing the aversion. It thus takes away some of the support on which the emotion is dependent. That emotion may therefore fade, together with other perceptions it was colouring.

In meditation we have the opportunity to explore this dependent arising and fading of phenomena through a greater range than would be available to a non-meditator, and into much more subtlety. As we do so, we realize too that clinging itself also has a range of subtlety, and that we must include as expressions of clinging more than just the palpable push and pull of the mind toward phenomena.

---

[2] '*sarvopalambhopaśamaḥ*', e.g. MMK 25:24. Developing the practices that have been outlined, it will be obvious that the 'pacification of perception' such texts draw attention to goes well beyond a dropping of the mind's verbal labelling of objects. Certainly, in the course of meditation a quieting of labelling may sometimes occur, and this may be felt as enjoyable, as 'fresh', or as just slightly odd. By themselves though, such experiences of a dropping of labelling do not open up any possibility of a radically freeing understanding. In contrast, experiences of the fading of perception that we are now addressing can extend into a range of much greater profundity; and more importantly, the fading of perception – to whatever extent – is a much more profoundly *significant* experience, as we shall explain.

Appropriating phenomena, grasping them as 'me' or 'mine', even unconsciously, is a form of clinging; and identifying with more subtle phenomena, such as consciousness, is a more subtle form of clinging. In fact, intuitively conceiving the inherent existence of any thing is also regarded as a form of grasping in the tradition – *avijjā* being perhaps the most subtle kind of clinging.

As skill with the practices is developed, one notices in meditation that phenomena fade to the extent that clinging is reduced through any insight way of looking. Less clinging in any moment fabricates less perception of objects. The continuum of self-sense we introduced in Chapter 11 is, on fuller investigation, also a continuum of perception of all phenomena. More gross, solid, separate, defined, and intense-appearing at one end, less and less so as clinging in all its manifestations is attenuated.

Cessation and 'reality'

At the extremity of the more subtle end of the continuum, in a moment when clinging, identification, and grasping at inherent existence are pacified, there is the *cessation* of perception – the phenomena of the six senses do not appear at all.[3] The Buddha stressed the importance of such cessation many times:

> That sphere should be understood where the eye ceases and perception of forms fades away. That sphere should be understood where the ear ceases and the perception of sounds fades away. That sphere should be understood where the nose and… smells… tongue and… tastes… body and… perception of tactile objects fades away. That sphere should be understood where the mind ceases and perception of mental phenomena fades away.[4]

Through letting go of clinging more and more totally and deeply, the world of experience fades and ceases; and seeing and understanding this is of great significance:

> I say that the end of the world cannot be known, seen, or reached by travelling. Yet… I also say that without reaching the end of the world there is no making an end to *dukkha*.[5]

---

[3] We will return to discuss the theme of cessation of perception at greater length in Chapters 28 and 29. Here it will be helpful to make just a few remarks relevant to this stage of our exploration.

[4] SN 35:117.

[5] SN 35:116.

In the *Samādhirāja Sūtra*, too, it says:

> With perfect understanding that things are empty, dualistic perceptions fade away and the wise abide within a state devoid of every feature.[6]

And Nāgārjuna, likewise, pointed out the dependence of cessation on an absence of clinging:

> One who sees the absence of 'mine' and the absence of I-making does not see.[7]

Witnessing again and again the movement along this continuum of appearance in dependence on clinging, we may ask, as we did of the similarly dependent appearance of the self: Which perception reflects 'reality'? Exactly what amount of craving, identification, or *avijjā* reveals the 'real' thing, the 'real' world, the way things 'really' are?

We may be tempted to answer that an absence of craving, identification, and delusion will reveal the world 'as it is'. But equanimity – the dying down of the mind's push and pull with respect to phenomena – does not reveal a world of things, in their pristine 'bare actuality', 'just as they are', stripped only of the distortions of ego projections and gross *papañca*. Rather, as meditative skill develops, we see that without clinging phenomena do not appear at all. Not only *how* they appear, but *that* they appear is dependent on the fabricating conditions of clinging.

To be sure, one could go to the other extreme then. Since the cessation of perception comes about through a dying down of fabricating (with all the implications of falsity that that word carries), this non-appearance of phenomena could be construed as more 'real' than any appearance of things. This is one way to interpret the many statements in the tradition such as:

> To see nothing is to see excellently,

from a *Prajñāpāramitā Sūtra*; or, from the *Dharmasaṃgīti Sūtra*:

> When all phenomena are not seen, one sees them perfectly.

---

[6] Translation from the author's notes.
[7] MMK 18:3.

We will see later, though, why even the experience of cessation cannot be objectified and taken as an ultimate truth.[8] For now, however, we will simply say that the two statements just above declare the importance both of cessation, and, more primarily, of the seeing that there are no 'real' things. Cessation can make clear the extent of fabrication, and that without being fabricated by the mind a phenomena does not appear and is not any thing in itself. We will take from fading and cessation the understanding that all phenomena are empty, that there is no objective stance on how a thing is. It is this *understanding* of cessation that is most important, not simply the experience itself. This it is crucial to emphasize. The fading of perception implies that the thing-ness of things is dependent on the perceiving mind's clinging. We begin to realize that things do not have any existence as 'this' or 'that' independent of the mind. As Hui-neng stated,

> From the first, not a thing is.[9]

In practice, the more appearances fade along this continuum, the more chance there is of seeing the emptiness of *all* phenomena. A range of experience comprising only a limited amount of fading may leave unexposed the fabricated nature of certain phenomena, and so may leave the assumption of their inherent existence unchallenged. Then an intuitive leap of understanding, or some other means, is needed to extend the insight into fabrication and dependent origination to embrace all phenomena, including awareness and the present moment, the last phenomena to fade. Such a leap of intuition is certainly possible, but exploring and understanding a fuller range of this continuum of fabrication of perception may be a surer bet.

A fuller understanding of dependent origination

Referring these observations back into the context of the map of *paṭiccasamuppāda* can be instructive. A few points are important to make. First, through this meditative experience of fading, it is clear that not only does craving depend on *vedanā*, as in the more commonly received formulation, but also that *vedanā* depends on craving.

Although we did acknowledge, in Chapter 10, a certain non-linearity of the links, this kind of non-linearity we are now discovering is more surprising and

---

[8] In Chapter 29.

[9] Translation by D. T. Suzuki in *The Zen Doctrine of No Mind* [London: Rider, 1972] p. 22.

undermining of our common-sense notions. A seemingly basic experience is revealed to be dependent on the reaction to it. Considered from a point of view that would see the links of dependent origination as a sequence happening in time, this does not even make sense. But revealing, as it does, the emptiness of *vedanā* – the very experience of any sensation is revealed to be not at all independent of the way the mind is looking at it – it opens up a powerfully liberating new avenue for deeper insight, as we shall explore.

Second, we can include perception – that is, the experience of phenomena – more fully and centrally now in our understanding of dependent origination. The Buddha in fact listed perception as one of the factors comprising the fourth link, *nāmarūpa*. It is the forming of the appearances of definite things, not only their labelling with words, that is more accurately meant by the term *nāmarūpa* when used in the context of the teaching of dependent origination. Thus the colouring of appearances, the colouring of the perception of things and situations in different ways, is taken account of in the map.

Not only this though, the fading of experience – the rise and fall in the intensity of perception dependent on other links – is taken account of too. From the map of *paṭiccasamuppāda*, understood non-linearly, the role of both craving and *avijjā* as fabricators of perception is evident. And this mirrors meditative experience. Practising a view which manifests less *avijjā* – for example dropping the *avijjā* of identification in the *anattā* way of looking – fabricates less perception and *vedanā* in that moment. In moments of less *avijjā*, the rest of the links are fed less, so perception and *vedanā* are fabricated less, and they fade. Our meditative investigation and the Buddha's teaching of dependent origination both reveal that the fabrication of any experience at all is dependent on craving and on *avijjā*.

Now we can also better understand why in the sevenfold reasoning practice a vacuity opens up in place of the perception of the self or of whatever object is being analysed. When the analytical investigation sees the lack of inherent existence of the self or object, *avijjā*, which habitually assumes the inherent existence of things, is lessened. With *avijjā* thus lessened, the perception of the self or object is lessened correspondingly. As Śāntideva wrote in his *Bodhicaryāvatāra*:

> When an object of analysis is analysed, no basis… remains.
> Deprived of a basis, it does not continue.[10]

[10] All translations from BCA are the author's own, made also with reference to the translation by Kate Crosby and Andrew Skilton in Śāntideva, *The Bodhicaryāvatāra* [Oxford: Oxford University Press, 1995].

The perception of any phenomenon is dependent on *avijjā* as a basis, as the teaching of *paṭiccasamuppāda* makes clear.

To conclude that this fading of appearances we have been describing is merely "because things are impermanent" would betray an incomplete investigation of the conditions on which appearances and disappearances actually depend, and particularly, here, the relationship with clinging. For in such cases of fading it can be seen that the perception in question does not disappear randomly. Rather, it fades as clinging is reduced; and it can reconstitute and become more pronounced when clinging is stronger. If we see this enough times the dependent arising of perception becomes evident.

This is why it was stressed earlier to practise the ways of looking not just with a wider attention but also with attention focused more narrowly on one object. Then the fading of any particular appearance is clear and obvious, and its relationship with the release of clinging is more evident. Right here as I am looking at this particular thing, it fades. I cannot miss it. And I cannot conclude that it is simply because the focus was elsewhere. The dependency on clinging becomes apparent, whereas in a wider attention the particularity of the connection may get diffused.

To take only the conclusion of impermanence from this observation would be like concluding that when something falls from the hand it is only "because the positions of objects are impermanent". They *are* impermanent. But one has failed to notice a more significant law at work – that of gravity. The motion of the object released from the hand is not random; it follows the laws of gravity. Likewise here, a phenomenon in consciousness fades not simply because it is impermanent, but because its appearance is dependent on clinging, and when clinging is reduced enough the appearance is not supported and it dissolves. An object still in my hand does not fall because the hand is applying a force to keep it from falling. Similarly, as more skill in releasing craving is developed through the various insight ways of looking, we come to see that when a phenomenon does not fade in such practices, it is because it is being sustained as a perception by some clinging that we are perhaps not yet aware of, or not yet able to release.

On encountering such fading of perception, one might alternatively want to conclude that in meditation the brain chemistry or neurophysiology is somehow affected, resulting in 'distorted' perceptions. But when considering practice, it should be clear that all a meditator meditating in these ways is doing is paying attention, and letting go of clinging. As pointed out in Chapter 4, letting go of craving is actually not doing more, but doing less. Even looked at from a materialist bias, the dependency of perception on habitual clinging is still revealed.

For the sake of a fullness of realization of emptiness, we seek a profound and firsthand understanding of dependent arising. On several occasions the Buddha and others, giving instructions for higher insight, encouraged practitioners to

> abide contemplating increase and decrease with regard to the five aggregates of clinging: Such is form, such its origin, such its disappearance. Such is *vedanā*, such its origin, such its disappearance... Such is perception... Such are mental formations... Such is consciousness, such its origin, such its disappearance.[11]

It is not just the fact of impermanence that is being called to our attention for investigation here. Not only *that* the aggregates arise and pass, increase and decrease, but *how* and *why* they do: "*Such* is its origin, *such* its disappearance."

Insight into Fading Brings the Possibility of a More Powerful Way of Looking

With repeated experience of this fading of perception in meditation, the corresponding insight – that objects of perception are fabricated by clinging, and are thus empty of inherent existence – is consolidated more and more. At some stage this insight will reach a point of conviction. A practitioner is then able to adopt a meditative way of looking that takes this insight of emptiness as its principal lens, rather than the insight emerging only as a result of other ways of looking. One may now practise a view that more directly regards phenomena (at least, at this point, some of them) as 'empty' or 'just a perception'.

Notice that exactly what is included in the meaning of the view 'empty' here is different than previously – for instance when regarding phenomena as being empty of possessing a different 'substance' than awareness, or dualities being dependent at a fundamental conceptual level. Now, evidenced by countless instances of dependent fading, the tacit understanding that underlies this newly possible view is: 'empty because dependent on clinging and *avijjā*'. And similarly the articulation 'just a perception' implies here: 'just something fabricated through clinging and *avijjā*'.

As explained, sustaining any way of looking that constitutes a reduction in clinging and in *avijjā* will lead to less fabrication, and so to this fading of perception. Since viewing things as 'empty' or 'just a perception' as described

[11] E.g. in SN 22:89 and SN 22:101.

above actually comprises even more insight, and thus less *avijjā* and less clinging, than practices such as the three characteristics, this way of looking will also cause objects of perception to fade, and perhaps even more powerfully now.

Whatever way of looking one employs at any time, in practice such fading is usually gradual, along the continuum mentioned earlier. Taking physical pain again as an example, there may initially be a decrease in the intensity of the unpleasantness of the experience. It is quite possible that pleasant sensations take their place, but as these too are regarded as empty (or viewed with any other way of looking that decreases fabrication) they will also in time tend toward more neutrality of *vedanā*. Then, if the releasing way of looking is sustained on the neutral sensations, even they begin to fade. The perception of solidity is thus reduced until what remains is only a perception of space instead. It may grow vast, or it may just be that where there was sensation the perception is now of space. This space may be perceived as having different qualities, as we described a little in Chapter 15, and particularly may be perceived as having the quality of awareness. But now this awareness has no form or shape at all as its object. If this space too is then regarded as 'empty' or 'just a perception', it will also fade – into a nothingness, where even the perception of space seems to have collapsed. That perception of nothingness in turn can eventually be regarded also as 'just a perception', and it too will fade, for similar reasons.

Emptiness and the *Jhānas*

Understanding the jhānas as stages of progressively less fabrication

One may recognize in this continuum of unfolding experience a parallel with progressively deeper states of *jhāna*. This is worth some elaboration. In *samādhi* meditation, after any pain and hindrances subside, there is the arising of pleasure of different kinds, which gradually becomes more and more refined and subtle until the deep end of the third *jhāna*. This refinement continues until the loveliness of the fourth *jhāna*, where the *vedanā* have become "neither pleasant nor unpleasant". The body sense and the perception of form disappear in the fifth *jhāna*, the sphere (or 'realm') of infinite space. And by the seventh *jhāna*, the sphere of nothingness, any perception of space is replaced by a sense of nothingness.

What is happening here is most accurately regarded as a progressive non-fabrication of perception. Indeed the Buddha called the *jhānas* 'perception attainments'[12] – not because higher states of *jhāna* are fabricated more and more, but because progressive states of *jhāna* are fabricated *less and less*, and themselves fabricate less and less. (To fabricate more, as we described earlier, would be to move in the direction of more *papañca* and agitation – in extremis, a tantrum, for instance.) Here then, the perception of space, for example, becomes primary because the more gross perception of form (*rūpa*) is not being fabricated and so falls away. Even when the perception of space is no longer being fabricated and is replaced by a wonderful sense of nothingness, this nothingness too is actually still a very subtle object of perception. It is transcended by the sphere of neither perception nor non-perception, the eighth *jhāna*, more wonderful still, where the fabrication of perception reaches its minimum limit. At this point no perception is being fabricated other than the perception that awareness is not landing on any object as a perception in the present moment. However, there is as yet not the complete fading of perception that occurs in cessation. For in the eighth *jhāna* there is still a sense of awareness, albeit extremely refined; and still a sense of a present moment, in which this inability to conclusively form a perception, is perceived.

When contemplated from this perspective, the spectrum of the eight *jhānas* itself offers profound insight into the fabricated nature of the perception of things. And with this understanding, there will be less likelihood of reifying any of the stages of *jhāna*, or any similar openings of perception, as something ultimate.

Insights from the formless realms

It is sometimes claimed that the *jhānas* in themselves bring no insight. However, related to the above, a range of observations can render them immensely helpful for deepening understanding. As we have touched on before, emerging from such states as the formless realms the perception of things is often transformed, for a time, in accord with the particular *jhāna* one has just experienced. Exploring this can help consolidate insight into the fabricated nature of all perception.

Emerging from the sphere of infinite space, for example, the perception of substantiality is usually much reduced. This is because in that particular *jhānic* state this perception of substantiality, of solidity or "obstruction", was not being

---

[12] E.g. in AN 9:36. All the *jhānas* are referred to as 'perception attainments', except for the sphere of neither perception nor non-perception. This last, as explained below, cannot properly be said to involve perception of an object.

fabricated[13] and its fabrication has not yet recovered to more habitual levels. There may be a mystical appreciation opened within the way of looking then, in which things are seen in some way to have the nature, or substance, of space. One may vividly sense that despite the re-forming perception of solidity the essence of things is, 'more truly', space. Things can now be seen both ways, though – as solid, and as space – at once.

Often, as a result of an experience of the sphere of infinite space, a strong, deeply moving sense of the oneness of all things can open up afterwards. Although arising primarily through seeing that all phenomena share this 'essence' of space, this sense of oneness can sometimes be flavoured slightly differently as well. For the sphere of infinite space may also make available and impress upon us, as an after-effect, a parallel and complementary insight: that cosmically 'all is one' in some *material* sense. After the experience of the *jhāna*, there can be in the seeing and in the heart a keen appreciation, a joyful resonance with the knowledge, for instance, that the atoms and molecules that form my body and those that form yours or that form this miraculous flower in front of me were all forged in the very same stellar explosion billions of years ago; and that all the matter and energy that currently exists shares a common, unified origin, way before that, as the undifferentiated and super-compacted stuff that underwent the process of the Big Bang in the birth of this universe. Naturally resonating now with such knowledge, exhilarating feelings of wonder, delight, and love, as well as a certain liberation, pervade these openings of the seeing.

Whether through the perception that all things share an 'essence' of insubstantial space, or through this perceived oneness at the level of materiality, the sense of the separateness, too, of material forms is not being fabricated then as much as it normally is. Thus in moving in and out of the *jhāna* or its after-effects we realize that perceptions of solidity and of separateness, as well as of non-solidity and of oneness, are fabricated.

Similarly, coming out of an experience of the sphere of infinite consciousness, all things can appear to have the nature of consciousness. (And here, through and after this *jhāna*, the sense of oneness that so touches the heart and informs the seeing is no longer a oneness of materiality but rather a oneness of consciousness, sometimes a kind of cosmic consciousness.)[14]

---

[13] Cf. AN 9:37, DN 15, etc.: '*paṭighasaññānaṃ atthaṅgamā*', which may be translated as 'the disappearance [or: setting down] of perceptions of obstruction'.

[14] In practice, there are actually a cluster of states quite similar to the sphere of infinite consciousness, but subtly differentiable nonetheless, that all involve the sense of awareness as the principal perception. In these cases therefore there can and will be a range of correspondingly nuanced diversity to the sense of things in their mystically flavoured after-effects on perception.

Emerging from the sphere of nothingness the view of things can be that while they are clearly 'things', they are also 'nothing', they somehow lack the reality we have typically ascribed to them. (Here the sense of oneness present in the after-effect comes from seeing that all things share this essence of 'being no thing, really', an 'essence' of nothingness, of emptiness.[15]) If one has entered the *jhāna* without an understanding of emptiness, one might feel this insight – that things lack inherent existence – intuitively, but it might be difficult to articulate. Although one has not understood yet quite *why* and *how* things are empty, there is insight there nevertheless, and it will bring, along with a sense of awe and beauty, a profound and even exciting sense of freedom.

This applies also to the sphere of neither perception nor non-perception. Accessing the state without previous insight, on emerging to the perception of differentiated things, one might somehow comprehend that these things are 'all just perception'. No longer unquestionably 'the real world', this world might appear as merely one of the 'realms of perception', in contrast to the realm of neither perception nor non-perception.

Thus the states themselves can in fact bring insight and open up insight ways of looking, if one knows how to capitalize on the perceptual transformations. Rather than concluding that any state itself is ultimate or ultimately true, with repeated practice one may come to understand that the conventional and normal perception of things, though shared by most, is actually fabricated, and is just one way of fabricating perception. Repeated experience of any of the formless *jhānas* may reinforce the particular insight views connected with that *jhāna*. As long as these are not taken as being ultimate truths, preventing further investigation, such insight and undermining of habitual views can only be helpful.

Using insight to access the formless jhānas

We can begin to see now more fully how insight and *samādhi* are actually intertwined, and feed each other. In fact, among a range of means he taught for deliberately attaining various higher states of *jhāna*, the Buddha outlined exactly these insight ways of looking which we have been exploring.[16] For example, one way he taught for reaching the sphere of nothingness is to sustain a moment-to-

---

[15] Cf. the references to and brief discussion of an 'essence of emptiness' in the *Exchanging Self and Other* section of Chapter 24.

[16] See MN 106.

moment view of any phenomena present as "void of self or of what belongs to a self". This may certainly be construed as a description of the *anattā* practice. And without doubt, since it causes a reduction in fabrication, the *anattā* practice can lead to states of *samādhi*, as discussed, and may sometimes even lead to the realm of nothingness.

It is also possible, however, to take this instruction of the Buddha to mean repeatedly regarding whatever arises as being empty of its own phenomenal self, and also empty of belonging to, or being an aspect of, any other reified phenomenon – in the manner we have just introduced in this chapter. This would prevent the establishment of a view of phenomena as 'belonging to awareness' or 'being an aspect of awareness', where awareness is reified and assumed to possess phenomenal selfhood. It would thus allow the perception to go beyond states of vastness of awareness, such as the sphere of infinite consciousness or its satellite states, which support, and are sustained by, such a view of awareness. Practising the Buddha's instruction this way, rather than as only an *anattā* practice, will probably be more powerful and is more likely to issue in the seventh *jhāna*.

Additionally, it is not only that each of the formless *jhānas* has particular insight perceptions that emerge from it, as explained above. Each will also be *supported* most by those particular insights. For each particular formless *jhāna* is allowed predominantly by a way of looking that involves insights deep enough to cease fabricating the particular perceptions that must be dropped for that *jhānic* perception to emerge. Thus each *jhāna* and its particular insights have a mutual reciprocity. Particular insights lead to particular *jhānas*; and particular *jhānas* bring, and reinforce, those particular insights. Since, as described above, the primary insight that emerges from the sphere of nothingness is that 'there are no things *really*', a view that sees the emptiness of things, and not just that they are 'not me, not mine', is more likely to belong with this *jhāna*.[17]

Another possibility the Buddha offered is to view phenomena through the lens: 'all are perceptions'. This will also issue in the sphere of nothingness. While seeing things as perceptions already supports a degree of holy disinterest toward them and so will support fading, filling out the implied meaning (as suggested

[17] Likewise with the third option the Buddha offered for using insight to reach the sphere of nothingness – the curious sounding formula for the meditator to "*Consider that 'I am not anything belonging to anyone anywhere, nor is there anything belonging to me in anyone anywhere.'*" In practice, it will usually be more effective to interpret this formula in a way that includes more of the emptiness of *phenomena*. The implied understanding might then be that anything which appears, or which I might take myself to be, is empty in itself, and does not belong, in any way, to any other thing – including a vast awareness, for this is empty too.

earlier) with an understanding that all perceptions are *fabricated*, in the way that we have discovered, will give this practice much greater power. They are 'just perceptions'. As described, if the very perception of nothingness is then viewed as 'just a perception', it will fade into the sphere of neither perception nor non-perception. That is not possible if one has not quite seen that nothingness is still a perception.

Fading Opens Choices

Of insight ways of looking and samādhi

Thus in practice this spectrum of fading can be approached in a number of ways. Similar to what was described in earlier chapters, at every stage of fading, one potentially has a choice. When, for instance, an area of bodily discomfort fades, one may choose to focus on, and spread, the well-being or pleasure that has replaced the discomfort, and then stabilize that into a state of some *samādhi*. Alternatively, one may keep regarding that area of the body with the insight way of looking, and the perception there may fade further down the continuum.

At each stage then, one may keep pressing on with the insight way of looking, or choose to spread and stabilize whatever perception is now there into a corresponding state of *samādhi*. Sometimes the view may lead straight into a state of *jhāna*; at other times the perception will need to be tuned into, spread, and stabilized before a more fully *jhānic* state can arise. One possibility, therefore, is to occasionally use the ways of looking with the deliberate intention of reaching a specific *jhāna*, as outlined above. Even if the full *jhāna* does not quite stabilize then, it can still be very helpful to linger at that stage of perception, since the particular insights that are involved with that *jhāna* will be reinforced by doing so. And of course, typically these insights and any such states themselves are profoundly beautiful.

The malleability of perceptions

Aided by the novel realization that *vedanā* are not independent of the reaction one has to them, with practice it also becomes possible, to a degree, for a meditator to transform, at will, unpleasant *vedanā* into pleasant or neutral. This malleability of perception further reinforces the insight that *vedanā* are, to a certain extent, what the mind makes of them. And the consolidating of this understanding allows in turn for a greater facility in shaping the perception of *vedanā*.

In the service of what the Buddha called "a pleasant abiding in the here and now"[18] – collecting the mind and body in a state of well-being and *samādhi* – this shaping of perception is certainly skilful and wholesome. But it is important not to neglect the insight aspect here, and to use such playing with the malleability of perception to consolidate and deepen insight into emptiness and dependent origination.

For some it may occasionally be necessary to take care in this respect. Discovering that phenomena are likely to fade if I look at them in certain ways I have developed, it is possible that the intention of practice slips at times, becoming instead only an attempt to get rid of what is not pleasant. Aversion has then hijacked the practice. This we have drawn attention to before, and it is worth a reminder that holy disinterest is also a disinvestment, a relinquishing of any investment in whether a phenomenon is present or not, or in how it appears.

Actually, if, from seeing phenomena fade dependently, the implications of their emptiness have been understood, this hijacking by aversion to try to make things fade should not arise too often. Nevertheless, in some moments one may find it helpful to gently encourage the realization that *because* things are empty, they can come, or go, or stay, no problem.

We should also point out that a curiosity about the dependent origination of phenomena is perhaps the most desirable intention behind watching things fade with certain ways of looking. It is this curiosity, therefore, that should be prioritized and nurtured.

Seeing Dependent Fading Opens Up Emptiness as the Middle Way

Generally, with a greater degree of fading of both the self-sense and the perception of phenomena there is a greater, and more lovely, sense of liberation and release in the moment. We have mentioned, though, that fear can sometimes arise in these deeper states. Here then, it is useful to reiterate the importance of balancing the insight practices with *samādhi* or *mettā* practices; and also of working skilfully with fear when it arises, as described in Chapter 14. But at any rate, as familiarity is gained with such experiences of less self and less world we begin to feel immensely nourished by them, and to recognize them as profound resources. We

---

[18] MN 53, AN 7:63.

come to realize there is nothing at all to fear, and that, in any case, the perception of things will always reappear later.

It is just at this stage of practice, moreover, that it begins to dawn on us, through the very insight which is taking place, that what is fading away is void anyway, and that therefore we are not really losing anything.

This is not to say that there is a sense that phenomena are without value. A lack of inherent existence does not imply that a thing is worthless. In fact, usually this way of practising to see the emptiness of phenomena will not lean over into *any* kind of nihilism. Seeing things appear and fade dependently, we cannot conclude that things simply do not exist, are not real at all. Yet we see clearly firsthand that they do not exist in the way that we had previously assumed. They do not have the kind of reality they seem to. Witnessing and understanding fabrication, fading, and dependent origination for ourselves opens up the Middle Way:

> For one who sees the origination of the world with right insight as it actually is, [the view of] non-existence with regard to the world does not occur. For one who sees the cessation of the world with right insight as it actually is, [the view of] existence with regard to the world does not occur.[19]

In this approach to gaining insight into the emptiness of objects, we see their intimate connection with, and non-separation from, the perceiving mind in a way that ensures the heart stays open and connected. We also see how the *citta* is, to some extent at least, responsible for what it perceives. Seeing all this, fear and nihilistic views are much less likely; and we can let go of phenomena, and let go into these more empty states, with greater abandon.

The Freedom of Different Ways of Looking

In realizing for ourselves this dependent arising and fading of phenomena, understanding its implication of emptiness, and then gaining some familiarity with viewing things directly as empty, a range and freedom of view is opened up to us. Describing how he practised, the Zen Master Lin Chi said,

> Sometimes I take away the person. Sometimes I take away the situation or the thing. Sometimes both. And sometimes neither.

[19] SN 12:15

By 'taking away' is meant 'seeing the emptiness of'. Thus, among the options he listed, the first corresponds to a way of looking that sees the emptiness of self; the second to viewing phenomena as empty; the third to a lens that sees both the personal self and phenomena as empty; and the fourth takes both self and phenomena at face value. Not impelled to always pick up and use the view of emptiness, free to look in any of these ways, we are freer, as understanding matures, to respond to any situation in any way that seems most helpful and appropriate.

§

Practice: Viewing phenomena as 'empty' because they fade dependently

When you have seen many times that perceptions fade dependent on the release of clinging of various kinds, and when you have understood the implication of their emptiness, you may sometimes now wish to practise a way of looking that views perceptions more directly as 'empty', or 'just a perception'.

As you practise this view, be clear that the understanding tacitly incorporated in the view is that their perception is dependent on clinging, fabricated by clinging.

As before, practise this way of looking with both a narrow attention focused on one object, and a wider attention more inclusive of the totality of experience. You may also experiment with focusing on one sense sphere for a period. Include both objects that are more fleeting and those more prolonged in duration.

Even as an object fades, experiment with sustaining the way of looking unremittingly on whatever more refined perception replaces the initial one.

At other times experiment with resting in whatever state opens up.

In any way of looking that causes a fading of perception a range of meditative stances is actually available – between, on the one hand, resting in the state of *samādhi* that comes through the way of looking, and, on the other, continuing more intensely to view things as empty. It can be useful, and fun, to explore the balance between these two aspects of the practice at any time.

Even if an object of perception does not fade so much, viewing it as 'empty' and 'just a fabricated perception' can still bring a great sense of freedom, and may be very useful in consolidating the view of its emptiness. In these practices, insight and liberating understanding may come at times through experiences where the fading is not so intense, or absorption in a particular *jhāna* not so steady or deep.

20

Love, Emptiness, and the Healing of the Heart

The Colouring and Shaping of Experiences

That appearances are thoroughly dependent on the *citta* can be seen in countless ways. The various practices that cultivate beautiful qualities of mind and heart, such as *mettā*, compassion, and joy, are particularly valuable in this respect. Thus they offer, along with their other blessings, potential avenues for insight into emptiness. While this might be the subject of a whole other book, let us briefly at least highlight some of the principles involved.

Of others

In devotion to any of these heart practices, the *citta* state inevitably moves through a wide range with the natural ups and downs of the meditation. Then we cannot help but see how variable is the perception of an other, and how coloured dependent on conditions. As we practise *mettā* toward someone, for example, our feeling for and perception of them changes. In the times when the *mettā* is strong, their beauty perhaps more apparent to us, they actually seem more loveable, and even though we may not know them well at all, we feel a kind of deep friendship and bond with them. As we experience this more often, the opposite views will stand out more in contrast too. The shaping of perception by the mind becomes obvious. And we can begin to question the truth of our conclusions about others.

We may recognize then that ordinarily our own past experiences and conditioning greatly influence how we tend to assess others. And from a more spacious perspective, the normal and understandable tendency to categorize others dependent on whether the self feels it has derived any benefit or harm from them, or whether we identify with them somehow, may be seen to be given too much weight in our conclusions about, or felt sense of, what they are like. Through acknowledging just this much dependent arising of our perception, a little space may be opened for looking more mercifully.

But we can go slightly further. Seeing over and over, in formal meditation and also in relationships in the world, how the perception of others is dependent on the mind, I may see too how, in some sense, the other is not separate from my mind. I can only know them through my perception, which will always be coloured in some way by the *citta*. Just in this respect, one who is 'other' for me is actually empty of independent existence.

And recognizing all this, we may again experiment with the malleability of perception. We can practise choosing to see others – even strangers and those with whom we feel we have difficulty – as 'friends'.

Such a practice, without the insights we have been discussing, may initially seem quite naïve. As understanding develops over time, we see that it is in fact the opposite; and that a belief that others are objectively and simply how they appear to us would, rather, be naïve. Moreover, choosing to see an other as a friend actually brings joy through the very perception. It is a very lovely, and usually very beneficial, way of relating. Here once again then, instead of waiting for a shift in view to emerge as a result of practice in any meditation period, we may implement such a shift deliberately, knowing that it is helpful, and in this case as true as any other view.

Of the world

With practice it becomes more and more evident not only how our sense of others is dependent on the *citta* but how our sense of the world is too. When qualities such as generosity, *mettā*, and compassion are strong, *all* perception is coloured. We see beauty everywhere, in other sentient beings, in nature, in the most mundane and ordinary situations and objects. Things can seem to be lit from within themselves with a quality of love, peace, or joy. And as mentioned in Chapter 15, that quality can seem to pervade the universe, to be mystically woven in to the very fabric of the cosmos, and to hold all things within it.

When, on the other hand, the *citta* is contracted in self-centredness, even mildly preoccupied with acquisition and possessiveness, things seem otherwise. Perception is primed by the dualities involved in these notions, as described in Chapter 18, feeding at least some level of fear, for instance; and through all this the world appears differently. Even at this level it might be said that 'we make our world'.

Karma and the malleability of perception

The qualities and impulses of the *citta* that so shape the perception of the world in these ways we could say are aspects of mental *karma*. Thoughts and acts of generosity, for example, sow seeds in the *citta* – of generosity, and also of related positive qualities – making such qualities more likely to arise spontaneously in the future. When they do, they colour and shape our perception and sense of ourselves, of others, and of the very world we feel ourselves moving in.

Thus we can see how influential are the habitual dispositions of the *citta*. The qualities and impulses that have been reinforced through habit will tend to arise more frequently and with more force, and shape our perceptions of things accordingly. These colourings and shapings of perception can then become habitual too.

Past conditions do not fully determine the future however. The seeds planted in the present also have a potent influence in the present, as we have discussed. Perception is pliable. The more insight we have access to, and the more we have cultivated beautiful qualities of the *citta*, the more malleable perception can be for us with practice.

This malleability of perception is depicted poetically in the story of the night of the Buddha's Awakening. Sitting under the Bodhi tree, striving for liberating insight, he is assailed by *Māra*, who is desperately trying to prevent the Bodhisattva's enlightenment. At one point *Māra* summons his armies, who unleash a furious hail of arrows and missiles toward the would-be Buddha. These are transformed in mid flight though, into flowers, beautifully coloured and scented, which then rain gently down on the meditating Bodhisattva. What appeared as hard and harmful now appears softened, and as a blessing. The qualities of the *citta* colour and shape experience.

Emptiness and ethical care

Realizing the emptiness of phenomena through exploring how perception is fabricated keeps emptiness inextricably connected to care. At times there has understandably been a concern in the tradition that some may grasp at an interpretation of emptiness which is nihilistic in some way, and deems a care for ethics unimportant. Tsongkhapa stressed that one's understanding of *śūnyatā* needs, sooner or later, to be integrated with one's understanding of *karma* and one's commitment to ethics. And that if it is not, the understanding is incomplete:

> If, from within [the understanding of] emptiness, you know the

> mode of appearance of cause and effect, then you will not be captivated by extreme views.[1]

More than any other avenue of insight into voidness, seeing the dependent arising of perception in the ways that we have been exploring ensures against a mistaken view that emptiness means ethics and love are irrelevant. This approach makes manifestly clear that what I perceive is greatly dependent on the state of my *citta*. And that in determining the qualities that arise in the *citta*, how I act, how I think, and what I cultivate will all determine what exactly I experience. Caring for ethics and for the cultivation of what is beautiful are thus naturally integrated, from the beginning, into the very mode of insight that shows the emptiness of things. Nāgārjuna, too, emphasized and praised this integration of understandings:

> Those who understand this emptiness of phenomena but also believe in [the law of] *karma*, of actions and their effects, they are even more wonderful than the wonderful, more amazing than the amazing.[2]

Deeper Insights From Love: Seeing Fading Through *Mettā* and Compassion

It is not only the *colouring* and *shaping* of perception that practices such as *mettā* can reveal. Employed in certain skilful ways they can open up a level of insight into dependent arising as profound as that available through practices such as the three characteristics views.

In the *Akṣayamati Sūtra* it says:

> At first… love has beings as its object. For bodhisattvas who have practised [further] on the path, love has *dharmas* (i.e. phenomena) as its object. And for bodhisattvas who have attained receptivity to the truth of non-origination (i.e. voidness), love has no object.[3]

---

[1] From his *Three Principal Aspects of the Path*. (Translation from the author's notes.) Here, 'cause and effect' refers to the workings of *karma* – the ways seeds in the *citta*, of thought, intention, and action, bear results, as described above.

[2] *Bodhicittavivaraṇa*. (Translation adapted from Chr. Lindtner's in *Nagarjuniana*, p. 211.)

[3] (Author's own translation.) The original Sanskrit of this passage admits of several variant renderings, each carrying different implications. In part this is due to the fact that the Sanskrit word *dharma* has a number of meanings. Among these, it may mean 'teaching' or 'doctrine', of course, and at times 'the Truth', 'the Unfabricated', or '*Nibbāna*'. But it may also mean 'phenomenon'. This last gives us the sense on which the following practice and insights are based.

Let's explore the second of these possibilities as a meditation instruction; and return to the third possibility in Chapter 24.

Once one has some familiarity with directing *mettā* or compassion in the more usual ways, i.e. towards beings, and some momentum has gathered to these practices, it is possible to practise directing such love toward *phenomena*. This may involve focusing the energy or stream of intention of *mettā* and compassion, with or without phrases, on an experience, just as one would do towards a mental image of a being; or it may involve welcoming an experience into the space of kindness and compassion in the *citta*.

With a little experimentation a meditator can soon enjoy the beauty and healing tenderness that characterize this practice. Even more importantly though, as (s)he acquires some facility with this approach the same fading of perception that we described in Chapter 19 will quickly be noticed.

Seen now from our greater understanding of dependent origination, this makes sense. Whether directing *mettā* and compassion toward an object of perception, or receiving it into a space imbued with those qualities, there is effectively less clinging then toward that object. Just as with kindness to a person, kindness to a phenomenon means that it really is welcome, fully accepted. *Mettā* and compassion involve a softening of aversion, by definition. But they also involve a softening of grasping. For these kinds of love have peace in them – they are not agitated and contracted in craving for the object. Practising directing love towards objects of perception this way can reduce clinging to a much greater degree than simply being mindful, and so deprived of their support through grasping and aversion, perceptions of phenomena fade.

If you have been developing *mettā* or compassion practice in the traditional ways towards beings for a while, you may like to experiment with the following practice. In the context of this particular practice, keeping a distinction between the qualities of *mettā* and compassion is not so important.

Practice: Directing love towards phenomena

In a meditation session, practise directing *mettā*, or compassion – or a mixture of the two – towards experience, moment to moment. Begin with whatever experience is prominent at that time. If nothing is particularly prominent, begin with the body sensations.

Experiment with different ways of doing this. You may find that using the traditional method of phrases of *mettā* or compassion is helpful. But whether with or without phrases, in a more directed or a more receptive mode, over and over tenderly bathe and hold all phenomena in kindness.

Through the *mettā* or compassion, gently try to sustain a relationship with experience that is as genuinely and totally welcoming as possible of their arising, their abiding, and their passing. Let all the emphasis be on the qualities of love and acceptance.

As before, practise this with both an attention focused more narrowly on one experience at a time, and with a wider, more inclusive attention.

Include experiences in all the sense spheres.

Make sure also to include both unpleasant and pleasant experiences, as well as more neutral ones.

If there is resistance, see if it is possible to hold the *felt experience* of that resistance in love and complete acceptance. Whatever is experienced can be included.

The self-sense or image, when it is noticed, can be regarded as just another perception, and likewise be bathed in kindness and compassion.

Experiment also with including less obvious objects of perception. For example, kindness can also be directed in this way to the very experience of kindness in the moment; and also to the moment-to-moment intentions for kindness.

As always, notice what happens to perception when you do this, and how it feels.

In the last chapter, we saw that when grasping, aversion, identification, and *avijjā* are lessened, perception of self and of world is lessened too. From this perspective it could be said then that these factors – craving, identification, and *avijjā* – are 'builders of the self and the world'. In contrast, *mettā*, compassion, *samādhi*, equanimity, and even generosity, build less self and less world.

Thus it is not just because they bring clarity, steadiness of attention, and a sense of well-being that these beautiful qualities are so valuable on the path. They also contribute significantly to a deeper understanding of dependent origination. And this understanding is indispensable for the liberation of awakening. The Buddha said:

> The wise one ponders dependencies. Knowing them, he is released… Enlightened, he does not encounter 'existence' or 'non-existence'.[4]

[4] Sn 4:11.

Sometimes he referred to dependent origination with the epithet 'the constancy of the Dhamma', and declared that:

> First there is the knowing of the constancy of the Dhamma, after which there is the knowing of *Nibbāna*.[5]

And also that:

> Whoever sees dependent arising sees the Dhamma; whoever sees the Dhamma sees dependent arising.[6]

Fading, Fabrication, and Healing the Past

A question of catharsis

Whichever practice is used to support it, the observation that perceptions of phenomena fade when clinging is reduced has significant, and sometimes surprising, implications in all kinds of domains.

Assumptions around emotional healing, and particularly, for instance, notions of purifying the residues of the past through catharsis, may need to be revisited. Although here we can only touch on that whole area in brief, let us try to carefully inquire at least a little into this particular theme. Whether inside or outside of a formal session, frequently or only occasionally, experiences of eruptions of difficult physical sensations or difficult emotions at times can be a common feature of meditation practice or other kinds of inner work. With training, the courage and ability to be with such difficulties with some mindfulness and a degree of patience grows.[7] Often though, a meditator will not notice anything in the present causing such eruptions. They may seem to come from within unprompted.

In the absence of any immediately discernible cause in the present, it is frequently tempting to assume that something must be 'coming up' from the past,

---

[5] SN 12:70.

[6] MN 28.

[7] As stressed in earlier chapters, the material in this book, and particularly the discussion that follows, actually assume, for the most part, even more than this: they presuppose that various skills and capacities that enable a practitioner to work well and helpfully with a range of emotional states have already been developed.

or perhaps that old 'stuff' or *karma* is being purified. And since, when the difficulty subsides we feel lighter, and as if something has been released, the interpretation that something was stored inside, came up, and has now been released is quite understandable.

There are numerous variations of this view that can be adopted. With some of them, the associated task might be to patiently allow the storehouse of such imprints from the past to be emptied, perhaps simply to create a space for this process to happen without impediment. Or these hidden wounds and knots might actively be sought out somehow. Perhaps fully feeling the difficulty is seen to be what is required for healing. And it may be that identifying an incident or situation in the past that was the cause for this *dukkha* in the present is regarded as necessary. Whatever the variations, in this view the release of such difficulties is seen as a basic aspect of the path. Though challenging, it is a good thing that they come 'up and out'.

Such assumptions and views may certainly be helpful at times, and at a relative level may possess a degree of truth. But they might also now be critiqued from the perspective of the understanding we have gained of the fabricated nature of phenomena. We notice that abiding in meditation in a state of reduced clinging – for instance in the *anattā* or *dukkha* practices – such difficult experiences arise less. Less 'stuff' comes up. As skill in such practices develops further, we find that generally *no* difficult experiences arise while these ways of looking are engaged. And as described, eventually less and less of anything arises at these times. Difficult experiences are usually central to a sense or notion of purification though, so their non-arising would need to be explained.

One might want to assert that practices such as those we have introduced are somehow repressing what is difficult, doing something to block the process of its arising and release. But as has already been discussed, in relinquishing clinging these practices involve a relinquishment of doing. It is clinging that is actually a doing. Less clinging is less doing. And if, additionally, we consider that seeing *not* in terms of self is actually more true than, or at least as valid as, seeing in terms of self, it becomes clear that notions of purification cannot be ultimately true.

It turns out that I only experience a sense of purification when there is aversion or grasping or self-view; and the more of these, the more 'purification' I seem to experience. We could, then, also ask again: "How much clinging or self-view will reveal the real emotion or experience or phenomenon stored within?" But of course there is no answer to this question. We can find nothing that exists inherently as this or that stored inside us. Without being fabricated by clinging in the present, this difficult experience cannot arise. In fact, nothing at all from the past is anything *in itself*, because it needs fabricating in the present to make it any thing in particular. What 'comes up' is built – shaped, coloured, and concocted – to a large extent by factors in the *citta* in the present.

This is not to say that the past has no influence; just that any experience at all – of the present *or* of the past – arising in the present moment can be seen to depend on past conditions *and also* on present conditions. It requires both. It does not exist independently of the way it is fabricated in the present. Without being fabricated by the present conditions of the *citta*, it does not arise, and is not this or that, or any particular way.

To illustrate this fact that what is actually experienced from the past is dependent on the state of the *citta* in the present, the Buddha used an analogy:

> "Suppose that a man were to drop a salt crystal into a small cup of water. What do you think? Would that salt crystal make the small amount of water in the cup salty and undrinkable?"
> "Yes, venerable sir. Why is that? Since there is only a small amount of water in the cup, it would become salty because of the salt crystal, and undrinkable."
> "Now suppose that a man were to drop a salt crystal into the River Ganges. What do you think? Would that salt crystal make the water in the River Ganges salty and undrinkable?"
> "No, venerable sir. Why is that? Since there is a great volume of water in the River Ganges, it would not become salty and undrinkable because of the salt crystal."[8]

He then explained that, likewise, when the *citta* is restricted and there is smallness of heart, an imprint from something "trifling" in the past can result in dramatically difficult experiences in the here and now. When, however, the *citta* is unrestricted – when there is largeness of heart, and one is dwelling in one of the Four Immeasurables (*mettā*, compassion, joy, or equanimity) – a similar imprint from the past can often just result, in the present, in an experience that "hardly appears even for a moment".

The power of views and beliefs

In addition to the influence of the *citta* state, the *view* that is operating at any time will also be a decisive factor. Experimenting in practice we may discover that the

[8] In AN 3:100, the *Loṇakapalla Sutta* (A Salt Crystal). This *sutta* is sometimes listed alternatively as AN 3:101 or AN 3:99.

very *belief* in a store of past wounds or a notion of purification actually perpetuates the experience of 'difficult stuff coming up'. Beliefs inevitably function as views – they shape the way of looking – so will always affect what is fabricated, and thus what is experienced.

And depending on the exact view adopted, the mind might also tend to reach out towards certain associations, weaving in remembered, or even conjectured, incidents from the past, near or distant. In doing so, it further constructs and solidifies a particular way of looking – all the while believing in the objectivity of what it experiences.

Of course, a person might admit to having some reactions of fear or of other kinds of craving in the present in response to what is coming up. Without insight, however, the extent and significance of the effects of any clinging usually goes unrecognized, and it is assumed that essentially 'what has been buried is simply being uncovered'. So accustomed to this set of assumptions, we may fail to recognize that such an excavation model is, at best, only one possible view of what is happening.

If the dependently arisen nature of experience is not seen and understood, processes that seem to be purifications or releases of old hurts may actually be never ending. Convinced of its reality and necessity, we will try, with the best of intentions, to 'be with' our experience, and not realize that subtly woven into our 'being with' and our mindful attention are factors which construct that very experience. It may seem that we are simply being passive and open, not doing anything. But we have failed to see the subtle clinging and views present; that these most certainly constitute a doing; and that they shape and concoct experience. Difficult experiences thus being unwittingly fabricated again and again in the present, there is nothing that will exhaust a 'storehouse' such as this.

Shapeable pasts

These insights may be taken slightly further. As we experience the range of *citta* states opened up through practices such as *mettā*, we witness, too, how our *view of the past* is dependent on the state of the *citta* in the present. We mentioned briefly in Chapter 9 how often our story, our version of the past, gets petrified and believed in unquestionably as the truth. As the quality of *mettā*, for instance, ebbs and flows in the *citta* over time, we can see how the emotions, memories, conclusions, and stories related to the past shift also – unless we are clinging rigidly to some previously consolidated version of it. Again we may ask which view of the past corresponds to 'reality'. This is one way of beginning to realize, at a certain level, the past's lack of inherent existence. The more such dependency is seen, and the more its implication of emptiness understood, the more it is possible to realize a freedom from any sense of being burdened by the past.

Open-mindedness, and levels of view

We must tread carefully here though. In the realm of emotional healing, as in so many other areas, it may be wise to exercise a range and flexibility of view. To always regard what arises as empty will not be appropriate. But to always believe that what arises has some kind of existence independent of how it is seen in the present moment is mistaken, and can become a trap, as we have pointed out. With open-mindedness, curiosity, and practice, however, it is quite possible for us to develop the ability to relate to difficult and painful experiences in different ways at different times. Yet each of these ways of relating can, in its own particular fashion, express both a caring and a measure of insight at once.

Such a breadth of exploration takes skill and sensitivity, and a great deal of honesty and courage. We may fear acknowledging and opening to what arises as a difficulty from the past, and fear feeling the emotion it involves. On the other hand, for various reasons, we may also fear questioning its inherent existence, disturbing the sense of its seemingly unshakeable truth.

If the latter is the case, it might be important to remember not to simply jump to a position denying any reality to the past, or denying that conditions from the past contribute to present experience. One need only admit the possibility that fabrication in the present has a role too in what arises, and then experiment to find out just how much it contributes. An open question. The implications of what is discovered can then be pondered. Whatever our leaning, sooner or later we must experiment; and eventually, able to approach what arises from either angle, we can experiment in any moment to find out which approach is most helpful at that particular time.

Notice, in the analogy of the salt crystal, that the reality of the salt crystal itself is not questioned. In this particular teaching, the Buddha did not highlight the emptiness of the past per se. His illustration shows only that the influence of the past in giving rise to experience may be dwarfed by influences from the *citta* in the present. As discussed earlier, a respect for the conventional truths of *karma* and the workings of cause and effect is a necessary foundation for the path; and proclaiming the emptiness of *all* phenomena runs the risk of being interpreted by some to negate any concern with goodness. But teachings at different levels are given depending on the audience. On other occasions, the things of the past and whatever effects they have on the present, although appearing, are declared to be completely empty:

> Afflictions, actions,… agents, and results – all these are like fairy cities; they are like mirages, and dreams.[9]

And also:

> *Karma* is empty… *karmic* formations are like illusions… [10]

Different teachings and different views for different occasions.

In exploring the realm of emotional healing, we might inquire too then whether we are free to approach things from different angles and levels, or whether we have some resistance to one or another. For freedom, ultimately, includes a freedom to see in different ways, knowing that ultimately none reveals an objective truth. Any view is limited. Yet we are obliged to engage views, for when there is perception of any kind, there is always a view, a way of looking, involved. We are always participating in what we experience.

From this perspective it is a release of our *clinging to views*, rather than anything else, that actually allows the fullest emotional healing. Instead of crystallizing views of the self, the past, or 'Life', we can – based on profound insight and compassion – exercise a far-reaching pliability of view, and so open up the possibility of a lightness, a tenderness and blessedness to existence.

[9] MMK 17:33.

[10] *Śūnyatāsaptati*. (Translation adapted from Chr. Lindtner's in *Nagarjuniana*, pp. 51 – 53.)

21

Buildings and their Building Blocks, Deconstructed

Meditating on the implications of the fact that phenomena fade as clinging is relinquished begins also to expose the emptiness of things we might have considered more fundamental building blocks, or foundations, of existence. Let us start to explore a few of these.

Before we do, though, it should again be pointed out that the insights elaborated here and in many of the following chapters rest on the meditative seeing of fading, and the felt comprehension of the voidness of objects that it implies. Without such a firsthand understanding through meditation, the discussions of any consequent insights may seem abstract or unconvincing, and the freeing power of these next stages of insights and practices is much diminished. Take whatever time is needed, therefore, to allow the insights and practices explained so far to be planted and watered well, to mature and ripen.

The Illusion of 'Just Being'

Several times already we have alluded to the notion of 'just being'. A practitioner might recognize the *dukkha* in continuously pressuring himself to be different than he thinks he is. He might recognize too the *dukkha* inevitably involved in effort and striving; or in endlessly reacting to things by trying to change them into what is more agreeable. Seeing this, and growing tired of it, he might understandably hold up the concept of 'just being' as a goal of practice, or at least as a preferable state.

Here, *being* will usually be conceived in contradistinction to *doing*, or *becoming*, or both. Thus it may involve the idea, and even the impression, of not doing anything in practice – simply allowing awareness to happen naturally and effortlessly, as it seems to anyway. And since the sense of self will be less grossly inflated through the directing of intention and doing with respect to experience, it might also seem at such times that self is not fabricated at all. Because of all this, it might appear that a more fundamental or natural state is thus allowed than any that may arise through doing. 'Being' is elevated over 'doing' for these reasons.

Something in these conceptions may *on occasion* constitute one among a range of provisionally helpful views for a beginner in meditation. But by now, the problems with such assumptions and impressions should be easily evident. Already in Chapter 11, we pointed out that what might initially seem, as above, an experience of 'no self' is in fact merely an experience of a somewhat less fabricated sense of self. Our observations there demanded that we include and account for a much wider range of self-sense in our investigations.

And having seen and contemplated the fading of phenomena, we might now question the whole notion of 'just being' even more cogently. For we can ask: would any such experience of 'just being' really be an experience of non-doing?

Something has to give me the sense of experiencing being. To experience being, I have to experience something. To 'be' is to 'see'. But as practice reveals, to 'see', or experience, something – any thing, 'inner' or 'outer' – a degree of clinging is needed. And as has been made clear, even the subtlest clinging is a doing. A sense of being requires some perception, some experience; and any experience involves the doing of clinging. To be is to see; and to see is to do. Thus although it might at first seem compelling, on deeper investigation the apparent dichotomy between being and doing is in fact illusory. Being is not any more fundamental than doing, because being is doing.

Very similarly, from all that we have discovered and discussed so far, it is obvious that various related notions – such as 'Pure Awareness', 'basic mindfulness', 'The Natural State', or 'Presence' (as something basic, pure, and 'non-interfering') – are simply no longer tenable. They cannot be ultimately true. Whenever anything is perceived, that perceiving involves fabricating through clinging and *avijjā*. And what is perceived is always coloured and shaped by the *citta* in some way or other; there is no state of the *citta* even conceivably able to reveal an objective, independently existing, reality of things as they are in themselves.

The Emptiness of Clinging, and of Mind States

Through practice we have seen now that things – objects of perception – depend on clinging. For a thing to be a thing it depends on the mind's relationship with it, on grasping and aversion. We should ask next what clinging depends on. Certainly it depends on *avijjā*, fundamental delusion. But it is also impossible for clinging to exist without an object of that very clinging. Grasping and aversion are in relation to some thing. Clinging needs some thing to cling *to*. It depends on, and is in fact inseparable from, an object of perception. Now we have already determined that objects are empty because they are dependent. Clinging, therefore, is dependent on and inseparable from something empty. Thus intertwined with and leaning on a void, its existence is based on nothing real. It too is empty. Ha!

In the *Chandrapradīpa Sūtra* it says:

> On the ultimate level, one sees neither attachment, nor any thing to be attached to, nor anyone who harbours such attachment.[1]

Likewise, Nāgārjuna wrote:

> That by means of which there is grasping, and the grasping, as well as the grasper, and that which is grasped, are all peace. Therefore grasping is not found.[2]

Now we are journeying deeper into the mysteries of dependent origination. Not only is the object empty because it is fabricated, but the very fabricator is empty too. What was conceived of as a cause, support, or ground for the phenomenon is revealed to be void as well. No ground for the object. And no ground for the clinging either, since the clinging is dependent on the empty object. Here then it is not merely that the realization of voidness has been extended to embrace a greater range of phenomena, it is also made considerably more profound, as we shall shortly discuss further.

Once some familiarity has been gained with seeing perceptions fade in meditation, and the implications for the emptiness of objects digested, it is possible to add this deeper comprehension to the way of looking. We may contemplate the mutual dependency and emptiness of clinging and objects. In practice this may allow an even more intense fading of perception, and a thrilling and powerfully liberating sense of the groundlessness of phenomena.

Related to this we will need to reconsider our notion of *citta* states too. Typically we might conceive of equanimity, for instance, as an attitude to, or a relationship with, what is difficult or attractive. To be equanimous about this or that situation or thing is to have little or no grasping and aversion towards it. But the perception of

---

[1] Translation by Padmakara Translation Group in Shantarakshita and Mipham, *The Adornment of the Middle Way: Shantarakshita's Madhyamakalankara with Commentary by Jamgön Mipham* [Boston: Shambala, 2005] p. 339.

[2] MMK 23:15.

a thing will soften and fade as clinging is reduced. Without an object, can I be said to be equanimous *towards* a thing? The original object is no longer appearing. What am I equanimous *about*? Or even if the perception only fades a little, with a less intense, more diffuse object, equanimity, then, will not be in relation to the thing originally assumed to be its object. What appears in any state of more equanimity is an object that seems in itself an easier perception to be less reactive to.

Similarly with anger. My anger 'about' a situation or thing colours the perception of it. And without the perception coloured thus, there can be no anger. My anger needs an object. These two, anger and object, are not really separate though. I cannot find an anger separate from this perception, nor this perception separate from anger.

In fact, the same is true of any state of the *citta*. It will form one inseparable package with its object. Separate *citta* states are not findable, nor are objects findable separate from a *citta* state. In any state, what appear are objects of perception, fabricated together and empty.

For as much as it is a fabricator of perception, a *citta* state is also itself an object of perception. Or rather it is a conglomeration of perceptions – those perceived as internal (for example, the perceptions of heat, calmness, agitation, or pleasure in the body and mind), and those perceived as external. In fact, just like a *jhāna*, any *citta* state could accurately be said to be a state of perception.

And the whole show – *citta* state and object – forms an inseparable gestalt of empty appearances. Depending on and inseparable from an empty object, the *citta* state is empty. Depending on and inseparable from the *citta* state, the object is empty. From this perspective, states of suffering or states of mystical love are both appearances, ultimately groundless and empty. *Śūnyatā*, the magical nature of things, is revealed equally everywhere, in the appearances of heaven *and* in the appearances of hell.

We can see the emptiness of clinging from other angles too. In the discussion of duality, it was mentioned that clinging, like any dualistic concept, cannot stand on its own. It is relative to non-clinging. Just like 'left' and 'right', clinging and non-clinging are meaningless without each other; they rest on each other. They lack independent existence.

We can also see that, as movements of mind, aversion and grasping are not actually separate. Aversion for one thing implies grasping after another. Moving away from 'this', the mind seeks 'that', even if it is not aware of doing so. Aversion to pain is at the very same time grasping after comfort. They are not really two different things as they might initially seem to be. We may perceive one or the other at any time, but essentially the same movement is merely being interpreted differently.

The Voidness of the Aggregates

In the system of classification comprising the aggregates, clinging would fall into the category of the fourth aggregate – *saṅkhārā*, or mental formations. The Buddha taught that *all* of the aggregates are empty of inherent existence. Not only are they 'not self' in the sense of not belonging to a personal self or making up such a self, but they are also void in themselves. He used various images to communicate their empty nature:

> Form is like a glob of foam; *vedanā*, a bubble; perception, a mirage; mental formations, a plantain trunk; consciousness is like a magic trick – this has been taught by the Kinsman of the Sun. However you think about them, investigate them radically, they are empty, void, to whoever sees them wisely.[3]

The *Prajñāpāramitā* texts echo this frequently. In the *Mahāprajñāpāramitā Sūtra*, for example, it says:

> The Bodhisattva who [engages] in the perfection of wisdom [teaches the Dharma] to beings. [He tells them:] Empty is all this that belongs to the triple world; therein there is no form, no *vedanā*, no perception, no mental formations, no consciousness; no aggregates, no elements, no sense spheres… All these [phenomena] are nonentities and have non-existence for own-being.[4]

Chandrakīrti, too, stressed that "the emptiness of phenomena" means that they are "empty of themselves", "empty of their own entity", not merely of a personal self that might somehow own them. Addressing a variant possible classification of the totality of all phenomena, he confirmed that

> The eighteen constituents, the six types of contact, the six *vedanā* that arise from contact, physical phenomena, non-physical

[3] SN 22:95. The trunk of a plantain tree has no heartwood. Peeling off layers of bark, one will not find any pith or central core; it is 'empty'. "The Kinsman of the Sun" is an epithet of the Buddha.

[4] Translation by Edward Conze in *The Large Sutra on Perfect Wisdom* [Delhi: Motilal Banarsidass, 1979] pp. 573 – 574.

> phenomena, and conditioned and unconditioned phenomena – all of these phenomena are void *of their own entity*.[5]

Discussing the five aggregates he declared that

> The emptiness of those five aggregates *of themselves* is explained to be the emptiness of things.[6]

This phenomenal emptiness of the aggregates it is vital to see. In the *Mahāprajñāpāramitā Sūtra* is the instruction:

> Form should be seen as empty of form. *Vedanā* should be seen as empty of *vedanā*. Perception… as empty of perception. Mental formations… as empty of mental formations. Consciousness should be seen as empty of consciousness. It is thus… that the Bodhisattva… should train.[7]

Nāgārjuna, in his *Ratnāvalī*, explained in part why this is necessary:

> The conception of I does not exist without depending on the aggregates… As long as the aggregates are conceived, so long thereby does the conception of I exist.[8]

To leave the reality of the aggregates unquestioned is to leave the deeper seeds of self-view and *dukkha* unchallenged. Without realizing that the aggregates are themselves totally void, a subtle conception of an inherently existent self will remain. For those committed to practising, this will most usually involve (consciously or unconsciously) conceiving of the self as a process of impersonal aggregates. The later tradition in particular has stressed repeatedly, therefore, that practitioners, eventually,

> must eliminate… grasping at the aggregates as true [things]…

---

[5] MAV 6:200 – 201. The 'eighteen constituents', 'six types of contact', and 'the six *vedanā* that arise from contact' were explained briefly in Chapter 14, footnote 7. And the feasibility of categorizing phenomena in different ways through different systems we pointed out in Chapter 11.
[6] MAV 6:219.
[7] Translation by Edward Conze in *The Large Sutra on Perfect Wisdom*, p. 512.
[8] Translation by Jeffrey Hopkins in *Nāgārjuna's Precious Garland*, p. 98.

> because grasping at the truth of the aggregates is the ever-present power that is the direct cause of the apprehension of the self of the person.[9]

And it is from this apprehension of an inherently existing self that more gross levels of grasping and aversion, and so *dukkha*, ensue. Seeing that the aggregates themselves are void of inherent existence opens a fuller, more radical, and more wonderful liberation.

The emptiness of the first aggregate, the body and form, we will consider more completely from various perspectives in the next chapter. The emptiness of the second and third aggregates – *vedanā* and perception – we have already seen in different ways.

Let us stress again though that 'perception' here means more than the act of verbally labelling an object in the mind. Animals do not have vocabulary. Yet still they perceive and discriminate. And at times they feel fear and suffer in relation to what they perceive. We have a perception of an object even when we have no word for it, or when the mind is free of thought. Perception is experience. And the *act* of perceiving is the forming of experiences. Language certainly may be a *part* of this process of fabricating experiences. Indeed this fabricating role of words may also be explored in practice: with mindfulness it is sometimes possible to separate the labelling of an experience from the experience itself. For instance, one may see the mental labelling 'pain' as separate from the sensations. Or see the labelling 'fear' as separate from the bodily experience of the emotion. Doing this, sometimes the unpleasantness of the sensations is reduced. Or what was interpreted and felt as 'fear' becomes 'excitement', for example. It is evident then how the labelling consolidated and intensified the experiences. But such verbal labelling is only one ingredient in the fabrication of experience, one ingredient of what is involved in perception; and then only sometimes. As we have stated several times, perception is experience, or appearance; and we have uncovered much more fundamental ways that it is fabricated, empty, "a mirage". For we have seen that the appearance of an object depends on the way of looking. A pain can be perceived as a pain, as flickering atoms of sensation, as an impression in awareness, as nothing, or as unfindable, dependent on how it is fabricated by the view.

In addition to the emptiness of perception and of *vedanā*, we have now also seen the emptiness of clinging, an element of the fourth aggregate. And part of realizing its emptiness was realizing its inseparability from *vedanā*. At first,

---

[9] From Gorampa's *Distinguishing the Views*. (Translation adapted from Jose Ignacio Cabezón and Geshe Lobsang Dargyay's in *Freedom from Extremes*, p. 219.)

clinging and *vedanā* appear to be two separate phenomena. Indeed it is helpful for practice to view them that way, in order to be able to release clinging. But as insight deepens we see that they are in fact mutually dependent, as described in the last section. And it is not possible to say where one ends and the other begins.

To say that they are one entity, however, would not be accurate. We might say that, ultimately, they are 'not-two', non-dual. Their existence as separate things is illusory. This inseparability of the aggregates is an aspect of their emptiness. They are simply not sharply defined things.

In fact, with regard to the discussion above on perception, it would actually be more accurate to say that perception and *vedanā together* constitute the object of experience. As long as there is an object of perception it will have a *vedanā* tone inextricably wrapped up with it, even if that tone is 'neither pleasant nor unpleasant'. Although they are divided in the list of the aggregates, perception and *vedanā* are actually inseparable. Whenever we are conscious of any experience, the object of that consciousness is perception *and vedanā*. Moreover, as the subjective aspect of experience, consciousness is also inseparable from this object. As the Buddha suggested, experience may be *conceptually* divided up into the aggregates, and doing so forms a very helpful guide for practice; but the distinctions are not ultimately real. This fundamental inseparability was declared by Sāriputta:

> *Vedanā*, perception, and consciousness – these phenomena are conjoined, not disjoined, and it is impossible to separate each of these phenomena from the others in order to delineate the difference between them. For what one feels, that one perceives; and what one perceives, that one cognizes.[10]

We have already mentioned the inseparability of consciousness and perception in previous chapters. However, merely to realize *intellectually* that "because consciousness arises with an object it is empty of inherent existence" will not be enough. Meditative ways of looking with the power to dissolve that level of subtle and intuitive *avijjā* are needed. We will explore such practices and consider the emptiness of consciousness, the fifth aggregate, in much more detail in Chapters 25 to 27. We will also point out other inseparabilities and mutual dependencies among the aggregates later. For now though, let us begin to ponder at least a little some of the ramifications of this fact of reciprocal contingency.

---

[10] MN 43.

Mutual Dependency and the Emptiness of Cause and Effect

We see that perception, *vedanā*, and clinging are inseparable, as are *vedanā*, perception, and consciousness. These aggregates are not one thing, but they depend on each other and they arise together. In the Pali word *paṭiccasamuppāda*, the preposition *sam* means 'together'. *Paṭiccasamuppāda* thus means 'arising *together* dependently', 'dependent *co*-origination'. We might wonder how it is possible that two things can arise together dependent *on each other*. Usually when we think of some thing being dependent on some thing else, we consider the latter a cause of the former. But if they are mutually dependent and neither precedes the other in time, which is cause and which effect here?

Cause and effect, it is crucial to point out though, are not ultimately what is being pointed to by the Buddha's teaching. Revealing that two things are mutually dependent in fact reveals their emptiness. It is impossible for them to really be two separate inherently existing things if they are never found apart and neither arises before the other; yet nor can they be said to be truly one entity. This revelation of voidness is the fuller purpose of the teachings of dependent co-origination. Seeing the mutual dependency of phenomena, their emptiness is exposed, and thus clinging and *dukkha* are radically undermined. Only to a limited extent is *paṭiccasamuppāda* intended as a thorough explanation of a causal process.

Moreover, the whole *mechanism* of cause and effect, though appearing and functioning on a conventional level, is also declared to be empty. For many reasons, inherently existing cause and effect will be found to be impossible. We can see this if we consider their temporal relation for instance. As above, cause and effect cannot come into being at the same time, for then one would not have the time to produce the other. The other, the 'effect', would already be there. They cannot exist simultaneously and maintain a cause-effect relationship. One may instead want to suggest that the effect exists before the cause, but then that 'effect' would have arisen without a 'cause', which is obviously impossible. The only other possibility is that a cause exists before its effect. But a cause is only a 'cause' when it has produced an effect. Otherwise we cannot call it a cause. That which exists before the effect is not at that time a cause, because it has not yet done what causes do – that is, produce an effect. However minutely this is pondered, in terms of moment-to-moment manifestations of a process of cause and effect, the same conclusions will be reached. As Mipham wrote in his commentary to Śāntarakṣita's *Madhyamakālaṃkāra*:

No examination... will lead to a coherent account of causality.[11]

The same will apply equally even when the cause is conceived as a combination of conditions. Reasoning through these possibilities, Nāgārjuna concluded:

> An effect is not made by a combination [of conditions]; an effect is not made without a combination [of conditions]. In the absence of an effect, where can there be a combination of conditions?[12]

Just like singular causes and effects, combinations or 'webs' of conditions and their results are empty too.

Yet the mechanism of cause and effect is valid on a conventional level if not probed and analysed too deeply. Indeed, as Haribhadra explained:

> Only when one is satisfied with not analysing it [can one speak of] 'a relationship of cause and effect'.[13]

And also Śāntarakṣita:

> Agreeable only if not examined, things based upon foregoing causes arise as though they were the causes' subsequent effects.[14]

Cause and effect appear to us, and reliably, but they, together with the whole process, lack inherent existence. Chandrakīrti wrote:

> Both terms, cause and effect, are like illusions.[15]

---

[11] Translation by Padmakara Translation Group in Shantarakshita and Mipham, *The Adornment of the Middle Way*, p. 290.

[12] MMK 20:24.

[13] From his *Abhisamayālaṃkāra-Sphuṭārthā*. (This line translated by Jose Ignacio Cabezón and Geshe Lobsang Dargyay in *Freedom from Extremes*, p. 175.)

[14] MA 65. In general in this book, translations from MA are composites of translations by the following: Padmakara Translation Group in Shantarakshita and Mipham, *The Adornment of the Middle Way*; Thomas H. Doctor in Ju Mipham, *Speech of Delight: Mipham's Commentary on Śāntarkṣita's Ornament of the Middle Way* [Ithaca, NY: Snow Lion, 2004]; James Blumenthal in *The Ornament of the Middle Way: A Study of the Madhyamaka Thought of Śāntarakṣita* [Ithaca, NY: Snow Lion, 2004].

[15] MAV 6:170.

§

Practice: Contemplating the emptiness of clinging

(When you have seen many times in practice that objects of perception fade as clinging is released in various ways, and when you feel that you have digested the insight that things are thus empty, you can add this next step.)

Reflect on the fact that clinging needs an object. And that if the object is empty, that means clinging is dependent on something that is empty, illusory. Clinging must then be empty too.

Once settled in meditation, choose any object present in the moment to hold lightly in attention. Based on conviction from previous practice you can briefly regard it as 'empty because it is dependent on clinging of different kinds'. But then, as you are viewing the object, add to the view the understanding that clinging is empty too, since it depends on this object.

As with all ways of looking, there is plenty of room for experimentation with the approach and the emphasis. At times, you may wish to focus more on the voidness of the clinging; at other times, that of the object. Seeing the emptiness of clinging deepens the sense of the emptiness of the object. If clinging is void, the object is realized to have even less basis.

It is important to let the comprehension of the *mutual dependency* of object and clinging infuse the view. The object is empty because it is dependent on clinging, and clinging is empty because it depends on that object. They are both empty. Being mutually dependent and both empty, no ground for appearance can be found.

Notice how it feels to see this.

With practice, you may also pick up the view of the mutual dependency and emptiness of object and clinging more immediately, and then sustain this view while attending to both the object and the clinging together.

As always when a wider and deeper emptiness is contemplated it is possible that a greater degree of fading occurs. If so, again you may choose at times to continue this way of looking on the now less fabricated object of perception.

At other times, either deliberately relaxing the intensity of the contemplation a little or as you leave the meditation session, pay attention to the appearances of things. Perhaps you can notice the quality of groundlessness pervading experiences, the empty and magical quality of appearances. Notice how seeing this feels too.

At times, both in and out of formal meditation sessions, you can experiment with supporting such a perception without fully entering into focused contemplation of mutual dependence. For instance, letting the attention move from object to object as it will, you can allow the previously gained insight into mutual dependency and emptiness, which in meditation has been seen and contemplated more intensely, to gently inform the view in a more relaxed way.

PART SEVEN

Further Adventures, Further Findings

22

No Thing

Different Tracks to a Conviction in Emptiness

The Buddha said,

> For one who sees, there is no thing.[1]

And in the *Vimalkīrtinirdeśa Sūtra* there is the instruction:

> Just as in the conception of 'self', so the conception of 'thing' is also a misunderstanding, and this misunderstanding is a grave sickness… Strive to abandon it.[2]

We have already mentioned how counterintuitive is this realization of the comprehensive voidness of all phenomena, and the need, therefore, to expose their lack of inherent existence from multiple angles in order to give fullness and thoroughness to insight. We mentioned also that the variety of practices used here can broadly be split into two groups: meditations that explore fabrication, and analytical meditations.

The exploration of fabrication we may call a *directly phenomenological* approach. That is to say, it is an almost purely meditative examination of phenomena as they present themselves, and it deliberately tries to leave aside any further assumptions or speculations about them.

Regarding the world of things, all we can ever actually experience is the world of phenomena we perceive. (Indeed that is most often the meaning of the term 'the world' when used by the Buddha in the Pali Canon.) There is never

[1] Ud 8:2. (All translations from Ud are the author's own.)

[2] Translation by Robert Thurman in *The Holy Teaching of Vimalakīrti: A Mahāyāna Scripture* [University Park, PA: The Pennsylvania State University Press, 2003] p. 45.

the possibility of knowing precisely how things are 'in and of themselves', independent of perceptions. Of course, we typically assume that for the most part we perceive 'the objective world out there' exactly as it is. So adopting a phenomenological mode is already a significant shift.

This shift alone though will not reveal how the appearances of things, selves, time, and awareness arise interdependently, concocted by the mind. Meditative approaches such as those included in this book thus press further than most phenomenological approaches. For as the practices are developed, and especially as they elicit the fading of objects of perception, we see how phenomena are constructed, and we begin to see that the whole structure of experience is fabricated. Such comprehensive and profound seeing radically affects the mind and the heart, the relation with, and view of, existence.

Analytical meditation, on the other hand, though it is also for the most part a kind of phenomenological approach, reaches out in a slightly different way. The various reasonings each prove that the inner and outer things of the world cannot possibly exist in the way they appear to. They cannot have inherent existence. This much *can* be known of the ontological status of things. And knowing this fully is enough to liberate the heart.

Through teaching and listening I have often observed that many practitioners tend to be drawn to one of these styles of approach more than the other. Their preference arises not merely because they find that approach easier, but also because it seems to them more convincing than the other. The whole question of what suffices to provide conviction for any individual practitioner is a huge and fascinating one that we do not have the space here to go into.[3] It is interesting and important at least to notice, though, what relative weights of authority we each give to different kinds of knowledge in the quest for truth. Some of us give most or more authority to meditative experiences; some to logic; some to intuitive hunches and intimations; some to sources outside of ourselves – scriptural or

---

[3] Readers with a tendency to probing questioning may have realized already that *epistemological* questions – that is, questions about the very nature of knowledge and about the actual extent to which anything can be known, about gaining knowledge, making inferences, drawing conclusions, and so forth – must arise inevitably in any deep inquiry; and that their answers (*or* any assumptions in place, and there will always and unavoidably be some) form the necessary foundations not only for the whole endeavour described in this book, but also for *any* path of insight, and for much else too. How do we know anything? What can we know? What knowledge is trustworthy? Addressing questions such as these – more generally and not just in terms of personal preference – comprises an element of the exploration of epistemology, which came to be widely regarded in the later tradition – from Dignāga and Dharmakīrti to Śāntarakṣita, Sakya Paṇḍita, Tsongkhapa, and Mipham – as being of fundamental importance to travelling the path. As mentioned, however, this is a vast area and would really require the space of a whole other book to explore properly.

scientific, for instance; and some to the overwhelming human consensus – of 'common sense' and unexamined everyday perceptions.

Of course, many of us will arrive at an attitude whereby we depend on some or other differentially weighted combination from within this range of approaches. Indeed, as mentioned, realizing voidness from a number of different directions will, for most, add helpful weight to the conviction in the insights. And as we have also already mentioned, in practice the two approaches we are discussing here – the meditative investigation of the fabrication of experience, and the analytical meditations – will support each other well. Moreover, they can also be combined at times even within one way of looking, as we saw for example with the sevenfold reasoning and the *anattā* practice.

In addition to those practices we have already explored, there are many other skilful ways the emptiness of phenomena can be contemplated. Before we pick up again and take further the main thread of the inquiry into fabrication, let's introduce a few of these complementary meditations here and at various points in some of the chapters that follow. It won't be necessary for everyone to learn all of these practices, or even any of them, before moving on. But I would encourage experimenting with these meditations at some point at least, for each of them can be a powerful aid in developing the capacity to see that "there is no thing". It is said, too, in the tradition that a bodhisattva is one who approaches the realization of emptiness using an extensive array of different reasonings.[4]

An Inquiry into Parts and Wholes

One possibility available to us is a contemplation of parts and wholes. It's clear that without the parts of any thing, there can be no whole. A thing can be said, therefore, to be dependent on its parts. We can recognize further, though, that the very *concepts* 'whole' and 'part' cannot exist independently. Indeed not just the conception, but the *perception* of a part, *as a part*, is dependent on the conception and perception of the whole to which it is seen to belong. Whole and part are mutually dependent. Now in the abstract such a contemplation may not be that liberating. So let us follow our principle of applying emptiness meditations at first to where we experience more obvious *dukkha*.

Particularly useful whenever there is a sense of solidity to a difficulty, the 'dot-to-dot' meditation of Chapter 7 may be extended through the contemplation

---

[4] E.g. in the *Madhyamakāvatārabhāṣya* (Chandrakīrti's auto-commentary to the *Madhyamakāvatāra*).

above to provide a more thorough and freeing insight into emptiness.

In Chapter 7 we saw how close mindfulness can illuminate the ways the mind stitches the dots together in any experience to fabricate a solidified whole. This insight – that perceptions of solidified wholes are fabricated by the mind – may be strengthened also by asking a hypothetical question: How many of the dots could possibly be removed or absent and a perception of the whole still remain? If random moments of the experience of this fear or this illness, for example, were magically changed into more neutral experience, at what proportion of changed moments would we no longer solidify the whole as fear or illness?

The answer will vary of course and depend on all kinds of factors in the moment. But what is clearly suggested by the question, and seen through mindfulness, is that the apprehension of this whole is dependent on the mind. So when, with regard to some experience, we see that the mind joins the dots to fabricate a whole, the voidness of that whole is evident, and there can be some release. Seeing this repeatedly and more widely, over time this insight is consolidated and a conviction is developed that wholes are empty fabrications. With that as a foundation, an accessible conviction we can draw on, we can look again at the parts.

For we can recognize too that when there is a sense of a whole, the dots are also themselves *interpreted as parts of that whole*. As the 'whole' is concocted, individual moments of experience or individual spatial points of experience are not perceived discretely, separately from, or independently of, the sense of the whole. They are given from the intuited impression of the whole a weight and significance that they do not have in themselves. When that whole is felt to be emotionally loaded and burdensome, this instant of difficulty or this smaller region of discomfort in the body will be experienced more unpleasantly, with more of a load, and as more of a burden, than it would in isolation. A moment of pain, for example, will not be felt as just a single, momentary experience without further significance. Rather, it will seem heavier and more painful in itself, since it seems to instantiate something heavier and more oppressive – the whole.

Now this perception of the parts – as carrying the extra weight of the significance of the whole to which they are taken to belong – supports and reinforces the perception of that heavier whole in turn. Heavier-seeming parts make a heavier-seeming whole. And vice versa of course: this now weightier perception of the whole supports and reinforces that weightier perception of the parts. They support each other. Such a mutual dependence of whole and parts can be seen equally when something is craved. Whole and part are perceived, fabricated, and inflated, *together*.

From the dot-to-dot meditation we have the conviction that the whole is empty. Now we can bring this realization into the meditative process. We can contemplate that if the whole is void, then the parts (the dots) that are dependent on that 'whole' are *dependent on something that is an empty fabrication*. The way they are construed and experienced as parts is fabricated based on an illusory whole. They must be empty. Both whole and parts, then, are empty.[5]

In practice one might take this a small step further, and deepen the freeing effect by following the contemplation round one more time. Since, now, the whole can also be seen to be fabricated dependent on *empty* parts, that whole is in fact even 'more empty' than we initially had realized.

With regard to part and whole then, seeing the emptiness of one reinforces the realization of the emptiness of the other. And here again, mutual dependence entails mutual emptiness. Both the larger image drawn and the individual dots are illusory constructions.

Some reflection and some meditative attention may be needed to develop the insight that the perceptions of the parts depend on the perception of the whole in the ways that we have discussed. This insight can then be brought in quite easily and used in the way of looking. With practice, this entire approach may be employed quite quickly in meditation and without a great deal of thinking at all. Like any contemplation of emptiness, it will open a sense of freedom in the moment and may also lead to a fading of the perception involved. And because of the mutual dependence and mutual emptiness, it can bring too a wonderful and exhilarating sense of groundlessness to experience. Two empty appearances rely on each other, each thus depending on something that is not real. There is no basic ground of experience.

---

[5] It might be objected that, if extricated and considered independently of the whole, a part's basic reality will be evident; it will be found not to be empty. It is tempting to assume in this way that the 'dots' have an inherent existence in themselves. However, even though the dot-to-dot meditation reduces the fabrication of a sense of a whole, in actuality no experience can ever be completely isolated from its relation to its context. A moment, or a region, of experience is always perceived as part of, or in contrast to, its surroundings in time and space. We cannot know it in itself, independently. The mind conceives and perceives the things of the world in wholes and parts and relations. (In fact, always woven into our intuitive conception of any thing is a notion of whole, parts, and relativities.) Just like dualities, the cognition of whole and part, as well as the very concepts 'whole' and 'part', rely on each other and are inextricable.

Anyway, as we have already seen in previous chapters, the conjecture that there are fundamental building blocks of experience which exist independently and at which we could finally arrive in some mode of objective perception is not tenable. It is not borne out by any more thorough investigation of experience. 'Clearer' and 'deeper' seeing reveals only that what is perceived is dependent on the way of looking.

Practice: The emptiness of parts and wholes

(If you need to, spend some time with the dot-to-dot meditation in Chapter 7, witnessing how the mind joins the dots of experience to fabricate a solidified whole. Notice how this recognition undermines, to some extent, the perception of solidity and continuity of the object, and so brings some relief.)

Whenever there is a sense of solidity to a difficulty – whether it is a *citta* state, a bodily condition such as physical discomfort or illness, or an external situation that feels oppressive, such as busyness or a relationship difficulty – see if it is possible to directly view it as 'empty', based on the conviction that it is the mind that joins the dots to fabricate a solidified whole.

Experiment with dots which are *spatial regions* connected to form a larger whole – for example, viewing a region of physical discomfort as comprising smaller areas of discomfort joined together by the mind. Experiment also with dots which are *temporal moments* connected to form a more continuous whole – seeing, for example, the individual instances of a particular emotion stitched together.

Notice how it feels to do so, and what effects it has on the perception.

Once you have gained some facility with this, experiment – attention all the while remaining focused on the experience – with very lightly adding the contemplation that the perceptions of the dots (parts) are thus 'dependent on an empty whole'.

Notice how this way of looking at the experience feels, and also what effects it has on the perceptions.

As you hold attention on the experience, you may, if you like, follow the reasoning round once more. You can add the recognition that the perception of the whole is then 'fabricated in dependence on empty parts'.

Sustaining this awareness of the mutual dependence and mutual emptiness of whole and part, notice how it feels and what the effects are.

The Emptiness of the Body and of Material Forms

The Buddha taught that the body and all material forms are empty of inherent existence.

> Suppose that a big glob of foam were floating down this River Ganges, and a man with good eyesight were to inspect it, reflect

> on it, and examine it radically. To him – inspecting it, reflecting on it, and examining it radically – it would appear void, hollow, without substance. For what substance could there be in a glob of foam? In the same way, a monk inspects, reflects on, and radically examines any form, whether past, future, or present, internal or external, gross or subtle, common or sublime, far or near. To him – inspecting it, reflecting on it, radically examining it – it would appear void, hollow, without substance. For what substance could there be in form?[6]

And Chandrakīrti, reiterating the teachings of the *Prajñāpāramitā* Sūtras, stressed that

> According to its very nature, form is void of form.[7]

The emptiness of the body may be meditated upon in numerous ways. For example, when probed a little it becomes clear that the body is not as separate from its environment as it seems; its boundaries are not as clear-cut as they appear. At all levels in a constant and fluid exchange of elements across apparent edges, the body is not, upon closer inspection, a thing sharply defined from what it is not. Again, certain kinds of questions begin to point to its lack of inherent existence, and suggest the mind's role in reifying the body. Even leaving aside the absence of inherently existing boundaries and exact locations that is more openly evident at the subatomic level, when exactly does the water I drink, or the porridge I eat, become part of my body? Are the faeces in the bowels and the urine in the bladder part of the body or not? When precisely does a teardrop or a bead of sweat falling from the face stop being part of the body?

What is true of the body is true of all material forms, and we can extend the investigation to include any material thing. If various parts of a car or a human body were progressively removed, at what point would someone, shown what remains, not consider it 'a car' or 'a body'? And if parts of the body or the car slowly migrated to exchange places with other parts – the steering wheel gradually migrating to where the engine was, the wheels up to the roof, the seats upside down propping up the chassis, the engine to be perched above the wheels on the roof – again, at what point would someone no longer say it's a car? The mind imputes 'car' or 'body' to a perception.

---

[6] SN 22:95.

[7] MAV 6:183.

One might want to proffer as a response that fulfilling its specific function is what qualifies it as this or that. When we look at a car that is not able to drive or transport anyone, however, we typically still regard it as a car, just one that happens not to function. Where, then, is the 'car-ness'?

It is also possible of course to analyse a body or any other material object and realize its lack of inherent existence with the sevenfold reasoning, as outlined in Chapter 17.

In that case, the last of the seven possibilities – that the car is the *shape*, or arrangement, of its parts – we have just addressed. But in refuting the possibility that the shape or arrangement of a thing is what gives that thing an inherent identity and makes it 'what it is', we may also use another tack – the reasoning of neither-one-nor-many (explained more fully in the next section). Like everything else, the shape of a body or of any material form can be recognized through that reasoning to be neither inherently one nor inherently many, and so recognized not to have inherent existence. Therefore shape, itself lacking inherent existence, cannot be put forward as the inherently existing essence of any object, and that final possibility in the sevenfold reasoning is thus refuted. Here again we see how emptiness practices may profitably be combined with, or incorporated into, each other to give a fullness and thoroughness to realization.

Deeper teachings stress as well the voidness of matter even at the level of its most elementary and basic building blocks, or indeed however its most fundamental level might be construed. In a *Prajñāpāramitā Sūtra* it says:

> The element of earth has no nature of its own.

And the same is taught for the elements of air, fire, water, and space. Thus the *Vimalkīrtinirdeśa Sūtra* states that

> Matter itself is void. Voidness does not result from the destruction of matter, but the nature of matter is itself voidness.[8]

Used skilfully in meditation, both the neither-one-nor-many reasoning and the sevenfold reasoning are among the practices capable of revealing the emptiness of matter even at the most basic levels. Insights at such fundamental levels will naturally open a more fundamental, but also a more comprehensive and a more mystical, sense of liberation.

---

[8] Translation by Robert Thurman in *The Holy Teaching of Vimalakīrti*, p. 74.

The Neither-One-Nor-Many Reasoning

Though it may of course be used in combination with another practice, the neither-one-nor-many reasoning is actually complete in itself, and does not necessarily need to be supplemented by any other practice. Much simpler than the sevenfold reasoning, once the argument has been understood and some familiarity with it has been gained, it can be employed in meditation quickly and easily on any phenomenon with powerful and profound results.[9] Āryadeva, Dharmakīrti, Jñānagarbha, and numerous others put forth the reasoning in many different texts. Here is Śāntarakṣita's version from his *Madhyamakālaṃkāra*:

> Those entities affirmed by our own [Buddhist schools] and other [non-Buddhist] schools have no inherent nature at all, because in reality they have neither a singular nor a manifold nature. They are like reflections.[10]

We may consider the body, or any material thing at all; or we may consider something like a bodily pain, or the pattern of bodily sensations of an emotion. With only a little inspection it is clear that none of them is inherently 'one', is truly single in nature. The body has many parts – hair, skin, nails, teeth, kidneys, etc. Indeed for any material object, there will be this part and that part. And for any spatial perception, there will be different regions. If I have a pain in the area of my stomach, there is a region of the pain that borders an area of less or no pain around my throat, for example, and a region that borders an area of less or no pain in my lower belly or groin.

Seeing this, we may wish to simply admit instead then that the true nature of these things is manifold. However, for anything to be *really* 'many', there need to be things that are *really* 'one'. For 'many' is, by definition, a collection of 'ones'. Nothing, though, can be found that is truly singular. A hair, a tooth, a nail – none of those are inherently singular things. An atom of anything also has a nucleus and electrons, it is not essentially one. Even if we imagine down to the level of subatomic particles, these will necessarily have parts facing in different directions, or interacting with other particles in this or that direction. Anything that occupies space must have parts.

---

[9] Here, we apply the argument primarily to the spatial extension of phenomena. In Chapter 26 we will apply it to temporal duration, where it potentially has an even more fundamental and pervasively powerful effect.

[10] MA 1.

Postulating the existence of a partless particle that would be truly singular will not work. It would be impossible to arrange or amass such partless particles in order to form any thing from them. Having no differentiable sides, other particles could not be arranged either side of it. Such a particle would not be able to bond or interact with other particles in any direction. All the surrounding particles would contact the central particle at the same point, and all effectively occupy the same place. Nothing with any extension could ever come to be. Something that is really 'one' is impossible.

Since nothing that is truly one can possibly exist, it automatically follows that nothing that is truly many can exist either. As explained above, 'many' means a grouping of 'ones'. This body or this thing cannot therefore be *really* many, as we had initially assumed or been forced to propose.

One may want to say simply that a thing is what it is, and we can see it as one or as many. But if something is inherently existent, it means that it has to be how it is inherently, in itself, not dependent on the mind seeing it this way or that. Nothing inherently singular nor inherently manifold can be found to exist, and these are the only possibilities for an inherently existing thing. Exhausting the possibilities, we must conclude, therefore, that things lack inherent existence. They appear as one or many, but in reality they cannot be either.

§

In relation to practice, we should state again a few points we have stated before. Most of the meditations in this book will require a little patience and experimentation before they click. The sense of freedom and wonder that can come from these ways of looking, though, makes them well worth the investment of time and effort. With practice, we make these reasonings our own in meditation. Although they may seem formulaic at first, different routes through the same reasoning can creatively be followed at different times. And once digested they can be used very fluidly and lightly in meditation. Lastly, when employing any reasoning in meditation, a degree of *samādhi* in the moment ensures that the mind does not spin off out of control into an unhelpful proliferation of thinking.

Practice: 'Neither one nor many'

Take some time to reflect on the neither-one-nor-many argument until it makes sense to you.

Once the *citta* is somewhat settled in a meditation session, choose an object to view through the lens of this reasoning. It may be the physical body, or any material object, or an area of sensation in the body.

As you hold it in the attention or in the mind's eye, lightly reflect and recognize that it is clearly not one, for instance because it has parts.

Then see that actually nothing that is *really* singular could exist. A partless particle is impossible, since nothing could be formed from such particles.

If nothing that is *really* one can be found, this object now scrutinized cannot be *really* many.

As you hold the object or its image in attention, recognize then that it is neither one nor many. Recognize too that these are the only possibilities.

Since nothing that is truly one exists, there can be nothing that is really many, so all objects, being neither one nor many, lack true nature. All things lack inherent existence.

As you view the object with the help of the reasoning, notice what effect this way of looking has on the perception of the object contemplated. Notice too what effect it has on the sense of other objects.

When you leave the meditation session, be sensitive to the way things appear, noticing if there are any after-effects on the perception of things.

23

The Nature of Walking

All of the practices in this book may of course be explored in any of the four postures (sitting, walking, standing, and lying down). But in walking meditation it is possible too to contemplate the emptiness of walking itself. Let's consider a few of the many approaches available.

Sustaining a view of the experience of walking through a lens which in any manner deeply releases clinging, the very perception of walking will begin to dissolve in some way. For example, in walking and regarding as *anattā*, over and over, all the aggregates involved in the experience – the body, the sensations and perceptions through the different senses, the intentions, the awareness of all these – solidified perceptions, including those of walking, can begin to disband and to melt. As before, this fading reveals that the perception of walking is dependent on clinging.

It is also possible, walking with mindfulness and sensitivity, that other intuitive realizations similar to ones we have previously discussed begin to dawn. Paying attention to the whole of experience when walking, we may get the sense that the mind is cutting out certain elements of perception and conceiving of 'walking' separately. When we actually try to find 'walking' though, it is not so easy. We see that walking is dependent on, and actually *inseparable from*, a much wider field of conditions than it might seem to be at first. It is dependent on, and inseparable from, for example, the body, the earth, gravity, and our intentions. None of these may be removed to leave an independently existing walking. It is not the separate and self-contained process that we typically assume it is.

Encouraging this contemplation and this opening of the awareness can at times unfurl a different appreciation, a mystical sense that the whole universe is somehow involved in the walking. From this perspective, as has already been suggested, emptiness can also mean 'fullness'. No thing is as small, limited, and sharply defined as it seems. Its nature is in some ways infinite, full of the totality of other things. And these other things too are not separate, not isolatable. They are mutually defining, mutually supporting, interpenetrating.

We can extend this contemplation and recognize also that 'walking' is always in relation, or opposition, to 'non-walking'. The artificiality of these distinctions may be exposed through inquiry. If we are walking extremely slowly in meditation, at what point precisely is it *not* walking? When exactly does such walking become standing? Or walking very fast in meditation, when precisely does 'walking' become 'running'? When does running become jumping?

The Unfindability of Beginnings and Endings

A powerful reasoning can be extrapolated from questions such as these, and used in meditation.[1] We may, while walking or standing ready to walk, inquire into the beginning of walking. Walking, indeed any motion, cannot begin when stationary, since to be stationary is to be unmoving. Nor can motion begin when moving, since any moving thing is already in motion. Conversely, stopping – the ending of walking – also cannot happen when stationary, nor when moving.

One might try to say that starting to walk happens in some moment "before which there is no movement, but after which there is movement". Such an attempted solution fails, however. If the whole of that moment involves walking, then walking does not start in that moment. And if no walking happens in that whole moment, then obviously walking does not start in that moment either.

Two options remain for that postulated moment. Either that moment has no duration. Or there must be a portion of that supposed moment when there is no motion, and a portion when there is. Considering the former possibility, a moment of no duration cannot effectively exist. It would itself have no beginning or ending, and that is not possible, as we shall see in Chapter 26. In the latter possibility, the proposed moment of the beginning of walking has actually merely been postponed and shortened slightly. The same process of questioning could be repeated on this shorter moment, and then again, and again, until a moment of no duration would have to be postulated, which, as we have said, cannot exist. Of course, the same reasoning will apply to stopping. In any moment either there is motion or there is not. No beginning nor ending of walking can be found. And to say that "there is always walking" would be absurd. Without a real beginning and a real ending, motion lacks inherent existence.

---

[1] The reasonings presented here are adapted from Nāgārjuna's *Mūlamadhyamakakārikā* (MMK) – principally the second chapter, the whole of which is devoted to an examination of motion.

Notice that a reasoning like this may be extended beyond its original instantiation. Not just walking, but any event or situation, any emotion or state of the *citta*, any activity at all – whatever involves a process in time can be subjected to the analysis and way of looking described here. And in fact, the starting and ending moment of any thing can be seen in this way to be unfindable. Nāgārjuna wrote:

> Not only is the beginning of *saṃsāra* not found, but also the beginnings of all things, whatever objects there are, are not found.[2]

And also:

> It may occur to you that both coming into existence [of an entity] and passing out of existence are seen. But coming into existence and passing out of existence are seen only through delusion.[3]

Employing this analysis as a way of looking, the perception of things is *softened* at the very least. Instead of hard edges defining them, events and processes can be seen as having a more open nature. Then, where there might have been difficulty or a feeling oppressed by some thing, there can be feelings of freedom and lightness. And rather than the contraction of aversion and grasping that comes with reification, the heart too softens in relationship to the thing contemplated.

The *Saptaśatikā Prajñāpāramitā Sūtra* says:

> To the extent that a bodhisattva… does not see the production of [any phenomena], nor their stopping,… he shall, in [patiently growing receptive to] that, know full enlightenment.[4]

The Unfindability of Walking

We can borrow another analysis of motion from Nāgārjuna to use in meditation. In practice, this may be used in conjunction with the preceding analysis or on its own; and it too can be extended beyond walking. He wrote:

---

[2] MMK 11:7 – 8.

[3] MMK 21:11.

[4] Translation from Edward Conze in *Perfect Wisdom*, pp. 102 – 103.

> The gone-over is not being gone over; the not-yet-gone-over is also not being gone over; a being-gone-over separate from the gone-over and the not-yet-gone-over is not known.[5]

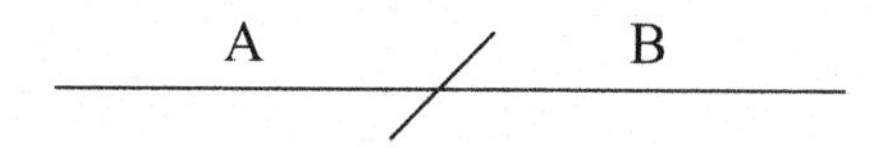

At any point on a walking meditation path, the section of the path that one has already traversed (A) is not 'being gone over'. Walking is not occurring there. Nor is the section of the path (B) that one has not yet traversed 'being gone over'. Walking is not occurring there either. Outside of A and B – what has already been traversed and what has not yet been traversed – there is no third part of the path where motion might be found. This observation holds, as Chandrakīrti pointed out in his *Prasannapadā*, even when analysed down to minute particles. On close inspection, walking cannot be found anywhere.

A similar reasoning might be applied temporally. Walking that is past no longer exists. Walking that has not yet taken place does not exist either. One might assume it exists in the present, but that assumption would be problematic too. Motion is defined as a change in position over time. This means that it cannot exist at any exact present moment. For if the position of an object changed in that moment, that moment would actually be at least two moments – one moment in time when the object was at one position, and another when the object was at a different position.

This conclusion would in fact be true of any point in time – not just the present moment, but moments that are now past or future too. We cannot just say, "Okay, motion doesn't exist in the present, but there was (or will be) motion *then*." There is actually no time findable at which a thing is in motion.

Walking and the elements that seem to make it up may be analysed as well with the sevenfold reasoning. It may also be subjected to the neither-one-nor-many analysis. Or to variations and combinations of these analyses. For example, walking – indeed any notion involving location and time, even the notions 'here'

---

[5] MMK 2:1. There are actually several possible ways of translating this verse. An alternative, for example, might read: *What has been moved is not being moved; what has not been moved is not being moved; apart from what has been moved and what has not been moved, moving is not known.* These various viable translations allow us to approach the argument from slightly different angles – considering the mover or the path, and each both spatially and temporally. Actually these subjects of the argument are inextricably related anyway, so that pulling on any of the threads is helpful. Followed to their inevitable conclusions, they will all eventually yield the same totality of insights into emptiness.

and 'there' – can be seen to be composed of parts. But then that conceived entity – the whole – has to be either one with or different from its parts. If it is separate from its parts, then that thing would be findable as something other than its parts when the parts are removed. But this is not the case with walking, nor with anything else. If it is the same as its parts, it would be 'many'. Indeed, how many, *really*? The parts could be considered to be infinitely many. Where then is 'walking'? And actually, each part could be seen to be many too. Yet an infinitely small, partless part cannot exist and such parts could not be amassed to form a larger entity. Again, where is walking?

Considered from these perspectives the notion and the sense of walking begins to dissolve, and we can taste the fruits of the analyses. For as we have stressed, the point of analytical meditations is not to remain caught in a web of logic, bound at the level of thought. And it certainly is not 'cleverness'. The point of practice is release, and it is this that is delivered in the dissolution of reified concepts. The world of things opens out, and with it, feelings of release and perhaps of quiet exhilaration – strong or subtle – are often opened too.

Resting in, enjoying, and consolidating the view

During any analytical meditation, once the analysis has been worked through and has given rise to a vivid sense of the emptiness of the object, it is important to *rest for a while in that view of emptiness*. Such seeing might be limited to the voidness of the thing analysed, or it might spill over naturally to other objects. Or, without actually analysing them, it can be extended more deliberately to other things. Whichever is the case, it is vital, as we have just implied, to enjoy this view – the sense of the magical quality of appearances, or the dissolving or unbinding of perception. Then when the sense of emptiness begins to wear off, the analysis can be repeated.

Practice: Analysing walking and finding it empty

Take a little time in a walking meditation session to first focus on the sensations of walking and so allow mindfulness to gain some stability and strength.

Then, perhaps standing at any point, ready to walk, imagine and carefully consider the beginning of walking. See that it cannot begin in a moment when the body is stationary. Nor can it begin once in motion. Realize that there is no third option, so the beginning of walking cannot be found. Subject an imaginary micro-moment to as much analytical scrutiny as it takes for you to be convinced that this is so.

Contemplate stopping, the ending of walking, in a similar fashion.

Notice what effects it has to see this: walking has no findable beginning or ending; but it is not permanent either – it lacks inherent existence.

You may also contemplate where, or when, walking is actually happening. As described, by mentally dissecting the walking path – and realizing that walking is not happening on the path ahead nor on the path behind, and that there is no part left where it may happen; or that it is not happening in the past nor the future, and cannot be happening in the present moment – see that walking is unfindable.

Having considered the present moment, see also that it must be true of *all* points in time – whether past, present, or future – that it is not possible to find walking at that time.

As always with the different insight ways of looking, be patient and gently persistent as you apply them. Often they will begin to have an effect only after a little while. Once they do deliver a realization of the emptiness of walking, notice how this feels. Rest in this view a while, relaxing the analysis, and enjoying the perception and feeling. When this sense begins to lose its vitality, run through the analysis again to re-ignite the realization.

These analyses may be combined once they have become relatively quick. And once some fluency with the sevenfold reasoning or the neither-one-nor-many analysis has been gained, you may also use either of these, or a combination, to contemplate the parts of walking and see that it has no inherent existence.

Make sure you experiment with subjecting other processes and phenomena to these ways of looking. Particularly if there is some activity that is feared, or experienced as *dukkha*, these analyses can be helpful in dissolving the perceived solidity of that thing. But any process in time – breathing, for instance, or a *citta* state or emotion – may usefully be regarded in these ways.

Subtle dukkha, and sweet relief

In practice it is interesting to notice the effects of seeing the emptiness of walking. Unless there is some physical discomfort or the mind is agitated or troubled in some way, we typically would not consider, or feel, walking up and down to be *dukkha*. Yet as the emptiness of it is seen – either through such analyses or some other means – and the perception of walking begins to be unbound and to open out, there will be a sense of unburdening to some extent, even where we had not actually been conscious of feeling any sense of burden. When we walk realizing that walking lacks inherent existence, the heart can be touched with a sometimes awesome sense of freedom and joy. It recognizes, in the very lightness of things that it apprehends, an inexhaustible beauty and wonder.

Similarly we can recognize the subtle *dukkha* of any binding of any perception – of self, of thing, or of event. The more tightly and solidly it is bound as this or that, the more *dukkha*. It is only because we are accustomed to perceiving everything this way, and that we have nothing to compare it to, that we do not recognize the *dukkha* therein.

Beyond Motion, Process, and Change

By looking for walking, or something similar, in any of these ways in practice, we can realize that the processes and events of the world, although they certainly appear and function, are not ultimately findable. They are empty of inherent existence. Of course, we *can* regard selves and things as processes. But this will only ever be a helpful way of looking at a conventional level. It is not the ultimate truth of things. And relative to a more profound view of emptiness, the level of liberation any process view delivers will be limited.

Actually, these arguments and ways of looking can be generalized to reveal that not only motion, but change and impermanence also are empty. For without real beginning, real ending, or real movement of transition, impermanence and change cannot be real in the way that we assume. Later, particularly in Chapters 26 and 27, we will see the emptiness of impermanence from other angles too. Through all of these means we eventually come to understand why it says in a *Prajñāpāramitā Sūtra*:

> Not of anything has its production or destruction been expounded.

As well as in the *Yuktiṣaṣṭikā*:

> What is dependently co-arisen is actually devoid of origination and destruction. Those who have come to comprehend this have crossed over the ocean of realist views.[6]

And in the *Mūlamadhyamakārikā*:

> Unarisen, unceased, like *nirvāṇa*, is the nature of things.[7]

---

[6] '*dṛṣṭibhūtabhavārṇava*'. (Translation adapted from Chr. Lindtner's in *Nagarjuniana*, p. 109.)
[7] MMK 18:7.

24

Emptiness Views and the Sustenance of Love

That insight into voidness naturally feeds beautiful qualities such as *mettā* and compassion will probably be evident to a meditator through practice by now. Since clinging is a contraction and a kind of tension, any view that releases clinging will also soften in that moment the closed- and brittle-heartedness that inevitably to some degree accompany and form part of clinging. Often then feelings of openness and tenderness arise in their place. As we have also witnessed, ways of looking which release clinging concoct less self in the moment and, with that, less sense of separation between self and other. Because this perception of non-separation is itself an aspect of the experiences of love, compassion, and generosity, such qualities are easily engendered then.

Over the longer term too, emptiness practices can play a very significant role in opening, deepening, strengthening, and purifying these lovely qualities and their manifestations in our life. The more we digest a genuine understanding of the voidness of self and of phenomena, the more our capacity for compassion and service, for example, is freed. We become less afraid of the suffering of the world, and more able to respond without feeling burdened. And we realize as well the folly of a life devoted only to self-interest.

But there are also ways we can *deliberately* bring in the various views of emptiness to support and empower practices like generosity and the *brahmavihāras*.[1] Let us explore a few of the many possibilities that exist.

Opening Love Through Loosening the Self-view

Even just with respect to insight ways of looking at one's own self, there are many options. Some of these relate to how one actually feels in the course of practice. For example, if on some occasion I am practising *mettā* or compassion towards

[1] The four *brahmavihāras* ('divine dwellings' or 'heavenly abidings') are *mettā*, compassion, appreciative joy, and equanimity. As mentioned in Chapter 20, these four are also sometimes known as the four immeasurables.

another, and I feel unwell physically, one possible response at times might be to gently encourage a view that embodies the attitude 'it's not about me'. In other words: 'right now, how *I* feel is not so important, it's *your* well-being that I am nourishing in this meditation'. Having seen from previous practice that the self-sense is fabricated, an empty appearance, there is more freedom to choose to regard the experience of self sometimes as not so significant, not so much at centre stage, where it is usually placed. Such letting go of self-interest in that moment can open the heart and energize the *mettā*. At the same time, as we would expect by now, my own weight of *dukkha* will be lightened.[2]

We may also use the faculty of the imagination at times to take such a shift of attitude a little further. Since it is understood now that there is no *real* way the self is, there is the possibility to imagine ourselves skilfully in different ways that might be helpful. Knowing that all self-views without exception are fabrications, we are free to play with different images of self without taking any of them literally as the truth. When we are experiencing *dukkha* then in practice, to lightly, playfully even, introduce the imagination of oneself as a hero or heroine, a *bodhisattva*, who is willing to endure and open to this discomfort and these difficulties for the sake of all beings, may be a very skilful way of looking. Because it can also bring in a heart element of devotion in some way or other, such a view can transform, even bless, the sense of the whole situation. To the extent that this kind of play of imagination is mixed with the view of one's self, of one's aggregates, and even of the imagining, as void, this becomes an immensely powerful practice.

The particular skills developed in the various emptiness meditations may also be employed to *ignite* the practices of *mettā*, compassion, or the cultivation of other beautiful qualities. Here too there is great scope for creativity. Again if I am unwell for instance, I might deliberately use those very sensations and experiences to imagine that I am dying. In so doing, I might also view the process of death as a giving back of 'my' aggregates, elements, and constituents to the universe. Essentially this is only a slight variation of the *anattā* practice. But here the relinquishment involved in the view of the aggregates as 'not me, not mine' is being supported by and opened to a sense of connection with the vastness of the universe. Such giving back can bring much needed qualities of tenderness and of healing to the heart. Love and compassion also arise naturally, and a sense

[2] Of course in suggesting this tactic I am again assuming that a meditator already has an ability to listen with compassion to, and generally care for, herself; and in particular too, that she has already developed the skills to open to, hold, and work helpfully with difficulties of body and mind when she wants to.

of devotion, prayerfulness, and great beauty may be unlocked. Then I might tune in to, and encourage in different ways, any of these qualities I choose.

With previous experience in practices such as the *anattā* way of looking it is highly unlikely that viewing things in this way will lead to feelings of existential angst. Those kinds of feelings, as well as the kinds of existentialist notions that sometimes underpin them, actually rest on other, usually habitual and unconscious, views which have not been examined deeply enough and which effectively grasp at the true existence of things and of a self. It is in fact only when viewed through the lens of self that the vastness of the universe can appear cold, hostile, or oppressively meaningless.

Once enough familiarity and skill with any particular emptiness practice is gained, it may be incorporated into a whole host of other practices, such as *mettā*, compassion, or various practices of generosity, to deepen those other practices. For example, while directing *mettā* to another, I may *simultaneously* work to sustain some emptiness view moment to moment – for instance, of my experience as '*anicca*'; or my aggregates as '*anattā*'; of my self as 'empty'; or of everything as 'having the nature of awareness'.

With a little experimentation, this is certainly less difficult or cumbersome than it might sound, and the two practices can be blended together easefully so that both are empowered. As mentioned in Chapter 20, qualities such as *mettā*, compassion, and generosity fabricate less self in the moment. Then as less self is constructed, it becomes more readily *apparent* that the aggregates are not-self, for example, so the *anattā* way of looking is supported right there. And conversely, as mentioned above, when there is less self-sense there is then less sense of separation and almost effortlessly love arises. The practices can thus feed and support each other quite naturally in the moment.

Practice: Deepening *mettā* and compassion by fabricating less self

(If you are already quite familiar with *mettā* or compassion practice, and if you have developed some facility with any emptiness practice which fabricates less sense of self in the moment – for example, one of the three characteristics or the sevenfold reasoning – you may wish to explore the following practice.)

Spend some time at the beginning of a meditation session cultivating either *mettā* or compassion in your usual way. When you feel ready, bring in one of the emptiness ways of looking, and gently try to sustain it moment to moment, as you continue directing love to a being.

One possibility is viewing all that you experience as you practise – the sensations of sight and sound, the sensations of the body, the mental perceptions and images, even the intentions, attention, and consciousness – as *anattā*. Notice the effects this has on the whole practice.

Experiment with the balance of emphasis between the two ways of looking in any moment. Here, the primary intention is the strengthening of the *mettā* or compassion; the emptiness way of looking is being used to support this.

The second *dukkha* method may be incorporated by repeatedly tuning in to the sense of clinging and relaxing it.

If you are using the *anicca* characteristic, experiment to find which approaches best support the *mettā* or compassion. If needed, you may gently guide the *anicca* view so that it brings, for instance, an opening out, or a diffusion, of the sense of self – subtly steering the unfolding towards more softening and love in the moment.

Perhaps, on encountering nothing but momentary perceptions, the self is sensed to be almost nothing, 'paper thin'. Existing through perceptions, it is inseparable from what it perceives, and so inseparable from the world. Love opens naturally with this awareness of non-separation.

If you are incorporating the sevenfold reasoning, it is probably best not to try to analyse while doing the *mettā* or compassion practice, but rather to draw on the conviction in the emptiness of self given by past practice of the reasoning. Based on this past insight, bring in the sense that the self is void, and allow the love to be directed from there. When the sense of the emptiness of self weakens, you might run through the analysis again briefly to rekindle it. Alternatively, you might start a session with the analysis, and then, holding the view of voidness, move into a *mettā* or compassion practice.

There are many other possibilities too beyond these. Ways of looking which view the aggregates themselves as empty will open even more depth to the *mettā* and compassion practices. By this point it may anyway be the case that the three characteristics or the sevenfold reasoning already lead into views of the voidness of phenomena in various ways. If so, this seeing can be included in the practice.

Since such ways of looking will also lead to a fading of perception, some care must be taken to *modulate* the degree of fading so that the sense of love itself does not totally fade, but is still palpable in some way. Learning to play with this modulation can be a lot of fun.

Eventually, any of the practices in this book may be used to support *mettā* and compassion practices. As you learn new ways of looking you may wish to return to this exploration.

The View of the Other

We may also turn the emptiness ways of looking toward the other. When there is judgement, ill-will, or anger at another, I might ask, for instance: Who am I angry with exactly? My anger requires that I am viewing this other as a solid self. Without a sense of their self as an object, the anger cannot be sustained. But when, asking this question, I look more closely I cannot find this self of theirs as an object for my anger. Nor can I find any part that justifies my anger. Considering their body, I find I cannot be angry at their body, or the parts of their body – the spleen or the lungs, the hands or the brain. Whatever part I consider, it does not seem to make sense for me to be angry with that part. I might think I am angry at this person's feelings, thoughts, or intentions. But even these, as discussed earlier, arise out of conditions – inner and outer, past and present – and then evaporate. There is no self in them, and contemplated this way these parts don't seem to fuel my negative feelings. Dissecting the other (merely metaphorically, that is!) and asking who exactly I am angry with, my anger cannot find a base for support, and so it dissolves.

In a somewhat similar vein, Śāntideva began to reflect on his anger when a person beat others with a stick. Realizing it simply makes no sense to be angry at the stick, he reasoned further:

> Having disregarded… the stick, I am angry at the person who impels it. But he too is impelled – by hatred. It is better, then, that I hate hatred.[3]

It will not be possible, though, to sustain hating a hatred that is unattached to a self. Deprived of the fabrication on which it depends – the self of the other – hatred collapses and disbands. Relieved then, we can thankfully taste some openness again.

Often, too, when there is anger or judgment of another the perception of what we share in common with this other is reduced, while the perception of the differences between us is intensified. And this very priming of the perception of dissimilarities tends in turn to support the judgment or anger. Differences and diversity exist, of course, but one helpful possibility when there is judgment is to shift to a way of looking that focuses on what we have in common.

Here again the aggregates can provide a useful framework. Looking at the other I see there is body there, and body here; *vedanā* there and *vedanā* here; perceptions, mental formations, and consciousness – there and here. And going

[3] BCA 6:41.

through the aggregates one by one, I realize too that, although there certainly are differences, essentially the aggregates over there and over here are quite similar.

Focusing on the aggregates of myself or an other pries the perception of those aggregates loose somewhat of their adhesion to fixed and solid selves. Instead of being obscured by or subsumed into the perceptions of the selves we have constructed, the aggregates can be seen more freely. And seeing the aggregates as more autonomous in this way allows their essential similarities to be acknowledged more easily. With less sense of separation then, as well as less solidity of the other's self, judgment can dissolve, and feelings of warmth and friendship can flourish.

Practice: Searching for the object of negative feeling

When there is some kind of negative feeling, such as anger or judgment, toward another, practise holding this person in the attention and asking, for instance, "Who exactly am I angry with?"

View each part of them in your mind's eye and see if that part is the object of your negativity.

Notice what happens to your perception of the other and your feelings about them as you do this.

You may also analyse the person with the sevenfold reasoning. Notice what happens to your feelings about them when you view them as empty of inherent existence.

Practice: Using the aggregates to recognize commonality

Both in and out of formal meditation sessions, practise viewing an other – whatever your feelings toward them at that time – in terms of the aggregates. *Khandha*, as we have said, literally means 'heap', and here it can be helpful to indeed view each aggregate as a collection – as a stream of momentary instances, or a collection of smaller parts such as the organs and elements that make up the body.

As you contemplate each aggregate in the other, recognize at the same time that this aggregate or collection exists also in yourself. Even though there are differences, is it possible to see that there is no difference in essence between the aggregates 'here' and 'there'?

Notice how it feels to sustain a viewing of the other in this way.

If some manifestation of love arises in the heart, you may wish to focus on, and gently encourage, that feeling.

Ways of looking at the other in mettā and compassion practices

It is possible too, when actually practising *mettā* or compassion, for example, to make the other – who is the object of the practice – also the object of an insight way of looking at the same time. Again there are many options. I may bring in a view of *anicca*, for instance, by simply holding the knowledge in the heart that this being, to whom I am directing love, is *subject to death,* and *subject also to all kinds of uncertainty and change*. Partly because it reminds me, as above, that we share these fundamental facts of existence in common, and partly because it reminds me of their vulnerability, this awareness will feed the love and compassion.

Alternatively, the *moment-to-moment impermanence* of the other may be tuned in to as one directs love to them. Then again the view of the other changes. We see their flickering and ephemeral nature, and this opens the flow of compassion. Not only because there can often be an intuitive view of what is fleeting as being worthy of compassion; but also because the perception of the other is lightened. And where the perception is lightened, there will be a lightening of the heart. Love and compassion arise naturally in such a light space, for they share this quality of lightness.

Of course this lightening of the perception of the other occurs also because seeing their moment-to-moment impermanence breaks down the habitual view of them as a solidified self. In fact, particularly when there is suffering, compassion can be empowered by viewing the object of compassion not so much as the person, but as *the individual mind moments of suffering. This* momentary gestalt of mental impression, of consciousness and experience, with its perception and feeling, is actually where the *dukkha* is. Even an experience of physical pain is, like all experiences, an experience experienced through the mind as a perception of consciousness. Viewed this way, and broken down into moments which can each be focused on and held in care, the self-view is dissolved to an extent, as if these mind moments were ownerless, each just floating alone somehow, and deserving of tenderness.

Here then it is not so much the rapidity of moments that is attended to. Rather, the view extricates these moments from the projected solidity of the self of the other.[4] The perception of other is lightened, but the compassion will often become stronger.

---

[4] The view described here as underpinning this practice may also be credibly derived as one of the potential variant meanings of the *Akṣayamati Sūtra* passage we quoted in Chapter 20. That passage stated the possibility at times of love taking as its object, not beings, but *dharmas* – a term which can sometimes carry the particular meaning, as described above, of our ephemeral states of being.

Viewing as *empty* the one to whom I am directing the *mettā* or compassion will empower the love even more profoundly than focusing on their impermanence. Chandrakīrti alluded to this in his *Madhyamakāvatāra*. Most of that text is devoted to an exposition of the view of emptiness, but it begins with a moving homage to compassion:

> … At the start I praise compassion.
>
> Beings think 'I' at first, and cling to self. They think 'mine' and are attached to things. They thus turn helplessly as buckets on a waterwheel. And to compassion for such beings, I bow down.
>
> Beings are like a moon in rippling water, fleeting, evanescent, and empty in their nature. Bodhisattvas see them thus, and yearn to set them free. Their wisdom is beneath compassion's power.[5]

In his auto-commentary on these verses Chandrakīrti explained that compassion may be practised at three levels. The first takes as its object beings in the ordinary sense, suffering through their inexorable vulnerability to all sorts of shifts of fortune ("turning helplessly as buckets on a waterwheel"). Compassion at this level also includes an understanding that ignorance and clinging fuel *dukkha*. This level of compassion is the most commonly practised.

The second level of compassion practice takes as its object beings viewed through the lens of momentary *anicca*. One directs love towards beings while sustaining a view of their "fleeting, evanescent" nature – a nature like the flickering reflection of "a moon in rippling water". These first two levels we have discussed above.

The third level of compassion practice takes as its object beings regarded through a lens which understands that they are "empty in nature". We have available to us by now many possible ways of going about this. For example, I may use the sevenfold reasoning to see the emptiness of the other, and then hold that sense of her emptiness in the view as I offer her love. Or I may bring into the view the sense of the body of the other as permeable, not truly a thing separate from the universe, as discussed in Chapter 22.

But I may also add to this last the understanding that her mental aggregates, equally, are dependent on, and inseparable from, the universe. She is not findable

[5] MAV 1:2 – 4.

apart from her perceptions. Without any perceptions would she be at all? Perceiving any object, that very perception is not her, but also not other than her. It forms a part of a fabric on which she is imputed as a self, and without which she is nothing at all. Now since most of her perceptions are directly or indirectly perceptions of outer objects, these perceptions themselves are not separate from the universe. And since the other mental aggregates always accompany perception and are not separable from it, her mind, as well as her body, may be regarded as dependent on, and inseparable from, the universe.

We discussed previously too how the mind now – including its perceptions – is shaped by its past and present intentions and movements; and how in turn, the mind now and its perceptions help shape the future of the mental aggregates. Thus her mental aggregates in the present may also be seen as not truly separable from her mental aggregates of the past and the future.

Regarded in all these ways, she is unfindable as a separate thing. She is seen to be 'infinite' in some sense, 'full of the universe'. Although it might initially be surprising, when she is viewed like this – as unfindable, as empty – *mettā* and compassion toward her are effortlessly opened and deepen to another level.

Practice: Viewing the object of love and compassion in different ways

As you direct *mettā* or compassion to another, hold lightly in your awareness at the same time a knowledge of their mortality, and also of their vulnerability to all kinds of changing circumstances, inner and outer. Gently encourage this view to help open and deepen the flow of love.

At other times, based on your own experience seeing the rapid impermanence of your own aggregates, view an other, as you direct love to them, through a lens that sees the momentary nature of their aggregates. Notice what effects this has on the practice.

If they are suffering, experiment, as described, with a view of their mind moments as the object of compassion.

Once you have developed any other way of looking that can see deeply the emptiness of the self of another, you can experiment with incorporating it into the *mettā* or compassion practice. This may be the sevenfold reasoning, or the sense of their being 'infinite' and unfindable as some thing separate from the universe, as described.

You may also view their aggregates as empty of inherent existence, using any of the insights or practices we have discussed. (Later, when we see that consciousness is void too, that insight can be incorporated into the view as well.)

Notice what effects seeing the other as empty has on the experience of love, and also on perception. It is very likely that the perception of the other will fade to some extent when viewing them as empty. Again, the extent of the fading can be played with. Even when the appearance of the other to the mind dissolves to a great degree, one may still retain a sense of them as the referent of the emptiness. Rather than an absence of connection, seeing their emptiness should support the opening of a beautiful and mystical quality of union and love.

Voidness and the Spectrum of Love

With practice, it is possible to work to sustain a view of *both* self and other as empty while engaging practices such as *mettā* or compassion. Again then it will be necessary to play with the degree of fading, sensitive to what is helpful; and sensitive, too, to the variations in the experience of love along this continuum of fading.

Focusing on the emptiness of self, other, or both, it may be that the experience deepens to a transcendent sense of non-referential love, a love that has no object.[6] This should not be confused with love for all beings, which takes all beings as its object. In this non-referential love, the object of love has dissolved. Actually, while the perception of the other has faded, the sense of emptiness has become vivid through the perception of a vacuity imbued with the meaning of emptiness, and this emptiness forms a *kind* of object for the love. In seeing the voidness of all things though, it will include love to all beings implicitly, since all beings share the nature of voidness.[7]

It may be at times, however, that as things fade the very perception of love begins to fade too. Initially becoming more subtle, it may move toward equanimity as it does so. This need not always be a problem. As before, we can learn to play with modulating the degree of fading, if we wish to, so that different qualities and flavours of love manifest more or less. But it becomes clear to us through all this that love too is empty, and that its boundaries with other qualities are not in truth rigidly definable.

Exploring different ways of looking allows different experiences of love, and of many other exquisite qualities of heart, to arise and be explored as well.

---

[6] This was the third possible kind of object of love referred to in the passage from the *Akṣayamati Sūtra* we quoted in Chapter 20 – "for those who have attained receptivity to the truth of [voidness]… "

[7] A somewhat similar state of "love without an object" may also arise from the meditation outlined in Chapter 20 on directing love towards phenomena, when perceptions fade to a certain degree. These two states will become more similar when the fading gives rise to a cognition 'empty', for then, as explained above, emptiness becomes a kind of object for the love.

Through practice we can open to the great range in the manifestations of love – from the more everyday sense of 'love of one self for another', for example, through to this most refined perception of 'love without an object'. It is actually part of our humanity that the whole range of these shades is available to us; and that our experience in practice inevitably moves back and forth along this spectrum. In time, nurtured by and nurturing them all, we recognize that *all* have their beauty, their blessedness, and their place.

Giving and the Emptiness of What Is Given

We can also consider some of the ways emptiness views may be incorporated into other heart-based practices. Generosity – the giving of what we value – is for many reasons always lovely, whether mixed with the understanding of voidness or not. We have already mentioned how, like other qualities such as *mettā*, compassion, and devotion, giving fabricates less self, and lightens the perception of the world. When infused with some understanding of emptiness it becomes an even more powerful practice. Chandrakīrti, echoing the teachings of the *Prañāpāramitā Sūtras*, wrote:

> Giving, void of giver, receiver, and gift, is called a transcendent perfection. Giving in which there is attachment to these three is taught to be a mundane perfection.[8]

Generosity may take many forms. Certainly, giving in actuality is crucial – of money and material goods, of time, attention, and whatever else may be helpful. But there are, in addition, many forms of giving that are mostly practised within a meditative imagination, and these too can be of great benefit. The practices of dedicating merit and of exchanging self and other, like *mettā* and compassion practices, both involve this kind of imaginal giving. Numerous variants are possible for each, so let us consider just a few options.

Dedicating merit

In the practice of dedicating merit we reflect on the beautiful qualities we are cultivating through practice. We see that mindfulness, *mettā*, and *samādhi*, generosity, wisdom, and the rest all contribute significantly to happiness. Indeed

[8] MAV 1:16.

we realize that happiness is actually dependent on these qualities. No matter what else we have in life, if these qualities are lacking, happiness is simply not possible. In a sense then, they may rightly be regarded as causes of happiness.

At the beginning or end of a day of practice, knowing that we will be, or have been, working to cultivate these causes of happiness, we may – in our minds – offer them, and the experiences of happiness they bring, to others. Wedded to an attitude of devotion this is a lovely, heart-opening, and helpful ritual in its own right. And again, just as with so many other Dharma practices, with sensitivity we can also feel how the self, as a result, may be fabricated less in that moment.

Exchanging self and other

Like the practice of dedicating merit, the practice of exchanging self and other emerges from the ideal of the bodhisattva who dedicates her existence to awakening for the sake of others. One of the ways such a selfless motivation is supported over the long term is by working to cultivate an attitude of the *equality* of self and other – that is, a vision and feeling that the happiness of others is just as important to me as my own happiness, that they matter equally to me.

Such an attitude can also be augmented in meditation by imagining exchanging the happiness of self and other – giving away one's happiness to another, and taking on suffering so that they might be spared it.[9] This meditative imagination, open to all kinds of empowerment through emptiness views, forms a beautiful and potent way of looking.

In practice one can imagine giving one's pleasure or happiness to others somewhere else, whether there is an experience of pleasure or happiness in the present or not. What is more important is giving away *specific* experiences of happiness or pleasure, rather than a vague, abstract happiness or pleasure. The happiness in this pleasant sight, these body sensations, this feeling of joy – one can be very creative here, but tuning in to the actual or imagined experience is vital. This is in part because then we can see the happiness or pleasure *as* an experience, a perception, and already that can support a different relationship with it. Through the mindfulness there can be at least the intimations of the fleeting or not-self nature of these perceptions – naturally loosening the self's grip on them, supporting an ability to let them go, as well as opening at least some sense of lightness of being.

---

[9] There are other approaches possible to the practice of exchanging self and other which involve exchanging the sense of *self*, but here we will only consider exchanging the *happiness* of self and other.

And when we offer this happiness to others, we will typically find that our own experience of happiness is increased in the moment. Perhaps it is surprising at first, but rather than diminishing our store, giving happiness away reveals a sweet and inexhaustible well-spring of joy that is available to us. With practice over time we grow to trust this.

The ease with which we are able to give away like this our happiness and the qualities which cause it, and also the joy we experience in doing so, are both increased through incorporating any emptiness way of looking into the process. As the above passage from Chandrakīrti indicates, not only self and other, but also that which we are giving may in practice be lightly viewed through any emptiness lens. In fact, any combination of these can be subjected to a view of voidness. There are many possibilities and permutations. We may more deliberately regard the perceptions of happiness and pleasure as *anicca* or *anattā*. Or they can be viewed as empty in themselves in any of the ways we have explored. Since it comprises a more profound insight, this last will open the greatest ease and joy, and the greatest capacity for giving.

Actually, not just happiness and the causes of happiness, but also other phenomena may be regarded as empty and dedicated in meditation to others. One may sustain a view of the emptiness of the aggregates, for example, while prayerfully offering them to all beings. Again it will be helpful to focus the attention on the *experience* of each aggregate and the sense of its emptiness as you do this, so that the giving feels alive and not abstract: "My body, which is empty, exists for your sake." Similarly with the activities of the body, with *vedanā*, perception, intentions, and consciousness. The six senses and the pleasure in each of them may also be viewed this way.[10]

Such offering need not involve any words, even mentally. But the movement expresses an intention and a view that radically places one's own empty aggregates and the constituents of one's being in the service of the ultimate welfare of others. For example, one may contemplate just the visual sense and dedicate all that is involved there: "These empty *vedanā* and perceptions of sight belong to you; they exist for your benefit. Because they are empty, and also because they do not exist to give *me* pleasure, I do not mind whether they are pleasant or unpleasant." Practising in such ways can really be like practising an art. Again, there is great scope here for creativity and improvisation.

As any of these phenomena are offered and viewed as empty, their perception will fade to some extent, and seeing this should reinforce the very sense of their

---

[10] Cf. Śāntideva's inspired resolve for practice (in BCA 8): "*I abandon this heap... to the service of the world.*"

emptiness. As they fade and as we see their emptiness, we appreciate too the *equality* of all things. For in having no own-nature, all things have the same nature – of voidness. Or we might say that, lacking any essence, all things share equally an 'essence' of emptiness.[11] If helpful, the perception of the vacuity into which they all fade may be used – merely as part of a skilful way of looking in the moment – to support the sense of 'equality of essence', without actually reifying either the vacuity or an essence of emptiness.

Then, everything, even that which we would conventionally regard as worthless or undesirable, may be meditatively offered to the welfare of all beings. Greed, anger, and delusion, as well as insight and beautiful qualities; doubt, dullness, and heaviness, along with commitment, effort, and energy – the essential sameness of all can be perceived, and this seeing of the non-duality of things allows a total giving, a dedicating of one's entire being. The view of emptiness thus consummately supports the opening and deepening of devotion.

Much of this will of course apply to the complementary aspect of exchanging self and other – the taking on of *dukkha*. As with the giving of happiness, this can be a remarkable practice even before any emptiness view is added. I may, for instance, whenever there is any discomfort in meditation, play with imagining that my taking on this experience magically somehow takes it away from someone somewhere else: "I will take this headache, this heartache, this situation, so that you can be spared this pain, so that you have ease."

Opening to the difficult experience thus, we are practising a kind of release of aversion very similar to the 'welcoming' of the second *dukkha* method. But here there is a holding of both the difficult experience *and* the sense of an other or others, so that, just as in the giving of happiness, the release of clinging is being coupled with a well-wishing towards another. As we would expect, since there is, through the welcoming, a reducing of aversion towards the *dukkha* one is experiencing, it is possible that the perception of the difficulty will fade to some extent, rendering it also easier to open to as a consequence. Perceptions of self, other, and phenomenon – all are softened, and peace and freedom may arise.

Again the fading points to the voidness of the phenomenon. And again, difficult experiences may be deliberately viewed as void in many ways. Then they seem less substantial and problematic, and I am more able, and willing, to

---

[11] Cf. Nāgārjuna's *Bodhicittavivaraṇa* v.57: "*Just as sweetness is the nature of sugar and heat that of fire, so the nature of all things is proclaimed to be emptiness.*" (Author's own translation.) Here the word rendered as 'nature', *prakṛti*, may be translated as 'essence' as well, and also as 'fundamental condition'.

welcome them like this and to take on *dukkha* for the sake of others. So the sense of the emptiness of these perceptions intensifies, and the sense of love and non-separation deepen. Emptiness and compassion are thus blended in a powerful way.

As we have mentioned in other chapters, seeing phenomena fade, and seeing their voidness deeply, not only do things appear much less solid and more insubstantial, but perception may often become quite malleable. There may be, with practice, the possibility to transform perceptions, so that what initially appeared one way may be experienced very differently. The deeper the views of emptiness incorporated, the greater the possibilities here. In the practice of exchanging self and other, the nature of an experience can sometimes be transformed from painful to blissful, and its very appearance changed to blessèd, or 'divine', appearance. The same is true of the perception of ourselves, and of an other. Just as we may choose to see an other as a friend, we may, seeing their emptiness deeply, choose to see them as translucently beautiful, luminous, and divine.

Sometimes such a transformation will happen by itself in the practice as the love and the emptiness ways of looking are mixed. At other times it may be more deliberately supported as a skilful and lovely, mystical way of looking. Emptiness ways of looking thus deliver us to the threshold of tantric practices. Then also the facility and the liberating power available to us there will be dependent on the depth, and the degree of consolidation, of our insights into emptiness. The artistic nature, too, of all these practices becomes even more apparent.

Creative play in practice

By this point in our journey, and as is evident from the foregoing discussion, any practice involving imaginal giving – such as dedicating merit or exchanging self and other – admits many possible variations. Although you may develop a favourite way of engaging these practices, it can also be very beneficial to retain a flexibility and fluidity of approach. Trying different things at different times, mixing different emptiness views together, and improvising your own methods can all contribute to ongoing discovery and an aliveness to these practices. The following is therefore only a framework, a general list of elements which may be combined and experimented with in practice.

Practice: Exchanging self and other

When there is a moment of happiness, whether in or out of a formal meditation session, practise tuning in to the experience and offering this happiness or pleasure to others. This movement of offering can be very quick and light, and does not necessarily need any words to support it.

Practise also giving away an *imagined* experience of pleasure or happiness, as well as the causes of happiness that you are cultivating through practice.

When there is some *dukkha* present, tune in to the experience, and then experiment with imagining that your taking it on relieves an other or others elsewhere of similar *dukkha*. With a little practice the various elements involved here – the sense of the other, the sense of wishing them well or giving them love or happiness, and the sense of welcoming the difficult experience – can all be easefully held together.

Notice the effects on your feelings and on perceptions.

Experiment with incorporating different emptiness ways of looking into these practices. Experiment also with different combinations of objects viewed through these emptiness ways of looking. You may view your self or the other – the receiver – as empty; or both. You may also view as void, in any number of ways, that which is given or taken.

Again notice the effects this has on your feelings and on your perceptions; and also on the capacity to give and to take.

Whether actually experienced in the moment or only imagined, remember to make the object specific, by focusing on a particular happiness or *dukkha*, or the experience of the particular aggregate or sense sphere that is being dedicated. Breaking up the field of possibility, and offering this or that part at a time – for example, the happiness and pleasure of one of the senses – may thus be helpful. Even if offering the totality of being, connecting with the phenomena that comprise this totality, and with a sense of their emptiness, brings the practice alive.

Emptiness and Equanimity

Views of emptiness also help love by supporting a degree of equanimity in relation to the suffering of beings. Love and compassion need such equanimity to give them strength, stability, and durability. Even without invoking the deeper levels of insight into emptiness, this support can be seen in countless ways. While caring deeply for the suffering in the world and working to ameliorate the many conditions contributing to it, we can, for example, still recognize that, from one perspective at least, any conditions we human beings encounter are not inherently favourable or unfavourable. What seems negative and difficult is not necessarily so in itself, since much that is positive may come from it – if it is met with mindfulness, curiosity, and wisdom, for instance. Similarly, what is pleasant and seems like a boon is not inherently so in itself, for it may spawn all kinds of negativity and *dukkha* if met with grasping and carelessness and without investigation. There may be occasions when our best efforts have not prevented a particular suffering, and yet some unforeseen blessing or growth of being emerged from the painful situation. Witnessing this can allow a little spaciousness and equanimity to come into our compassion.

We can reflect too that whatever actions we take in trying to alleviate the suffering of others, the effects of these actions have no independent existence, for many reasons. Inevitably, for example, from the time of their instigation they will ripple out to meet and interact with innumerable other factors, other effects from other actions, past, present, and future, in the world. The effects of our actions are thus not simply isolatable as separate entities. They rapidly become mixed, infinite and unknowable. Seeing this I can only keep doing what seems most helpful, but I cannot become too attached to the effects of my individual actions.

§

Understanding the voidness of things, we discover, opens the heart in so many ways. And generally we find that the more profound the view of emptiness, the more it will strengthen and support the blossoming of love and compassion. It is *ultimate bodhicitta* – the realization of *śūnyatā* – that allows the fullness of *relative bodhicitta* – the dedication of one's existence to the welfare of all beings. When self, time, separation, and even suffering are seen to be empty, a devotion to the endless commitment of love is felt without burden.

PART EIGHT

No Traveller, No Journey – The Nature of Mind, and of Time

25

Emptiness and Awareness (2)

What then of awareness? However we conceive of it, whether as one of the aggregates, as the collection of the four mental aggregates, or as something other than the aggregates, and whatever we call it – Awareness, Consciousness, Mind, *Citta*, 'That which knows'[1] – it too is void of inherent existence.

The subtle binding involved in any reifying of awareness cannot be loosened, though, merely by adopting a belief in, or an intellectual view of, its lack of inherent existence. Normal and habitual, this level of clinging will remain fundamentally untouched unless the emptiness of awareness is seen for oneself through practice. That requires very deep and subtle insight. For to say that consciousness is empty means more, we know, than merely saying it is 'not me, not mine'. The possibility – as the *anattā* way of looking is developed – of dropping the identification with consciousness already constitutes quite a subtle level of practice. Realizing in meditation the *voidness* of consciousness is an even more subtle affair. Such insight, striking near the roots of delusion and bringing a profound freedom and unburdening, is certainly available however. In fact, with all the tools and insights we have already developed, it is perhaps only a small step from the point we have now reached.

There has been in this area, though, a considerable amount of controversy in the tradition, and it is easy to become confused. Added to this, a meditator's view of the nature of awareness may well evolve through various stages over time. As we have mentioned, some of these will actually be supportive in opening a great degree of freedom; and they may also provide provisional, but necessary, platforms for deepening insight.

Many of these views, suggested by relatively common meditation experiences,

---

[1] There is not always a consistency of terminology across the relevant literature in the tradition. In order that the essential insight here not elude us – that we have a tendency to reify 'that which knows', 'awareness', 'consciousness', 'mind', and that we need to realize its emptiness – these terms are used interchangeably in this chapter. Otherwise, generally in this book 'awareness' and 'consciousness' are used synonymously and differentiated from terms like 'mind' and '*citta*'.

seem to correlate too with what is expressed in a number of texts. On closer inspection however, the language in these texts is often being used in very particular ways, so that it is expressing insights other than what we might first assume. Sometimes too it is necessary to differentiate in the texts between those statements expressing partial or provisional insights, and those expressing fuller and more ultimate insights.

It might be useful then to examine briefly one or two of the more common notions of the nature of mind and of its emptiness, and see just where they are helpful and where they are limited.

Mind as mirror

One conception of awareness is that it is somehow like a mirror that reflects the objects of the world. A large part of our task in practice then would be to 'clean' the mirror so that it might reflect things clearly and truly. 'Emptiness of Mind' in this view is sometimes taken to mean a state of no thought. For thoughts would be like spots of dirt on the mirror's surface, distorting and obscuring the reflection of things. The mind in itself, like the mirror, might be regarded as inherently empty of these adventitious stains, these thoughts and other impurities: its true nature is to simply and naturally reflect things as they are.

Such a notion may perhaps be helpful partly because it carries an implication of the unaffected nature of awareness. A mirror is not troubled in any way by what passes before it. It continues to reflect whatever is there, whether beautiful or ugly. Encouraging this view of awareness can thus support a deepening of equanimity – a letting go, in the moment, of a degree of reactivity to appearances.

However, two problems with this notion will be immediately clear from all that we have discovered through practice by now. First, implicit in this idea is the belief in an objective reality, the mirror-mind reflecting 'things as they are'. Second, there is the assumption that, like a mirror, awareness reflects things effortlessly, passively. From our more thorough investigation of fabrication though, we have seen that objects of perception are concocted, through various forms of clinging, to appear as this or that, and that without clinging – which is not passive, but a doing – they are not anything objectively in themselves.

Our realization of the nature of awareness needs to go beyond this level of understanding that construes mind as a mirror. In response to Shen-hsiu's verse:

> Our body is the *Bodhi* tree, and our mind a mirror bright –
> carefully we wipe them hour by hour, and let no dust alight,

Hui-neng expressed a much more profound insight into the fundamental emptiness of mind:

> There is no *Bodhi* tree, nor… a mirror bright.
> Since all is void, where can the dust alight?[2]

Vast Awareness as Source of all things

Another view which may emerge from practice was among the cluster of variations explored in Chapter 15. Sometimes when there is a sense of the vastness of awareness, it can seem that this vastness is the transcendent 'source' of all other transient phenomena. As was mentioned, things seem to arise out of, and disappear back into, this space; and this sense of things may be profoundly helpful in supporting equanimity, love, and freedom. Here again, awareness seems free and independent, uninvolved in and unperturbed by the movements and machinations of 'small mind', of reactivity and thought.

However, this notion of awareness as a source of appearances was repudiated by the Buddha. In relation to any such perception of vastness of awareness – or indeed to *any* perception or notion, even of *nibbāna* – he said that one who is awakened

> does not conceive things about it, [and] does not conceive of things coming out of it.[3]

If one seeks the fullness of insight it is not ultimately helpful to regard awareness, or anything else, as the source of appearances. To be locked into that view would be to perpetuate a sense of the inherent existence of that phenomenon, missing and preventing the more radical freedom of insights into emptiness, dependent arising, and the ultimate groundlessness of all things.

With careful and open-minded investigation in practice we will notice something interesting, though, that can help us move beyond many of these kinds of views: *The way awareness seems at any time is dependent on the way of looking*. Practising in certain ways, awareness will likely seem vast and imperturbable. On another occasion, or even at another point in the same

---

[2] Translation adapted from Wong Mou-lam's in A. F. Price and Wong Mou-lam (translators), *The Diamond Sutra and the Sutra of Hui-neng*, pp. 70 – 72.

[3] MN 1.

meditation session, practising with a narrowly focused attention and tuned in to the rapidity of moment-to-moment *anicca*, it is quite possible to have a sense of consciousness not as vast and imperturbable but as arising and ceasing together with different phenomena with immense rapidity. Which is the 'real' way awareness is? As we have already mentioned, awareness is bound up with perception. Through the way of looking then, it merely takes on the aspect of perception at any time. What is perceived in any such manner cannot be regarded as the true nature of awareness.

In fact, a sense of vastness of awareness is still itself an object, a perception, which includes, woven into it, a perception of space. As discussed in Chapter 19, the spectrum of fading reveals that any such perception of space is still fabricated. This appearance of a vastness of awareness is then a fabrication. It is not ultimate. Without the support of a certain level of clinging it too will fade. And this will of course be true of *any* perception. Nothing that is perceived can be taken as the nature of awareness, nor regarded as ultimate in any way.

Thus, for example, although many texts speak of the 'luminous nature' of awareness, this does not mean that awareness is bright in the commonly understood sense. For that kind of luminosity could only be known as an object of perception. To be sure, experiences of inner light and brightness in meditation are quite common, most often when there is a degree of *samādhi*, but they too, it is easy to see, are fabricated objects of perception. The luminous nature of the mind refers merely to its ability to know, to perceive and experience.

Likewise, we may also encounter many texts where it is actually declared that the nature of awareness, and of other phenomena too, is "like space". The *Prajñāpāramitā Saṃcayagāthā*, for example, says that

> Seeing reality is like seeing space and cannot be expressed by another example.

Care needs to be taken, however, in the interpretation of such statements. 'Space' has a different meaning and connotation in these texts than what we might normally assume. As Mipham points out in his commentary to Śāntarakṣita's *Madhyamakālaṃkāra*:

> 'Space' is the mere designation for the quality of absence of physical obstruction or contact.[4]

[4] Translation by Thomas H. Doctor in Ju Mipham, *Speech of Delight*, p. 451.

It is a kind of negation then, an "absence of physical obstruction" – that is all, not something that is given any real existence. For this reason the *Prajñāpāramitā Saṃcayagāthā* adds:

> People speak easily enough of 'seeing space'. But how does one see space? Examine carefully the meaning here.

'Seeing space' means a kind of non-seeing, a non-encountering of any thing. 'Space', regarded as a kind of absence only, a lack of physical obstruction, is used in these texts as an analogy for the lack of inherent existence.

If, then, 'space-like' is a synonym for 'empty', and 'luminous' means 'cognizing', to say that "the true nature of awareness is like space but still luminous" means: *There is knowing but it is empty of true existence.* Buddhist teachings on the nature of mind are pointing out that there is no inherently existing entity – 'mind' or 'awareness' – that cognizes, nor any truly existing 'process' of consciousness.

Other *Prajñāpāramitā sūtras* and texts declare that

> Mind does not exist as mind. The nature of mind is luminosity.

Here the meaning of 'luminosity' deliberately includes both the fact of cognizing *and* the emptiness of that cognizing, implying in one word the indivisible unity of those two aspects. A profound and astounding understanding is being expressed here, one that shatters all of our intuitive conceptions of the nature of consciousness. Let us unfold the fullness of what it means, and what it implies, gradually over the next few chapters as we explore various ways of looking that may be conducive to this realization.

Stepping-stones to Deeper Insight

'Mind Only' and the unfindability of mind

Whatever approaches or practices are used, realization of this radical emptiness of awareness almost always rests on previous realizations of the emptiness of phenomena. Thus, for example, Śāntarakṣita wrote:

> By relying on the Mind Only [system], know that outer things do not exist. And by relying on this [Madhyamaka] system, know

> that mind too is utterly devoid of self-existence.[5]

And Rangjung Dorje, the Third Karmapa, echoed this:

> Looking at an object, there is none; I see it is mind.
> Looking for mind, mind is not there; it lacks any essence.
> Looking at both, dualistic clinging is freed on its own.[6]

Statements that outer objects are 'mind only' may be taken at different levels. Some practitioners may feel comfortable with the insight described in Chapter 15 – that all things are of the same substance or nature as awareness. Others may feel more comfortable with the more sophisticated insight that objects do not exist in themselves without being fabricated by the mind, as explained in other chapters. Here, what is actually of greater significance is the next step – recognizing that this mind also has no inherent existence. For then clinging to awareness dissolves as well as clinging to objects. And realizing that awareness is empty, one cannot continue to cling to a notion of a substance of awareness. Thus, despite the reservations expressed, insights such as those around the vastness of awareness can prove very useful and need not be limiting, as long as it is eventually recognized that awareness too is thoroughly empty.

Having seen, through developing various ways of looking, that objects are empty, how then might we realize that mind "lacks any essence"? One possibility is through recognizing that the mind or awareness cannot be found. Many texts lend support to this approach. For example, Śāntideva wrote:

> Mind has not been seen by anyone.[7]

And,

> Mind can be found neither inside, nor outside, nor elsewhere. It is not a combination [of the aggregates] and neither is it something separate… It is not the slightest thing. The very nature of beings is *nirvāṇa*.[8]

---

[5] MA 92.
[6] In his *Aspiration Prayer of the Mahāmudrā of Definitive Meaning*. (Translation by Lama Sherab Dorje in The Eighth Situpa and The Third Karmapa, *Mahāmudrā Teachings of the Supreme Siddhas: The Eighth Situpa Tenpa'I Nyinchay on The Third Gyalwa Karmapa Rangjung Dorje's Aspiration Prayer of the Mahāmudrā of Definitive Meaning* [Ithaca, NY: Snow Lion, 1995] p. 24.)
[7] BCA 9:22.
[8] BCA 9:102 – 103.

The *Dharmadhātuprakṛtyasambhedanirdeśa Sūtra* expresses this more fully:

> Investigate whether this thing you call 'mind' is blue, yellow, red, white, maroon, or transparent; whether it is pure or impure, permanent or impermanent, and whether it is endowed with form or not. Mind has no physical form; it cannot be shown. It does not manifest, it is intangible, it does not cognize, it resides neither inside, outside, nor anywhere in between. Thus it is utterly pure, totally non-existent. There is nothing of it to liberate. It is the very nature of *dharmadhātu*.[9]

And the *Mahāvairocanābhisaṃbodhi Sūtra* says:

> How should one properly understand one's mind [to be]? Like this: even if you search for it thoroughly as having an aspect, colour, shape, or location; as a form, *vedanā*, perception, mental formation, or consciousness; as a self, or possessed by a self, as something to grasp or apprehend, as pure or impure, as a constituent or sense field, or in any other way at all, you won't observe it. This lord secret one is the portal to the totally pure *bodhicitta* of a bodhisattva.[10]

Here again, however, care needs to be taken. For as Mipham pointed out in this context:

> It is a very great mistake to think that merely not seeing [some thing] is the same as being introduced to its emptiness. Though you examine your head a hundred times, a ruminant's horns cannot be found. To say that not seeing something is to realize its emptiness – wouldn't that be easy for anybody?[11]

The fact that when we look for the mind we cannot see anything that has colour,

---

[9] Translated by Ken and Katia Holmes in Jé Gampopa, *Gems of Dharma, Jewels of Freedom*, pp. 239 – 240.

[10] Translation adapted from Lama Sherab Dorje in The Eighth Situpa and The Third Karmapa, *Mahāmudrā Teachings of the Supreme Siddhas*, p. 71.

[11] *Beacon of Certainty* 3. (Translation from John Whitney Pettit in *Mipham's Beacon of Certainty*, pp. 204 – 205.)

shape, or form does not go very far at all in demonstrating its essential unreality. That a thing is not tangible or visible does not necessarily imply its emptiness. The mind's existing as an entity of mere knowing – its non-existence as anything physical, together with its capacity to know objects appearing to it – is in fact only a conception of the nature of mind at a *conventional* level. Some much more powerful and profound way of looking is required to penetrate the ultimate truth of its nature and give a fuller comprehension of its unfindability. We need somehow to understand the statements in the above texts asserting, for instance, that the mind "does not cognize", or that it is not any of the aggregates, nor a combination of them, nor apart from them.

Awareness is void, for it is dependent on what is empty

One more compelling avenue available to us relies much more integrally on previous insights into the emptiness of objects, and also on insights into mutual dependence which we have already touched on.

The word for consciousness in Pali is *viññāṇa* (Skt: *vijñāna*), which means 'knowing'. The fact that it is a verb form, a present participle, and not, like the English words 'consciousness', 'awareness', 'mind', etc., a noun, points away from the conception of some kind of entity with an ethereal substance that 'does' the knowing, or 'is' aware. More importantly even, 'knowing' needs a 'known'. Thus awareness is awareness *of* an appearance, a perception. No matter how subtle or seemingly all-inclusive the perception, or how refined or expansive the awareness seems, without a perception, an object known, 'knowing' is meaningless. And conversely, for something to be an object, a 'known', it needs knowing. Like *vedanā* and clinging, and also like any duality, consciousness and its object depend on each other. Such contingency cannot ultimately be one of cause and effect though. Being mutually dependent, each would have to precede the other in order to be a cause for the other, which is clearly impossible. Rather, they always arise together. Arising simultaneously, there is no time for either to cause the other. Knowing and known, awareness and perception, always go together. They cannot be separated so that we have one without the other. They are not truly separate phenomena; yet they cannot be said to be 'one' either. As we have seen before, two things that are mutually dependent cannot have inherent existence. Both consciousness and perception are thus empty.

This understanding that consciousness is void because it is mutually dependent on perception can be given further depth and power by more fully relying on previous insights into the emptiness of objects of perception.

Chandrakīrti explained that:

> "Once objects of cognition are disproved, consciousness is easily refuted," so teach the Buddhas. Since the non-existence of objects of perception also refutes the existence of consciousness, objects of perception are refuted first.[12]

If the 'known' is an object of perception, and if we have seen repeatedly that these are empty, then we may realize too that knowing, awareness, depends on what is empty. Just as we explored with regard to clinging, consciousness is contingent on, inseparable from, and jointly fabricated with, something that is not really real. Ultimately groundless and unsupported, it is leaning on, and intertwined with, a void. It too can only be empty.

It may be that in order for this insight to render a more radical freedom in meditation, insight into the emptiness of perceptions needs to have reached a point of conviction and gained a certain depth through practice. Whether through analysis revealing the impossibility of their inherent existence, or through investigation of dependent arising, or both, the emptiness of perceptions is then intuitively understood to mean more than that they are fabricated and illusory in the way that, for instance, a movie is. For the events of a movie may be acknowledged to be illusory fabrications without detracting from the reality of the consciousness watching that movie. But if, for example, we have seen deeply the fading of perception for ourselves firsthand, we understand how knowing and known, consciousness and perception, are inextricably bound up together – they are fabricated together, and they fade together. We may also have seen, as we shall shortly explore, how time – past, present, and future – is inseparably fabricated in the process. This is quite unlike recognizing the illusory nature of a movie or a hologram (as in Chapter 1). Seeing emptiness deeply leaves nothing untouched. We comprehend that rather than any one element, such as awareness, being real while others are fabricated, the whole show is concocted together, like "a magician's trick".[13]

Mutual dependency – a mystical groundlessness

That perception and consciousness are mutually dependent and that they are fabricated together was communicated by the Buddha and others in various ways

---

[12] MAV 6:96.

[13] SN 22:95.

on a number of occasions. The obvious dependence of perception on consciousness is expressed in the most common formulation of *paṭiccasamuppāda*: "Dependent on consciousness, there is *nāmarūpa*." (*Nāmarūpa*, we have explained, includes perception and refers to the forming of appearances.) But the reverse, less obvious, dependency was also pointed out: that without *nāmarūpa* – the forming of appearances, of objects of perception – there can be no consciousness, for consciousness is always consciousness of some thing:

> And what, monks, is consciousness? There are six categories of consciousness: visual, auditory, olfactory, gustatory, tactile, and mental. When *nāmarūpa* arises, consciousness arises; when *nāmarūpa* ceases, consciousness ceases.[14]

The fabrication of any object of experience is also the fabrication of a consciousness. And when *nāmarūpa* is pacified through a deep release of clinging, perception fades, as we have repeatedly seen, and consciousness must then fade too:

> When one neither intends, nor arranges, nor has a tendency toward [anything], no sense-object arises for the stationing of consciousness. There being no object, there is no support for consciousness.[15]

Being inseparable and mutually dependent, knowing and known, we see, are concocted together, and fade together. It is clear then also that awareness, the knowing of any object, is not an unfabricated phenomenon. Fading together with the perception of objects, it too is fabricated by clinging.

In addition, though, to the fabricated nature of both consciousness and perception, something amazing and mysterious is also implied by all of this. For we have just said that perception and consciousness are dependent on each other; and that both are dependent on clinging. But clinging, as we explored in Chapter 21, is empty, and dependent itself on an object of perception. It must also be dependent on consciousness. Perception, consciousness, and clinging thus all lean on each other, without true separation, and without any other basis. Being mutually dependent, they are all ultimately groundless and empty.

---

[14] SN 22:57. Here we are primarily considering the dependent co-arising of consciousness and *perception*. We will explore the other elements of *nāmarūpa*, their emptiness, and their mutual dependence with each other and with consciousness more specifically in Chapter 27.

[15] SN 12:38.

Insight into this mutual dependence of *nāmarūpa* and consciousness was at the very heart of the Buddha's breakthrough on the night of his Awakening. He described how in meditation his probing questioning into the origins of *dukkha* began to open up the understanding of dependent origination. Recounting his investigation of *nāmarūpa*, he said,

> Then the thought occurred to me, '*Nāmarūpa* exists when what exists? What is the necessary foundation for *nāmarūpa*?' From my radical examination, there came the breakthrough of discernment: '*Nāmarūpa* exists when consciousness exists. Consciousness is a necessary foundation for *nāmarūpa*.'[16] Then the thought occurred to me, 'Consciousness exists when what exists? What is the necessary foundation for consciousness?' From my radical examination there came the breakthrough of insight: 'Consciousness exists when *nāmārūpa* exists. *Nāmarūpa* is a necessary foundation for consciousness.'
>
> Then the thought occurred to me, 'This consciousness comes back to *nāmarūpa*. It does not go beyond it… *Nāmarūpa* is a necessary foundation for consciousness, consciousness is a necessary foundation for *nāmarūpa*. From *nāmarūpa* as a necessary foundation come the six sense spheres… contact… *vedanā*… Thus is the origination of this entire mass of *dukkha*… ' Vision arose, gnosis arose, wisdom arose, higher knowledge arose, illumination arose within me in regard to things never heard before.

Likewise inquiring into the cessation of *dukkha*, he discovered that

> 'From the cessation of *nāmarūpa* comes the cessation of consciousness, from the cessation of consciousness comes the cessation of *nāmarūpa*. From the cessation of *nāmarūpa* comes the cessation of the six sense spheres… of contact… of *vedanā*… Thus is the cessation of this entire mass of *dukkha*… ' Vision arose, gnosis arose, wisdom arose, higher knowledge arose, illumination arose within me in regard to things never heard before.[17]

---

[16] This might also be rendered: "*From what as a necessary condition* [or: *support*] *is there nāmarūpa?... From consciousness as a necessary condition* [or: *support*] *comes nāmarūpa*." We will use both variations in order to more fully convey the radical insight here and its implications.

[17] SN 12:65.

In response to questions from Mahā Koṭṭhita, Sāriputta elaborated further on this mutual dependence:

> It is not, Koṭṭhita my friend, that *nāmarūpa* is self-made, that it is other-made, that it is both self-made and other-made, or that – without being self-made or other-made – it arises spontaneously. But from consciousness as a necessary condition comes *nāmarūpa*…
>
> [Nor] is it that consciousness is self-made, that it is other-made, that it is both self-made and other-made, or that – without self-making and other-making – it arises spontaneously. But from *nāmarūpa* as a necessary condition comes consciousness…

Mahā Koṭṭhita, understandably, was perplexed by this, so Sāriputta gave an analogy:

> Just as two sheaves of reeds might stand leaning against one another, in the same way, from *nāmarūpa* as a necessary condition comes consciousness, from consciousness as a necessary condition comes *nāmarūpa*. From *nāmarūpa* as a necessary condition come the six sense spheres… contact… *vedanā*… Thus is the origination of this entire mass of *dukkha*. If one were to pull away one of those sheaves of reeds, the other would fall; if one were to pull away the other, the first one would fall. In the same way, from the cessation of *nāmarūpa* comes the cessation of consciousness, from the cessation of consciousness comes the cessation of *nāmarūpa*. From the cessation of *nāmarūpa* comes the cessation of the six sense spheres… of contact… of *vedanā*… Thus is the cessation of this entire mass of *dukkha*.[18]

Notice that Sāriputta's analogy does not suggest a temporal relation of cause and effect. Although it is not stated explicitly, the implication, as we have discussed, is that these phenomena – leaning only on each other and fabricated together – are fundamentally groundless, and are not truly separate. In other words, that they are empty of inherent existence; two voidnesses depending on each other. Thus even the most basic notion of a cognizer is revealed through

[18] SN 12:67.

practice to be inadequate as a statement of the true nature of mind. For the whole structure of knowing and known collapses through insight. As Nāgārjuna wrote:

> For the Tathāgatas, mind is not understood in the form of cognizant and cognizable. Where there is [a belief in the view of] cognizant and cognizable, there is no awakening.[19]

And although only expressed here in relation to consciousness and *nāmarūpa*, we have seen this mutual dependence and its implications between other links in the web of dependent origination. Eventually it can be realized that this wondrous and mystical groundlessness extends to all things in existence. As the *Saptaśatikā Prajñāpāramitā Sūtra* says:

> All [phenomena] lack objective support.[20]

§

Certainly, if it is pondered well, an experience of the cessation of the six sense consciousnesses can make the emptiness of all consciousness clear. But it is possible to sustain a liberating view of the emptiness of awareness in meditation well before this – by contemplating the emptiness of perceptions, and the dependence of consciousnesses on those empty perceptions. Objects depend on mind, so they are empty. Mind, or consciousness, depends on objects which are empty, so it too is void.

Practice: Meditating on the mutual emptiness of consciousness and perception

(Initially, this practice will be easier if a relatively steady perception is taken as an object, such as the perception of a state of *samādhi*, or a sight or sound that is not so fleeting. Eventually, it can be sustained too even as the attention moves between different momentary perceptions, resting in a view that sees their emptiness and the emptiness of awareness at once.)

Hold any perception in attention. Then, based on your conviction from past insights into the emptiness of objects of perception, introduce the view of that object as 'empty'.

[19] *Bodhicittavivaraṇa*. (Author's own translation.)

[20] Translation by Edward Conze in *Perfect Wisdom*, p. 84.

As you continue to do so, tune in as well to the sense of consciousness, of knowing, that goes with the perception in the moment. Gently introduce the understanding that this knowing is dependent on, and inseparable from, an empty known, so that it must also be empty. (This will also require a previous familiarity with focusing on the inseparability of consciousness and perception.)

Alternatively, you may sustain the view of consciousness as 'not me, not mine' and then add the understanding that it is dependent on empty perception, so that it is empty too. (Here the *anattā* view merely helps loosen the clinging to consciousness, making the contemplation easier.[21])

It is also possible, seeing that awareness is dependent on and inseparable from fabricated perceptions, to view awareness as 'fabricated' over and over, moment to moment.

Experiment both with using a more narrowly focused attention and at other times a wider, more spacious, attention. If a sense of vastness of awareness arises, see that too as empty, as described.

Notice what this way of looking feels like and what its effects are. As always though, make sure that at least sometimes the view is sustained through any fading or transformation of perception that occurs.

As emphasized before, unless we deliberately and thoroughly see for ourselves the emptiness of some thing, it is safe to assume that we are ascribing inherent existence to that phenomenon, whether we realize it or not. Without doubt, the degree of *dukkha* involved in reifying awareness is in itself quite subtle. We will generally not even notice it until we experience the deeper, more extraordinary level of freedom that comes with realizing the emptiness of awareness. Seeing this level of voidness also opens up a more profound realization of the fundamental groundlessness of all things. And such insights have the power to radically alter and free up our whole sense of existence.

---

[21] Likewise, once this practice is developed, the view of consciousness as empty of inherent existence, dependent on and inseparable from the factors of *nāmarūpa*, can also be used (if desired) when returning to the *anattā* practice, to help in seeing consciousness as 'not me, not mine'.

26

About Time

Another, immensely powerful, approach to the realization of the emptiness of awareness is made available through seeing the emptiness of *time*. So basic to our very sense of the existence of any thing, time intuitively appears to us as having itself an independent reality. It seems obvious that the flow of time is simply there, absolute, a kind of container for phenomena and events, steadily continuing irrespective of the way of looking, or of what appears or does not appear within it.

Profound insight, though, can see through, melt, rupture, or open out the seeming reality of time. And it would be a shame to live a whole life and to die without tasting the mystery and freedom that come when there is some sense of release from the apparent confines of this relentless and inescapable flow. Perceptions of the flow of existence – or of surrendering to or letting go into that flow – may be felt as liberating at a certain level, it is true. But with a deeper understanding we realize that all such perceptions remain, at another level, stubbornly and subtly oppressive unless their emptiness is fully known.

And since time is such a fundamental notion, insight into its lack of inherent existence has other momentous and far-reaching consequences that can be comprehended and sensed immediately. As alluded to above, seeing the voidness of time implies and reveals the voidness of awareness too. In fact it essentially undermines as well the reification of all kinds of phenomena. Further, a sense of the emptiness of time or its transcending can, if desired, cogently open the doors to the realms of imaginal or tantric practices, and contributes, perhaps more than any other insight, to the power and possibilities of such practices.

How then might profound and fundamental realizations of the voidness of time be nurtured? The beginning levels at least of such insights often happen naturally through basic mindfulness meditations. Typically, as a meditator learns to settle the attention (s)he sees how much the sense of past and future is constructed by thought, and also how much *dukkha* is often wrapped up in thinking about the past and the future. Inhabiting the present more fully can feel wonderful and vivifying. 'Past' and 'future' may seem to drop away at times, and then seem illusory, leaving only the reality of the present.

But although it can be a helpful way of looking for a while to see that "it's always the present", that "only Now exists", or even that "Being is endlessly Now", such notions reify and sometimes eternalize 'the now'. Just as with perceptions of flow, eventually the present needs to be seen through also. 'Being in the now' is most certainly not the goal of practice. Realizing the emptiness of *all* time – past, future, *and* present – is essential to a more radical liberation. Such insight is accessible through a range of means and will ultimately take us even deeper into the mystery of dependent origination.

Two Analytical Meditations

This moment is neither one nor many

One possible approach is to apply the neither-one-nor-many reasoning to the present moment in meditation. If this, or any, moment really has inherent existence, it has to be one or many. If it is one, then either it is divisible into a beginning, middle, and end, or it is not. If it is divisible, then that one moment is not in fact one but three moments. The beginning must come before the middle and the end, and so it is really a different moment in time. But if the moment cannot be divided, it must be nonexistent, infinitely small. Without any differentiation between beginning and end, it would be impossible to arrange such singular moments in order of time, of happening. Therefore a moment that is truly one is not possible. We can't now say then that the present moment is many, for 'many' is only possible as an accumulation of 'ones', and we have just found that a moment that is truly one cannot exist. Since it cannot be either one or many, and there are no other options, the present moment cannot have inherent existence.

Some might be tempted to object that this has merely refuted the true existence of 'moments', but not of time. However, central to our intuitive sense of time is the perception and felt notion that there are portions of time that are existing or happening now, and others that are not; and that these others not now existing fall into two discernible groups – the past, which is gone, and the future, which is yet to come. The meaning here though is essentially the same as what is meant by 'moments'. Time *means*, *unavoidably*: past, present, future; beginning, middle, end – whether we use words like 'moments' or not for this. Language is not actually the problem, and nor is thought. However we try to express it, we have a deep habit of perceiving, and intuitively, silently even, conceiving of, time in this way as real.

Once digested, and with a little practice, the neither-one-nor-many analysis of the present moment can be used extremely effectively and quite quickly in meditation, without feeling cumbersome at all. Contemplating this *moment* of consciousness and seeing that this moment has no inherent existence, we automatically see that consciousness lacks inherent existence. And this applies too to whatever phenomena involve and exist in time, since, for *any* thing to be, it needs a time to be 'in'. Without a reality to the time that it exists in, a phenomenon is without fundamental basis. Seeing this in meditation can open up a wondrous, thrilling, lightening, and profoundly liberating sense of the groundlessness of all things.

Diamond slivers

The emptiness of this moment can also be realized through other meditative analyses. One of these, called 'the diamond slivers' (because, like a sliver or shard of diamond, it is said to be able to cut through anything) is based on the first verse of Nāgārjuna's *Mūlamadhyamakakārikā*:

> Neither from itself, nor from another, not from both, nor without a cause does any thing arise anywhere at all.

We can apply it here to the arising of this present moment of time. This moment cannot possibly arise *from itself*. Arising is meaningless for something which already exists; and to exist before it arises is clearly not possible. If it arises from something *other*, that other would have to be either some other thing, factor, force or energy in the present moment, or any past moment. It cannot arise from something other existing in the present moment though: being in the same moment, that would be a case of the moment arising from itself, which we have just said is meaningless for anything. But it cannot arise from a past moment either, since any past moment must have completely disappeared before the present moment can arise, and if it is totally gone, how can it be said to give rise to anything?[1]

[1] One might feel drawn to try to find a way to conceive of the past moment not having wholly disappeared before the present moment. A strange moment that is really two moments, past and present somehow overlapped, is nonsensical though. And analysing the point of contact between past and present moments yields no coherent solution either. That point of contact becomes, under analytical scrutiny, itself a third moment with two contact points – one touching the 'past' moment, and one touching the 'present' moment – and those contact points would themselves constitute micro-moments each having two contact points, and so on. There would be an infinite regress to a non-existing moment an infinite number of moments away from the present moment. Or, put another way and more simply: whatever contacts the present can only do so in the present, and so itself becomes the present. When analysed, past and present can have no contact in any way that makes sense.

As Chandrakīrti pointed out, the third possibility – that the present moment arises somehow both from itself and from another – merely accrues the problems associated with each of these possibilities when they are considered singly.[2] The fourth option – that this moment arises neither from itself nor from another – would, if moments are assumed to have inherent existence, be equivalent to saying that this moment arises without causes and conditions. But this moment clearly depends on other moments preceding it.

These four options exhaust all the possibilities. Since none are ultimately tenable, the only conclusion is that the arising of this moment has no inherent existence. Without a real arising, and by definition not permanently existing, this moment must also lack inherent existence.

§

These two analyses may each be used on different occasions with slightly different intentions – in order to realize the emptiness of time more generally, or in order to realize the emptiness of any phenomenon, such as consciousness or any object, through realizing the emptiness of this moment of time.

As always, carefully ponder for yourself, in and out of formal meditation sessions, any analysis you wish to explore, until you are satisfied with the conclusion. Then in applying it meditatively, experiment to find ways that work for you. The ordering of the argument can often be varied, and you may insert any considerations that you feel are necessary or helpful in bringing conviction and a sense of freedom. The following are therefore only outlines providing reminders of the essential points.

Practice: This moment is neither one nor many

Focusing on a sense of the present moment – as a moment of time, or as a moment of consciousness or of some other phenomenon – bring into the view the understanding that this moment cannot be one, since it must have a beginning, a middle, and an end, and these must occur at different times.

Maintaining the focus on the present moment, gently reflect that if it did not have a beginning, middle, and end, it could not really exist. It would be infinitely small; and it would be impossible to arrange such moments in any sequence of time.

[2] MAV 6:98.

See also that this moment cannot be truly many. This 'many' would have to be comprised of moments that are truly one. Since no moment can exist without beginning and end, however, there can be no moments that are truly one which could be aggregated to form the many.

Sustain a view of the moment as thus being neither one nor many, and so being empty of inherent existence.

Whatever phenomenon you were contemplating, see how this way of looking fundamentally undermines the sense of its inherent existence, and notice how this feels.

Practice: Diamond Slivers – this moment does not truly arise

While maintaining a focus on the present moment, consider that it cannot arise caused by itself, since, as described above, that would make no sense.

Consider also that its arising might be caused by something other, and see that that too is not possible. Something other in the present would still be the present moment and so another nonsensical case of self-causation. Nor can it arise caused by the past (as 'other') since the past is gone, and without contact there cannot be true causation.

As you maintain a focus on the moment, consider the third possibility: to say that it arises 'from both self and other' is not tenable, since that would in no way overcome the deficiencies of each of the first two possibilities already considered.

Reflect that the fourth possibility – that it arises independent of any causes and conditions – is not true of anything in the world. At the very least, the present moment needs the past to have preceded it.

Hold the moment in attention with the understanding that, for a present moment considered to have inherent existence, all the possible modes of arising have been exhausted. Therefore neither the arising nor the abiding of this moment can possibly have inherent existence.

Notice the effect of this way of looking.

As with any insight, once the sense of emptiness is relatively strongly established, you may experiment sometimes with allowing the attention to move between different phenomena. In a now more relaxed way, view each and all through a lens that knows the emptiness of the moment, and thus of the phenomenon in that moment.

Time and Mutual Dependency

Interdependent notions

In addition to such analytical meditations, other possibilities abound for realizing time's emptiness. We can, for example, consider that just like 'left', 'centre', and 'right', the very notions of 'past', 'present', and 'future' depend on each other. None of these three has any independent existence. Each is meaningless without the others. And trying to hold up the reality of one while dismissing the others is not viable. If a meditator is tempted to say from experience that past and future are illusory constructs with no real existence, then the present must equally be seen to be illusory, since it depends on the illusions of past and future. The mutual contingency of past, present, and future entails their lack of inherent existence; and the sense that past and future have no real existence further implies the voidness of the present. When investigated, the assumption that the present, the now, is ultimately real cannot be sustained.

Clinging and concoction

That a sense of time is dependent also on clinging is uncovered through our phenomenological inquiry into the fabrication of perception. A relatively gross level of this dependency is quite easy to see. Both in and out of meditation, we can notice that the sense of time becomes more prominent when there is a greater degree of craving or aversion to something. Having to queue when we don't want to or when we want to be somewhere else; dreading or hankering after an event in the future; or aversive to discomfort and waiting for the end of a meditation session – time then seems to have more weight and intensity. Conversely, when grasping and aversion are relaxed the sense of time becomes much lighter.

As meditation deepens, and our skill in relaxing the push and pull of clinging grows and becomes more subtle, various experiences of timelessness may be allowed as the perception of time is fabricated less and less, or not at all. We see for ourselves then a strange truth: all sense of time – of past, of future, and of present – is fabricated by clinging.

Self, things, time

Before we explore the various possibilities though, the investigation of this dependency may be opened up further. For we know, by this point, that any dependency invites an awareness of other dependencies also. Clinging, we have discussed, is dependent on the perception of a thing. It is also dependent on a sense of self. As Dharmakīrti made clear:

> When there is the perception of self, there is the perception of other. From the distinction between self and other there is grasping and aversion. Bound up with these two, all faults are born.[3]

('Other' here can mean other selves, and also everything that is other than the self, i.e. the things of the world, that the self may desire to have or to avoid.) So clinging depends on self and things; and self and things, we have already seen, are dependent on clinging.

Seeing now that the sense of time is dependent on clinging ties the sense of time itself therefore into this web of mutual contingency. *The perceptions of self, of things, and of time all rely on and feed each other.* This can be seen at any level of subtlety, and is evident from every angle.

We can notice, for instance, that the sense of time is given substance and significance when substance and significance is given to things, to objects of perception. For when things are given substance and significance, then measurement and comparison between things *over time* – from past to present to future – becomes important. And so the perception of time gains weight and significance.

We can notice too that the perceived importance of such measurement and comparison is usually for and in reference to a self that is also intuitively conceived to exist in time, and to continue in time. Any clinging always and inevitably involves measurement and comparison. And as Dharmakīrti asserted above, clinging is the intrinsic reflex of the self-sense. Even if it is not present as a thought, at least a very subtle perspective of self-investment accompanies any sense of self: How *will* this thing be for me? What will its *changing* or its *continuing* mean for me? What can I get? As we have seen, looking through a lens of belief in a self, things are made to stand out to perception; they are given substance. And so is time.

---

[3] *Pramāṇavārttika*.

Equally though, the sense and conception of self is given substance as things and time are given substance. We already know that since it is fabricated through clinging, the self-sense requires some thing to be given significance, to be clung to. It also needs a sense and conception of time. At a relatively gross level, we can see that our habit of mentally stretching out into past and future some personal difficulty or prospect of progress intensifies and solidifies the self-sense. But who am I if there is only an ungraspable present?

We fabricate a greater burden and solidity to *things*, too, by mentally extending them in time in the same way. Things, whether they be 'issues' or objects, would also have little significance without a conception of time stretching from past through the present to the future.

All this must be witnessed, but also thoroughly explored in meditation. We can play there with the dependencies more deliberately, approaching from any of the three angles – self, things, or time – in order to deepen and consolidate the insights.

Fabricating less sense of self – for example either through contemplating the emptiness of self or through the *anattā* practice – we see how perceptions of things lose their solidity and then fade, and this we have already discussed. But the perception of time can lessen also.

Or when, through seeing their voidness or through a release of the push and pull of clinging to them, the perception of things fades, we may see too how the perception of self and time fade also.

Similarly, ways of looking that contemplate the emptiness of time to some extent will be found to calm the fabrication of objects of perception and of self. Even just letting go of the past and future – mentally chopping them off, and bringing a simple, bright mindfulness to the present – will considerably lighten the sense of self, and take some solidity out of the perception of things.

As our meditative investigation becomes more subtle, it becomes more and more clear that, at the most fundamental level even, self, things, and time are all mutually dependent. Like in Sāriputta's analogy of the sheaves of reeds, these three lean against each other, as three sticks might form a somewhat fragile tripod. Co-arising in any moment of perception, none can actually stand alone. But unlike in the analogy of the sticks – where it might be conceived that the individual sticks could exist separately and might be found fallen on the ground – here none can possibly be found alone, nor have any real existence alone. Rather, whether intensely or more subtly, they are fabricated together as aspects of a single experience. Thus as before with what is mutually dependent, although they seem to be three separate phenomena with independent existence, all three are in fact interpenetrating, not-separate, groundless and empty.

In practice, experiences of seeing the emptiness of time, or of fabricating less perception of time, may manifest in many different ways and with a range of intensities. When they are strong, language will falter in trying to adequately capture such mystical experiences. It may be that all perception – of self, objects, and the present – fades in an experience of cessation. Or, despite the fact that all three elements of the tripod are essentially fabricated together, it may be on occasion that some elements fade more than others. For example, perception of forms may remain, while time seems to stop somehow. We have a glimpse of eternity – or rather of timelessness, for we see through and beyond any meaning of 'eternity' as a continuous flow of time without end. It may be too that the felt sense of time opens out in a kind of infinite way so that all time, past, present, and future, is somehow intuited to be 'here'. Or it might collapse into a zero point, so that we see there is no time, really, for anything to be in.

Time is dependent on what is empty

Let's inquire further into this mutual dependency and emptiness of time. Because of the fundamental duality intuitively and habitually conceived between existence and non-existence, the very *perception* of any thing in the present subtly and implicitly weaves in a conception of time – at least of present and future. Where there is a thing, there is immediately implied and intuited the possibility, in time, of 'not that thing', of its non-existence – its end or its transformation into some other thing. In other words, the perception of any thing involves a conception of fundamental duality; and involved in this conception of duality is a conception of time.

Conversely, without a thing – and thus also without the potential of comparison and measurement between things – time is not perceivable. Not even a present moment, a 'now', would be perceivable, because a sense of the present comes only with the perception of some thing. 'This moment' is delineated by perception. In some sense, 'this moment' is 'this perception'. Any perception of time is dependent on a perception of a thing. As mentioned earlier though, things need a time to exist 'in'. It can therefore equally be said that any perception of any thing is dependent on some perception of time.

From this direction too then we may arrive at an understanding of what we explained earlier was discoverable through a very deep release of clinging. At the most basic and subtle levels, the perceptions and conceptions of time and of things are wrapped up in, and mutually dependent on, each other. But as before, such mutual dependency is not dependency in the usual sense of the word – of one real phenomenon on another. Something more astounding, mysterious, and profound is implied by their leaning on each other this way. Time and object are essentially inseparable; one cannot be found without the other. It might even be said that time is in some sense an 'aspect of the object'.

And here again we can invoke the implications of mutual dependence. As before, two phenomena that are mutually contingent are actually both empty. Further, if things are empty then time is seen to be dependent on and inseparable from what is empty. In its dependence on an empty self too it is likewise reliant on what is void. Nāgārjuna wrote:

> How could time exist without an entity? Time is dependent on an entity. If no entity exists, how will time exist?[4]

So, in practice, not just time past and future, but this very moment – the present – can be contemplated as being dependent on self and objects, with the knowledge that both of these are empty. Or it may be viewed through a lens that knows that this moment of time, concocted with this experience, is dependent on clinging, so it is fabricated and empty. This last insight may be taken to another level by adding to the view the understanding that the very clinging on which this present moment depends is also void, as we have already seen. Through all of these means, the conviction that time is empty of inherent existence grows.

Eventually that conviction can be used to further deepen the insight into the emptiness of the self and of phenomena. Self can be contemplated as empty since it depends on time and on things, which are both empty. Things can be contemplated as empty because they depend on time and on self, which are both empty. And as mentioned, like any other phenomenon, consciousness too can be viewed this way in meditation. It can be understood to be dependent on time. Awareness needs a sense of the present moment. The present, we have seen, is dependent on past and future, and also on the perception of an object. Since these all are empty, consciousness must be empty. Thus almost all the *Prajñāpāramitā sūtras* contain statements such as:

> The nature of everything is emptiness. Everything… [including] consciousness… is empty of itself.

[4] MMK 19:6.

Beyond 'Permanent' *and* 'Impermanent' – The True Nature of Things

Just in case it is not already clear through witnessing the fading of perception in meditation firsthand, realizing the emptiness of time can add another more profound and more radical dimension to our understanding of the emptiness of objects of perception.

Much earlier we said that objects are empty because they are fabricated by and dependent on mind. As alluded to in the last chapter though, to say that perception is fabricated and empty means more than might be conveyed by analogy to a movie or hologram as a fabricated illusion. For there it might be assumed that, although fabricated, the perception itself still exists in time; it is only that it is a mistaken perception, or that it does not somehow correspond with reality. If it was not evident before, now we can see a deeper and more complete emptiness of perceptions. Because time is empty, perceptions are, in a sense, "empty of themselves". It is not simply that they are conveying 'objective illusions'. When, we may ask, does a perception really exist – in one moment or in many? As was explained more generally earlier, by seeing the emptiness of time we can see that there is not really any time for perception to really be 'in'. Time, we come to understand, is actually fabricated *with* the perception of an object. And this realization takes our insight into the voidness of things to another level, opening up a greater depth, beauty, and mystery to our sense of that voidness of things.

Realizing the emptiness of time, we see too more fully and more deeply what we began to see in Chapter 23. For if time is empty, then production, arising, and ceasing must also be empty. As it says in the *Mūlamadhyamakakārikā*:

> Like an illusion, like a city of fairies, like a dream,
> thus have arising, abiding, and ceasing been explained.[5]

And in the *Vimalakīrtinirdeśa Sūtra*:

> All things are without production, destruction, and duration.[6]

And again, without an ultimate reality to things or time, neither permanence

[5] MMK 7:34.

[6] Translation by Robert Thurman in *The Holy Teaching of Vimalakīrti*, p. 31.

nor impermanence can be an ultimate truth. A belief in *anicca* as ultimately true implies, as well as a belief in the ultimate reality of time, a belief in, and a seeing in terms of, the existence and non-existence of things – the two extreme views avoided by the Buddha's 'Middle Way' of emptiness. And if things do not either really exist or really not exist, then an assertion of their impermanence is ultimately untenable. Thus the *Sārdhadvisāhasrikā Prajñāpāramitā Sūtra* declares:

> Form, *vedanā*, perception, mental formations, and consciousness
> are not permanent or impermanent.[7]

And the *Mahāprajñāpāramitā Sūtra*:

> The perfection of wisdom… does not describe [any phenomenon]
> as permanent or impermanent.[8]

Nor, when it is seen that time is not ultimately real, is it possible to adopt or maintain a position that views things as "having ultimately only a momentary existence". The voidness of time radically undermines the reality of moments, and makes such a statement essentially meaningless.

Likewise, we cannot believe ultimately in any conception that would explain the nature of things and selves as processes in time:

> The stream of existence is not acceptable in the three times.
> How can there be a stream of existence if it does not exist in the
> three times? [9]

The true nature of things is neither permanence nor impermanence. Rather, everything – including arising and ceasing – is dependently arisen, and thus empty. The *Mūlamadhyamakārikā* points to this in its wonderful opening homage:

> I praise the fully enlightened Buddha,
> the best of teachers,
> who taught the dependently arisen,

[7] Translation adapted from Edward Conze's in *Perfect Wisdom*, p. 24.

[8] Translation by Edward Conze in *The Large Sutra on Perfect Wisdom*, p. 265.

[9] MMK 21:21. '*na yuktā bhavasaṃtatiḥ*': There are many possible renderings here – 'The flow (the 'stream', 'continuity', 'succession', 'series', 'process') of being ('existence', 'becoming') is not acceptable ('proven', 'established', 'right', 'proper')… ' The essential meaning is the same in any case.

> unceasing, unborn,
> not annihilated, not permanent,
> not a unity, not a plurality,
> with no coming, and no going,
> the auspicious, free from conceptual elaboration.

Later in the same text it says:

> Whatever exists dependently, such a thing is essentially peace.
> Therefore both what is arising, and arising itself, are peace.[10]

There is a need, though, to differentiate between levels of truth, and Nāgārjuna and others repeatedly drew attention to this:

> [In a relative sense] everything is impermanent, but [in the absolute sense] nothing is permanent or impermanent.[11]

Of course at a certain level teachings about impermanence and the arising and passing of things are enormously important. And as we have seen, these concepts and perceptions can serve to form helpful provisional ways of looking that may eventually lead to more profound insights. But in itself, a view of impermanence is not a view of the ultimate and true nature of things. In the *Dharmasaṃgīti Sūtra* it says:

> Those attached to the world take arising and ceasing to be real. Therefore the Tathāgata, the Greatly Compassionate One, in order to lead them around… their fear… has taught, in accordance with conventional manners of speaking, that [phenomena] 'arise and cease'. [In reality] though, for any phenomenon there is neither arising nor ceasing.[12]

And Nāgārjuna reaffirmed this understanding:

> There is no origination. There is no destruction. The customary usage of origination and destruction [however] has been expounded [by the Buddhas] for practical purposes.[13]

---

[10] MMK 7:16.
[11] *Śūnyatāsaptati*. (Translation by Chr. Lindtner in *Nagarjuniana*, p. 61.)
[12] Author's own translation.
[13] *Yuktiṣaṣṭikā*. (Translation adapted from Chr. Lindtner's in *Nagarjuniana*, p. 109.)

Ultimately, it is said:

> That which is dependently born is unborn.[14]

And,

> Unarisen, unceased, like *nirvāṇa*, is the nature of things.[15]

Practice: Approaches to the emptiness of time

As is evident from the discussion in this chapter, it is possible to arrive at a realization of the voidness of time through many different means:

- You may have found that in releasing clinging more and more deeply – through the *anattā* practice or through any other practice that fabricates less self – glimpses of timelessness emerge in various ways, and the dependence of the sense of time on self and clinging is seen.

- You may also cultivate either or both of the analytical meditations outlined earlier. Additionally, a moment – of consciousness or of any other phenomenon – may be subjected to the sevenfold reasoning by analysing its relationship to its parts, particularly its beginning, middle, and end.

- Or the understanding may be developed that, as explained, time depends on the perception of things; and that if things are empty, then time also is empty. Like the analyses, in order for this to be an effective way of looking in meditation, the present moment needs to be focused on quite intently. Then the understanding of this moment's inseparability from and dependency on empty, fabricated perception can be brought in and sustained as a view. (A conviction in the emptiness of objects of perception needs therefore to have developed from previous practice.)

Whichever means are used, notice what it feels like to see that time is empty.

Since, generally, the assumption of the reality of time is so deep-rooted, it may be most helpful if eventually all three of the above approaches are developed and employed. And as always, the insight needs repeating. It is usually not enough to see the emptiness of time in any of these ways just once or twice.

Growing accustomed to the insight, a conviction is gradually established that time is empty; and this conviction can then be used in meditation as a platform for further ways of looking:

---

[14] Ibid. (Author's own translation.)

[15] MMK 18:7.

- It is possible to focus on any object of perception and sustain a view of it as 'empty because it depends on time, which is empty'.

- The emptiness of self can also be contemplated in this way.

- Since clinging too needs a sense of time – at least of the present and the future – as well as (like everything else) a time to be 'in', it also can be regarded as 'empty because time is empty'. Here the focus may be any felt sense of clinging in the moment; or it may be the clinging that we know must be present to support the fabrication of the moment's perception.

- Consciousness, the sense of knowing that is present with any object of perception, may also be repeatedly viewed in this way moment to moment.

In each of the above cases, when you feel ready, it is possible to extend the way of looking to include an appreciation of the mutual dependence and interpenetration of time and the phenomenon focused on. The tacit understanding in the view then might be expressed, for instance, as: 'This present moment of time is empty. It is dependent on and inseparable from empty perception (or consciousness, or clinging). This empty perception (or consciousness or clinging) is dependent on this moment of time, which is empty.'

As always, notice how these ways of looking feel and what their effects are.

With practice, an appreciation of the mutual dependence and emptiness of self, things, and time grows, and this understanding can further creatively inform approaches to these meditations.

27

Dependent Origination (2)

As suggested through the discussion in the last chapter, a realization of the emptiness of time allows a practitioner to quickly intuit and meditate on the emptiness of *any* phenomenon at all. When honed, a single, simple meditative tool such as the neither-one-nor-many analysis of the present moment – or any other way of looking that fully reveals time's voidness – may be all a practitioner needs in order to realize the emptiness of *all* things.

Nevertheless, for the sake of moving toward a consummation of insight and of penetrating the mystical depths in the Buddha's teachings we can take our exploration of dependent arising further still. In the later tradition dependent co-origination is often called the 'King of Reasonings',[1] and we have already explained some of the reasons why it offers the best mode of approaching emptiness. Now though, like a beautiful sculpture or a multifaceted jewel we may find that its mystery yields itself to us more fully as our contemplative gaze is directed from a number of different vantage points. Probing further and more comprehensively with our inquiry in this way will further illuminate and unfold its structure and its marvels, so deepening our insight into the wonder of emptiness – of mind, of time, of all things.

The illusion of elements of mind

Let's begin to examine more closely the first few links in the map of *paṭiccasamuppāda*. Having already explored the mutual dependence between consciousness and perception, we can now take a closer look at some of the other mental factors of *nāmarūpa*. As well as *vedanā* and perception, these include intention, attention, and contact.[2] They are all involved in any process of cognition, and, as we have stated before, in the shaping and fabrication of appearances.

---

[1] See, for example, Tsongkhapa's *Praise to Dependent Arising.*

[2] These five factors are specified in MN 9, SN 12:2, etc.

Again, as we inquire into these elements, rather than isolating exactly definable entities or factors, we find the opposite – that they are actually inseparable and mutually dependent. When we ponder what attention is, for example, we see that it is comprised of intention and consciousness. This is so even for the most fleeting moment of attention. The intention places or holds the consciousness on an object, we might say. Of course, in any moment we may or may not be aware of this intention. But without it, or without consciousness, attention has no meaning. Attention is not separable in any way from either its intention or consciousness.

Further, when considered at the most subtle and fundamental level, we can see that this intention that goes with attention is actually a mental movement toward some thing, and a grasping, a holding on to some object of perception. Thus it is essentially indistinguishable from the movements of craving and clinging. And just as grasping at some thing implies aversion to another – and vice versa, as was mentioned in Chapter 21 – we can see too that in attending to some thing, the mind fastens onto that object and rejects other potential objects. On closer inspection then, the dividing lines between clinging, craving, intention, and attention are not clearly or inherently demarcated. The differences between these factors are not fundamental, but only a matter of degree.

Our discovery that objects of perception are dependent on the push and pull of clinging, and that, reciprocally, clinging needs an object, can also be extended to the phenomenon of attention. An object of perception is dependent on attention. And attention, reciprocally, needs an object. Attention and object are mutually dependent and thus mutually empty.

In meditation one can again empower the insight here even further by holding within the view another layer of understanding. If the object is void, attention is dependent on and inseparable from what is void. Then it too can only be void. Seeing this deepens the sense of the emptiness of both attention and object.

Likewise, since the perception of time is inseparably woven into the mutual dependencies involved in the perception of things, other contingencies can also be uncovered here quite easily. We have seen how a sense of time, of this moment, is delineated by the perception of some thing – in other words, by what is known. Since known and knowing are mutually dependent and inseparable, this means that this moment is dependent on knowing. That is, time is dependent on consciousness. The reverse dependency we already explored in the last chapter: knowing, consciousness, is dependent on this moment, on time. So, the present moment depends on consciousness, and consciousness depends on the present moment. Consciousness and time, therefore, are mutually dependent and mutually empty.

The same must be true of attention. Since attention, perception, and consciousness are inseparable, we can see that this moment (time) is dependent on attention, and attention is dependent on this moment (time). As before, their mutual dependence implies their emptiness. Moreover, each being empty means that the other is dependent on, leaning on, an empty thing. From many angles then, it is possible to contemplate that attention too is void of independent existence.

Contact – defined as the coming together of sense base, sense object, and consciousness[3] – is likewise not findable as a separate thing, and it can also be seen to be empty for many reasons. We need only invoke, for example, the emptiness of consciousness to realize that contact too must be void. We can also see how, as clinging and identification are released, for instance through a deepening of the *anattā* practice, contact fades together with perception. As the Buddha alluded to, contact, rather than having some kind of objective existence, is actually fabricated by clinging (which includes identification and *avijjā*) together with a sense of self and perception of the present moment:

> Contacts make contact dependent on attachment. When there is no attachment, contacts would make contact with what?[4]

As before it should be stressed that contact, attention, and the other factors are of course all useful concepts at one level. When we investigate them more thoroughly, however, we find that they are void. No perception. No *vedanā*. No attention. No contact. Not *really*... Wonderful, mysterious, and, with practice, profoundly liberating – we are uncovering even more completely the radical groundlessness of existence.

Saṅkhārā and avijjā

In some instances, the Buddha's more detailed outline of the principle of dependent origination ended with the mutual dependency of consciousness and *nāmarūpa*. On other occasions, more frequently recorded, two links – *avijjā* and *saṅkhārā* – precede consciousness, as we have briefly discussed.

By this point on our journey, we can see that what is meant by *avijjā*,

---

[3] MN 111.

[4] Ud 2:4. The word rendered here 'attachment' – *upadhi* – is used almost synonymously in the Pali Canon with words such as *taṇhā* – usually translated as 'craving'. It also has the meaning 'foundation' or 'ground'. Whichever way it is rendered, the fundamental insight pointed to by the Buddha here is the voidness and groundlessness of contact.

'delusion' or 'ignorance', must encompass a range of mistaken intuitions, from a relatively gross lack of understanding to the most subtle and deeply rooted misconceptions. For example, *avijjā* includes: not knowing which kinds of action, speech, and thought lead to increased suffering and which lead to an alleviation of suffering, to greater peace and happiness; not viewing things in terms of the Four Noble Truths; not being aware of the impermanent nature of things. *Avijjā* also includes believing in the reality of the self, and viewing existence from that perspective. This too has a range of levels, from the grossest solidification of personality view to an intuitive, unnoticed assumption of the independent existence of the most subtle sense of self – perhaps a momentary consciousness or a vast, extremely refined awareness. Ignorance about the nature of self also includes ignorance about the mutual dependence of subject and object. And as we have discussed, wrapped up too with this delusion of self are the most basic assumptions of the inherent existence of phenomena and of time. A lack of awareness of the ultimate nature of all things is the deepest level of *avijjā*.

The term *saṅkhārā* also encompasses a broad range in its meaning. And here again we will uncover a blurring of boundaries and definitions between the links of *paṭiccasamuppāda,* and also between the aggregates. Up to now, I have for the most part translated *saṅkhārā* as 'mental formations' in its context as the fourth aggregate, and as 'concoctions' in the earlier chapter on dependent origination (Chapter 10). There the term was explained through several illustrations highlighting the grosser obsessions, tendencies, and predispositions of reactivity, impulsivity, assumption, and perception brought to any situation. These all, certainly, constitute a part of what is meant by *saṅkhārā*.

More fully though, the term *saṅkhārā* refers to the manifestation, through body, speech, and mind, both of fabrications – that is, phenomena that are fabricat*ed* – as well as the forces and movements of fabricat*ing*.[5] Mental formations of thought and the movements of intention are not only formed (fabricated), but they also form (fabricate). Thus, similarly, perception and *vedanā* are categorized as *saṅkhārā* too.[6] They also both are concocted *and* concoct. As we have seen, fabricated phenomena are not ultimately isolatable as merely the results of fabrication. Being mutually dependent with other phenomena, they also play a part in fabricating the present and the future.

> And why do you call them 'fabrications'? Because they fabricate fabricated things, therefore they are called 'fabrications'. What

[5] SN 12:2.

[6] MN 44.

> do they fabricate as a fabricated thing? For the purpose of formness, they fabricate the fabrication of form. For the purpose of *vedanā*-hood, they fabricate the fabrication of *vedanā*. For the purpose of perception-hood… For the purpose of formation-hood… For the purpose of consciousness-hood, they fabricate the fabrication of consciousness. Because they fabricate fabricated things, they are called fabrications.[7]

The category of *saṅkhārā*, since it includes mental factors that contribute to fabrication, also includes the more subtle instances of intention and of ways of looking and conceiving, which, as we have seen, fabricate the aggregates – that is, the awareness of experience in the moment. (The next section pursues this exploration into an even greater level of subtlety.)

Probed a little more searchingly then, *saṅkhārā* too are not essentially distinguishable from other factors that are involved in the fabrication of experience but which might be more usually categorized within *nāmārūpa* or as other links of the web of *paṭiccasamuppāda*.

Subtle dependent origination

When we consider a relatively gross level of *avijjā* – for instance, a lack of clarity about what leads to happiness and what leads to *dukkha* – it is quite easy to see how such ignorance impels and directs the forces of fabrication that make up *saṅkhārā*. Convinced, for example, that we need the approval of others in order to be happy, certain intentions, thoughts, and ways of looking will be triggered and attention channelled in certain ways on entering into certain situations. Intentions and attention will be determined and propelled to some significant extent by such *avijjā*.

But this is in fact evident at a much more basic and subtle level too. Whenever there is *any* sense of self, *any* perception of an object, and *any* sense of time, there will be intentions, perhaps subtle, to maintain, remove, or transform that perception for the sake of self. In other words, dependent on fundamental *avijjā* – that is, on not comprehending the emptiness of subject, object, and time – there are intentions of the self, in regard to objects of perception, in time.

Even at the most subtle level, with the intuitive conception and belief in a real consciousness (subject) knowing a real object in a real present moment and

[7] SN 22:79. With its use of the dative of the abstractive noun form of each aggregate, *rūpattaya* etc., this is a difficult passage to translate. For our purposes, the main point is that *saṅkhārā* (fabrications) are so called because they fabricate experience.

a potentially real next moment, there will arise the intention for attention to the object in the present moment and the next moment. The belief in their reality fuels a subtle investment which locks subject, object, and time together as conventional experience, through the force of intention and attention. Subject, object, time and the present, along with intention and attention, are woven together and bound in each others' grip – under the spell of even the most subtle reification, the action of fundamental delusion.

The *avijjā* is in the *conception* – of an object being known by a subject in time. And as we have discussed, implicit in this conceiving are various dualities. From a certain perspective and in a manner of speaking – for here we may be at the limits of possibility for any positive conceptual assertion – we could say that the movements of intention (the *saṅkhārā*), coming from this conceiving of the existence and non-existence of subjects, objects, and moments of time, fabricate *this* moment; and that in conceiving of a *next* moment of subject and object, the intention 'leans forward' and rolls the whole dynamic constellation into the fabrication of that moment too. *Saṅkhārā* thus work at the most fundamental level as kinds of cohesive, or binding, forces, concocting the perception of the present and the continuity of perceptions in time – concocting, or weaving, in other words, even the subtlest perception of *bhava*, 'existence', 'being', 'becoming'.

Saṅkhārā is in fact often translated as 'volitional formations', which stresses the centrality of the factor of intention in fabricating any and all experience:

> What one intends, what one designs, and what one has a tendency towards – that is a basis for the stationing of consciousness. There being a basis, there is a support for consciousness. When that consciousness is supported, there is the production of renewed existence in the future. When there is the production of renewed existence in the future, there is future birth, aging and death, sorrow, lamentation, pain, distress, and tribulation. Such is the origination of this entire mass of *dukkha*.
>
> But when one does not intend, design, or have a tendency towards [anything], there is no basis for the stationing of consciousness. There being no basis, there is no support for consciousness. When that consciousness is without support, there is no production of renewed existence in the future... Such is the cessation of this entire mass of *dukkha*.[8]

[8] SN 12:38.

No ground, no centre

Again though, examining *saṅkhārā* and *avijjā* more closely, we find only mutual dependencies, only entities that are empty of inherent existence and lacking true separation. A *saṅkhāra* such as the intention to pay attention, for example, is dependent on a sense of a subject, no matter how subtle. It is also dependent on a perception and conception of an object; and on a sense of a present and a next moment. In fact *any* intention, since it is an intention *for* something, is always in relation to an object and always involves a sense of time, of the present and at least the next moment. And these are all void. Time, we have said, is dependent on consciousness, and on the movements of intention that are the expression of the investment of the subject. It is also dependent on perceiving and conceiving of an object. These too are all void. Consciousness, we have seen, is dependent on an object, on attention, intention, and time. Again, all void. Depending on these phenomena that are void, *saṅkhārā* too must be empty.

> *Saṅkhārā* are like a city of fairies, like illusions and mirages… [They] are like dreams.[9]

No matter how finely one probes the mind, no really existing element is arrived at, and thus also none that can serve as a real basis. There is nothing there that is not empty. Rather, all of these elements are mutually dependent and mutually empty. And saying they have a ground in *avijjā* is not ultimately tenable either, because *avijjā* is mutually contingent and void too. It does not exist in some kind of abstract way, removed from *saṅkhārā* and clinging, from consciousness, mind, and perception of phenomena. It exists only with, and inseparably from, these other factors. Nāgārjuna stressed this point:

> *Avijjā* does not occur without *saṅkhārā*; and without it *saṅkhārā* do not arise. Since they are caused by one another, they have no own-being. That which is not established in own-being, how could it create others? Conditions created by others cannot create those others.[10]

We can understand even more fully now the meaning of the mind's

---

[9] *Śūnyatāsaptati*. (Translation adapted from Chr. Lindtner's in *Nagarjuniana*, p. 65.)
[10] Ibid., pp. 39 – 41.

'unfindability'. Wherever we look for some thing to form a building block, a platform for or a constituent of mind, we find only empty phenomena. Mind is thoroughly void and thoroughly without foundation. And this level of insight is indispensable for a fullness of realization.

> Mind has a merely illusory own-nature... From the very beginning it has been without any own-being... [For it] lacks substantial foundation... [And] those who do not know this emptiness are not liberated.[11]

Typically, the intuitions of *avijjā* have us believe and feel insistently that mind or 'that which knows' must somehow have foundations and also a centre, and thus in some sense be 'findable'. At a very subtle level, however, any notion that mind exists in any findable way at all will form a basis for *dukkha*. Even though it might be extremely refined, any sense of a centre to knowing is a kind of contraction, providing a seed for *dukkha*, or a point on which more *dukkha* can be built.

But we can see now that, in reality, knowing has no centre. It has no centre in a self, certainly, because the self is empty. More than this though, since space and time (including the present moment) are empty and fabricated perceptions, knowing cannot really be said to have any centre in space or in time. How amazing!

And now we have seen too that no mental factors or combination of mental factors can provide a centre or ground. Awareness is not separate from empty perceptions. It is not separate from attention, intention, perception, *vedanā*, *saṅkhārā*, past and future, or *avijjā*. No inherently existing dividing line can be found between any of these elements. Not truly separable from each other, they are all mutually interdependent, and they are all empty.

More generally, whatever one might pick up to consider, on investigation it will be found to be fabricated, empty, dependent on and inseparable from other empty phenomena and concepts. Voidness, groundlessness, is the nature of the mind and of all things. The *Aṣṭasāhasrikā Prajñāpāramitā Sūtra* says:

> All [phenomena] are... unknowable and imperceptible, because they are empty and they do not lean on anything.[12]

---

[11] *Bodhicittavivaraṇa*. (Translation adapted from Chr. Lindtner's in *Nagarjuniana*, pp. 197 – 207.)

[12] Translation by Edward Conze in *The Perfection of Wisdom in Eight Thousand Lines and Its Verse Summary* [San Francisco: Four Seasons Foundation, 1983] pp. 178 – 179.

And Nāgārjuna's *Śūnyatāsaptati* emphasizes and reiterates this insight:

> Things that arise dependently are groundless.[13]

§

Many possibilities for meditation are presented to us through the web of mutual dependencies we have been describing. In practice any *individual* element may be picked up and held within a view that comprehends its contingencies, inseparabilities, and emptiness. And ways of looking that contemplate the voidness and groundlessness of all the interpenetrating factors *at once* can also be sustained.

As always, the ability to develop these ways of looking will generally rest on the skill one has developed, usually gradually, in earlier practices. And as before, various practices may be combined to bring greater power and depth to the way of looking.

Outlined below are examples of a few of the many accessible threads that may be explored. But here there is great scope for experimentation and for investigation of other possibilities suggested by the preceding discussion.

Practice: Meditating on the voidness of attention and of the elements of mind

Once the *citta* is somewhat settled in meditation, choose a relatively steady object to attend to. As the attention is held on the object, introduce into the way of looking the understanding that this object depends on this attention; and that conversely, this attention depends on this object. Allow the sense that they are therefore mutually dependent, inseparable, and mutually empty to permeate the way of looking. You may find that including such an understanding in the view may involve a very light thinking, which may be dropped once the view is established. Alternatively, it may feel fine to continue with that light thinking to support the view.

(When contemplating these subtle factors of mind, it can also be helpful, *before* contemplating their emptiness, to spend a little while regarding them as *anattā*. The

---

[13] '*animitta'*, which may also be rendered 'uncaused'. A commonly used term in the tradition, *animitta* is often translated as 'signless'. While that is usually a quite appropriate translation, the larger context of this particular verse suggests that its other possible meanings – 'groundless' or 'uncaused' – better convey the insight Nāgārjuna intended to express here. (This translation is adapted from Chr. Lindtner's in *Nagarjuniana*, p. 37.)

release of clinging and identification this allows can render the new way of looking more workable in the initial stages. Find out what is helpful for you.)

This way of looking may be made more powerful. Choose a relatively steady object, and based on conviction from previous practice, view it through a lens which knows that it is empty. As you do so, gently begin to include an appreciation that the attention in the moment is dependent on this object. Thus the attention is dependent on and inseparable from what is empty, and can only be empty.

This contemplation of mutual dependence on an empty object may be repeated with any factor of mind.

Practice: Meditating on the mutual emptiness of subject, object, and time

Once you are familiar with a way of looking that sees time and this moment as void, this may be incorporated into the view.

Choose an object, and begin to regard it as 'empty' or 'just a perception'.

Then, as you continue to do so, begin to include also in the way of looking the understanding that mind is empty too, since it depends on the empty object. (Here you can see the mind as a whole as empty; or choose to focus on any of the individual mental factors, as above; or, regarding the mind as a collection of mental factors, allow the understanding of emptiness to include them all.)

When you feel ready, you can then gently add the contemplation of the emptiness of time and the present moment. (It will be easier if this insight too has reached a point of conviction already. Then that conviction can simply be summoned and incorporated, without having to go through an analysis of the moment or reflect much on why the moment is empty. Still, it is certainly possible, and can be very powerful, to introduce an analysis or a light reflection at that point.)

As always when the emptiness of phenomena is contemplated at a deep level like this, there can be a fading of the perception of phenomena. As perception fades, you can practise sustaining the view – of the emptiness of the object of perception, of the mind that knows it, and of the present moment – as far down the continuum of fading as possible.

You may also experiment with various different orderings as you combine different insights. For example:

Regarding the object of appearance as just a fabricated perception – since it is dependent on clinging and self-view, for instance – the understanding can then be added that this moment of time must be empty too, because it depends on this object of appearance.

Including then the sense of attention to the appearance and the moment, the dependence of this attention on this appearance and on a sense of this moment (time) may be contemplated, so that attention is understood to be empty.

Then, the mutual dependency can be followed around again. Since this moment and this object of appearance are dependent on attention, they can be seen to be dependent on what is empty. A deeper sense of their emptiness can thus be obtained.

Practice: Contemplating the dependencies of *saṅkhārā* and consciousness

The mutual dependencies of *saṅkhārā* – specifically here, intentions and the intentions to pay attention – can also be contemplated. For example, as you hold attention on an object, you can tune in to the subtle sense of the intention to pay attention. Then, just as before, a way of looking can be sustained which understands that the object is empty because it depends on the intention, and that the intention is empty because it depends on the empty object.

To this view may be added the understanding, as discussed, that consciousness is dependent on intention, and, also, that intention must be dependent on consciousness.

This way of looking too may be further empowered by gently introducing the understanding, based on previous insights, of the emptiness of either consciousness or the intentions to pay attention, or both.

It is also possible to delicately incorporate into the view the contemplation that *saṅkhārā* are dependent on *avijjā*, in other words on the *conceiving* of consciousness (or any kind of subject), object, and time (this moment and a next moment).

(Again, experiment to see if you find it helpful to begin these practices by viewing the intentions as *anattā* for a little while.)

Working in meditation with these extremely subtle conceptions and perceptions – of the various factors of mind and of the most refined sense of subject, object, time – is a delicate art, definitely requiring a lightness of touch, which comes with practice. This level of insight plays with conceptions and perceptions at the very minimum limits of their constellation and the edges of their use. As mentioned, because of the depth of insight involved a depth of fading is eventually inevitable, and at times that may dissolve even this subtlest level of conventional perceiving and conceiving. Such fading constitutes a deepening, certainly, but it is not the sole purpose of such practices. The heart's understanding is deepened too in the very engaging of the ways of looking that incorporate these subtle conceptions and perceptions. It will be most helpful, therefore, to resume these ways of looking, if possible, once conceiving is workable again and appearances re-manifest to a degree after fading. A meditator may sometimes find that experience seems to dance lightly back and forth across this boundary of the fading of conception. Taking the above advice on board, this is not a problem, for experience on both sides of this boundary can be fruitful.

Entering the Mystery of Dependent Co-Arising

The realizations discussed in this chapter open a much deeper and more mysterious dimension to the understanding of dependent origination than any we might initially have entertained. For we typically tend to assume that some basic entities must truly exist, even if only momentarily, and that these basic entities are at least conceivably findable and separable. We also assume that they can give rise to other such truly existing entities. And we assume that this process happens in time. Ultimately though, the teaching of *paṭiccasamuppāda* is not an attempt to describe a process whereby sharply defined, potentially separable, and really existing elements arise in time. Rather, an understanding significantly beyond our usual conceptions is being pointed to.

To begin with, as we have seen, the mutual dependence of the elements in the web of *paṭiccasamuppāda* means they are inseparable and interpenetrating. In the *Mūlamadhyamakakārikā* it says:

> Whatever arises dependent on some thing is not the same as that thing, nor is it different from it. Therefore it is neither annihilated nor permanent.[14]

This 'non-sameness and non-difference' is a crucial point, vital to the very purpose of the teaching of *paṭiccasamuppāda*. The need to grasp it has been emphasized many times in the tradition, since it radically opens up the meaning and the implications of dependent origination. Thus Mipham, for instance, wrote:

> Those who believe in a substantial reality may, when something is produced from a cause other than itself, believe this is a case of dependent origination. They may think like this, but they misunderstand... Dependent arising is the complete antithesis and negation of production by any of the four possible ways [i.e.

[14] MMK 18:10.

> production from self, other, both self and other, neither self nor other]. To understand this is of the highest importance.[15]

As we probe any of the dependencies of *paṭiccasamuppāda*, we find more than 'dependence' in the ordinary sense of that word. We discover a profound *mutual* contingency and a fundamental *inseparability*, so that the dependent co-arising of things means much more than that they are caused by other things. It means, more fully, that things are ultimately unfindable and inconceivable, that they are void, that phenomena have no real existence.

Moreover, although we can gain much from a level which interprets the teaching of dependent origination as the operation in time of a rapid and complex mechanism of feedback loops, we have seen through deep practice that dependent arising cannot ultimately be viewed as a process which happens in time. It would be more deeply true to say that *time is, itself, a dependent arising*. And since time is a notion so fundamental to our conceiving of the arising and existence of things, such a startling realization simply short-circuits any conceptually based attempt to fully map out a process of how phenomena arise. Seeing that time is a dependent arising places severe limits on any endeavour to grasp *paṭiccasamuppāda* in terms of more conventionally understood assumptions of arising and dependency.

It is partly for these reasons that when Ānanda reported to the Buddha that dependent origination now seemed to him "as clear as clear can be", the Buddha cautioned him against assuming prematurely that he had understood it:

> Don't say that, Ānanda. Don't say that. Deep is this dependent co-arising, and deep its manifestation.[16]

The most profound import of the teaching of dependent origination is not yet reached if there remains a belief in any view that would reduce it finally to a mechanism involving basic elements in time. Nāgārjuna wrote:

> He who imagines that even the most subtle thing arises, such an ignorant man does not see what it means to be dependently arisen.[17]

---

[15] From his commentary to Chandrakīrti's *Madhyamakāvatāra*. (Translated by Padmakara Translation Group in Chandrakirti and Mipham, *Introduction to the Middle Way*, p. 279.)

[16] DN 15. (All translations from DN are the author's own, made also with reference to the translations of Thanissaro Bhikkhu in *Handful of Leaves, Vol. 1* and *Vol. 5* [Redwood City, CA: Sati Center for Buddhist Studies, and Valley Center, CA: Metta Forest Monastery, 2003 and 2007].)

[17] *Yuktiṣaṣṭikā*. (Translation adapted from Chr. Lindtner's in *Nagarjuniana*, p. 107.)

And:

> Those who imagine that what is fabricated possesses origination or decay do not comprehend the movement of the wheel of dependent co-origination.[18]

It is, instead, a more mystical understanding that is ultimately revealed in penetrating dependent origination. The *Anavatapta-paripṛcchā Sūtra* says:

> That which arises due to conditions does not arise. It does not have the nature of arising. That which depends on conditions is taught to be empty.

And included in a fuller insight is the comprehension that *everything* is dependently arisen, *everything* is empty. There is nothing that, even momentarily, forms a real ground or basis for phenomena:

> Neither that which arises dependently nor that which it arises dependently from exists.[19]

This radical and complete groundlessness that the teaching of *paṭiccasamuppāda* reveals is also part of what is so hard to accept at first, without profound practice. Even with practice it is hard to fathom. Dependent co-origination points to insights beyond the grasp of language, logic, and our usual conceptions. Thus the Buddha reported that shortly after his Awakening he felt reluctant to teach it, doubting the possibility that others would understand:

> This Dhamma that I have discovered is deep, hard to see, hard to comprehend, peaceful, sublime, beyond the reach of logic, subtle, to be experienced by the wise. But mankind is intent on a base, delights in a base, is gratified with a base. And for mankind, intent on a base, delighting in a base, gratified with a base, this dependent co-origination, the contingency of this and that, is hard to see… [20]

---

[18] Ibid., p. 107.

[19] *Śūnyatāsaptati*. (Ibid., p. 41.)

[20] SN 6:1. The word translated here as 'base' (*ālaya)* is listed in the Pali-English dictionary as meaning 'abode', 'roosting place', 'perch'. Its etymological root (*ā-lī*) means 'to settle'. So, 'a place to settle'. The English word 'base' helps to convey the meaning too of a 'ground' – a 'basis' – for things. At the most subtle and fundamental levels it is this that "mankind" typically and

He considered it "deep" and "hard to comprehend" not, ultimately, because it is complex in the way a machine with many parts may be complicated, where understanding might mean carefully discriminating each small part and its precise functions in the overall working of this machine. Instead, dependent arising is deep because it radically and pervasively undermines our typical assumptions and even our most basic intuitive sense of things. In melting such conceptions and perceptions, it transcends them to reveal the astounding and mysterious way things are.

Rather than providing an ultimately intelligible map of a truly existing process, then, the purpose of the Buddha's teaching of *paṭiccasamuppāda* is actually to lead to a realization of the profound and total emptiness of all phenomena, and their absolute lack of any true foundation. Magical, void, utterly without ground is the nature of all things, and the heart knowing this is touched by a sense of great beauty and joy. The Buddha's intention in expounding dependent co-origination was to open a powerful tunnel into the freedom of *śūnyatā*. Thus Chandrakīrti, too, stressed the necessity of realizing that even what seem to be the basic building blocks for the process of existence are empty and groundless:

> One who sees dependent arising correctly does not perceive a substance even in subtle things.[21]

If what one is seeking is a final, intellectual understanding of 'how it all works', then there may be frustration. A view which comprehends the emptiness of all phenomena does not, and cannot, give an ultimately coherent explanation of the functioning of conventional reality in conceptual terms. Any such hypothetical account could only be available from views which reify at least some thing as elementary, including time. In seeking a full explanation then, we may be missing the point of the teaching. For explanation is not the task of emptiness; liberation is.

---

intuitively seeks and assumes; and this conception which is primary in engendering clinging and *dukkha*. *Ālaya* can also mean 'desire' or 'attachment'. Rendering it as such would point not only to the fact that delighting in attachments generally impedes the path, but also that, when one remains intent on clinging, the understanding of dependent origination through the understanding of the fading of perception that occurs with clinging's release is obviously impossible. Interestingly, *ālaya* can mean 'pretence' too. Thus it perhaps also carries the implication of being intent on and grasping after things that are somehow false, not ultimately real.

[21] In his *Prasannapadā*. (Translation from the author's notes.)

Conversely though, and as we have suggested before, simply shrugging and declaring 'unknowing' too early would also be a mistake. A premature retreat from knowing, before one has probed such mysteries as mutual dependency and the emptiness of time, can only deliver a limited freedom. Unknowing is not in itself, therefore, the point of the path. It is thoroughly *knowing* voidness that brings a fuller release.

However, at least one of these two tendencies – on the one hand, wanting the 'clarification' of a reductionist explanation, and on the other, wanting to abandon concepts too early – is usually very strong for most people. One person may be attached to descriptions of atomized items neatly categorized with their well-delineated functions within a mechanism, and believe such descriptions to be reality. Another may be attached to the concept that all concepts are burdensome and that they block any possibility of opening to reality. Sometimes a practitioner's tendency careens back and forth over time between these two extremes. More often we each sustain a certain disposition to one or the other. This pair of views and tendencies are like Scylla and Charybdis, and somehow a middle way between them needs to be charted.

Perhaps the most skilful use of the teachings of *paṭiccasamuppāda* is to regard the terms and the relations between them as offering powerful ways of looking for meditation. What we actually require is just enough clarification to enable us to meditatively work with the map so that it begins to lead beyond its own terms, its own conceptual structure dissolved in the radical freedom and emptiness into which it opens.

Now contemplating in meditation the mutual contingency and emptiness of the elements of dependent origination is, in effect, a way of looking with a drastically reduced level of *avijjā*. As we have suggested, at its most fundamental levels *avijjā* includes ignorance of emptiness, of dependent origination, and of the kinds of mutual voidness and interpenetration we have been discussing in this chapter. And since, more than anything else, it is the element of *avijjā* – this fundamental delusion – that (conventionally speaking) supports the other elements such as perception, *vedanā*, and clinging, these all fade profoundly. The whole edifice can collapse. The whole structure itself can melt as *avijjā* melts.

Thus, by pointing out various dependencies which could be realized and contemplated more deeply in meditation, the Buddha made available the means for unfabricating *dukkha* and exploring the unfabricating of experience. And through this mystical unbinding of the world of phenomena are provided avenues too for a more profound and fuller realization of emptiness.

This, I think, was the purpose of the teaching, and for this it suffices. The various mutual dependencies, rather than presenting a hopeless complexity and an insurmountable barrier to clarification, offer numerous diverse approaches for beginning to play with dependency and fabrication in order to realize the liberation that insight into emptiness brings.

The teaching of dependent origination is thus purely a "skilful means". It uses concepts and conventionalities, but sets up contemplations of their relationships in ways that eventually melt and transcend those very concepts and perceptions.[22] Nāgārjuna wrote:

> Inasmuch as all things are empty of their own-nature the incomparable Tathāgata has taught this dependent co-origination… The ultimate meaning consists in that![23]

And:

> For those imprisoned in the conceiving of things the unsurpassed medicine is the ultimate truth – the teaching that things are without own-being… O Refuge, the teaching about origination and cessation… has been declared by you to be only of provisional meaning, and a convention.[24]

Using the concepts of conventional reality, the exploration of dependent origination and fabrication forms the raft necessary to reach the ultimate:

> Without relying on conventions, one cannot realize the ultimate.
> Without realizing the ultimate, one cannot attain liberation.[25]

---

[22] It is perhaps not insignificant in this respect to note historically that all the actual terms of the individual links in the map of dependent origination were already being used, before the Buddha, in Vedic and Upanishadic thought. Sometimes they were even grouped together, as elements in a process describing a cyclical chain of creation and causation. The Buddha picked up and utilized these conventions and concepts, which would have been familiar to the greater part of his audience, in a radically different way – *not* to reify the links, but rather to show the emptiness and groundlessness of all things. The fact too that sometimes he taught ten links and sometimes twelve also suggests that his intention was not to concretize an explanation, but was instead purely pragmatic – to provide the keys that can unlock a freedom beyond concepts.

[23] *Śūnyatāsaptati*. (Translation by Chr. Lindtner in *Nagarjuniana*, pp. 65 – 66.)

[24] *Acintyastava*.

[25] MMK 24:10.

28

Dependent Cessation – The Unfabricated, The Deathless

As discussed, habitually and usually without realizing it we view things as having inherent existence; some degree of *avijjā* and clinging are woven into our typical ways of looking. Therefore any way of looking that sees the emptiness of phenomena will be manifesting less *avijjā* and clinging than our normal ways of looking. The deeper the level of emptiness it sees, the less *avijjā* and clinging are expressed and created in the looking. With less and less *avijjā* and clinging, there is less and less fabrication of perception, so that consciousness and appearances become more and more refined, until eventually even the most refined and subtle perception of subject, object, and time ceases.

Learning to fabricate less and exploring this letting go of fabrication are part of the journey of discovery in practice. While the fabrication of lovely and wholesome perceptions and states – such as *mettā,* compassion, and *samādhi* – is certainly vital to the path, on the continuum of fading discussed in Chapter 19 these are actually states of *less* fabrication than usual, and these 'superior' perceptions can fade and be transcended eventually too:

> There is the inferior, there is the superior, and beyond there is the giving up of this entire field of perception.[1]

The Buddha emphasized often the value of such a cessation of conventional perception:

> Where *nāmarūpa*, together with impingement and the perception of form, cease without trace, it is there that the tangle is cut.[2]

---

[1] MN 7.

[2] SN 7:6.

And the *Prajñāpāramitā Saṃcayagāthā* echoes this:

> Wherein there is no seeing of form, no seeing of *vedanā*, no seeing of perception, no seeing of volitional formations, no seeing of consciousness, mind or mentality, this has been taught by the Tathāgata as the seeing of reality.[3]

As did Nāgārjuna, in one of his hymns of praise to the Buddha:

> You have said that there is no liberation without realizing the signless.[4]

And of course this dependent cessation was repeatedly referred to by the Buddha in his teaching of *paṭiccasamuppāda*:

> With the remainderless fading and cessation of *avijjā* comes the cessation of fabrications; with the cessation of fabrications, the cessation of consciousness; with the cessation of consciousness, the cessation of *nāmarūpa*; with the cessation of *nāmarūpa*, the cessation of the six sense spheres; with the cessation of the six sense spheres, the cessation of contact; with the cessation of contact, the cessation of *vedanā*; with the cessation of *vedanā*, the cessation of craving; with the cessation of craving, the cessation of clinging; with the cessation of clinging, the cessation of becoming; with the cessation of becoming, the cessation of birth; with the cessation of birth, aging and death, sorrow, lamentation, pain, distress, and tribulation cease. Such is the cessation of this whole mass of *dukkha*.[5]

Reading such passages a few things should be obvious based on all that we have discussed and explored in practice up to now. The words above are not describing a kind of comatose state of utter oblivion, total unconsciousness.[6] Yet nor are they

---

[3] Translation from the author's notes.

[4] *Lokātītastava*. We mentioned in the last chapter (in footnote 13) that 'signless' is the more usual translation of the word *animitta*, and here it captures well Nagārjuna's intended meaning for this verse. A 'sign' (*nimitta*) is any object of perception at all, gross or refined, inner or outer. 'Signless' (*animitta*) therefore means 'without an object of perception'. As will be inferred from our discussions the two meanings overlap, since without an object of perception there is not a support or ground for consciousness.

[5] In AN 10:92, MN 115, etc.

[6] This fact is also made clear through the wording of other passages, for example AN 10:6 and AN 10:7.

pointing merely to a fading and ceasing of only the grosser manifestations of self and *papañca*. Phrases such as "cessation of consciousness", "cessation of *nāmarūpa*", and "cessation of *vedanā*" clearly indicate something more than a cessation of only the grosser *distortions* of consciousness, *nāmarūpa*, contact, etc. What the Buddha was describing here is not a state of 'equanimous objectivity' with regard to the things of the world – a state of perceiving things 'purely' because the accumulated residues, encrustations, and biases from the past no longer flow into the present to influence or veil perception. Here we have gone beyond what might be termed a 'calming of reactivity', and beyond merely a pacification of the extremes of *vedanā* – whether unpleasant or pleasant. Rather, what is being referred to is a complete fading and cessation of all appearances, and of all the elements that make up conventional experience – including *all six* sensory consciousnesses together with all their associated contacts, *vedanā*, perceptions, etc. All are utterly transcended.

> Here, Sandha,… with regard to earth, the perception of earth has disappeared; with regard to liquid, the perception of liquid has disappeared; with regard to fire, the perception of fire has disappeared; with regard to wind, the perception of wind has disappeared; with regard to the sphere of infinite space, the perception of the sphere of infinite space has disappeared; with regard to the sphere of infinite consciousness, the perception of the sphere of infinite consciousness has disappeared; with regard to the sphere of nothingness, the perception of the sphere of nothingness has disappeared; with regard to the sphere of neither perception nor non-perception, the perception of the sphere of neither perception nor non-perception has disappeared; with regard to this world, the perception of this world has disappeared; with regard to the next world, the perception of the next world has disappeared; whatever is seen, heard, sensed, cognized, attained, sought after, or explored by the mind: the perception of that has disappeared. Absorbed in this way, [one] is absorbed dependent neither on earth, liquid, fire, wind, the sphere of infinite space, the sphere of infinite consciousness, the sphere of nothingness, the sphere of neither perception nor non-perception, this world, the next world, nor on what is seen, heard, sensed, cognized, attained, sought after, or explored by the mind — and yet one is absorbed. And to this [one] absorbed in this way, [all] the gods pay homage even from afar: 'Homage to you… you of whom we don't know even what it is that you are absorbed dependent on.'[7]

[7] AN 11:10. Sometimes this *sutta* is listed as AN 11:9.

Conceptions of the Unfabricated: Words Pointing Beyond Words…

An experience wherein conventional perception ceases is not really describable. Since conceiving and language are based on notions of subject, object, and time, how can what remains when they collapse possibly be conceived by the mind or conveyed in words? The Buddha said:

> Where all phenomena are removed, all ways of speaking are removed as well.[8]

When questioned on the matter Sāriputta explained that, with the remainderless fading and cessation of the six sense spheres of contact, any statement that "there is anything else", or that "there is not anything else", that "there both is and is not anything else", or that "there neither is nor is not anything else", is to "*papañc*–ize non-*papañca*". His explanation makes clear the more complete meaning of the word *papañca*. More than just gross ego-proliferation, it refers at its most subtle level to *objectification* – the construing and differentiation of objects (and a subject) that is part of conventional perception, the 'making manifold' of things:

> However far the six spheres of contact reach, that is how far objectification (*papañca*) reaches. However far objectification reaches, that is how far the six spheres of contact reach. With the remainderless fading and cessation of the six spheres of contact, there comes to be the cessation of *papañca*, the pacification of objectification.[9]

Many teachings thus confine themselves to speaking in negative terms, making clear what is *not* there, and what has been left behind. To speak in terms of 'cessation' is to speak in terms of known conventions, using a negative formulation – the ceasing or non-fabrication of perception – without affirming anything about what remains. The word *nirvāṇa* is also in fact a negative formulation.

But sometimes the Buddha spoke in more affirmative terms as well – of that which is opened to. For example:

> Knowing the destruction of fabrications, you know the unmade.[10]

---

[8] Sn 5:6.

[9] AN 4:173.

[10] Dhp 383. (Translations from Dhp are the author's own.)

And:

> There is, monks, an unborn, unbecome, unmade, unfabricated. If there were not that unborn, unbecome, unmade, unfabricated, no leaving behind of the born, become, made, fabricated would be discerned. But because there is indeed an unborn, unbecome, unmade, unfabricated, a leaving behind of the born, become, made, fabricated is discerned.[11]

Sometimes he used the word '*nirvāṇa*' synonymously with 'the unfabricated'.[12] And because it is not fabricated, he also called it 'the truth':

> That which has a deceptive nature is false; but that which has an undeceptive nature – *nibbāna* – is true. A monk possessing [this truth] possesses the highest position of truth. For this is the highest noble truth – *nibbāna*, which has an undeceptive nature.[13]

Among the other synonyms he used for 'the unfabricated' were: 'the uninclined', 'the subtle', 'the very difficult to see', 'the unaging', 'the stable', 'the unmanifest', 'freedom', 'the peaceful', 'the sublime', 'the auspicious', 'the amazing', 'the deathless'.[14]

Other formulations, though, stress the fact that an experience of cessation does not involve the perception of any kind of object. In the *Pañcaviṃśatisāhasrikā Prajñāpāramitā Sūtra*, for instance, it says:

> A bodhisattva who is endowed with that wisdom eye does not cognize any phenomenon – be it fabricated or unfabricated, wholesome or unwholesome, faulty or faultless, defiled or undefiled, mundane or supramundane. With that wisdom eye he does not see any phenomenon, or hear, or consider, or perceive one. This is the perfectly pure wisdom eye of the bodhisattva.[15]

And in the *Dharmadharmatāvibhāga* it says:

---

[11] Ud 8:3; Iti 2:16.
[12] SN 43:14 – 43.
[13] MN 140.
[14] SN 43:14 – 43.
[15] Translation from the author's notes.

> Original nonconceptual wisdom... is defined with the utmost precision as that which involves no object, no focusing, no attributes on which to focus at all.[16]

A sensitivity and subtlety of discernment is needed to navigate the apparent diversity of these statements. When the emptiness of any object is contemplated intensely in meditation, the object fades. If the vacuity that appears in place of the object is pregnant with the meaning of emptiness, then emptiness can be said to be the object of consciousness at that time. As the meditation deepens, however, the conceptual and perceptual construction of subject and object, knower and known, begins to collapse and there begins to be a blending of this consciousness and this emptiness. With the collapse of both subject and object, it cannot be accurate to say that there is a knowing of some thing, or object, by some consciousness. Chandrakīrti pointed out that it can, nevertheless, be spoken of this way, as long as we recognize that we are using the language of 'as though' – that is, a manner of speaking paralleling the perspective of conventional reality, where consciousness knows an object:

> Suchness is unborn, and mind itself is also free from birth. And when the mind is tuned to this, it is as though it knows the ultimate reality.[17]

Language and concept, as we have said, necessarily involve notions of subject and object. Sometimes the language used in teachings describing this level of realization will lean toward emphasizing more the conception of a known, an 'object'; and at other times, toward the conception of a knowing consciousness, a 'subject'.

Choosing a word such as 'unbinding' to translate *nirvāṇa* – from tracing its etymology to *nir* ('un') and *vāna* ('weaving' or 'binding') – may help take the conception away from any kind of object. Similarly, at a certain level at least, it might be more accurate to speak of 'unfabricating'.

But still, conceiving will usually enter quickly and habitually even for a meditator working at this level. Especially when it is a momentary glimpse, an experience of cessation may be interpreted *after the fact* in terms that conceive of it as a knowing of an unfabricated 'object'. Or it may be that the knowing consciousness is assumed to have an inherent existence somehow. Or the insight that led up to the experience might be reified and clung to. Several passages

---

[16] Translation by Jim Scott in *Maitreya's Distinguishing Phenomena and Pure Being* [Ithaca, NY: Snow Lion, 2004] p. 179.
[17] MAV 11:13.

suggest that there is a fuller liberation when attachment to such conceiving is dissolved through insight.[18] As we shall discuss though, these may still be very helpful stages of insight to pass through.

Sometimes the Buddha did describe what remains with the cessation of perception in terms of a consciousness that is released, unbound from any object:

> Clinging, one is unreleased; not clinging, one is released. Should consciousness, when standing, stand clinging to form, supported by form [as its object], established on form, infused with delight, it would exhibit growth, increase, and proliferation.
> Should consciousness, when standing, stand clinging to *vedanā*… perception… mental formations, supported by *vedanā*… perception… mental formations [as its object], established on *vedanā*… perception… mental formations, infused with delight, it would exhibit growth, increase, proliferation.
> Were someone to say 'I will point out a coming, a going, a passing away, an arising, a growth, an increase, a proliferation of consciousness apart from form, from *vedanā*, from perception, from fabrications', that would be impossible.
> If a monk abandons desire for the element of form… abandons desire for the element of *vedanā*… perception… fabrications… consciousness, then from the abandonment of desire, the support is destroyed, and there is no foundation for consciousness. Consciousness, thus unestablished, not proliferating, not performing any function, is released.[19]

On another occasion he gave the analogy of a ray of sunlight that does not land on any wall, ground, or water to describe a consciousness which, with the release of craving, finds no object of support anywhere.[20]

The Zen Master Huang Po also pointed to such a consciousness that is not of objects in the usual sense. He called it the 'Pure Mind', or the 'Real Mind':

> This Pure Mind… the people of the world do not awaken to it, regarding only that which sees, hears, feels, and knows, as mind. Blinded by their own sight, hearing, feeling, and knowing, they do

---

[18] E.g. MN 64.

[19] SN 22:53.

[20] SN 12:64.

> not perceive the spiritual brilliance of [the Pure Mind]... Realize that, though Real Mind [or: Pure Mind] is expressed in these perceptions, it neither forms part of them nor is separate from them.[21]

At times the Buddha spoke of what remains with the cessation of the six sense consciousnesses and their respective objects of knowledge as a

> Consciousness without attribute, without end, luminous all around. Here water, earth, fire, and air have no footing. Here long and short, subtle and gross, pleasant and unpleasant, and *nāmarūpa* are all destroyed. With the cessation of consciousness [i.e. the six sense consciousnesses] here each of these is destroyed.[22]

In addition to what we explained in Chapter 19 about the spectrum of fading, the Buddha's teaching to Sandha (cited earlier in this chapter) together with a number of other passages[23] make it clear that this "Consciousness without attribute" cannot be equated to any of the formless *jhānas*. Nor can it be equated to the vastness of awareness we explored in Chapter 15. As Huang Po's words indicate, this "Consciousness without attribute" is not an open awareness that embraces or takes in everything in the senses. The Buddha said it is "not experienced through the all-ness of the all",[24] that is, through the six sense bases.

Furthermore, in an experience of a vastness of awareness as we described it in Chapter 15, perceptions of time and space are still being fabricated. A practitioner might imagine that an experience of a vastness of awareness is an experience of the Unfabricated, since it seems 'eternal' and 'deathless' while other phenomena come and go within it. This Consciousness without attribute, however, is not 'eternal' and 'deathless' in that sense of 'existing continuously in time'. It does not 'continue'. But it is not momentary; nor is it totally non-existent. It is, rather, not of time, or space, at all. The Buddha said:

---

[21] Translation by John Blofeld in *The Zen Teaching of Huang Po: On the Transmission of Mind* [London: The Buddhist Society, 1968] pp. 36 – 37.

[22] DN 11. "Consciousness without attribute" (*viññāṇaṃ anidassanaṃ*) may also be translated "a consciousness that does not point out [or: 'indicate' or 'look at' anything]". Such a rendering would make clear and emphasize its difference from all other consciousnesses, which always have some kind of object.

[23] E.g. MN 59, AN 9:34, MN 137.

[24] MN 49. The 'all' refers to the totality of what can be known through the six sense bases. See, e.g., SN 35:23.

> There is that sphere where there is neither earth, nor water, nor fire, nor wind; neither sphere of infinite space, nor sphere of infinite consciousness, nor sphere of nothingness, nor sphere of neither perception nor non-perception; neither this world nor the next world; neither sun, nor moon. And there, I say, there is no coming and no going, no staying, no passing away, and no arising. It is without foundation, non-continuing, and objectless.[25]

Skilful Conceiving

We have already established that what is not of time does not exist in the way that we usually conceive of something existing. Ultimately, as Sāriputta pointed out, the Unfabricated cannot be confined to conceptual and linguistic designations of 'existing' or 'not existing'. It is evident, though, that in speaking of cessation and the Unfabricated, the language used in different teachings will often slant one way or another – sometimes towards negating and at other times towards affirming. At still other times the emphasis is on making it very clear that there is neither negation nor affirmation being taught.

For one dedicated to practice, all these may best be regarded as skilful means. Teachings which seem to lean this way or that may be regarded as skilful prods and goads to our practice. They are helpful responses to our usual conceptions and inclinations, which tend to gravitate toward affirmation or negation. Thus, for instance, Huang Po responded to the fear that can arise in relation to deep fading:

> People are afraid to forget their minds [the cognition of subject and object], fearing to fall through the Void, with nothing to stay their fall. They do not know that the Void is not really void, but the realm of the real Dharma. This spiritually enlightening nature is without beginning… subject to neither birth nor destruction, neither existing nor not existing, neither impure nor pure, neither clamorous nor silent, neither old nor young, occupying no space, having neither inside nor outside, size nor form, colour nor sound. It cannot be… comprehended by [intellect], explained in words, contacted materially, or reached by meritorious achievement.[26]

---

[25] Ud 8:1.

[26] Translation by John Blofeld in *The Zen Teaching of Huang Po*, p. 41.

Openly examining our own reactions to different teachings regarding cessation and the Unfabricated is important, and can be quite enlightening. Often we will discover that we do harbour a bias either towards affirming the existence of an Unfabricated or towards denying it. Such prejudices can be considerably charged with emotion too. And curiously, these opinions and feelings can sometimes be particularly strong for practitioners whose skill in meditation has not yet developed to the point where there is a deep enough fading of appearances to arrive at a view actually based on their own experience and understanding. The existence of such predispositions, however, is not in itself an insurmountable problem. But if they are there we need to be honest with ourselves about them and about their effects, and realize that such reactions are really not based on insight alone. We might ask ourselves frankly if we want a certain answer to be true, and why.

The common tendencies encountered here are expressions of what we might call spiritual, or metaphysical, or even religious, inclinations: on the one hand, a spirituality of 'That', where the heart is pulled towards a sense of something transcendent and tends to reify it; and, on the other, a spirituality of 'This', where a transcendent is denied and the heart devotes itself to 'this', the 'reality of this moment'.

Fear may have some part in either inclination. Those who gravitate towards a religiosity (however much denied) of 'This' may assume that those who are drawn toward 'That' are afraid of meeting and tolerating the impermanence and existential limitations of 'this', of 'concrete reality', and very occasionally such suspicions might be accurate. But one may cling then to a notion that 'this is it' out of some sense that this reality is what has to be faced up to.

Or there may be in the sense that 'this is it' a great sensibility to the beauty of the particulars of experience revealed by mindfulness in the moment – this sound, this sight, this touch. Usually woven into that sense, though, are all kinds of often unconscious assumptions about what is real. And there may be a hidden clinging to the belief in and prioritizing of 'This', because transcending it seems as though it would be 'life-denying' in some way, or might somehow undermine the ability to love, or deprive 'this' of any sense of meaning.

The assumptions of inherent existence in many of these notions about reality are easy to recognize. So it becomes evident that deepening insight here and journeying further must be connected with an understanding of the emptiness of 'This' and 'That'. Our path thus far has been one of progressively broadening, deepening, and refining our comprehension of voidness by relying on previous insights as stepping-stones. Let us continue to do so, and in keeping with our approach let us come at these issues and this level of insight pragmatically rather than dogmatically.

By this point in practice – if you have been developing the meditations outlined in this book, and have witnessed repeatedly the deep fading of phenomena and understood its implications, or if you have been using other practices that make the emptiness of phenomena clear – it is probable that the inclination to consciously espouse a view asserting the reality of 'this' will have been considerably weakened. Even if there is a tendency then to reify a transcendent Unfabricated, such a reification can be seen as a stage in practice, just as it might have been helpful for a while to reify awareness in various ways, as discussed in Chapter 15. If this reification of an Unfabricated helps in undermining a belief in the ultimate reality of the phenomena we *typically* cling to and construct *dukkha* around, it is serving a crucial function. And it may, therefore, be part of the path. The Buddhist teachings of emptiness are not aimed only at negating the reification of those notions and constructs that might seem (to some) more obviously 'spiritual' and then throwing us back to face the 'reality of concrete life'. Rather, stressing the realization of the emptiness of *everything*, the teachings focus repeatedly on pointing out the emptiness of what we are more commonly attached to and misconceive: the aggregates – the elements of experience, of 'Life'. For our *dukkha* is principally in relation to 'this', to these aggregates; and seeing their emptiness is what brings the most significant liberation.

If ultimately it cannot be said of the Unfabricated either that it exists or that it does not exist, then it cannot just be simply, quickly, and finally dismissed as non-existent and without value. Eventually, to be sure – despite the truth at one level in regarding it as an absence of fabrication – we shall see that ultimately the transcendent Unfabricated has no more existence than the mundane. However, it does not have any *less* existence. *Experientially*, it can be just as real and crucial as, for example, love, generosity, compassion, insight, and mindfulness. All of these are empty too. Yet they are all immensely valuable and perform vital functions on the path, even when they are reified – as for the most part they are. Likewise, opening to an experience of non-fabrication may be powerfully liberating, even when that experience is interpreted at first in terms which give some thing inherent existence.

Cessation and Insight

Whether or not there is a stage of reifying an Unfabricated, we have said before that fading and cessation need most of all to be understood in the context of dependent origination and fabrication – the building of subject, object, and time.

Since it is this understanding that brings freedom, this is most important. Phenomena fade and cease with the fading and cessation of the forces of fabrication in the mind, because then they are not being built by *avijjā*, clinging, and other *saṅkhārā*. Such realization can then be used to further develop skill in undermining and arresting fabrication. And thus deeper comprehension can evolve. It is because the Buddha had profoundly and thoroughly understood how the whole world of experience is built, and how it is dismantled through insight, that he could say upon his Awakening:

> House-builder, you are found out! You will not build a house again. All your rafters are broken, and your ridgepole disassembled. The mind has arrived at non-fabrication, has experienced the end of craving.[27]

As we have explained and witnessed in practice, insight ways of looking, to varying degrees, inevitably deconstruct the aggregates. That is to say, they undermine the fabrication of the whole show of conventional phenomena and the elements involved in fabrication. The Buddha taught that:

> You should smash, destroy, and demolish form… smash, destroy, and demolish *vedanā*… perception… *saṅkhārā*. You should smash, destroy, and demolish consciousness.[28]

For it is through these insight ways of looking, which naturally dismantle and dissolve the whole edifice of appearances, that we learn about fabrication and dependent origination.

In practice, a moment of cessation of consciousness and perception may come about through any way of looking which releases clinging deeply. Thus it can potentially be allowed by any of the three characteristics practices, or any further practice embodying what we have called 'holy disinterest'.

As has been mentioned though, clinging and *saṅkhārā* rest on *avijjā*. It is *avijjā*, gross or subtle, which impels the fabrication of consciousness and perception:

> If a person immersed in *avijjā* fabricates a meritorious fabrication, there comes to be a consciousness experiencing the meritorious.

[27] Dhp 153 – 154.

[28] SN 23:2.

> If he fabricates an unmeritorious fabrication, there comes to be a consciousness experiencing the unmeritorious. If he fabricates an imperturbable fabrication, there comes to be a consciousness experiencing the imperturbable [i.e. the four formless realms].[29]

We have discussed how, at the most subtle level, *avijjā* includes a conceiving of subject, object, and time (including the present moment) as real; and this conceiving involves a belief in dualities, of various kinds, between 'this thing' and 'not this thing'. With this conceiving and these dualities come intentions and fabrications that further drive the "conjurer's trick", that further fabricate and propel the world of appearances and time. As the Buddha said:

> Those who wander endlessly in birth and death, in *saṃsāra* – in 'this thing' and 'another thing' – that is only a journey of ignorance... [30]

And Nagārjuna wrote:

> Seeing the 'existence' and 'non-existence' of phenomena, those who are unwise do not see the auspicious, the pacification of appearances.[31]

As briefly alluded to in earlier chapters, on any occasion, therefore, when *avijjā* is dissolved deeply enough through an insight way of looking there will be a cessation of appearances, since at that time the whole web of *paṭiccasamuppāda* is being undermined most potently by the undermining of *avijjā*:

> "But when a monk has eliminated *avijjā* and aroused understanding, then, with the fading of *avijjā* and the arising of understanding, he does not fabricate either a meritorious fabrication, an unmeritorious fabrication, or an imperturbable fabrication. Neither fabricating nor intending, he does not cling to anything in the world... With the total non-existence of fabrications, from the cessation of fabrications, would

[29] SN 12:51.

[30] Sn 3:12.

[31] MMK 5:8.

> consciousness… *nāmārūpa*… the six sense spheres… contact… *vedanā*… [etc]… be perceived?"
> "No, Venerable Sir."
> "Good, monks, it is just so… Believe me, apply yourselves to this. Have confidence in this and do not be unsure. Just this is the end of *dukkha.*"[32]

This is why when we contemplate emptiness intensely appearances dissolve. As a significant reduction of *avijjā* in the moment, sustaining such a profound insight view withdraws the impetus from the fabrication of the aggregates so that they fade.

And seeing this fading further consolidates and deepens the understanding of their concocted and empty nature. Paraphrasing the Buddha's utterance about a 'Consciousness without attribute', Nāgārjuna explained this role of insight:

> Earth, water, air, and fire, long and short, subtle and coarse, as well as virtue and so forth are said by the Subduer to be ceased in that indeterminable consciousness, complete lord over the limitless… Here *nāmarūpa* has ceased. All these that earlier appeared to consciousness because of non-wisdom later cease for consciousness in this way because of wisdom. All these phenomena… are pacified through being burned by the light of true insight. Thus the reality is later ascertained of what was formerly imputed through *avijjā.*[33]

In his *Yuktiṣaṣṭikā* too he wrote:

> Just as the Buddhas have spoken of 'my' and 'I' for pragmatic reasons, thus they have also spoken of the aggregates, the sense bases, and the elements for pragmatic reasons. Such things spoken of as the great elements etc. are absorbed in consciousness. They are dissolved by understanding them. Certainly they are falsely imagined.[34]

---

[32] SN 12:51.

[33] *Ratnāvalī.* (Translation adapted from Jeffrey Hopkins's in *Nāgārjuna's Precious Garland*, p. 107.)

[34] Translation adapted from Chr. Lindtner's in *Nagarjuniana*, p. 111.

Insight Is Empty Too

As alluded to, although it is not always a problem, experiences of cessation can for some become focal points for attachment, both subtle and not so subtle, in a number of ways. This is understandable. The unbinding and melting of subject, object, and time that occurs in cessation can be an awesome and profoundly moving experience. And in a practice session when there is again and again a deep fading of appearances it can also be quite common that a meditator feels 'on the edge of a breakthrough'. Then, especially if there has been exposure to teachings that place a great emphasis on achieving an experience of cessation, it is very easy for an element of chasing or pushing for such an experience to creep in to the meditation, sometimes unnoticed. But of course, as a manifestation of clinging at that point it is likely that such pushing will actually prevent a cessation experience. Even when a practitioner knows this though, and knows better, the pushing can repeatedly arise.

As always, it is helpful to develop our sensitivity to levels of effort, and to the relationship with and conception of practice, in any moment. And when this kind of grasping arises in deep meditation it is possible to gently remind oneself that it is the understanding of emptiness and dependent origination that is the most important thing. Then the attitude to and the inclination of the practice in the moment can get back on track. We can trust that through simply sustaining, developing, and consolidating insight ways of looking, what needs to happen is happening – the understandings that liberate are taking root in the heart.

More significantly in the long run, a little reflection reveals that insight ways of looking are in fact empty too – for many reasons. And this understanding can be deliberately included in practice, in the very view at that moment. Then not even insight and the way of looking can form an object of grasping and become a ground for *dukkha*.

Practice: Meditating on the emptiness of insight

Once you have gained some facility in meditation contemplating the emptiness of time and consciousness, it is possible to contemplate the emptiness of insight also.

In a meditation session choose any object of perception. For a little while sustain any insight way of looking at it that sees its emptiness. If you wish, you may also include insight into the emptiness of the mind that is looking.

When you feel ready, include the awareness of the insight way of looking. Then begin to include in the view an understanding of its emptiness too.

This may rest on the understanding that it exists in time, but that time is empty.

Or that the way of looking is dependent on and inseparable from the object it is directed at, which is an empty appearance.

Or that it is dependent on and inseparable from consciousness, which is empty too.

You can also combine all three of these understandings, or find any other way of contemplating insight's voidness that feels helpful.

PART NINE

Like a Dream,
Like a Magician's Illusion...

29

Beyond the Beyond…

Beyond all duality

This fact that with a sufficient dissolution of *avijjā* and clinging there is a fading and cessation of perception demands of us further careful reflection. For not all the conclusions it seems to suggest are ones at which we can yet arrest our explorations. In particular, some of the understandings as they have emerged so far from our observations might set up an orientation wherein appearances are somehow denigrated. The appearances of the world may be viewed to be essentially the results and manifestations of ignorance. Cessation, on the other hand, might be seen as ultimately more true and desirable. And such a bias would reflect only a partial realization. Taking our inquiry into dependent arising, fabrication, and emptiness deeper still will open up greater and less dualistic insights.

To begin with we can investigate more searchingly the nature of delusion. Although on one level it can certainly be said that *dukkha*, self, and appearances arise in dependence on *avijjā*, *avijjā* – like all the other links in the web of dependent origination – is thoroughly empty also. This it is possible to see from many angles. For example, as we have already mentioned, while appearances are dependent on delusion, delusion is also dependent on appearances. It only exists with, and in relation to, appearances; and appearances, we know, are empty. *Avijjā* is also dependent on consciousness. Without consciousness there can be no delusion, and consciousness too is void. Seen thus to be leaning on and totally inseparable from what is empty, delusion is also seen to be empty. And of course *avijjā* must also be dependent on time. Like anything else, it needs a time to 'be in'; and because time is empty, *avijjā* can only be empty.

Chandrakīrti stressed that it would betray an incompleteness of insight to regard ignorance as something real and as really fabricating appearances which then need to be removed:

> Like a dense mass of clouds, the darkness of ignorance enshrouds the minds of worldly beings, and thus objects appear in an

> incorrect way. Just as, due to diseased vision, some people will incorrectly perceive strands of hair [i.e. black lines], double moons, eyes on peacocks' feathers, or bees – all of which are illusion – in the same way, due to ignorance, the unwise perceive the variety of fabricated phenomena by conceptualizing them.
>
> "*Karma* [actions of body, speech, and mind which fabricate appearances and *dukkha*] arises due to ignorance; when ignorance is banished, *karma* also" – to think like this definitely betrays the unwise. The sunlight of insight clears the thick darkness of ignorance. The wise have realized emptiness, and thus they gain liberation.[1]

In his commentary, Mipham elaborated on this last verse:

> [Those who understand the Middle Way] understand that, in the very moment in which deluded appearances manifest – as the result of their cause, namely ignorance – these same phenomena are without inherent existence. This is liberation. This is why Chandrakīrti's root verse says that they do not consider that the cause of appearance is something to be eliminated. The sunlight of their intelligence gives a complete view of the ultimate status of things and dispels the thick darkness implied in the assumption of true existence. Those who are wise realize emptiness. They understand that all things – cause and effect, defilements to be abandoned, and also the antidotes to these same defilements – are empty of inherent existence. It is thus that the wise gain freedom. One should not understand that the attainment of liberation comes through the exhaustion of ignorance.[2]

The implications here are subtle but momentous. Conventionally we can say that *avijjā* gives rise to *saṅkhārā*, perception, and the rest. Seeing that ignorance, *saṅkhārā*, and all the other links are empty, however, moves the whole understanding beyond dualistic notions. Any directing of practice towards the idea of finally pacifying the world of appearances is itself pacified through this insight. Rather than regarding appearances as ultimately inferior, when we dwell

---

[1] MAV 6:104 – 106.

[2] Translation by Padmakara Translation Group in Chandrakirti and Mipham, *Introduction to the Middle Way*, pp. 267 – 268.

in a realization that *everything* is empty, appearances may appear to us magical, holy even. They are no longer imbued with the sense of the taint of ignorance. For that is only possible when *avijjā* is reified. Now the reality of the notion of ignorance collapses, along with the subtly negative colouring of appearances that it entails. Such insight does not set up merely a return to ordinary unexamined assumptions though. Since by this point in practice there is a deep knowing of the voidness and dependent arising of all things, the view will not be limited that way. Rather, in their wondrous insubstantiality and their utter lack of any foundation now all appearances may be seen to express a profound and mystical blessedness and even bliss. In the *Pitāputrasamāgama Sūtra* it says:

> The Buddha has taught at length that ignorance itself is empty of ignorance. When one enters dependent arising, one enters the *dharmadhātu* (the sphere of ultimate reality). This the Teacher has set forth.[3]

All twelve, then, of the links of *paṭiccasamuppāda* are void. Nāgārjuna emphasized this insight repeatedly:

> The twelve members of relativity, starting with ignorance and ending with decay, which are subject to dependent co-origination, we maintain to be like a dream and an illusion.[4]

Arriving at and cultivating this understanding is now possible for us in many ways. And in turn this realization allows us to pursue our inquiry into dependent arising even more deeply. A fuller comprehension can grasp what was alluded to in Chapter 27, so that we begin to realize something more amazing still. For if all the links in the map of *paṭiccasamuppāda* are empty, and if time, arising, and ceasing are also empty, then *fabrication and dependent origination themselves must also be empty*. How, after all, could fabrication be something ultimately real, if its elemental building blocks, its results, and the time that it happens in are all void?

The arc of our long journey of insight is beginning in some ways to trace a spiral – progressing and evolving as if by circling back on itself but at ever more profound levels. And in doing so it opens out to an awe-inspiring depth of mystery. Having picked up the concept of fabrication and investigated it with

---

[3] Translation from Padmakara Translation Group in Shantarakshita and Mipham, *The Adornment of the Middle Way*, p. 295.

[4] *Bodhicittavivaraṇa*. (Translation by Chr. Lindtner in *Nagarjuniana*, p. 203.)

more and more penetration, we have eventually gone beyond even the very notion of fabrication. Fabrication and dependent origination are conceptual constructs that are immensely helpful at a certain level. But they are in fact only relative truths. What is extraordinary about them is that they have the capability to take the understanding beyond their own meaning in this remarkable way. They eventually negate even themselves.

We can take these astounding insights a couple of steps further too. If arising and ceasing are empty, and the fabricated is not *really* fabricated, then cessation also is not *really* real. Moreover, posited in duality with the fabricated, *the Unfabricated must be void as well.* Nāgārjuna wrote:

> Since arising, abiding, and ceasing are not established, the fabricated does not exist. When the fabricated is not established, how will the unfabricated be established?[5]

Many *Prajñāpāramitā Sūtras* stress the "emptiness of the unconditioned" and the "emptiness of the ultimate". Chandrakīrti also reiterated this, likewise listing the "emptiness of the unfabricated" as one of the "sixteen emptinesses" that need to be comprehended:

> That which is free of birth, of abiding, and of impermanence, is unfabricated. This being empty of itself is the voidness of the unfabricated.[6]

Understanding all this in a manner that can be brought into our ways of looking opens up an exquisite and profound beauty. For any reification of the Unfabricated will inevitably imply and support the conceiving of a real duality between the fabricated and the Unfabricated. And through this dualistic conception, the world of appearances – the fabricated – will inevitably be demeaned somehow, even subtly, relative to the Unfabricated. But reflecting further and exploring more deeply in meditation the nature of fabrication and dependent origination makes it less likely that an experience of the cessation of perception, should it come about, will result in such a hard duality being conceived between the fabricated and the Unfabricated. Then we are no longer constrained to seeing some thing as being *really* the product of the 'fault' of ignorance, whilst conceiving of another as 'pure'. Everything can now be seen

---

[5] MMK 7:33.

[6] MAV 6:192.

to be 'pure', wondrously so. For nothing, ultimately, is the product of anything. No thing is truly fabricated or truly unfabricated. Then also we are no longer constrained to seeing fabricated things as unreal, while regarding the transcendent Unfabricated, wholly 'Other', as real. All can now be seen to be equally 'unreal' or 'real', equally miraculous. Beauty and truth are everywhere.

The nature of nirvāṇa

Unfolding these understandings and practising them as meditative views can liberate a tremendous joy. But such insights have significant consequences for our overall conception of the path too. Realizing that fabrication, cessation, the fabricated, and the Unfabricated are all empty, a conception of *nirvāṇa*, the goal of the path, as some kind of cessation of appearances and manifestation is no longer ultimately meaningful. In the later tradition, a 'non-abiding *nirvāṇa*' – an awakening that is neither a dwelling in cessation nor a being mired in reifying the appearances of *saṃsāra* – is explicitly regarded as the aim of the path, the enlightenment of a Buddha. Not elevating a removal of appearances, it more fully embodies a non-dual understanding. In so doing, it leaves open an infinity of possibilities for the expression and activities of compassion. The wisdom that comprehends the world, and the compassion that acts in it are given equal emphasis, because in fact they are thoroughly united.

Moreover, through the insight that understands the emptiness of all things without exception the belief in any ultimately real duality between *saṃsāra* and *nirvāṇa* collapses. Nāgārjuna, for instance, wrote:

> If all this is empty, then there is no arising or passing away. From the relinquishing or cessation of what does one expect to obtain *nirvāṇa*?[7]

If craving and ignorance are void, then ultimately whatever is considered a defilement is not really real. And so the cessation of defilements in *nirvāṇa* cannot really be real either. In the *Ratnakūṭa Sūtra* it is written:

> The Buddha asked, "Mañjuśrī, where should the state of Buddhahood be sought?" Mañjuśrī answered, "It should be sought

[7] MMK 25:1.

right in the defilements of sentient beings. Why? Because by nature the defilements of sentient beings are inapprehensible."[8]

And the *Uttaratantra* says:

Because sentient beings are realized to be just the peaceful *dharmatā* [i.e. the true, empty nature of all phenomena] they are naturally completely pure, and they are primordially liberated from affliction.[9]

Any way it is considered, *nirvāṇa* – like all the phenomena of *saṃsāra* – can be realized to be utterly empty, beyond existing and not existing. Thus the *Aṣṭasāhasrikā Prajñāpāramitā Sūtra* proclaims:

Even *nirvāṇa*... is like a magical illusion, like a dream... Not two different things are illusion and *nirvāṇa*, are dreams and *nirvāṇa*.[10]

Nāgārjuna echoed this insight:

There exists no distinction at all between *saṃsāra* and *nirvāṇa*. There exists no distinction at all between *nirvāṇa* and *saṃsāra*.[11]

Those who do not see reality conceive *saṃsāra* and *nirvāṇa*; but those who see reality conceive neither *saṃsāra* nor *nirvāṇa*.[12]

Even more completely, when it is understood that the fabricated and the Unfabricated, ignorance, fabrication, and cessation are all equally empty, we understand why it can be taught that the nature of *all* things is *nirvāṇa*. The *Mahāprajñāpāramitā Sūtra*, for example, declares that:

All [phenomena] have non-existence for their own-being... they are the same as final *nirvāṇa*, because of their unreality.[13]

---

[8] Translation from the author's notes.
[9] Translation from the author's notes.
[10] Translation by Edward Conze in *The Perfection of Wisdom in Eight Thousand Lines and Its Verse Summary*, p. 99.
[11] MMK 25:19.
[12] *Yuktiṣaṣṭikā*. (Author's own translation.)
[13] Translation by Edward Conze in *The Large Sutra on Perfect Wisdom*, p. 571.

And similarly the *Saptaśatikā Prajñāpāramitā Sūtra*:

> Because everything is unconditioned, unproduced, and non-existent… all [phenomena] are the same as enlightenment.[14]

And in the *Ratnamegha Sūtra* it is said:

> Primordially peace, unarisen, naturally *nirvāṇa*, Protector, you taught all phenomena to be like that.[15]

Rather than pointing toward a final goal of cessation, delivering us to an ultimately real Unfabricated and to a view of all else as really fabricated, an unremitting exploration of fabrication and dependent arising opens a vision of the world as *nirvāṇa* – a world of magical appearances, groundless and thoroughly empty yet mystically appearing. At one level we can say that phenomena are fabricated, but not ultimately. At another level it can only be said that they are empty. We have used the concepts of fabrication and dependent origination to go beyond those very concepts of fabrication and dependent origination. As Chandrakīrti wrote:

> Conventional reality therefore becomes the means, and by this means the ultimate is reached.[16]

§

Sometimes in Dharma teachings there is an emphasis on reaching a state of "disenchantment" with the world and with all the things of the world. The bringing about of this disenchantment is then regarded by some as the purpose of practices such as the contemplation of impermanence or even emptiness practices at a certain level. But we need to investigate this kind of teaching carefully. For, first, experiences of disenchantment can often be merely expressions of the presence of aversion in the *citta*, rather than of any great

[14] Translation by Edward Conze in *Perfect Wisdom*, p. 105.

[15] This is one of the ways the word *nirvāṇa* came to be used in the later tradition. Since all phenomena without exception are empty, the nature of all things is 'natural *nirvāṇa*'. See also, for example, Chandrakīrti's MAV 6:112. (The translation here is by Tyler Dewar in Wangchuk Dorje, The Ninth Karmapa, *The Karmapa's Middle Way*, p. 321.)

[16] MAV 6:80.

insight. And second, even if there has been some sense of disenchantment brought about through practice, we can see now that going deeper into an experiential understanding of emptiness profoundly and wonderfully *re-enchants* this whole world of phenomenal appearances, as described. Now that we have seen the emptiness of fabrication, and so the emptiness of any duality between the fabricated and the Unfabricated, when we say that this or that is fabricated, it has a whole other sense, a whole other dimension of meaning. Now, from a poet's perspective, it is interesting to note that the Sanskrit word *saṃskṛta*, which we have been translating as 'fabricated' or 'concocted', with all the subtly negative implications of falsity that those translations carry, can also mean 'consecrated', 'sanctified', 'hallowed'. For this is the felt sense we have with a certain depth of insight into fabrication. Rather than only negative connotations, now the intimations in the sense of 'the fabricated' are of holiness, sacredness, purity, and mystery.

Skill in view

Regarding the relation of practice to all that we have just unfolded, something crucial should be explained here however. Even though ignorance, fabrication, and cessation are empty, it is still the case that when we actually engage in a way of looking that sees deeply the emptiness of phenomena appearances will fade. There will be at least some degree of movement towards cessation. This will be so even when we contemplate the emptiness of ignorance and fabrication.

It is said that only the non-dual wisdom awareness of a Buddha is able to fully know the emptiness of appearances without those appearances fading.[17] Only a Buddha can sustain perceptions while thoroughly cognizing the voidness of those perceptions. For all others, even those who have profound understanding and direct experiences of emptiness and cessation, practice must alternate between times of more fading and times when appearances are more manifest.

Experiences of the fading of perception, since they are so valuable in absorbing the understanding of emptiness deeply into the heart, remain immensely helpful and even necessary. However, because cessation can no longer be regarded as the ultimate goal and as the expression of awakening (as well as for many other reasons), practice periods with less fading are equally vital on the

---

[17] E.g. in the *Mahāyānasūtrālaṃkāra* and the *Mahāyānasaṃgraha*. This proclamation is reiterated by many later teachers too – for example, Tsongkhapa, in his *Illumination of the Thought* (his commentary on Chandrakīrti's *Madhyamakāvatāra*), and Mipham, in his *Beacon of Certainty*.

path. In earlier chapters, we described how at times meditation might skilfully incorporate an intentional modulation of the fading of appearances, so that a practitioner decides where to be on the spectrum of fading at a particular time. Additionally now, within that spectrum one possible range we have also already mentioned can be refined and becomes even more important.

If we have understood the emptiness of phenomena deeply through experience, and also understood the emptiness of ignorance and of fabricating, then a way of looking may be practised which holds these understandings within it, but lightly. It may well be that such a way of looking is most accessible directly on emerging from more in-depth contemplation of the emptiness of all things – where there has been a considerable fading, but where now there is a re-forming of the world of appearances. Or it might be that perceptions are not fully dissolved in the first place. However it is arrived at, through the view of this lens the thoroughly empty nature of appearances is acknowledged to a certain extent, but not focused on too intensely. Things can then still appear. Yet they appear groundless, magical, less substantial. The deep understanding of their empty and insubstantial nature also then renders appearances much more malleable, more able to be seen, for instance, as 'radiant' in their voidness, or even 'divine' – without reifying 'radiance', 'divinity', or the appearances themselves. Since a Buddha's mysterious ultimate gnosis somehow unites a full cognizing of both appearances and emptiness, a practice which sustains such a view and the possibilities which it opens would be a kind of skilful imitation of a Buddha's way of looking.

Practice: Viewing appearances, knowing that *avijjā* is void

As usual take some time to settle the mind at least a little in meditation.

Then, choose any object of perception and, focusing on that object, begin to view it through a lens that understands, from previous practice, that it is fabricated. Include especially the understanding that it is fabricated by *avijjā*.

When you feel ready, begin to include in the way of looking the understanding that this *avijjā* operating right now must be empty also.

(There are many insights that can be used here. You can bring in the insight that *avijjā* is dependent on and inseparable from this empty object, and so must be empty too. Or that it is similarly dependent on consciousness, which is also empty. Or that it must be void because it needs to exist in time, and all time is void. It is also possible to subject a moment of *avijjā* to some analysis or other, for instance the sevenfold reasoning. As always these other insights will probably need to have been practised with in advance and enough familiarity with them developed to be able to bring them to bear here in an uncumbersome way so that they can open further insight.)

This way of looking will naturally allow a deeper fading of perception. But play with modulating the fading so that appearances remain to some extent. Alternatively you may wish to enjoy for a while this deeper fading and relatively deeper pacification of concepts before allowing the world of appearances to return to some degree.

The important thing here is at some point to sustain the viewing of appearances through a lens which silently understands: 'The *avijjā* which fabricates these empty appearances is empty itself. These appearances are not *really* the product of a *real* ignorance.'

If you like, you may start to allow the attention to move between objects in a relaxed way, or take in a wider field of objects.

In perceiving various appearances and sensations now, notice the sense of things that this way of looking brings. Notice also the heart's responses.

The previous practice may be extended to include a contemplation of the voidness of fabrication itself, and thus of any duality between the fabricated and the Unfabricated. As above, you will need to play with modulating the extent of fading to allow this kind of insight.

Practice: Meditating on the emptiness of fabricating

Either focusing more narrowly on one object or working with a wider field of attention, begin to sustain a view that the object of perception is empty. When you feel ready, begin to gradually include in the way of looking the understanding that ignorance, consciousness, and time are all empty. This may be done in any order and through the means of your choice.

Holding these insights in the view, start to include in the way of looking the implication that follows: that there is no *real* arising or ceasing, no thing that is *really* fabricated, and no *real* source of fabrication – so that fabrication itself must also be empty. Then, since the fabricated is empty, the Unfabricated must be empty too, as they are posited in relation to each other. Let any sense of holding to a conception of a real duality between the fabricated and Unfabricated collapse.

Allow the attention to move in a relaxed way between various objects if you wish.

Here too, notice the sense of things that this way of looking opens. And notice also the responses of the heart.

30

Notions of the Ultimate

Beyond 'emptiness'

Reading Buddhist texts and listening to teachings, one typically meets a range of perspectives defining what is ultimate. Within that range of perspectives, one might occasionally also encounter instructions that seem to point beyond even the view of emptiness. A verse in Nāgārjuna's *Mūlamadhaymakakārikā*, for instance, reads:

> The Victorious Ones taught emptiness to be the relinquishing of all views. Those for whom emptiness is a view were said to be incorrigible.[1]

Since it may be interpreted in various ways, this verse has been the subject of considerable debate within the tradition. Let us briefly consider some of the possible meanings in the light of what we have discovered through practice up to now.

One way of clinging to a view of emptiness would be to conceive of it as a thing, a space, or a realm, with inherent existence. Such views, though, we have already discounted in discussing notions of the nature of awareness and of the Unfabricated. Our use too of the concept of emptiness in a more adjectival way, right from the beginning, ensures that the emptiness of emptiness is in fact relatively obvious. For if emptiness always qualifies some phenomenon or other, then it is always dependent on that phenomenon. It is not something with an independent or separate existence.

We may take this a little further though. If there are not really any things, then any attributes of those things, even attributes such as 'empty' and 'not empty', are not really real either, and cannot ultimately be clung to. Jñānagarbha wrote:

[1] MMK 13:8.

> Because the object of negation is not existent, it is clear that in reality, there is no negation of it.[2]

A similar insight was voiced by Śāntarakṣita:

> Origination and so forth have no reality, thus absence of origination and so forth are equally impossible. Since, in and of themselves, both are disproved, verbal statements are impossible. When there are no objects, there can be no arguments refuting them.[3]

From this perspective then we can understand such statements as:

> 'Empty' should not be declared. Nor should 'non-empty', 'both', or 'neither' be declared. It is spoken about [thus only] for the purpose of instruction.[4]

Ultimately any conceptual assertion, including the assertion of emptiness, must be relinquished. In the *Prajñāpāramitā Saṃcayagāthā* it says:

> If a bodhisattva conceives of form, *vedanā*, perception, fabrications, and consciousness as 'empty', (s)he is still engaged in signs (*nimittas*), and the path of the unborn is missed… When one has no concept of 'born' or 'unborn', one practises the highest transcendent wisdom.

Here then, the ultimate view is described as transcending the concepts 'empty' and 'emptiness'. It is the "unspeakable, inconceivable, inexpressible perfection of wisdom".

Working with such teachings and texts, it is helpful to know that words such as 'ultimate' and even 'emptiness' may be used in different ways at different times. Sometimes the ultimate truth of things is declared to be their emptiness of inherent existence. But at other times the ultimate is declared to be beyond all assertions and

---

[2] In his *Satyadvayavibhaṅga*. (Translation from Karma Phuntsho, *Mipham's Dialectics and the Debates on Emptiness* [London: Routledge, 2005] p. 138.)

[3] MA 71 – 72. In the texts of the later tradition, terms such as 'absence of origination' and 'non-production' are used often, not only to qualify some thing as lacking findable or true arising etc., but also more broadly – since the voidness of the thing thus qualified naturally follows – as synonyms for 'emptiness'. 'Unborn', likewise, is frequently employed almost interchangeably with the word 'empty'.

[4] MMK 22:11.

conceptual designations, *including* emptiness. Moreover, since, as we have just seen, a full understanding of the implications of emptiness eventually leads to a transcending of all concepts and ascriptions, at still other times that very word 'emptiness' is used too, as Nāgārjuna used it above, to mean a 'relinquishment of all views'.

Of course all this inconsistency of terminology can be confusing. It is crucial therefore to consider in context any such passage which declares the need for a transcending of, or surrendering of, the view of emptiness. In this connection we should make a few important points here.

Teachings such as Nāgārjuna's above cannot be taken as general statements against views as ways of looking in practice. We have already said that ways of looking are anyway unavoidable, and that some kind of conceiving is wrapped up in all perceiving. Even though ultimately any assertion of emptiness must be relinquished, in practice the flexibility to use at different times different insight ways of looking – i.e. views – is vital.

In fact, one possible way of clinging to a view of emptiness might be through an overly rigid adherence to some particular way of looking. We have stated several times therefore that emptiness is just one way of looking among many that might be viable – to be picked up and put down as feels helpful and appropriate. Our approach follows and amplifies Āryadeva's wise advice regarding views:

> The alternatives of existence, non-existence, both existence and non-existence, and neither were taught in different contexts. From the perspective of the sicknesses they treated, are not all of these medicines?[5]
>
> That which benefits others for a while is 'truth'. That which does not is the opposite, 'falsity'.[6]

Within the gamut of potentially helpful ways of looking various views of voidness incorporating different levels of understanding undoubtedly have their place in opening freedom. They are necessary. For without emptiness ways of looking a genuinely radical shift in understanding is not usually possible. And although the ultimate nature of things is beyond what can be ascribed to them conceptually, it is nevertheless the case that a conceptual view of emptiness forms an indispensable step in this realization. Śāntideva wrote:

---

[5] *Catuḥśataka*. (Translation by Tyler Dewar in Wangchuk Dorje, The Ninth Karmapa, *The Karmapa's Middle Way*, p. 438.)

[6] Ibid., p. 438.

> The notion of things is removed through the notion of emptiness. Through training in the view 'no thing exists', even that will later be relinquished.[7]

And thus in the *Ghanavyūha Sūtra* it says:

> The teachings on emptiness were given so that all the views that sentient beings held, whatever they may be, might be relinquished and dismissed. If the view of emptiness thus heard is not itself refuted and destroyed, however, there is no remedy for such a view. One is then like a sick person forsaken by their nurse. But just as with a fire that does not remain once it has consumed all there is to burn, the fire of emptiness itself goes out once the views to be burned have been consumed. And when such views cease, the fire of perfect wisdom arises, defilements and afflictions are burned away, and then the mind in all its beauty manifests.[8]

Since a conceptual view of emptiness is almost always necessary to approach the non-conceptual ultimate, some schools refer to it as the 'approximate' ultimate. Śāntarakṣita, and, later, others such as Gorampa and Mipham for instance, thus delineated two tiers of the ultimate – the conceptual (or 'approximate', or 'concordant') ultimate, and the non-conceptual (or 'actual', or 'authentic') ultimate. In the auto-commentary to his *Madhyamakālaṃkāra* Śāntarakṣita wrote:

> The ultimate truth is beyond both thing and non-thing. It is beyond both origination and absence of origination, beyond emptiness and non-emptiness. It utterly transcends the entire net of conceptual constructs. Nevertheless, because 'absence of origination' and so forth are approaches to the actual ultimate, being harmonious with it, they are also referred to as ultimate. Without the stairs of real conventionalities, it would be impossible for a master to go to the top of the house of reality, that is ultimate truth.[9]

Within such a delineation, it can be said from one perspective that the approximate ultimate is still a conventionality, since it is still conceptual. From another perspective

[7] BCA 9:32.

[8] Translation adapted from Padmakara Translation Group's in Shantarakshita and Mipham, *The Adornment of the Middle Way*, pp. 306 – 307.

[9] Translation adapted from James Blumenthal, *The Ornament of the Middle Way,* pp. 149 – 150.

though, it can be said to be ultimate, since it is concordant with the non-conceptual ultimate, and a cause for its realization. A conceptual view of emptiness is a key that opens up the freedom of the Middle Way beyond all conceptual designations.

In this context, terms such as 'conceptual constructs', 'conceptual designations', or 'conceptual elaborations' all translate the word *papañca* (*prapañca* in the Sanskrit of the original texts). *Any* conceiving or conceptual position at all is regarded as a kind of 'proliferation', and any conceptual view as, effectively, a kind of extremity of view that cannot be the authentic Middle Way. The actual ultimate truth of things then is said to be beyond all *papañca*. And it is considered necessary to eventually actually experience this transcending, or pacification, of conceptual designations and extremes in order to understand emptiness fully.

Notice that this use of the term *papañca* is almost identical with Sāriputta's use of the term (see Chapter 28). Unlike Sāriputta and the earlier tradition, however, in the later tradition an experience of transcending *papañca*, and thus an experience of the ultimate, is not always equated with a transcending of appearances and the six sense spheres.

The coalescence of emptiness and appearances

Within the later tradition, sometimes the ultimate is defined from the perspective of a Buddha's gnosis (wisdom awareness). Since that gnosis is regarded as the highest wisdom and the ultimate view, the characteristics, contents, and perceptions of that wisdom awareness are taken to determine what is ultimate.

Such an approach has many significant consequences. Let's just consider it briefly here inasmuch as it is relevant to our exploration at this point. It is said that, along with its characteristic of non-conceptuality, a Buddha's gnosis embodies a completely non-dual realization of pure emptiness. Just as in the discussion of cessation, although we may speak about it in language that leans either at times towards notions of a subject, or at other times towards notions of an object, this wisdom awareness, itself void, is completely beyond designations of subject and object. In an inconceivable way, 'subject' (wisdom awareness) and 'object' (emptiness) are totally undifferentiated.[10] And yet, as was mentioned earlier, despite its utter non-conceptuality and its immovability from a non-dual cognition of emptiness, this gnosis mysteriously somehow also cognizes appearances. Thus Mipham, for instance, wrote:

---

[10] This ultimate, yet empty, non-dual gnosis was the original meaning of the term *dharmakāya* in the *Prajñāpāramitā Sūtras*. Within the tradition, a stream of texts – running from the *Aṣṭasāhasrikā Prajñāpāramitā Sūtra* through, for instance, the *Mahāyānasūtrālaṃkāra,* the *Mahāyānasaṃgraha*, Sthiramati's *Triṃśikāvijñaptibhāṣya*, Vasubandhu's *Trisvabhāvakārikā*, as well as the writings of Ārya Vimuktisena, Ratnakākaraśānti, Abhayākaragupta, and many others – has preserved this sense.

> In the mind of an ordinary person, the two realities [i.e. conventional appearances and emptiness] can only appear in alternation… But gnosis is beyond conceiving and does not abide alternately in the two extremes. It is the Great Middle Way. As long as one has not reached gnosis by means of alternation, however, it is not the ultimate Middle Way that is the heart of all Buddhas' realization… This gnosis may be considered the fruitional Middle Way… the coalescence of appearance and emptiness. But… for this great gnosis,… appearance, emptiness, and coalescence are not reified as having some essence.[11]

In this view then, the ultimate is not devoid of appearances. Nor can it be limited to a merely conceptual understanding of emptiness. That understanding has been absorbed and penetrated to realize the ultimate truth of things beyond all concepts.

Very much related to the insights and explorations of the last chapter, this approach of defining the ultimate from the perspective of a Buddha's gnosis may be converted into a skilful way of looking. Rongzom Chözang wrote:

> All apparent phenomena are just delusion. Moreover, there is no freedom from delusion to be achieved by dispelling delusion. But because the nature of delusion is totally pure, it has the nature of enlightenment. All phenomena are in this way primordially in the state of enlightenment.[12]

All defilements are empty, we have found, including ignorance. And realizing that ignorance is empty enables us to view a world of empty and magical appearances whose essential nature is not different from *nirvāṇa*. Moreover, these appearances are not separate from the mind that knows them; and this mind, or awareness, is empty too. Although the teaching of the voidness of mind might be grasped at in order to dismiss a reifying elevation of the mind or awareness, in practice realizing the empty nature of mind actually opens up a profound sense of its mystical nature. There is *knowing*, but it is void of inherent existence, without a real centre and not ultimately of time. Being empty, it is essentially free and its nature is beyond all conception.

---

[11] *Beacon of Certainty* 7. (Translation from John Whitney Pettit in *Mipham's Beacon of Certainty*, pp. 230 – 235.)

[12] In his *Establishing Appearances as Divine*. (Translation adapted from Heidi I. Köppl's in *Establishing Appearances as Divine: Rongzom Chözang on Reasoning, Madhyamaka, and Purity* [Ithaca: Snow Lion, 2008] p. 96.)

A way of looking which views awareness this way, and views appearances as empty, magical, and inseparable from it, may be immensely potent. Certainly it runs the risk that awareness is reified at times by the practitioner. But if, relying on previous practices and insights, the emptiness of mind is contemplated over and over as part of the way of looking, the Middle Way beyond existence and non-existence can be returned to fairly quickly whenever there is a leaning toward reification.[13] Doing so, and thus not losing touch with the mystical sense of the utter groundlessness of awareness, will also give more liberating power to the way of looking.

Sometimes, in the streams of the tradition that emphasize this kind of approach, the enlightened mind of a Buddha is taught to be innate within all sentient beings. Recognizing that the essential nature of 'ordinary' mind is actually 'clear light' – that is, empty knowing, an indivisible emptiness and cognizing – it can be said to be not fundamentally different from the empty essence of a Buddha's pristine wisdom. Mipham explained:

> Pristine wisdom is not arisen from the mind, but is the mode of subsistence of the mind, the clear light nature. This is to be understood as similar to how the emptiness that is the noumenon of all things is the mode of subsistence of all things, but is not arisen from those things.[14]

From this more mystical perspective a Buddha's gnosis, as much as it is something we are aiming to develop, is already here and now. It is only that we do not realize it.

With the unfolding of insight – into the voidness of awareness, of ignorance, and of appearances which are not separate from empty awareness – it may be

[13] Of course, a risk of leaning toward a reification of some or all phenomena is present anyway along with *any* practice. As we have repeatedly stressed, the tendency to reify phenomena is a deeply ingrained habit of mind. For some, a habitual tendency toward nihilism will also be noticed, and needs to be guarded against.

Related to these tendencies, an additional observation may be important to report here. It is often the case that, as insight into voidness is developed through meditation, a practitioner's understanding oscillates slightly over time – back and forth around the tightrope of the Middle Way – between views of 'it exists' and 'it does not exist' with regard to phenomena. This oscillation can be expected, discerned, and responded to skilfully in the course of practice. As practice deepens, such wavering and the imbalances of understanding it entails become less extreme and more subtle – closer to the actual Middle Way.

[14] *The Meaning of Fundamental Mind, Clear Light.* (Translation by Jeffrey Hopkins in Mi-pam-gya-tso, *Fundamental Mind: The Nyingma View of the Great Completeness* [Ithaca, NY: Snow Lion, 2006] p. 79.)

possible to intuitively glimpse a vision of all things as the empty manifestations of primordially enlightened wisdom-awareness, itself also empty. A song of Milarepa's describes such a vision:

> All things in *saṃsāra* and *nirvāṇa*... all existents, phenomena, appearances, and non-existents, all these functional realities are inseparably of one taste with the quintessential nature of emptiness... All share in the vastness of the great coalescence. The wise who realize this truth no longer see mind, but only wisdom-mind. They no longer see living beings, only Buddhas. They no longer see phenomena, only the quintessential nature.[15]

And as mentioned several times earlier, the more profound the insight into emptiness, the more the doors to tantric and imaginal practices are opened, and the more one is able to perceive all things as magical, empty, and divine. This potential is wonderfully expressed in the *Mystical Verses* of the Second Dalai Lama:

> The experience of the yogi is then this: The world is seen as the mystical *maṇḍala* and all living beings as tantric deities; everything that one eats and drinks becomes transformed into blissful ambrosia; all of one's activities become spiritual, regardless of how they conventionally appear; and every sound that one makes becomes part of a great *vajra* [adamantine] song.
>
> I, a tantric yogin, have a blissful mind; I, a tantric yogin, spontaneously generate goodness in everything I do. All male divinities dance within me and all female divinities channel their sacred *vajra* songs through me.[16]

The full reasonings behind this view, its vocabulary, its many avenues and ramifications are beyond the scope of this book. But given all the practices and insights we have developed, it may be quite possible by now to experiment and find one's way into a whole range of blessèd, beautiful, and very powerful ways of looking.

---

[15] Translation by Glenn H. Mullin in *The Six Yogas of Naropa* [Ithaca, NY: Snow Lion, 2005] p. 57.
[16] Translation by Glenn H. Mullin in *The Practice of Kalachakra* [Ithaca, NY: Snow Lion, 1991] pp. 66 – 67.

31

An Empowerment of Views

The fullness of emptiness

No matter how skilful, any way of looking at appearances which we employ is still in fact a relative view. Since, for us, there is always at least some conceiving whenever there are appearances, no way of looking at appearances should be clung to as literally being a non-conceptual ultimate view. Nor should any be clung to as being a kind of window revealing finally 'true' appearances, things which are definitively, singularly, actually, 'what is'. Insight into emptiness enables different ways of looking; and different ways of looking bring deepening insight into emptiness. Through all this, a profound freeing up of the whole sense of existence is possible.

The teachings of *śūnyatā*, as was stated at the beginning, exist only for the sake of this freedom; ultimately, they also should not be clung to. However, while we have considered now a number of ways in which it is possible to cling to voidness as one journeys on the path of insight, it is undoubtedly also possible, and much more common, to cling to reifications of conventional appearances or to reifications of other aspects of relative truth. In particular, emptiness teachings may sometimes be approached in ways that water down their meaning and their impact, leaving our habitual notions of the world, our deep-seated intuitive realism, essentially undisturbed, and so bringing very little liberation.

Some of these incomplete conceptions of emptiness we have already mentioned, at least in passing. Teachings on *śūnyatā* are not proclaiming that language or cultural assumptions are the primary problem. Nor that reasoning and logic are to be dismissed as unhelpful in the pursuit of freedom. Although, as discussed, the entire net of concepts is eventually to be transcended, texts by Nāgārjuna, Chandrakīrti, Śāntarakṣita, and others *use* reasoning and logic as tools to make evident that our most basic normal assumptions about things cannot possibly be true. Rather than the movements of reasoning, it is principally these more fundamental, habitual, and intuitive conceptions that imprison us, so they are actually the target of refutation in the teachings. As can be seen in practice, these binding conceptions operate in the mind below the level of language. Thus thought, too, cannot be regarded as the problem. Emptiness teachings are not saying "Don't think, just experience", or, ultimately, "Just stay at the moment of contact with things as they are", for fundamental delusion is woven right into our very experience, our 'basic' perception, even when there is no thinking.

We have explained also how insight into the voidness of things would be significantly incomplete if we were to equate emptiness with impermanence, and proclaim that "things exist, but only momentarily", or that "all that exists of things is a flux or process". Nor too should only those notions that are more usually deemed 'spiritual', such as Self or soul, an inherently existing Awareness, the Unfabricated, or the divine, be regarded as the primary targets of teachings on *śūnyatā*. Often when this is the case, ordinary experience, though it might ostensibly be proclaimed void as well, is left basically unchallenged – the designation of emptiness there merely nominal and essentially insignificant. Such a biased approach usually betrays a desire to simply retain already held views; and also a lack of the kind of deeper meditative practice necessary to go beyond such preconceptions. It is important too, of course, that the liberating view of voidness reaches eventually as well to even the subtlest level of intuitive reification of awareness or of any kind of notion of 'the ultimate'.

While there may be many motivations behind adopting any limited view of emptiness, all such positions share in the fact of leaving something not-empty. Perhaps the most common is a clinging to conventional appearances as somehow real. Maybe this is to be expected simply because these are the most common experientially. But there are other reasons too.

As alluded to there have been recurrent worries throughout the history of the Buddhist tradition that when teachings on voidness are heard but not understood, they may be interpreted in a nihilistic way and used as an excuse for ignoring ethics. Perhaps historically this concern has been justifiable at times. It has almost certainly on occasion led to a withholding of the teachings on emptiness. But in some instances it has shaped an expression of the teachings which strives to ensure that conventional reality is not disrespected. Then there may be a great emphasis laid on communicating that the conventional truth of things is not refuted through seeing emptiness. It may be said, for example, that "a vase is not empty of itself, it is only empty of inherent existence".

For someone who has explored fabrication and dependent arising extensively in their meditation practice, however, such a formula would be unnecessary, though at least not harmful. But for someone without such a depth of meditative practice, this language could draw an unhelpful distinction between a phenomenon and its inherent existence. It might suggest that seeing the emptiness of some thing refutes a part of it called its 'inherent existence', as if that were some kind of external and merely intellectual addition that may be removed without affecting the thing itself. Stressing that the conventional existence of the thing is not negated by realization of its emptiness might encourage a beginning practitioner to assume, even tacitly, that some objective basis within a thing remains, somehow separate from, untouched and unaffected by, the emptiness of that thing. Thus it might be assumed that a part of that thing called its 'conventional existence' is not empty. This leaving of something 'real' leaves something to cling to, and a basis for *dukkha*. Making such a mental distinction without experiencing emptiness deeply in practice, the basic habitual notion of the thing remains essentially undisturbed. Such an understanding of emptiness would bring very little freedom. As Gendun Chöpel wrote:

> It is the pot or the pillar that must be negated... What good is it to leave the pot aside and negate separately something called a 'truly established' pot?[1]

Dendar-hlarampa similarly taught:

> Except for refuting just these mountains, fences, houses, and so forth which so forcefully appear to exist concretely, we are very wrong if we search for some other horn-like thing to refute. [By 'horn-like' is meant something obviously protruding, separate from the object itself, which may be removed and still leave the object essentially intact.][2]

In Mipham's words:

> Phenomena... undeniably appear. If one then examines the status of the objects that are manifest to the senses and asks whether they have a real existence in themselves, one can investigate them using the reasonings of the Madhyamaka tradition. And one will find that, while conventionalities like pots and so on appear to us, they and their constituents, down to the tiniest infinitesimal particles, are

---

[1] In his *Adornment for Nāgārjuna's Thought: An Eloquent Distillation of the Profound Points of the Middle Way*. (Translation adapted from Donald S. Lopez Jr., *The Madman's Middle Way: Reflections on Reality of the Tibetan Monk Gendun Chopel* [Chicago: University of Chicago Press, 2006] p. 58.)

[2] From his *Presentation of the Lack of Being One or Many*. (Translation by Jeffrey Hopkins in *Meditations on Emptiness* [Boston: Wisdom Publications, 1996] p. 545.)

> unable to withstand analysis. This means not that they are empty of some extraneous true existence, but that, by their very nature, they abide in emptiness, the emptiness of being primordially unborn and unobservable. This is the emptiness that we need to establish. Phenomena that are empty from their own side are said to lack inherent identity… They are said to be impossible to define, void, without self, beyond the extremes of *saṃsāra* and *nirvāṇa*, space-like, and so on. All this is the same as saying they lack true existence. By contrast, if, on being subjected to absolutist analysis, a thing were found to resist such an investigation, it would necessarily be established as truly existent. But no phenomenon, compounded or uncompounded, is found to resist such an analysis… If it is imagined that true existence is being refuted somehow separately from the object being referred to, it is clear that clinging to the reality of the object will in no way be arrested. The whole point of establishing that things are empty will be lost.[3]

Explaining it logically, he also commented:

> Consider a pillar and the true existence of a pillar. If they are one, then refuting one [the true existence of the pillar] the other [the pillar] is refuted; if they are different, by refuting a true existence that is not the pillar, the pillar that is not empty of itself would be immune to analysis,[4]

which would mean that it is truly existent, that there is something not empty. When we see deeply into the nature of things though, we see that

> In the place of a pillar, primordially pure, there is nothing that is non-empty whatsoever.[5]

Perhaps there is only a real risk of being misled by language stressing the unassailable conventional reality of conventional appearances, and somehow separating it from a notion of inherent existence, when meditative analysis is the

---

[3] From Mipham's commentary to Chandrakīrti's *Madhyamakāvatāra*. (Translation by Padmakara Translation Group in Chandrakirti and Mipham, *Introduction to the Middle Way*, p. 215.)

[4] *Beacon of Certainty* 1. (Translated by John Whitney Pettit in *Mipham's Beacon of Certainty*, pp. 196 – 197.)

[5] Ibid., p. 196.

exclusive or main tool for contemplating emptiness. Indeed, if you have been following the avenue of practices which emphasize an exploration of fabrication and dependent arising, it might seem hard to understand how this debate over the 'object of negation'[6] – what actually is negated by the view of emptiness – has come to have such a long history in the later tradition. For in taking the more directly phenomenological approach and exploring the fabrication of appearances, it is exactly those appearances that are understood to be empty. Appearances are not denied; how could they be? As Mipham said, "phenomena undeniably appear"; but they are void through and through. Penetrating and comprehending deeply the dependent arising of appearances, one sees the emptiness of all things. And further, as we have explained before, there is unlikely to be any danger of neglecting ethics, goodness, and kindness through this approach to insight. For the role that the qualities in the *citta* have in colouring and shaping appearances becomes clear through the very approach.

The inclination to somehow grant a level of objective truth to conventional reality is understandable, and such a tendency is not always motivated only by ethical concerns. We humans seem to possess a hard-to-fracture clinging to the intuitive conviction that there *really is* something that exists in an independent way, and then want to know what 'really' is there. Rather than being able to establish and determine such a reality, however, the philosophical and scientific projects which seek to do so seem to reveal the opposite instead. As we probe, ask, and analyse more deeply, we find only dependency, relativity, emptiness. And whatever the linguistic and conceptual framework of our inquiry, eventually even the clear distinction between conventional and ultimate begins to blur. A bow begins…

In the Buddhist tradition, the notion of the 'valid cognition of conventional reality' has been influential and is emphasized by those who fear that conventional appearances may be disrespected in exploring emptiness. It is important of course to be able to distinguish between a person or object and a photograph or painting of that person or object; or to discern when an appearance is a mistaken perception resulting from some kind of organic disturbance or optical illusion. A picture or an optical illusion is generally unable to perform the functions of an actual person or object and so can be dismissed as not an 'authentic relative truth'.

Again though, while such an approach may seem perfectly reasonable common sense, when repeatedly stressed and grasped at without a deeper understanding it may bring with it the danger of assuming that conventional appearances are left essentially undamaged by the realization of emptiness. Since it may seem to a

---

[6] Sometimes 'the object of negation' is also referred to as 'the negandum', or 'the object of refutation'.

practitioner that things as they appear are receiving validation, it may be that things as they appear effectively end up being given an objective reality.

By contrast, other streams in the tradition do not condone any valid cognition of conventional reality. In the *Samādhirāja Sūtra*, for example, it says:

> The eye, the ear, and the nose are not valid cognizers. The tongue, the body, and mind are not valid cognizers. If these faculties were valid cognizers, what need of the Noble Path would there be for anyone?[7]

And Chandrakīrti, echoing this, wrote:

> If ordinary perception yielded true and valid knowledge, suchness [emptiness] would be seen by common folk. What need would there be then for Noble Ones? What need for Noble Paths? It is wrong to take the foolish mind as validly cognizing. Since, in every aspect, ordinary experience has no validity, it does not invalidate explanations of ultimate reality. Empirical phenomena consensus will approve, and all denial of them consensus will negate.[8]

Here then, instead of trying to establish conventional reality by valid cognition which distinguishes what is functional from what is not, conventional reality is merely pronounced to be whatever is the consensus of worldly view. He added:

> Vases, sweaters, canvases, armies, forests, rosaries, trees, houses, chariots, hotels, and all such things should be accepted in the way they are labelled by ordinary beings, for the Lord of Sages did not quarrel with the world. Parts and part possessors, qualities and qualified, desire and those desiring, defined and definition, fire and fuel – if analysed, like a chariot, with the sevenfold reasoning, do not exist. Apart from that, they exist by way of what is renowned in the world.[9]

The Ninth Karmapa elaborated on this:

---

[7] Author's own translation. The word rendered here as 'valid cognizer' is *pramāṇa*, which could also be translated as 'authority'.

[8] MAV 6:30 – 31.

[9] MAV 6:166 – 167.

> Without analysing... the followers of the Middle Way accept – from the perspective of others – whatever is asserted by worldly people on the basis of worldly ways. When analysing... however, one cannot find any thing apart from the suchness [emptiness] that is the true nature of those things. This suchness is the ultimate truth... The conventional should be accepted based on what is renowned to others... As explained, conventional reality, when analysed, is unfindable. This unfindability renders any presentation of the conventional inappropriate.[10]

A radical opening

Here, rather than attempting to proffer ultimately coherent explanations of the workings of conventional appearances, and reifying them in the process, what is deemed important is the realization of the ultimate nature of things. For it is this that liberates. Moreover, through refusing to give conventional, or relative, truth any objective status, any imputed sense of division between the conventional and the ultimate is dissolved. We arrive at an inseparability of conventional and ultimate truth, the inseparability of appearances and emptiness that was highlighted earlier as the highest view. The relative is what appears, the ultimate is its nature. There are appearances, and these appearances are empty.

Mipham, in his discussion of such questions, did not altogether dismiss the notion of valid cognition of conventional truth. Emphasizing, though, that there is simply not just one way of perceiving things, the approach that he adopted somewhat refines the debate by allowing for the possibility of a certain malleability of perception – just as we discussed, for instance, in Chapter 24 in the context of emptiness and heart practices. Although there are certainly limits to this malleability, there is no grasping at a singular determination or fixed view of 'what is' at a conventional level. His more flexible system admits a spectrum of valid relative truth, so that there can be the development of what he sometimes termed 'higher forms of seeing',[11] through tantric and emptiness practices, as alluded to in the song of Milarepa and the verses of the Second Dalai Lama cited in the last chapter. All of these perceptions, without exception, are realized to be

[10] In *Feast for the Fortunate*, his commentary on Chandrakīrti's text. (Translation by Tyler Dewar in Wangchuk Dorje, The Ninth Karmapa, *The Karmapa's Middle Way*, pp. 224 –225.)

[11] E.g. in *Beacon of Certainty* 6. (Translation by John Whitney Pettit in *Mipham's Beacon of Certainty*, p. 222.)

ultimately empty appearances however. Here then, conventional truth is still merely appearance, whose ultimate truth is emptiness. But rather than a supposed correspondence with, or mirroring of, an objective reality, what makes a perception valid *at one level* is its agreement with the perceptions of beings at a similar level. In this view it is understood that we share habitual tendencies to perceive in certain ways, and it is merely the stability of these shared perceptual tendencies that renders a perception valid conventionally at any particular level.

For some, of course, initially encountering either a refusal to establish any valid cognition of conventional truth, or a view such as Mipham's, which establishes it only contextually, may give rise to suspicion and even annoyance. Yet a profound meditative exploration of dependent arising will likely end up with similar sorts of conclusions to those of Mipham, or lead at least to a letting go of the felt need to define valid conventional cognition. At the same time, as we have repeatedly stressed, and as will be obvious to anyone practising this way, the understanding and freedom that are opened bring no irresponsibility with respect to conventional appearances, no behaviour that harms self or other.

Perhaps it could be said that, as beautiful as the inquiry may be, a clinging to wanting to determine what is 'really and unequivocally there' on a conventional level simply betrays a mistaken premise of fundamental delusion. Perhaps we may say, with the Buddha, that some questions do not need answers. What matters is the freedom and love that comes from realization of the emptiness of all phenomena. Still, our inquiry into emptiness involves inquiry into appearances; and since cessation is not regarded as the goal, that inquiry may become a kind of open-ended exploration – of ways of looking and the perceptions of their associated appearances. It is not the assumed objectivity status of its appearances at a conventional level, but the blessing and liberation that any way of looking effects that becomes the primary criterion for judging it.

As well as being ultimately pragmatic, the adoption of a core approach of exploring different ways of looking has been concordant with a fundamental and vital insight right from the start. For it is in fact the fundamental openness of things that allows us the possibility to play with ways of looking and to see their effects on the heart and on perception. From the perspective of this approach, the very least that can be said of a view which, understanding that objects, awareness, and ignorance are all empty, *does* see a world of magical appearances, inseparable from a mind that is ultimately groundless too and beyond time – and *does* sense all of it thus as 'holy', 'blessèd', or 'divine' – is that such a way of looking sees appearances skilfully. What is opened by a view is what is most important.

In the end, everything is empty. Heart, appearance, way of looking – these too are void, and actually inseparable. With respect to *how* things appear though, we can acknowledge the primary significance of ways of looking and their effects on the heart, and also some degree of flexibility in perception. At this level, it is certainly clear that the state of the *citta* shapes and colours perception. But the truth of the converse is easily recognized as well: perception shapes and colours the *citta*. Understanding all this opens a door. In practice we may, to a degree, shape empty perception in the service of freedom and compassion. When there is insight, we know that how and what we see are not simply givens, but are the colourable and malleable, magical, material of empty appearances.

There is space here, and space for reverence and devotion. When we see the void – the open and groundless nature of all things, the inseparability of appearances and emptiness – we recognize anyway just how profound is our participation in this magic of appearances. Then whether fabrication, which is empty, is consciously intended in a certain direction or not, the heart bows to the fathomless wonder and beauty of it all. It can be touched by an inexhaustible amazement, touched again and again by blessedness and relief. In knowing fully the thorough voidness of this and that, of then and now, of there and here, this heart opens in joy, in awe and release. Free itself, it knows the essential freedom in everything.

A Word of Gratitude

Many thanks to Robert Brodrick and Clare Brunt for initially suggesting that I write this book, and for their gentle persistence, over some years, in reminding me of that suggestion. And many thanks to Mark Øvland and John Stones for their help in overseeing this publication. For their careful editing and detailed feedback I am very grateful too to Mark Øvland, Robert Brodrick, Michael Swan, Nicola Oestreicher, Susan Crozier, Juha Penttilä, and Ramiro Ortega, who also suggested a number of general stylistic improvements. Several times, at different stages of its preparation, Kirsten Kratz very generously read through the entire manuscript, offering countless valuable critiques and all manner of support, for which I am profoundly thankful.

While translations from Pali or Sanskrit sources are for the most part my own, for Tibetan and Chinese texts, or in the instances where the original Sanskrit of a passage was not available to me, I have relied on the translations of John Blofeld, James Blumenthal, José Ignacio Cabezón and Geshe Lobsang Dargyay, Edward Conze, Tyler Dewar, Thomas Doctor, Lama Sherab Dorje, Malcolm David Eckel, Ari Goldfield, Katia and Ken Holmes, Jeffrey Hopkins, Heidi Köppl, Glenn Mullin, Gadjin Nagao, The Padmakara Translation Group, John Whitney Pettit, Kenneth Saunders, Jim Scott, Daisetz Teitaro Suzuki, Robert Thurman, Alex Wayman, and Wong Mou-lam. I humbly and gratefully acknowledge all their wonderful work. Should anyone feel that their work has been used and not fully acknowledged, please contact the publishers.

I am also indebted to the many students over the years whose questions have helped to shape and refine the presentation of this material. And to all the teachers mentioned in the preceding pages, as well as a great many that have not been, I feel that my debt is truly immeasurable.

Bibliography

Bhikkhu Bodhi (translator), *The Connected Discourses of the Buddha: A New Translation of the Saṃyutta Nikāya (Vols. I and II)*. Boston: Wisdom Publications, 2000.

—— *The Numerical Discourses of the Buddha: A Translation of the Aṅguttara Nikāya*. Boston: Wisdom Publications, 2000.

Bhikkhu Ñāṇamoli and Bhikkhu Bodhi (translators), *The Middle Length Discourses of the Buddha: A New Translation of the Majjhima Nikāya*. Boston: Wisdom Publications, 1995.

Blofeld, John, *The Zen Teaching of Huang Po: On the Transmission of Mind*. London: The Buddhist Society, 1968.

Blumenthal, James, *The Ornament of the Middle Way: A Study of the Madhyamaka Thought of Śāntarakṣita*. Ithaca, NY: Snow Lion, 2004.

Chandrakirti and Mipham (translated by Padmakara Translation Group), *Introduction to the Middle Way: Chandrakirti's Madhyamakavatara with Commentary by Jamgön Mipham*. Boston: Shambala, 2002.

Cabezón, José Ignacio and Dargyay, Geshe Lobsang, *Freedom from Extremes: Gorampa's "Distinguishing the Views" and the Polemics of Emptiness*. Boston: Wisdom Publications, 2007.

H. H. The Fourteenth Dalai Lama (translated by Jeffrey Hopkins), *How to See Yourself As You Really Are*. London: Rider, 2006.

Dorje, Wangchuk, The Ninth Karmapa, (translated by Tyler Dewar), *The Karmapa's Middle Way: Feast for the Fortunate*. Ithaca, NY: Snow Lion, 2008.

Dreyfus, Georges B. J. and McClintock, Sara L. (eds.), *The Svātantrika-Prāsaṅgika Distinction: What Difference Does a Difference Make?* Boston: Wisdom Publications, 2003.

The Eighth Situpa and The Third Karmapa (translated by Lama Sherab Dorje), *Mahāmudrā Teachings of the Supreme Siddhas: The Eighth Situpa Tenpa'i Nyinchay on The Third Gyalwa Karmapa Rangjung Dorje's Aspiration Prayer of the Mahāmudrā of Definitive Meaning.* Ithaca, NY: Snow Lion, 1995.

Jé Gampopa (translated by Ken and Katia Holmes), *Gems of Dharma, Jewels of Freedom: The Classic Handbook of Buddhism by Jé Gampopa.* Forres: Altea, 1995.

Garfield, Jay, *The Fundamental Wisdom of the Middle Way: Nāgārjuna's Mūlamadhyamakakārikā.* Oxford: Oxford University Press, 1995.

Gyamtso, Khenpo Tsültrim, *Progressive Stages of Meditation on Emptiness.* Auckland: Zhyisil Chokyi Ghatsal Publications, 2001.

—— *The Sun of Wisdom: Teachings on Noble Nagarjuna's Fundamental Wisdom of the Middle Way.* Boston: Shambala, 2003.

—— *Stars of Wisdom: Analytical Meditation, Songs of Yogic Joy, and Prayers of Aspiration.* Boston: Shambala, 2010.

Gyatso, Ven. Lobsang, *The Harmony of Emptiness and Dependent-Arising.* Dharamsala: Library of Tibetan Works and Archives, 1992.

Hamilton, Sue, *Early Buddhism: A New Approach: The I of the Beholder.* Richmond: Curzon, 2000.

Hopkins, Jeffrey, *Compassion in Tibetan Buddhism.* London: Rider, 1980.

—— *The Tantric Distinction.* Boston: Wisdom Publications, 1984.

—— *Emptiness Yoga.* Ithaca, NY: Snow Lion, 1987.

—— *Meditation on Emptiness.* Boston: Wisdom Publications, 1996.

—— *Nāgārjuna's Precious Garland: Buddhist Advice for Living and Liberation.* Ithaca, NY: Snow Lion, 2007.

—— *Tsong-kha-pa's Final Exposition of Wisdom*. Ithaca, NY: Snow Lion, 2008.

Köppl, Heidi I., *Establishing Appearances as Divine: Rongzom Chözang on Reasoning, Madhyamaka, and Purity*. Ithaca, NY: Snow Lion, 2008.

Lindtner, Chr., *Nagarjuniana: Studies in the Writings and Philosophy of Nāgārjuna*. Delhi: Motilal Banarsidass, 1987.

Lopez, Donald S. Jr., *The Madman's Middle Way: Reflections on Reality of the Tibetan Monk Gendun Chopel*. Chicago: University of Chicago Press, 2006.

Maitreya and Mipham (translated by Jim Scott), *Maitreya's Distinguishing Phenomena and Pure Being*. Ithaca, NY: Snow Lion, 2004.

Makransky, John J., *Buddhahood Embodied: Sources of Controversy in India and Tibet*. Albany: State University of New York Press, 1997.

Mipham, Ju (translated by Thomas H. Doctor), *Speech of Delight: Mipham's Commentary on Śāntarakṣita's Ornament of the Middle Way*. Ithaca, NY: Snow Lion, 2004.

—— (Mi-pam-gya-tso and Khetsun Sangpo Rinbochay, translated by Jeffrey Hopkins), *Fundamental Mind: The Nyingma View of the Great Completeness*. Ithaca, NY: Snow Lion, 2006.

Nagao, Gadjin M., *Mādhyamika and Yogācāra: A Study of Mahāyāna Philosophies*. Albany: State University of New York Press, 1991.

Napper, Elizabeth, *Dependent-Arising and Emptiness: A Tibetan-Buddhist Interpretation of Mādhyamika Philosophy*. Boston: Wisdom Publications, 2003.

Newland, Guy, *The Two Truths in the Mādhaymika Philosophy of the Ge-luk-ba Order of Tibetan Buddhism*. Ithaca, NY: Snow Lion, 1992.

—— *Introduction to Emptiness: Tsong-kha-pa's Great Treatise on The Stages of the Path*. Ithaca, NY: Snow Lion, 2008.

Payutto, P. A., *Dependent Origination: The Buddhist Law of Conditionality*. Bangkok: Buddhadhamma Foundation, 1994.

Pettit, John Whitney, *Mipham's Beacon of Certainty: Illuminating the View of Dzogchen, The Great Perfection*. Boston: Wisdom Publications, 1999.

Phuntsho, Karma, *Mipham's Dialectics and the Debates on Emptiness*. London: Routledge, 2005.

Rabten, Geshe (translated and edited by Stephen Batchelor), *Echoes of Voidness*. Boston: Wisdom Publications, 1983.

Rinchen, Geshe Sonam and Ruth Sonam (translator), *Yogic Deeds of Bodhisattvas: Gyel-tsap on Āryadeva's Four Hundred*. Ithaca, NY: Snow Lion, 1994.

Śāntideva (translated by Kate Crosby and Andrew Skilton), *The Bodhicaryāvatāra*. Oxford: Oxford University Press, 1995.

Maitreya and Mipham (translated by Jim Scott), *Maitreya's Distinguishing Phenomena and Pure Being*. Ithaca, NY: Snow Lion, 2004.

Shantarakshita and Mipham (translated by Padmakara Translation Group), *The Adornment of the Middle Way: Shantarakshita's Madhyamakalankara with Commentary by Jamgön Mipham*. Boston: Shambala, 2005.

Suzuki, D. T., *The Zen Doctrine of No Mind*. London: Rider, 1972.

Thanissaro Bhikkhu, *Handful of Leaves, Vols. 1 – 5*. (Five Volumes of Anthologies from the Pali Canon.) Redwood City, CA: Sati Center for Buddhist Studies, and Valley Center, CA: Metta Forest Monastery, 2002 – 2007.

—— *Wings to Awakening*. Barre, MA: Dhamma Dana Publication Fund, 1996.

—— *Selves and Not-Self*. Valley Center, CA: Metta Forest Monastery, 2011.

Thurman, Robert A. F., *Tsong Khapa's Speech of Gold in the Essence of True Eloquence: Reason and Enlightenment in the Central Philosophy of Tibet*. Princeton: Princeton University Press, 1984.

—— *The Holy Teaching of Vimalakīrti: A Mahāyāna Scripture*. University Park, PA: The Pennsylvania State University Press, 2003.

Tsong khapa (translated by Geshe Ngawang Samten and Jay L. Garfield), *Ocean of Reasoning: A Great Commentary on Nāgārjuna's Mūlamadhyamakakārikā*. Oxford: Oxford University Press, 2006.

Vose, Kevin A., *Resurrecting Candrakīrti: Disputes in the Tibetan Creation of Prāsaṅgika*. Boston: Wisdom Publications, 2009.

Williams, Paul, *The Reflexive Nature of Awareness: A Tibetan Madhyamaka Defence*. Delhi: Motilal Banarsidass, 2000.

Index

About the Author

Rob Burbea is Resident Teacher of Gaia House, one of the largest and most respected retreat centres in Europe. He is a co-founder of Sanghaseva, an organization dedicated to exploring the Dharma through service work internationally, and a co-initiator of DANCE (Dharma Action Network for Climate Engagement). Audio recordings of many of his Dharma talks, guided meditations, and meditation instructions are available at www.dharmaseed.org.